AMERICAN DESPERADO

MY LIFE AS A COCAINE COWBOY

JON ROBERTS
&EVAN WRIGHT

EBURY
PRESS

1 3 5 7 9 10 8 6 4 2

Ebury Press, an imprint of Ebury Publishing
20 Vauxhall Bridge Road
London SW1V 2SA

Ebury Press is part of the Penguin Random House Group of companies whose
addresses can be found at global.penguinrandomhouse.com

Penguin
Random House
UK

First published by Ebury Press in 2011
This edition published in 2018

www.penguin.co.uk

A CIP catalogue record for this book is available from the British Library

ISBN 9780091949419

Printed and bound in Great Britain by Clays Ltd, Elcograf S.p.A.

Jon Roberts was, prior to his incarceration, among the most successful drug smugglers in American history, at one point overseeing an operation that accounted for more than half of the cocaine entering the US. He collaborated with some of the most notorious criminals of his era, including Pablo Escobar and General Noriega, was a key player in the Iran-Contra affair, and starred in the hit documentary *Cocaine Cowboys*. Jon died in 2011.

Evan Wright is the author of *Generation Kill*, one of the most celebrated books on the Iraq War and adapted by David Simon into an HBO miniseries. He is a recipient of the National Magazine Award, a *Los Angeles Times* Book Award, a PEN/Faulkner Award and a Lukas Book Prize. He is also a contributing editor to *Rolling Stone* and *Vanity Fair*.

Also by Evan Wright

Generation Kill

Hella Nation: In Search of the Lost Tribes of America

How to Get Away With Murder in America

TO NOEMI AND JULIAN

Desperado, the horse that I thought would win the Derby and make me famous as something more than a gangster, was a baby when I got him. He hadn't been trained how to run, but he could already fly on the grass. He had good instincts. He didn't like other horses. You don't want a sociable horse. They stay in the pack. You want a horse who likes to run in front of all the other horses. Desperado was a killer. I named him Desperado because I saw myself in his eyes.

—JON ROBERTS

AMERICAN DESPERADO

1

EVAN WRIGHT (E.W.): During a break in the Heat versus Pistons game at Miami's American Airlines Arena, an announcer informs the crowd that a "very special celebrity" is in the house. "Ladies and gentlemen, we have Jon Roberts, Miami's original cocaine cowboy, with us tonight."

Live images of Roberts seated in the arena splash onto the screens in the arena: a physically fit sixty-year-old with silver hair combed straight back. Unaware that he is being filmed, Roberts gazes expressionlessly. Deepset eyes give his face a wolfish, predatory appearance. Fans seated near him stand with their camera-phones and take aim. Roberts notices his image on the screens and offers a pained okay-you-got-me grin. He puts his arm on his eight-year-old son, Julian, seated beside him. Julian ducks his head into his father's shoulder but peeks up, grinning, as cameras flash. His dad is the biggest star in the arena.

Little more than fifteen years earlier Roberts was a fugitive. His face was featured on FBI most-wanted posters at U.S. post offices across North America. He fled Miami after the U.S. government labeled him as top "American representative" of the Medellín Drug Cartel and charged him with overseeing the importation of billions of dollars of cocaine. Roberts and a small band of American partners had created a veritable FedEx of drug smuggling. They employed secret airfields, listening posts to eavesdrop on Coast Guard communications, and sophisticated homing beacons for tracking cocaine shipped by sea that stymied the U.S. government for nearly a decade. That part of Roberts's story—and the outrageous life he led that epitomized the excesses of Miami's cocaine-fueled boom of the 1980s—was told in the underground hit documentary *Cocaine Cowboys*, released in 2006.

Key aspects of Roberts's extraordinary criminal life remained untold—his rise in a powerful New York Mafia clan, the murders that prompted his exile to Miami, his involvement with a CIA official that led to a secret plea deal with the government.

Through it all, he possessed an asset not typical of admitted killers: charm. A man who did business with Roberts in his New York Mafia days—and later joined the priesthood as a result of the experience—told me, "Jon was extremely likable. He was fun to be around. Underneath that was a person capable of very bad things. He is an extreme dichotomy of good and bad. He is a very old story, Dr. Jekyll and Mr. Hyde."

Roberts's frankness about himself—usually blended with a sly, sardonic humor—can be disarming. In a phone call before we met to discuss telling his full story, he said, "I might be a sociopath. Most of the time I've been on this earth I've had no regard for human life. That's been the key to my success."

I ARRIVE in South Florida the spring of 2008 to begin interviewing Roberts for this book. He insists that I stay with him and his wife, Noemi, and son, Julian, at their house in Hollywood, Florida. He insists that I not rent a car. He'll pick me up. He'll drive, always.

"I don't ever want to be in a car with somebody else driving it," he explains.

Jon's accent is New York, but not the tough-guy dialect of the streets. He speaks an urbane New Yorkese, like Michael Douglas's Gordon Gekko in *Wall Street*. We do many hours of interviews in Jon's car, visiting old haunts—bars, smugglers' docks, murder scenes—with time out to pick up Julian at school and shuttle him to playdates and hockey practice.

When Julian is in the car, Jon drives at the proper speed and questions him about school, like any other involved parent. When Jon and I are alone in the car, he reverts to old habits. He seems to drive his car, a late-model Cadillac, at only two speeds, 75 mph on surface streets and 110 mph on freeways. As he darts in and out of traffic and squeals out of parking lots, driving with Jon feels like being dropped into a car-chase scene in a 1970s movie. I glimpse the rearview mirror, expecting to see elaborate car crashes in our wake and flashing red lights. But Jon is a precise high-speed driver, never reckless. Rocketing toward a parking space, he flicks the wheel with one hand and backs in. He always parks his car facing out, primed for a quick getaway.

Jon's home is an expansive Spanish modern, set against a lake on the Inland Waterway. Before we enter, he clips blossoms from a jasmine vine, then places them in a vase in the front hall. A friend from his New York days tells me that Jon has always liked flowers. "In his apartments he always had a bowl of water with a gardenia blossom floating in it."

Jon's hospitality is obsessive. Before my arrival he phoned me on a morning when I happened to be eating blueberries. Now a fresh basket of blueberries waits for me in the refrigerator. Every time I visit there will be blueberries.

In the Roberts household, Jon does the cooking—French toast for breakfast, pasta and baked fish for dinner. Unless there is an NBA game on, or a new episode of *Two and a Half Men*—his favorite show—meals are eaten at the long, plank-wood dining table. Noemi is responsible for setting it.

She is an energetic presence, thirty years younger than he. Noemi is African on her father's side and Hungarian on her mother's. She and Jon met shortly after she arrived in America, when she was training in a Miami park for a triathlon. There is an athletic bounce to her movements, and she speaks in an exuberant, bubbling accent—not always easily understood. She pulls me aside before my first dinner in the house and says, "I adore Jon. But the day I met him, he touched me and my body went numb, because his energy is black. Jon is not human. I love him, but I live as his prisoner. I cannot leave him because his evil is magnetic."

Overhearing his wife's commentary, Jon offers a *Father Knows Best* laugh. "Please, Noemi. You'll spoil his appetite."

Jon's older sister, Judy, who lives nearby, is a frequent dinner guest. A graduate of Emerson College, Judy was a personnel director at a large New York company while Jon pursued his criminal career. After the birth of Julian (by Jon's previous wife), Judy moved to Florida to help raise him. In her mid-sixties, Judy is slim and stylish. At the dinner table she speaks in a calming voice, directed at Julian when he mumbles about his schoolwork, then at Jon when he shouts at Julian for mumbling. "Let him speak in his own voice, Jon," she scolds.

Jon shakes his head and sighs, surrendering to his sister.

Julian smiles. You get the idea that agitating Jon is something he likes.

After dinner Jon and Julian shoot hoops in the driveway. When Julian runs for a layup, Jon grabs him and swings him in the air, closer to the rim. Julian makes the shot, and Jon releases him. Jon says, "He's a monster. He beats kids twice his size."

There are three dogs in the house. ("My first ring of defense for an intruder," Jon explains.) The biggest is Shooter, a 150-pound Presa Canario—a fighting breed banned in parts of the country due to the dogs' well-deserved reputation for fatally mauling humans. Shooter follows Jon everywhere and growls if I make a sudden movement. "He's very protective of me," Jon says. "Don't ever lift your hands high. Shooter doesn't like that."

"What will he do if I raise my hands?"

"Just don't do it. Trust me on this one, bro."

There is an awkward moment when Jon walks me into the guest room, where I'll sleep. The carpet is smeared with a five-foot-long trail of blood, bones, and animal guts. Jon curses. It's the neighbor's cat, whom Shooter has eaten and vomited up. "What a shame," Jon says, delicately scooping pieces of cat into a trash can. "I love cats."

Shooter has also killed two dogs on the block, a pit bull and a chow. Recently, he chased a Haitian gardener into a tree for whistling at Noemi. At sunset, when Jon and Noemi take Shooter for a walk, neighbors greet them with frozen smiles and retreat behind their doors. "Unfortunately, if a dog challenges Shooter, he will kill him. It's his nature," Jon says.

Late at night Jon scrubs the house from top to bottom. Judy says he has always been neat. His prison reports state that as a federal inmate, he "went beyond the call of duty in maintaining the sanitation of his sleeping area and the kitchen."

As he mops the floor one night, Jon explains the secret of a perfect shine, which he learned in prison. "Fill the bucket with ice, put the wax on when it's almost frozen. That's how you get the shine."

I joke that he cleans the house like it's a murder scene. Jon tilts his head back and laughs, while keeping his eyes on me. The eyes don't laugh. Jon is a formidable presence, even in his sixties. Though no taller than five foot ten, he wears tight shirts that show off a shredded and always deeply tanned physique. A few years ago, after his release from prison, Jon was involved in a petty altercation on the street. Police were called, and Jon found himself in the back of a squad car. With his arms cuffed behind, Jon kicked out the back window and escaped. When the two officers attempted to rearrest him, Jon badly beat one, and several more were called to subdue him with a Taser. "I overreact sometimes," Jon explains. "But I don't want to do that anymore, because of my son."

Jon avoids talking about his past in front of Julian. But the dark side of Jon's life intrudes. When Jon sends me to the store in his car to buy milk, I reach for sunglasses under the armrest—and a loaded

.45 falls out. Later Jon shows me the locations of two guns with silencers, sealed in plastic bags and buried not far from his house on somebody else's property. He says, "I'm not saying these are my guns, but now you know where they are, in case I ever tell you I need one. You can dig them out with your fingers."

While Jon keeps some secrets from Julian, he doesn't hide the positive attention he receives for his gangster past. Hollywood über-agent Ari Emanuel calls frequently to discuss Roberts's deal with Paramount Pictures and Mark Wahlberg, who plans to portray him in a film. During one such call, Noemi says, "See. People come to Jon because he is evil. Mr. Emanuel and the movie star Mark Wahlberg worship the power my husband has. They wish they could have even one pinkie full of the evil that Jon has."

Julian tells me, "Mark Wahlberg is going stay at our house. My dad's the cocaine cowboy." He adds, "Akon* wrote a song about my dad." And Julian sings, " 'Stone cold killer with a pocket full of triggers, movin' that shit by the pound, boy. Better watch out, my dad's the Cocaine Cowboy.' "†

Later in the week I enter Jon's home to find Akon himself sitting in front of the TV with Julian playing video games. Jon claims that Snoop Dogg, 50 Cent, and Lil Wayne have all made pilgrimages to visit him. As Julian explains, it's "because my dad's an original gangsta."

Jon and I begin our interviews each morning at eight-thirty, after he drops Julian at school. We sit in the living room by a window overlooking the swimming pool. Jon's recall of names, dialogue, and small details about people is impressive. Due to the notoriety of Jon's family and his own criminal career, there is a vast newspaper archive chronicling key events of his life—his name first appeared in *The New York Times* in connection with a murder shortly after

---

* The Grammy-nominated hip-hop performer and producer.
† The lyrics to the song "Cocaine Cowboys," written by Akon and performed by Akon and DJ Khaled, do not include the line "Better watch out, my dad's the Cocaine Cowboy." Julian added the line after listening to an advance copy of the song Akon gave to Jon.

his twenty-first birthday. The format of this book was originally intended to be strictly "as told by Jon," but when some of the stories he told stretched my credulity—from his tales of hanging out with Jimi Hendrix to his detailed account of committing a murder with a man who later became a high-ranking CIA officer—I sought other sources. Their voices are included here and serve to corroborate or at times challenge Jon's version of events.

Jon's language is direct, simple. He generally speaks in what could be called community college–level English, but when recalling past events, he often switches to a syntax of double negatives and *ain'ts* that's closer to the street. Like many people, when Jon tells a story from the past, he often slips into the present tense for the more action-oriented sequences. In writing the book, I occasionally changed the order of the narrative and cut for length, but I didn't invent flowery language or put false observations in Jon's mouth. In some instances, improper grammatical constructions used by Jon are preserved to maintain the authenticity of his voice. It is his story.

In pop culture the rough-edged but almost lovable gangster has almost become a stock figure. Jon does not fit that image. His self-portrait of violent and predatory behavior is far too frank. His is a story that deconstructs the myth of the honorable gangster and along the way does some serious damage to idealized views of American innocence. Jon thrived as a criminal by being a keen observer of people, and his narrative is filled with cutting portraits of the corrupt politicians, dirty cops, fallen celebrities, rogue CIA agents, and other members of the decadent ruling class who populated his world. His story ultimately stands as an unsettling social history of America, from the 1960s through the 1990s, as told from the perspective of a largely unrepentant criminal.

Jon assures me he has no interest in morality, but his conversations always turn to the moral puzzle of who he is. He begins our interview, saying, "If there is one thing my life has been about, it's the idea my father taught me when I was a boy: *Evil is stronger than good. If you have any doubt, pick the side of evil.* Those are the morals I lived by. It's how I got power in different situations. Evil always worked for me. My life is proof that my dad was right. But I hope he's wrong, too. For my son's sake. I don't want to raise my son like my father raised me."

"I don't like some of the things my son hears about me from other people. I think it's strange that we go to Miami Heat games, and when they announce I'm there, everybody applauds, like I'm a hero. If people knew the truth about me, I wonder if they would still be applauding my name.

"When I was born, America was a very straight country. A guy like me wouldn't have been applauded back then. But I hear the music my son listens to, and it's all garbage—this gangsta crap—where the singer doesn't even talk English. This is what people value today, so they probably will still applaud me. I don't care what they do. The important thing is my son will know the truth about me."

2

E.W.: Jon was born June 21, 1948, to Edie and Nat Riccobono. The Riccobono family, which included Jon's sister, Judy, five years older, lived on White Plains Road in the Bronx. Outside their apartment, the IRT train ran past on trestles. Beneath them the Bronx's Little Italy was crowded with Neapolitan bakeries, butcher shops, and olive oil merchants. The Riccobonos' apartment was above Luna Restaurant, a linguini house so quintessentially Sicilian that Francis Ford Coppola used it as the setting in *The Godfather* where Al Pacino marks his entry into the Mafia by murdering two men over dinner.*

Most of the residents in Little Italy were law-abiding citizens who wanted nothing to do with the Mafia. The

---

* Pacino shoots a mafioso named Virgil Sollozzo and the crooked cop, Captain McCluskey—played by Al Lettieri and Sterling Hayden—after retrieving a gun hidden in the restaurant bathroom. In the film, Luna is called Louis' Italian American Restaurant.

Riccobonos were not in that group. Jon's father and his uncles—his father's brothers, Sam and Joseph—claimed the Mafia equivalent of having come over on the *Mayflower*: They came to New York from Sicily allegedly on the same boat with Charles "Lucky" Luciano, a founding father of Cosa Nostra in America. Jon was born a Mafia blueblood.

Of the three Riccobono brothers, Joseph was the most infamous. Uncle Joe (as Jon calls him) made headlines in 1937 when New York special prosecutor Thomas Dewey indicted him as a member of "Murder Incorporated." Though Murder Incorporated was a mostly Jewish gang headed by Bugsy Siegel and Meyer Lansky, it worked closely with the Italian Mafia. Joseph served as Lucky Luciano's emissary inside the Yiddish gang. After his indictment, Joseph went into hiding for seven years. When he finally surrendered to authorities, the press noted that he was "one of the most fastidiously attired defendants arraigned in court in some time."* Joseph managed to wiggle out of those charges and went on to help engineer Carlo Gambino's bloody takeover of the mob after Luciano was deported by the U.S. government in 1946. He would serve Gambino as his top adviser—*consigliere*—until his death in 1975.†

Jon's other uncle, Sam Riccobono, was a capo and a successful businessman. While running a Mafia loan-sharking operation out of Brooklyn, Sam operated a taxi company and built a chain of dental labs that grew into a legitimate business.

Jon's father, Nat, was by all accounts the violent one. He served as one of Luciano's most trusted killers. By the time of Jon's birth, he was enforcing the Italian Mafia's rule over African American businesses. He ran numbers and loan-sharking operations from black bars in New Jersey.

Jon would be influenced by all three men. Like his uncle Joe, Jon developed a taste for flashy attire, an easy rapport with Jewish criminals, and an uncanny ability to slip out of seemingly impossible

---

* "Lepke Aide, Hunted 7 Years, Gives Up," *New York Times*, November 18, 1944.
† "Joseph Riccobono, Racketeer, Is Dead," *New York Times*, June 10, 1975.

legal difficulties. He acquired his uncle Sam's sense for business. Like his father, he would be violent.

Jon's mother, Edie, was a blond, blue-eyed knockout whose father was Polish and whose mother was Italian. Her parents had met in New York's garment center, where her father, Poppy Siloss,* was a fabric cutter and her mother, Honey,† was a seamstress. Though Honey had relatives in the Mafia,‡ she and Poppy lived a hardworking version of the American Dream. They raised Jon's mother in Teaneck, New Jersey, in hopes of shielding her from Honey's Mafia-connected relatives. Their effort failed. When Edie was in her late teens, she took up with Nat Riccobono and became pregnant with Jon's sister, Judy. Neither Jon nor Judy knows how their parents met.

JON ROBERTS (J.R.): My mother had nothing in common with my father. They were Beauty and the Beast. She looked like Marilyn Monroe. My dad was twenty years older. He was stocky, a balding guy. People who saw him on the street walked in the other direction. He barely spoke English. I don't think he had any formal education. He could write numbers and names on a piece of paper, and that was about it.

When I was little, I asked my mother what my dad did, and she got upset. She said, "I don't know. Don't ask me again."

In my house no one talked about the Mafia. I had to put it all together myself. In school I'd hear kids say, "His dad's one of those people." The teachers treated me differently. Nobody questioned me for being absent. Nobody yelled at me when I acted up.

I would find out my father was a "made" man. In movies they show being made as a big, holy ritual. That's the movies. When they made somebody in the Mafia, it was because a guy was bringing

---

* Though in records his surname was Siloss, Jon and his sister disagree about their maternal grandfather's first name. They called him by his nickname, Poppy.

† "Honey" was also a nickname used by Jon for his maternal grandmother.

‡ Honey's nephew Gerard "Jerry" Chilli was a captain in the Bonanno crime family whom Jon would become close to in his mid-twenties.

them a lot of money. They said a made man couldn't be killed. Not true. If they wanted to kill a made man, they could find a way. Being made mostly built ego in a guy so he'd be a better earner. The Mafia had a game just like any other organization. Burger King has its employee of the month. The Mafia had made men.

My dad's main job was controlling black bars in New Jersey. Out of the bars he loaned money and ran the numbers. The numbers game was started in Harlem way back in the early times, when the blacks were starving up there and needed a way to make money. Then it spread everywhere. Here's how it worked:

The New York *Daily Mirror* printed a circulation number that changed every day. To play the numbers, a person would guess tomorrow's circulation number. He'd write his guess on a scrap of paper, with his initials and his bet—one dollar or five dollars. Every bar had a cigar box where they'd put the bets. My dad drove around to the bars every day, paid the winners, and collected the next day's bets from the cigar boxes.

When I was about five or six, my dad started taking me around with him instead of driving me to school. My dad had a driver, Mr. Tut, who was always with him. Mr. Tut was a black guy who'd boxed in the ring but never made it big because whenever he started to lose, he'd revert to street fighting. He was a giant, with huge fists, and I liked him because unlike my father, he'd smile and seemed like a happy guy.

To my father, black people were "moolies."* That's not to say my dad was prejudiced. He didn't like anybody. He didn't even like himself, probably. To have a black driver served a purpose. It was a lot easier walking into a black bar with a black guy than with a white guy because then the blacks didn't get attitude. It helped that Mr. Tut was a tough man.

I don't want to dishonor my father, and I don't judge him, but I don't have fond memories of him. He wasn't a happy-go-lucky guy. He was not nice.

---

* An offensive slur for black people in Italian American slang.

My dad always had a big Mercury or Cadillac. He would ride up front with Mr. Tut and put me in the back. Some mornings they'd drive me to school. Other mornings my dad would take me with him to work. Since my dad didn't talk, I never knew where I was going until I looked out the window.

There was a day in about 1955 when we left early in the morning. We headed toward the bars in New Jersey. I was dozing in the back and felt the car stop. I looked up and saw my dad and Mr. Tut staring ahead.

We were in a half-residential, half-farm area of Jersey. The road led to a one-lane bridge. A car was stopped on the bridge facing ours, blocking the way. Mr. Tut started to open his door, and my dad said, "I'll take care of this."

My dad got out and walked up to the car on the bridge. He always carried a gun. I saw him take it out from his waistband and say something to the man in the car. Then he pushed his gun into the window and shot the man. *Boom, boom, boom.*

Mr. Tut said nothing. We watched as my dad opened the door to the guy's car, pushed the man he'd shot sideways, and got in. He backed the car off the bridge. We drove across it, and my father climbed back in our car.

My father turned to me and asked, "What just happened? Did you see anything?"

I said, "No. I didn't see anything."

I was lucky, I guess, because I made the right response. My father studied my face, the way you'd look at a map. I was studying him, too, like he was the map of my future. I was scared, but I felt close to him like I hadn't ever before. He'd done something that I'd have to keep a secret from everyone. I felt like he was treating me like a man.

I believe the shooting changed me. It made my reactions different from a normal person's. I learned not to get emotional. I learned to observe without reacting or crying. My father trained me in that incident to be like a soldier: not to let what I saw get to me, to move on. I was a little kid. I didn't reason this out. It seeped into me as instinct.

After the shooting I watched the news on TV. I expected to hear a story like "Man gets shot in the head," but there was nothing. I couldn't figure it out. In the movies it was a big deal if someone got shot. The police investigated. There were trials, arrests, headlines. I'd seen a real shooting, and nothing happened.

I became interested in holding a gun, to see what it felt like. We had a big, yellow-wood cabinet in the living room. I noticed my father put things behind the top ledge of the cabinet when he thought nobody was looking. I climbed up there and found a gun. It was a .38 revolver. I remember holding it, being amazed. When he shot that man in the head, it wasn't a little *pop* like in the movies. It was an explosion. I felt the tiny gun and thought, *This is unbelievable, the force of this.*

By doing a murder in front of me, my dad taught me another lesson. He showed me you can get away with things. It's not like they teach in school. My father did what he did, and he didn't go to jail. It wasn't like God punished my father, made him lose a leg or get cancer. What my father did made no difference to the universe. It showed me that if you're careful not to get caught, you can do anything. It was a very good lesson, maybe the best lesson I ever got. It made all the violence that was to come my way a lot easier.

AROUND THE time of the shooting, my family moved to Mulberry Street in Manhattan's Little Italy. It was a walk-up apartment in an old building. When you came in, you saw we had a lot of nice things. The furniture was new. We had two TVs. We had air-conditioning. It was obvious we were different. All of a sudden mink coats would show up in our house, guys with guns were dropping off expensive food, liquor. I'd go out on the street with my father, and people would move aside.

My parents fought constantly. I never saw my dad hit my mother. But she was afraid of him. I couldn't understand what put them together. What had attracted her to him? She never told me.

My mother and father's beliefs were at the opposite ends of the world. She had compassion for people. He had zero. All they had in common was that they made two children, me and my sister, Judy. She was a good girl. She didn't get into trouble. She liked school. She watched *American Bandstand*. As different as she was from me, Judy was always loyal. No matter what I did, she never looked down on me.

JUDY: Our mother was artistic. She could draw. She always had flowers in the house. Her parents, Honey and Poppy, were full of life. Poppy was born speaking Polish, but he learned to write poetry in English that he'd recite to Jon and me. Honey was a seamstress for Claire McCardell,* and she'd bring me beautiful dresses she made. Our mother drew so much from her own parents. When our father wasn't around, she had a wonderful sense of humor. She loved laughter and music. She taught me to play the piano.

Our mother worked at giving Jon and me a normal childhood. She and Honey used to take me to Philadelphia, where they filmed *American Bandstand*, so I could dance on the show.

Our mother adored Jon. He was obsessed with cowboys and Indians. He watched all the westerns on TV. She got him cowboy outfits, toy guns, and figurines. When Jon was sick in bed, she would sit with him for hours and play cowboys and Indians with his little stupid figurines.

Jon was generous with me. If he got a cookie, he'd share it with me, which is unusual for a boy and his older sister. He was physically rambunctious. He was a daredevil, always jumping off things, running all the time. He jumped off a ledge and split his head open. He came back from the hospital with giant clamps on his head and ran around like crazy. I worried the clamps would get stuck on something and his head would fall open.

Jon loved sports and memorized all the statistics. He had a very good mind for numbers. He was a little wild, but he had a sweet heart. He was a normal boy.

---

* A top, post–World War II designer.

Our home was not normal at all. We had a dual life. Our mother was light. Our father was darkness. When Jon was in grade school, he changed. He started to act out and scream and bully our mother. She shrank from him. She would not stop him from acting out. I asked her why, and she said, "I can't say anything to your brother. Your father won't let me."

I don't believe my father loved anyone, but he took an interest in Jon. I believe our father was pulling him into his darkness. Jon was so small, and such anger started to come out of him. It would grow and grow.

J.R.: My mother wouldn't tell me to do homework, to pick up my room, nothing. She stopped talking to me. I didn't understand. After I got older, I realized my mother was terribly afraid of my father. I was afraid of him, too. How could I not be? I saw him shoot a man because he blocked his way on a bridge. What normal person would not put the car in reverse and back up? Is it easier to shoot somebody in the head or back up? To my father, it was easier to shoot the guy. I did not ever want to piss this man off. Even when he would say or do something that made no sense, I never would say a word back, nothing.

But our bond was tighter after the shooting. He and Mr. Tut took me on their rounds more and more. I'd barely go to school. In the summer my dad took me to the Jersey Shore. I'd look around at other kids who were there, and they'd be with their mothers, playing little games. I'd be with my dad and his friends—guys with guns, monster bodyguards—all hanging out in the middle of the day playing cards. Nobody had a nine-to-five job.

Many days my father would take me to the racetrack. It was the one thing he did that made him look almost happy. He loved the horses and was an excellent handicapper. I got my love of horses from him. Years later, when I bought my first horse, I thought of my father. It's the one good thing he turned me on to that I thank him for.

My father really liked black music. Obviously, he ran the black bars, and that music is what we heard when we went in them. My father also liked black women. When he'd take me into the bars to collect the cigar boxes with the numbers money, he would tell Mr. Tut, "Watch Jon."

Mr. Tut would sit me at the bar, get me a Coke, and my dad would disappear with a woman. He liked black music and black, black women. Italians don't like to admit this, but in ancient times there was a black migration into Sicily. That's why you see a lot of Italians with very dark complexions. There's African blood mixed in all of us.

Another part of my father's job was looking for people who owed him "vig"—interest on the money he lent. My dad put a lot of money out on the street to blacks and whites. When a guy didn't pay on time, my father would have to chase him down and give him a beating.

It was easy to find people in those days. It was a simpler world. People didn't have the means to pack their bags and take off. If you owed my father money, he and Mr. Tut would drive around until they found you. They'd ask around in the bars. There was always somebody in the bar who would rat out a deadbeat. "The motherfucker that owes you the money is over here."

We'd drive to wherever he was, and my dad would beat the guy. He'd take whatever was in his pockets. If he had a car, he'd take that from him, too.

My dad had big arms and hands, but he didn't believe in using his hands on people. He always hit people with objects. My dad kept a baseball bat in the car. Sometimes he carried brass knuckles. If he had nothing else, he'd beat the guy with the end of his gun. He didn't believe in punching it out with the other guy. My dad was there to give a beating.

Even as a kid, I understood my father's thought train: *The quicker you do a beating, the less problems you're going to have.* If you stand there and punch somebody back and forth, you don't know how long it's going to last. My father's belief was to hit the guy with something hard and end it as quickly as possible. Make your point physically and move on.

My father was careful not to hit people in the face who owed him money. You hit somebody in the face with a baseball bat, you might kill him, and then you won't collect your money. My dad focused on breaking people's arms, or cracking their shins. I can tell you, when you break someone's bones, they will scream bloody murder. But I never saw my father get excited when he beat people. For him violence was a business tool.

My dad did some things that were a mystery to me. If the guy who owed him money was with a friend, my dad would beat the snot out of the friend, too. My dad would tell him, "This is what you get for being friends with a piece of shit who owes me money."

It made no sense to me. Why beat the one guy if the other one owes you money? But that was my dad's way to make his points to people. If he thought his way was right, then it was right. All my dad's friends and my uncles, they all thought the same way. To them, their way was the right way. There was no question about it.

I'm a person who's used to violence, inflicting it and taking it. I've been shot, had bones broken, and I have been tortured a few times. One time in Mexico dirty cops put jumper cables on my balls and electrocuted me. That was not a good day. But violence and pain don't scare me. They make me angry. They hurt. They force me to concentrate my reasoning and solve the problem of why someone is hurting me.

But you take a normal person, and you break his bones, or you make him watch while you break his friend's bones, or burn his skin with a lighter, he will become very frightened. He will follow the directions you give him. I learned this from the way my father used pain and fear. My father instilled in me that if you're doing something wrong, do it in a forceful way, and you'll come out way ahead. Way ahead.

My dad never explained his philosophy in words. I used to wish he would talk to me more, but he didn't. I had to watch him. I absorbed what I saw without reasoning or understanding. But what I saw entered my mind and changed how I looked at the world. On the playground I would see kids draw a little circle in the dust, and two guys would stand and fight each other. In my dad's world, there were no little circles.

As a nine-year-old, I couldn't put what he was teaching me into words. But as I got older, my father's philosophy became clear: evil is stronger than good. To kill, to hurt, to instill fear gives you power over situations and people. If you have a problem, choose the most evil way to solve it, and do the evil as forcefully as you can. That's how you come out on top. The evil path is the strong path, because evil is stronger than good.

That is what, unfortunately, my father taught me. Having a son of my own, I see that what you put into the eyes and ears of a child feeds his mind. His mind will grow different ways depending on what you feed it. My mind was fed the power of evil.

I'm not saying I agreed with everything I saw my father do. We'd go to the bar in the middle of the day, and my father would lend money to some poor fucker that didn't have a job. The guy borrowing the money was borrowing it to drink. My dad didn't give a fuck. When the guy couldn't pay him back, my dad would tell him, "You better go steal the money you owe me." And the guy would. That was my dad's business, taking money from poor people who had to steal from other poor people to pay him. What kind of business is that?

One time he lent money to a man who had a hardware store in Jersey. When the man couldn't pay, my dad took it over. Instead of running the hardware store, my dad had a fire sale. He went out with his guys, and they laid out boxes of screws, hammers, saws, cash registers—everything. Come and get it. Whatever people would pay for it, my dad put the money in his pocket. That was the end of the hardware store. He sold it out and burned it to the ground.

I saw other kids whose dads owned shops, and they lived in nice houses. I'd look at my dad and think, *Hey, Dad. Why not run the hardware business like a real business?*

I'm not judging my father, or looking down on him. He had the correct understanding about evil being stronger than good, but if you look at what he did with his knowledge, he was not at all smart. His business was based on poor people. You can only go so far with poor people. My outlook is, if you want to be a bank robber, don't just be a good one. Rob the biggest fucking bank you can rob.

I WAS ten years old when my father gave my mother a '57 Thunderbird convertible. It made my mother happy. I could see this in her: she hated my father, but she wouldn't turn down the nice things he gave her.

The flashy car made us stand out in the neighborhood. It made me think we were moving up in the world. Of course, my parents could leave it on the street with the top down and keys in it, and nobody would touch it. I was proud that my family was special.

After my dad brought home the Thunderbird, a strange incident happened. My father and Mr. Tut took me to a boxing match at Madison Square Garden, and a mob of reporters came up to him. They were shouting questions, taking pictures. They chased my dad out of there. I'd never seen my dad run from anybody.

A few days later my dad did a funny thing. He told me he had to talk to me. The only other time I remember my dad directly talking to me was after he murdered the man on the bridge. I was nervous when I walked out to the car with him and Mr. Tut. We got in, and Mr. Tut drove for a while. My dad turned to me and said, "The cops are going to take me away, and you won't see me for a long time."

Then the cops came to our house. Two men in suits, all the rest in blue. My mother let them in. My dad waited for them in the kitchen. He stood up when they entered and said nothing. It was very peaceful. My dad's attitude was, even though the police were against you, they were doing their job. When they got you, they got you. My mother was quiet when he walked out with them. Nobody ever talked much in the house when my father was around. This day was no different. As my dad walked out the door, he looked at me and said, "I'm gone."

3

J.R.: My father was deported to Sicily in 1959. Years later I found out what happened. When Lucky Luciano, the boss of all the Mafia families, was deported by the government in 1946, a man named Albert Anastasia took over. In 1957 Carlo Gambino, who my dad and my uncles were loyal to, decided to take over from Anastasia.

Albert Anastasia used to get his hair cut at the barbershop in the Park Sheraton Hotel.* One morning a couple of guys went in there and shot him to death in his barber chair,† and Gambino became the boss of everything. I don't know if my family was involved in whacking Anastasia, but after it happened my uncle Joe got a big promotion. He became Gambino's *consigliere*. I'm sure my dad got a promotion, too. Maybe he got my mother the Thunderbird to celebrate it.

---

* Now called the Park Central Hotel on 870 Seventh Avenue.
† On October 25, 1957.

The mistake that happened was, a few weeks after Gambino took over, he called all the top gangsters from around the country to meet with him. They gathered at a farm in upstate New York, a place called Apalachin. The meeting turned into a fiasco when a nosy cop saw all the flashy gangster cars parked at the farm and raided the place.* They caught dozens of top Mafia bosses there, including my uncle Joe and my dad. The Riccobono name was in the papers every day.† That's why the reporters chased us at Madison Square Garden. My uncle Joe became infamous as the head of the "Apalachin Five"—top Mafia guys arrested at Apalachin who refused to testify about what they were doing there.‡ He fought for his right not to testify up to a federal appellate court and won.§

My dad had a different problem after his arrest at Apalachin. Unlike my uncle Joe, who was an American citizen, my dad was what they now call an illegal alien. Everything he had—driver's license, leases, cars he owned—it was all fake names and forgeries.**

---

* The Apalachin Meeting raid on November 14, 1957, was a seismic event in the annals of American crime, prompting congressional hearings and a restructuring of the FBI, which for years under the leadership of J. Edgar Hoover had denied the existence of a nationally organized Mafia.

† Joseph Riccobono had been in the center of a few media storms ever since Thomas Dewey indicted him in connection with Murder Inc. in the 1930s, but his arrest at Apalachin gave him a degree of infamy that culminated in his being named as a top boss in Joe Valachi's testimony to the U.S. Senate in 1963. His name would surface again in 1978 congressional hearings exploring the assassination of John F. Kennedy, though no evidence was presented that connected him to the death of the president.

‡ "Apalachin 5 in U.S. Plea," United Press International, August 28, 1958.

§ Texts of Opinions Reversing Conspiracy Convictions at Apalachin Meeting," New York Times, November 29, 1960.

** Jon's own records from this era are incomplete. He has not produced a birth certificate, and his sister Judy's birth certificate, while it shows her birthplace as the Bronx, bears a Jewish surname. Jon states that his father acquired false birth certificates for both children. I interviewed many sources who knew Jon in his youth as "John Riccobono." In published accounts of Jon's criminal activities in the late 1960s, he is called "John Riccobono." But one source I interviewed claimed that Jon's father was a Jewish gangster affiliated with the Riccobonos named "Epstein"—a name that Jon also used as a criminal alias in the 1980s. Law-enforcement officials I interviewed who were involved in the 2005 arrest of Mafia capo Gerard Chilli—who Jon claims is his maternal uncle—believe that Chilli is indeed an uncle of Jon's and that he is Italian.

He and my mother weren't even legally married. The cops released him after his arrest at Apalachin, but later they decided to deport all the illegal aliens connected with the Mafia.*

My father was a made man. The son of a made man will usually become a made man. But when my dad was deported, his power went away. Because of who my family was, I was like a prince in the Mafia, but when he left, I was also a bastard.

I saw this right away in my house. As soon as my father disappeared, my mother turned on me. After not talking to me for years, now she followed me around nagging me.

"You don't want to be like your father," she'd say. "Go to school."

When I argued back, she'd say, "You're just like your father. You're bad like he is."

I realize now my mother was trying to correct me. But it was too late. I was already just like my dad. I could feel it inside. I'm sure I reminded my mother of the mistake she'd made in being with my father.

A few months after my dad was deported, my mother put me on a plane and sent me to Palermo. This was in 1960, when flying overseas was not an ordinary thing. I was twelve, and I flew alone. I was supposed to stay with my father so he could raise me, and I wouldn't be a problem for my mother anymore.

To me, going to Sicily was like traveling to the Stone Age. There was no basketball, no baseball, no TV. I missed *Sea Hunt* and *Bonanza,* my favorite TV shows. My father dragged me here and there, and nothing made sense to me. All I saw was old Mafia guys playing dominoes, drinking coffee. I didn't speak a word of Italian. There were no kids my age. I hated Italy. It was so bad even my father showed compassion. He sent me home after a few weeks. I never heard from him again.

I never loved my father the way a normal person is supposed to

---

* "U.S. Taking Steps to Deport Aliens at Gang Meeting," *New York Times,* November 24, 1957.

love their parent. I respected him because I feared him. I didn't feel any love from him. I don't think my father was capable of love. I know that because I grew up to be just like him. I had no love for anybody.

WHEN I came back from Italy, my mom had moved to Teaneck, New Jersey, with my grandparents Honey and Poppy. Their house was the first house I'd ever lived in. It felt like a mansion. I went back years later and couldn't believe how small it was. It was a narrow two-story house divided into small rooms—a sardine can divided into smaller sardine cans. Including my sister, Judy, there were five of us in there.

But I'm not complaining. It was a good home. The only problem in that house was me.

They put me in a local school. I hadn't really been in school for a couple years. My thought patterns were different from other kids'. The stuff they taught in class was ridiculous. The story of George Washington and the cherry tree, where he says, "I cannot tell a lie." You've got to be kidding me. I'd hear this shit and laugh my ass off.

I made friends with kids on my street, but I didn't know how to get along with them. One day I was playing basketball with a kid at a little hoop his dad made for him in the driveway. I punched the kid. In Little Italy it was no big deal to fight with your friends. In Teaneck it was a major offense. The kid's parents came to my grandparents' house. Everybody was yelling, "This boy is your neighbor. You can't hit your neighbor."

The neighbors said I was messed up because I didn't have a dad. A guy in the neighborhood felt sorry for me and put me on a baseball team. It was called the Firemen because we were sponsored by an engine house. Our team was all the messed-up kids from bad homes. We had a game against a team of normal kids, and a fight started. I wasn't involved at first. But no way would I miss a fight. I grabbed a bat and started swinging. Everybody else was using their fists. I'm swinging my bat. One of the fathers tried to grab my bat. I hit him in the face. Now I got all the fathers of the kids from good homes chasing me. They finally took me down with a baseball bat and sent me to the hospital with a broken arm. I was off the team.

Watching *Bonanza* on TV was one thing I had in common with normal kids. Everybody went nuts over that show. I loved Westerns. I wanted to be a gunfighter. Here was one thing I could relate to with the rest of America. But when I listened to how other people talked about *Bonanza,* I was amazed. We had a teacher in school who talked about the show in class. He explained how the Cartwright family* represented the good values of America because they were on the side of law and justice.

My way of seeing it was different. To me the Cartwrights had the might and power, and they used it to take over all that land on their Ponderosa ranch. Thousands of acres. You're telling me it's fair that one family gets so much land? Some poor asshole in his little covered wagon wanders onto the Ponderosa ranch, and the Cartwrights ride out with guns and chase him off. They had the sheriff paid off, too. Anybody the Cartwrights didn't like, he got thrown in the jail. No trial, nothing. From the way I saw it, the Cartwrights were the same as my father and uncles in the Mafia. They understood force.

Because of all the stories in the news about my family, Riccobono was a bad name. My mother told me I had to change my last name. I changed my name to Jon Pernell Roberts, after Pernell Roberts, who played the oldest son on *Bonanza.* I liked him the best because he wore black. His hat, his vest, his gun belt were all black. He was the top enforcer for the family. He was the kind of guy I wanted to be. I wanted to steal my own Ponderosa when I grew up.

JUDY: When we moved to Teaneck, I coped with the bad in our family by throwing myself into schoolwork and my social life. I made myself oblivious by being good and pretending everything was good. Jon was the opposite. My father was an unspeakably evil

---

* The fictitious ranching family on which *Bonanza* centered.

man. But he was Jon's dad, and Jon lost him. It hurt him. He fought in school. He argued with our mother. He was still a little boy, but he was already mad at society.

Our grandfather, Poppy, was the only positive influence Jon had. Poppy was a wonderful man, and Jon loved him.

J.R.: I didn't love Poppy. The concept of me loving a person was not a concept. But I liked Poppy.

Poppy was a straight old-country Polish guy. Didn't drink, worked his ass off. He tried to raise me properly. Everything was poetic to him. He would talk about shit like the beauty of the sky. He was the total opposite of my father. I thought he was strange. Not bad, but strange.

Poppy loved to fish, and this is something he passed to me: the love of the water. It helped when I got into smuggling. On the weekends we would go to the Bronx and get on a drift-fishing boat. We had to be at the dock at five-thirty in the morning so Poppy could get a special place on the boat. The way I looked at it, if you're going to catch fish, you're going to catch fish, no matter where you sit. But Poppy had his way of doing it.

We'd go toward the Jersey shore for fluke or bluefish, or up toward Connecticut, where we would get black fish and mackerel in the colder water. On the way out they'd have a poker game on the boat.

These weren't anything like my dad's games, where his friends would play for hundreds of dollars with their guns out. Poppy and his friends played for a few dollars. One time Poppy won the game, and another guy on the boat called him a cheater. Poppy said nothing to this man. He did not stand up for himself.

The way this man treated Poppy turned my stomach. I couldn't believe the weakness Poppy showed. I was twelve, but I went up to the man and said, "You think he's a cheat? You're a piece of shit."

I spat in his face, and the guy hit me.

There was a mate on the boat, a teenager who liked Poppy. When he saw me get punched, he started beating on the guy. I picked up a grappling hook and began swinging. All hell broke loose.

When we got home, Poppy didn't talk to me. The man wouldn't raise his voice. He showed his anger with silence. I couldn't understand him. He'd shown weakness, and I'd tried to back him up.

Poppy took me fishing again, and I got us banned from the boat. The men on the boat had a betting pool. Each man would put in a dollar, and whoever caught the biggest fish won the pot. I watched everybody putting in their money one morning, and I remember looking at these jerks, thinking, *I'm going to take their money.*

There was $52 in it that day. I caught a fish. He was big, but there were other fish equal to my fish. So I took some lead sinkers, stuffed them down my fish's stomach, and made him the winner. I got the $52, and I tossed my fish in the bucket. Poppy was proud. He told the mate, "Filet our fish, because we're going to eat it tonight with his grandmother."

I didn't pay attention. I got my $52. I'm happy.

Then the mate came back and said, "Gee whiz, we're going to have to disqualify your grandson. Jon cheated."

Poppy put his arm on my shoulder and said, "Give back the money."

I looked him in the eye. "I don't give a fuck. The money is mine."

I knew Poppy wouldn't do anything. He'd backed down at the poker game when the guy called him a cheater. He wasn't going to fight me. He paid back the betting pool out of his own pocket.

AFTER I saw how weak Poppy was, there was no controlling me. I'd come home with lunch money I stole from a kid at school, and Poppy would ask where I got it.

"None of your fucking business." I knew how to handle him.

My school was Thomas Jefferson Middle School in Teaneck. When I didn't want to go, I'd call in bomb scares. Eventually some idiot ratted me out. The police took me and my mom to the fire station so they could lecture me about the consequences of my actions.

One of the cops said, "All these firemen have to get on their fire engines and drive to the school because of what you did."

"Why am I supposed to feel bad for making firemen get in their fire trucks? Isn't that their job?" I thought I was hilarious.

At thirteen I was already hairy. I started to shave. I looked older. I felt older. I played basketball with older kids in the city court. I thought I was going to be a professional basketball player. I was not tall, but I was fast. I liked playing kids who were bigger than me and beating them.

There was a high school boy I played whose name I'll never forget: Ivor Swenson.* He was a Swede or a German, over six feet tall, a star on the high school football and basketball teams. No matter how cold it was, he'd always take his shirt off when we played because he liked to show off his muscles. He always beat me.

Then I got better and finally beat him. That day I could see in his eyes it bothered him that a small kid beat him, so I rubbed it in by laughing in his face. He lost control and punched me. One pop, and I had a bloody nose. I looked at the blood streaming into my hands and became angry.

Ivor believed he was so big, he could get away with hitting me. He was technically correct. I wasn't afraid to fight him. I would fight anyone. But there was no way I could take him. He was 180 pounds. I was maybe 100 pounds.

I would make my point to him a different way. After he hit me I acted apologetic. I said, "Ivor, maybe your game was off. Let's play again."

He agreed. The asshole wouldn't shake my hand, but that was okay. I had a plan.

There was a group of older Italian kids from around Teaneck that I was starting to hang out with. They were bad kids, and I went to them and asked if they could get me a gun to give somebody a little scare. They thought it was comical helping an eighth grader

---

* Ivor Swenson is a pseudonym to protect the identity of Jon's victim.

get a gun, so they gave me one. A few days later I met Ivor at the court. I carried the gun wrapped in a towel.

"You ready to play?" I asked.

It was a cold day. But it didn't matter. Ivor was going to take his shirt off to show off how big he was, and as soon as his shirt was over his head, I shot at his leg. It wasn't as easy as my dad made it look when he killed the guy on the bridge. I was only two or three feet away, and I shot a few bullets without hitting Ivor. He danced around with his shirt stuck over his head, yelling while I fired away. It was like a scene in the cowboy movies where they make the guy dance by shooting at his feet. Finally, the big kraut fell over. He's crawling around, his shirt still stuck over his head. I saw a red spot in his warm-up pants where I shot his calf. I put my foot on his back and told him I'd shoot again if he didn't stop moving. I watched the blood spot grow. It reminded me of a science-class film strip they showed in school of a flower opening up. It was beautiful. Ivor was shaking and crying under my foot. I will admit to you I got excited watching him suffer. I wanted to say something to him. Finally, it came to me like a line from a movie: "Let's see how much basketball you play now, you prick."

I kick him in the head, walk away, and throw the gun in a sewer.

That night, I went home, turned on the TV, and that was it. Nobody came after me. I never got charged with a crime. Nothing happened.* I felt nothing. It did surprise me that I shot Ivor. I wasn't sure I would actually shoot him. I had proved something to my-self. I didn't have a father anymore. But I was a man. I had my dad inside me.

---

* There is no record of this shooting. One of Jon's friend's from that era, Peter Gallione, whom I interviewed, recalled that Jon was involved in several shootings, but he did not remember this incident. Gallione added that Jon and the friends who gave him the gun had assaulted and terrorized so many kids, they were often afraid to report them to the police.

4

J.R.: My mother took a job at Revlon. She went to different stores in New York and showed makeup products. She told me, "I promise you, you're going to have a good life."

Her way of trying to improve our lives was dating rich men. For a while she was involved with one of the top guys at Revlon. Then along came this other man. His name was Arnold Goldfinger, like in the James Bond movie *Goldfinger*. He had a lot of money. He drove a new Cadillac and lived in a big house in West Englewood, which was the rich area near Teaneck. My mother had hit the jackpot.

JUDY: Our mother married Arnold Goldfinger in 1961. He owned a radio tube factory and was very wealthy. My mother believed having a better life would help Jon. Unfortunately, the marriage did not have a good effect on Jon. He felt betrayed by our mother.

J.R.: I never liked my mother being with that guy. She changed. All of a sudden she had a halo around her head. When my dad was putting furs on her back, getting her the nice car, she never stopped him. Now he was that terrible man, and Arnold Goldfinger was our savior. She told me, "Arnold is going to be your father. He owns a factory, and someday it will be yours."

The first time I met Goldfinger, he told me I shouldn't turn out like my father. God, I hated him. He got rich because he made a special radio tube that had to go in radar machines used by the military. My mother took me to his factory, and he showed me all the people working for him. My mother kept saying, "You see how smart he is? You should be just like him."

I looked at Arnold Goldfinger and said, "Who fucking cares about your money?"

Everybody kissed his ass. I wanted him to know I was never going to like him.

The feeling was mutual. When my mother told him how much I liked the Harlem Globetrotters, he offered to buy me tickets. But there was a catch. I had to write one thousand times on paper: "Please, Mr. Goldfinger, let me see the Harlem Globetrotters."

I wrote it, because I loved the Harlem Globetrotters. But it made me hate his guts even more.

JUDY: Excuse me for saying this, but when it came to Jon, our stepfather was a prick. He had money up the kazoo. He lived in a mansion. When we moved in, I was given my own bedroom. You know where he made Jon sleep? In a storeroom downstairs, where they had kept dogs.

J.R.: When they put me in the dog room, that's when I knew my mother had literally thrown me to the dogs. I decided, "Fuck my mother, fuck everybody."

I didn't talk to my mother. I didn't look at her anymore. A few weeks after we moved into the house, she and Arnold went to Europe on a honeymoon. Judy had graduated from high school and was dating a guy, so she was gone most of the time. I was in the house alone with my two older stepsisters. Barbara, the eldest, was nineteen, and she was put in charge of me. She worked in a bank and already had the attitude of a classic ballbusting Jewish broad. Her main rule was that I stay downstairs in my dog room.

The one bright spot of moving to West Englewood was a girl who lived down the street named Nancy. I was at the age where the stuff was pumping in me. Nancy was a couple years older than me. She was a blond bad girl who was into rock and roll. Her thing was teaching me to play doctor. She let me feel her titties, her ass. She showed me how she liked to be kissed. We were doing this one day, and suddenly it felt like the walls were moving. My pants got wet. I didn't know what had happened, but it felt good. All she'd done was use her hand, but it gave me an inkling how good a girl could make you feel. I never looked at girls the same way after that. One hand, and they could take you into a different world.

I still was hanging out with my older friends who'd gotten me the gun. These guys were seventeen and eighteen. They'd come over at night and drink beer in my little dog room. One night one of them said, "Hey, let's take your stepdad's car into Manhattan."

My stepfather drove a 1961 silver-blue Cadillac. It was a beautiful car. While he and my mom were in Europe, my stepsister Barbara had the keys. I waited until she went to sleep and took them from her purse. I met my friends outside, and I got into the driver's seat.

"You don't know how to drive," my friends said.

"Guess I'll learn real quick."

I'd driven around with my father and Mr. Tut for years. Driving was no big deal. Next thing I know, I'm on the highway driving across the George Washington Bridge into Manhattan. My friends are laughing. "You better let us drive home, because we're going to get you fucking drunk tonight."

Even though I was thirteen years old, my friends knew a shithole on the East Side called the Blue & Gold Tavern* where the

---

* The Blue & Gold Tavern is still on East Seventh Street.

bartender didn't care. I walked in and sat at the bar, and he said, "You want a beer, kid?"

I had no tolerance. I drank two or three beers, and I was history. Hours later I came to in the back of my stepfather's Cadillac. One of my friends was driving. Route 4 was the road to my stepfather's house. I was so drunk, when I looked out the window at the sign, I thought it read "Route 44." I was seeing double.

I start yelling that it's my car, I got to drive it. My friend pulls over. "Drive your fucking car."

I nearly made it to my stepfather's house, but when I reached his street, I drove on the sidewalk and hit a telephone pole. The pole broke over across the hood. We crawled out of the car laughing.

The next morning I woke up in my dog room. My stepsister Barbara was shaking me. "You wrecked my dad's car!"

"Come on, I'm thirteen years old. I don't even know how to start a car. Someone must have stolen it."

I tried going back to sleep. Then I heard my stepsister in the next room, calling our parents in Europe. I ran in, grabbed the phone from her hand, and smashed it. She tried fighting me, and I knocked her over. That put some fear in her eyes.

I told that bitch how it was going to be. "Don't make aggravation for our parents on their honeymoon. You let the car get stolen. You're the asshole. You fix the car."

For weeks and weeks my stepsister had thought she had the upper hand, that I was a dog living in the storeroom. Those days were done. She paid to repair the car and fix the telephone pole.

By the time my mother and stepfather returned from Europe, the car looked brand new. My mother was home a few days when she came into my room and said, "I'm going in the hospital tomorrow. I'm going to have an operation."

I said nothing. I still was not talking to her.

JUDY: Our mother had become pregnant by Arnold Goldfinger, and she decided not to keep the baby. In those days doctors would say they were doing a "hysterectomy," but it was a euphemism. She went to Fifth and Flower Hospital in Manhattan and had an abortion.

J.R.: A day after my mom went into the hospital, my stepfather told me, "Your mother's sick. There were complications. She has peritonitis, blood poisoning, and lobar pneumonia."

My stepfather wanted to drive me into the hospital to see her. There was no way I would visit her with that piece of shit. In my group of Italian friends from Teaneck was a guy named Jack Buccino, who offered to drive me.

Jack had a red Ford Fairlane convertible that I'll never forget. It was a nice day when we crossed over the bridge into the city. I had a very strange thought, a magical thought. My sister had told me the real reason our mother had gone to the hospital. Driving across the bridge, I thought maybe my mother had the abortion because she didn't want to be with our stepfather anymore. She was going to leave him. I thought by visiting her now, I was going to change everything. We'd start talking again. Everything would be different. I'd stop going down the path I was on. I'd be a normal kid.

When the nurse took me into my mother's room, I didn't recognize her. There were tubes sticking out of her. Her face was caved in. She was out of it. I didn't even try to talk. I went to a bar with Jack and got blasted out of my mind on beer.

A day later my stepfather came up to me. "Good news," he said. "Your mother made a great improvement. She's getting better."

What I didn't know—and what my stepfather didn't know—is that sometimes when somebody is really sick, they give it one last fight, to try to live. My mother did that. Everybody thought she was getting better. Next day she was dead.

My mother's death shook me for a long time. The last memory I have of my mother is a woman in the hospital with tubes in her who I could not talk to. That's the picture of her that stays in my eyes today.

JUDY: Jon did not shed a tear when our mother died. His reaction was not natural. Instead of going through grief, he filled with more hatred.

For all the bad things I can say about our stepfather, he loved our mother. After she died, he took her ashes to Florence, Italy, and buried her there. That had been her favorite city on their honeymoon, and he showed his devotion by taking her there one last time.

He treated Jon and me terribly. He gave away her jewelry to my stepsisters. He threw out photographs. He made me buy the piano my mother got for me when I was little. The only item of clothing I kept of my mother's was her plaid coat. It was red and black and had big buttons down the front. That coat was my mother: bright, bold, full of life. I don't think Jon knew that woman. She adored Jon, but he didn't see that. She died before he could figure her out.

J.R.: My sister was the one fucked up by our mother's death. She went insane over the piano. It was her only bond with our mother. She dragged that fucking piano from place to place for decades. She was never the same after our mother died.

As I got older, I stopped holding a grudge against my mother. I saw she made decisions for reasons I didn't understand as a kid. I don't hate her anymore. I thank her. She gave me my life. I regret now that I never said, "Hey, Mom, I love you."

But that new way of seeing her came years later. When my mother died, it reinforced the way I was. Her death made me stronger. I didn't give a fuck anymore about anything. My philosophy was, fuck the world.

5

J.R.: Both my father's brothers took an interest in me. My uncle Sam, from Brooklyn, was the only person on my father's side who had any heart. He was younger than my father and looked more American to me. He'd come out to Jersey to visit me, take me for a ride in his car. I'd tell him about the trouble I was making at school and he'd laugh and tell me to knock it off. I used to wish he was my father, but then he'd go away and I wouldn't see him for six months.

My uncle Joe, my dad's older brother, was bald and had a beak nose that made him look like a bird that could eat you. After my mother died, he had a car pick me up and take me to a restaurant in Little Italy. He had bodyguards sitting at the tables around him. He didn't laugh or smile like Sam. But as different as my uncles were from each other, both told me the same thing: I should stay with my stepfather because it was good to grow up in a rich man's house.

My stepfather drank and drank after he lost my mother. He was a wreck. As broken up as he was, and as much as we hated each other, he let me stay in his home. He tried to make rules. He'd say, "It's a school night. Be home early."

My older friends would come over, and we'd set back all the clocks and go out. I'd come home drunk, fucked up on weed, at two in the morning, and my stepfather would stumble out to yell at me. I'd point to the clocks set to the wrong time and say, "Fuck you. I'm home early."

My stepdad kicked me out of his house. My grandparents couldn't handle me. My sister had gotten married and moved out of state. So I was sent to a boys' home in Hackensack.

Being in the boys' home just made me closer to the older kids I'd been running with. The reason Ivor never ratted me out after I shot him on the basketball court was because he was afraid of these guys.* They were the worst kids in Teaneck.

They called themselves the Outcasts, but they were never a true gang. They were just a group of kids that ran together. They became my brothers. They didn't make me who I was, but they put a lot of craziness into me. God Almighty, what a crew they were. These guys were maniacs.

There was Frank Messina.† His father was a typical Mafia thug who weighed four hundred pounds. He owned a driving school. He had one of those cars with two steering wheels, but Mr. Messina was so fat they had to indent the dashboard and push it back so he could fit. His son Frank was a small guy who was so nuts he used to wear a cape, like he was a vampire. As we got a little older, Frank started to carry a sawed-off shotgun under his cape, so it came in handy.

Another Outcast was Rocco Ciofani.‡ Rocco was a tough, tough kid. His father was a straight Italian guy, a working man, who had an auto-body shop. I ran away from the boys' home and slept in his

---

* One of Jon's friends from this era says that they once assaulted Ivor Swenson for threatening to rat them out for a scheme to pass counterfeit money.
† Frank Messina is a pseudonym to protect the identity of Jon's friend.
‡ Rocco Ciofani is a pseudonym to protect the identity of Jon's friend.

shop until Mr. Ciofani threw me out. He knew we were no good. Rocco was a shorter guy. He was a trained boxer, and he was crazy with a shotgun.

Not everyone in the Outcasts was Italian. Bernie Levine* was a fat, spoiled Jewish kid who lived near my stepfather's house. All the Outcasts hung out in Bernie's basement because he got all the drugs—weed, speed, heroin. It's at his house that a bunch of Outcasts started shooting heroin. I took lots of drugs, but I never got hooked on injecting them.

Bernie became very important later in my life. In the early 1970s, he moved to San Francisco and ran a recording studio for bands like the Grateful Dead. I was living in Miami by then, and Bernie got me started supplying his bands in San Francisco with cocaine. That's how I first got big in the coke business. It started with an Outcast. These guys stayed with me through my whole life.

Jack Buccino, the kid who drove me to see my mother in the hospital before she died, was another Outcast. I stayed at his house after Mr. Ciofani kicked me out of the auto-body shop. What a weird family. Jack's mother was a half-baked lounge singer. His father sold fake aluminum siding. He believed he was really good-looking and dressed like he was Dick Clark on *American Bandstand*.

From his parents' stupid influence, Jack fancied himself an actor and a singer. That was his goal in life. Mrs. Buccino was a typical Italian mother who babied the fuck out of him and let him live in a fantasy world. Jack sang in bands and talked about being in the movies, but mostly he was a junkie thief who never moved out of his parents' house.

When I was in middle school, all the Outcasts were high school age or older. They thought I was amusing because I would fight anyone. I still went to school sometimes, and the Outcasts would come by and look for kids for me to fight. They'd stand by the playground and point at a big kid and say, "Go fucking slap him and tell him to meet you by the dugout."

---

* Bernie Levine is a pseudonym to protect the identity of Jon's friend.

That was the spot for fighting. I'd fight the kid, and if I started to lose, the Outcasts would all jump in and beat his ass.

There was a black kid at my school who had two first names—Herbert Peter.* He was a real wacko, a bad kid like me. He had been held back a few grades, and his muscles were overdeveloped. To be king of the school, I decided to fight him. Even the Outcasts thought I might be overreaching, and they were right.

Herbert Peter gave me the fight of my life. He knocked me down, stomped me. He beat the stuffing out of me. The Outcasts didn't stop that one. They stood back laughing their balls off.

AFTER I got my ass kicked, the Outcasts taught me how to really fight. The biggest Outcast was Dominic Fiore,† who was over six feet tall. He became my teacher. We'd hang out in his basement. We'd push all the furniture to the side, and he and the other Outcasts would beat the shit out of me.

Dominic's belief was: to give a beating, you got to learn to take a beating. I'd already been beaten by Herbert Peter. But Dominic believed I needed more. You learn to take pain so it doesn't make you curl up or run. Dominic and the other Outcasts beat me with their hands, with pool cues, belts, chair legs. Then they taught me how to use those tools properly.

I'd seen my father give hundreds of beatings with a baseball bat, but Dominic taught me how to really use one. There is an art to everything. You think you just grab a bat and start swinging? It doesn't work like that, bro. I mean, give a normal person a bat and give me a bat, and we'll see who does what.

You don't swing for the fences when you fight with a bat. I approach you carrying my bat pointed down so it matches my leg. You might not even notice it. When I come close, I bring my bat up, grip it in both hands, and swing it low at your knee. If I hit you near the knee with any force, I will put you on the ground. I don't care

---

* Herbert Peter is a pseudonym to protect the identity of Jon's schoolmate.
† Dominic Fiori is a pseudonym to protect the identity of Jon's friend.

if you're a guy who weighs four hundred pounds. A bat to the knee will drop Superman, and when you're on the ground, I own you.

When you're bat-fighting, as soon as you get your guy on the ground, you need to reverse your grip on the bat. Put your strong hand near the end of the handle and your weaker hand below it. Point the bat down like you're grinding herbs in a mortar and pestle. You're going to pump the bat up and down on the person underneath it. Focus on taking out the knees, elbows, and hands. After that they ain't running nowhere, bro. Now you can take your time cracking their ribs, busting their balls—anything you want. When you got a bat, you're king.

If you don't have a bat, no matter what the other guy is doing, focus on his weak points. Take away his legs by kicking his knees. Take away his eyes by sticking him with your fingers or something sharp like a broken bottle. Work on his shins. Shins are very sensitive, and you can hurt a person real bad on his shins. The shinbone is the strongest bone in the body, but the front edge is tender if you stomp it.

Even though I just said the fronts of a person's shins are sensitive, when I kick people in the balls, I will use my own shinbone. My shin hits with more force than my foot, and my shinbone won't hurt me because I'm kicking balls, which are soft. You can break someone's balls with your shinbone. When you're fighting, look for every opportunity to hurt the other guy's eyes and knees and shins. And no matter what, always be kicking his balls.

Use gravity when you fight. Punch down, not up. When I'm fighting, I always beat down, and I always stab down if I have a knife. I do not stab up, I do not stab straight. I always stab down.*

Dominic taught me everything about fighting.

PETEY GALLIONE is the last Outcast I got to know, but he stayed my friend my whole life. Petey was like a brick with feet. He was

---

* Jon insisted we clarify this: "I don't do any of that shit now, but that's how I used to stab people."

five-nine and weighed 190 pounds. Later he played semiprofessional football, but he kept getting sent to prison, which stopped his career.*

I met Petey at a party in West Englewood. There was a rich kid who had a party at his house when his parents went out of town. He was a popular athlete, so all the popular kids showed up in their letter jackets, with pretty girls and nice cars.

I walked up with my Outcast friends, and the kid hosting the party came out on the lawn and said, "You're not welcome."

Jack Buccino was always comical. He says to this kid, "How about if you box our friend Petey. If you win, we leave. If Petey beats you, we stay."

I'm wondering who Petey is. Then I see the brick with legs waddle out of the darkness. It's Petey. He was seventeen or eighteen back then, and he did not talk. I later found out he was already a strung-out junkie. He drank fifteen bottles of opiated cough syrup a day. This was his secret weapon. Nobody could hurt him because he was full of painkiller in advance of being hit.

Petey steps up to the kid hosting the party. The kid shakes Petey's hand, as if they're going to fight like gentlemen. They circle around, throw a few punches. But boxing takes a long time. Petey got bored. Out of nowhere, he kicks the kid in the balls, knocks him down, and drags him onto the street. Petey goes nuts. He climbs on top of the kid and starts strangling him. He isn't fighting no more. He's just trying to kill him.

Girls start screaming. Kids pile onto Petey to stop him. But Petey's like the monster in the *Frankenstein* movie. Not even a whole crowd with pitchforks can stop him. Finally someone gets in a car and rams into Petey. That's how they save their friend.

To me, Petey was beautiful. He was the most crazed Outcast there was. But because he was still serious about football, he attended high school so he could play on the team. I started working out with him at his high school gym, even though I was still in

_____
* Gallione played in a local league on a team called the Bergen County Chargers.

eighth or ninth grade. Back then they used to have fraternities at the high schools. They were organized to keep kids out of gangs. Fraternities were mostly groups of popular kids who looked down their noses at kids like us, who didn't have families or whose dads were in illegal lines of work.

All the fraternity kids worked out together at Petey's high school gym. They'd hog the equipment. They acted like they owned the place. One day a fraternity kid said something to me under his breath. I confronted him and his friends, and they giggled at me like a bunch of girls.

Next day I came with a gun. The fraternity kids started to say something to me, and I took the gun out and started shooting into the ceiling. I wasn't going to hit no kids, but they didn't know that. *Boom, boom, boom.* They hit the floor, screaming. It was hilarious.

When I told the Outcasts what I did, nobody said, "You did a wrong thing." They laughed. We were like a pack of mad dogs running the street. There was no reasoning among us. I don't know what made us flip out so bad, but we were all gone.

PETER "PETEY" GALLIONE: Jon was a wild kid. He looked two feet tall when I met him. But he would take out a gun and start shooting like a cowboy in a Western.

I have tried to figure out what made us so crazy. Jon had lost his parents. His Italian family, his father and uncles, were well known in the streets, but Jon was alone. It made sense why he was wild, but only up to a point. All of us went so far beyond "normal bad" behavior.

Teaneck was an ideal place. There were rich areas, middle-class areas, and poor neighborhoods. It was a well-balanced city. I was from across Windsor Road in Teaneck, the wrong side of the tracks. My family was poor, but it's not like I starved. The schools were of high academic standing. My group of friends and I should not have turned out as we did. When I look back on what put us over the edge, I believe it was drugs. In the early 1960s a wave of drugs came through, and we all got wacked out of our minds. The drugs accelerated our craziness. Drugs lowered everybody's inhibitions for violence and crime. Drugs allowed us to put guns in our hands and not give a shit.

Some of the kids in the Outcasts had parents in the Mafia. But we didn't want to be a part of that. To us, the older generation of Mafia men were like company men at IBM. We didn't want to have bosses. We wanted to be our own bosses.

The Outcasts was a gang that was organized to be against organized gangs. What the Outcasts were about was we disliked society.

J.R.: In the early 1960s people were square. Kids were into the Beach Boys. I didn't want to run around like a Beach Boy. I dressed weird. I wore suede boots with points, velvet pants. I wore a beret. I carried an umbrella. The umbrella looked good, and I sharpened the tip so I could stab people with it. Nobody thinks of an umbrella as a weapon, but it's a very good one. You can kill somebody with an umbrella.

All of the Outcasts wore crazy, crazy outfits, with umbrellas and capes. Some Outcasts got pachuco tattoos—the cross with slashes on it—that Mexican gangs used. So-called normal kids in their ironed pants and shirts with button-down collars looked at us like we were weird, but to me, they were the weird ones.

We disliked people, but we all had dogs. That was the funny thing about the Outcasts. Even when I was roaming around the street, sleeping in different places, I got a Doberman. Our dogs were gods.

PETEY: Dogs were trust, loyalty, unconditional love. You didn't have to be anything for your dog to love you. We loved our dogs. If my dog wanted meat, I'd do a stickup to get meat for my dog.

When the Outcasts came together, we were just kids who liked to fight. But as drugs spread on the streets, we started robbing people who were buying or selling them. Drug rip-offs were ideal because the people we robbed couldn't report us to the police, since they were doing an illegal thing in the first place.

It's easy to rob a drug buyer. We'd offer to sell him some shit, and when he showed up with the money, we'd rob him. At first you could take someone's money, slap him in the head, and it was over. Then you had to start carrying a gun because other people were carrying guns, and it became something different. It got violent very quickly.

We justified the bullshit we did. We had a code: only rob street people. Never rob a house. Never stick up a liquor store. Those people are civilians. You don't touch them. But if it's street people, I can do anything. If I have to hurt you to do what I got to do, that was not a problem in my mind.

J.R.: We liked to do robberies inside cars. We'd get the kid we were going to rob to get into a car with us. I'd say, "We got to drive to see the guy who has the weed."

The kid gets into the car with me and the Outcasts. We start driving and tell him to hand over his money. Usually, the kid cooperates because we're such mad dogs. When he gives us the money, we throw him from the car.

Rocco loved to hit people because he knew how to professionally box. Even if the kid was cooperating, Rocco liked to try out new punches. He'd see how hard, or fast, he could hit somebody in the face before we threw him out of the car.

After a while we changed up how we robbed people. Northern New Jersey was like one big small town, and the guy we robbed last week might see us again next week. Or maybe the kid we robbed had rich parents, and we knew we could rob him more times in the future because of his parents' money. So we did a new setup, where I would get the kid in the car and make it look like I was being robbed, too. If the kid believed I was also a victim, it would keep the trust between us, so I could rob him again in the future.

ONE DAY Jack Buccino brought a black kid into our group, Freddy Wilbert.* Freddy was a real skinny kid who talked in a soft voice. Jack said, "Freddy's crazy. He'll do anything."

Freddy was perfect, because with America being as prejudiced as it was, he could pretend to rob us and everybody would believe it was real. Nobody would think a bunch of Italians were partners with a black kid.

I set up what was for us a big deal. I convinced a guy in his twenties that I could get him a thousand dollars' worth of heroin. I was fourteen and too young for a license, but I'd started driving an old Chevy Impala station wagon with a V8 and the shifter on the column. I picked up the guy we were going to rob. I had Petey in the back carrying an empty gym bag that we said had the heroin in it.

Petey acts uptight and says he won't open the bag until I drive to a safe place. I drive to a woods in Fort Lee. The plan is Freddy, the black kid, is supposed to jump out of the trees with a shotgun and rob us.

But when I pull up, no Freddy.

Petey is so wacked out on cough syrup, he gets confused and almost hands the guy we're robbing the empty bag. I pretend to accidentally honk the horn. Freddy finally runs out of the woods with his shotgun. He's supposed to get in the car, so people don't call the cops about a black kid running around on the street with a shotgun. But Freddy is so excited, he stands outside the window pointing the shotgun at Petey's head.

I roll down my window and tell Freddy, "Hey, bro. Could you get in the car so nobody sees that gun and calls the cops?"

Freddy says, "Oh, yeah. I'm sorry."

As soon as Freddy gets in, our victim just hands him his

---

* Freddy Wilbert is a pseudonym to protect the identity of Jon's fellow thief.

thousand dollars. Freddy starts to get out before he takes Petey's bag. That's key to the robbery. We don't want any chance the guy we robbed sees there's no heroin in the bag. I turn to Petey and say, "This robber's really fucked up. Give him your bag so he don't get angry and shoot us."

Freddy takes the hint. He grabs Petey's bag and jumps out of the car. I peel out. I'm sure the guy by now must have figured out we were all in on this. But he's so scared of seeing a black kid with a shotgun, he didn't notice all the mistakes we made. The next day I call the guy and say, "I'm sorry, man. We have a business relationship. I'm going to work with you to get your money back."

"What do you mean?"

I tell him whatever money he can get his hands on, I'll give him heroin at a discount that he can sell at his mark-up until he earns back the money he lost. This guy is so grateful about what a good guy I am, he agrees to meet me with $500 to buy more heroin.

I pick him up that afternoon. This time I have Rocco and Dominic with me. They don't want to go through no complicated bullshit. So as soon as the guy gets in the car, they beat the shit out of him, take his money, and throw him from the car. That was the end of our business relationship.

6

J.R.: In the fall of 1963 my sister did an intervention. Everybody knew I was turning out wrong. My sister wanted to try to be a mother to me. She decided the way to fix me was to have me move in with her and her husband. She had married a pilot in the Marine Corps, and they were living in Texas while he trained near Corpus Christi. Poppy came and got me from Jack Buccino's house and put me on a Greyhound bus to Texas.

I liked Texas. My sister and brother-in-law had a little house near the water. My sister helped me get a job on a commercial fishing boat. It was called the *Captain Maddox** after the name of the man who owned it. I got friendly with his son, Billy, who was a few years older than me. We worked long hours on the boat. Then Billy

---

* *Captain Maddox* is a pseudonym to protect the identity of Jon's former employer.

would take me around to beer places. It's a funny thing, being an Italian from New York, but I got along with rednecks.

Me and Billy had great experiences.* He got me laid the first time. Billy took me to a whorehouse filled with white-trash Texas girls and Mexican whores. For a couple of dollars, the Mexican broads would fuck you dry. That was the first time I got laid. A Mexican girl fucked my brains out.

I WAS only in Texas a few months when my sister's husband was transferred to Brunswick, Maine. So I moved up there with them. They enrolled me in high school and tried to make me into a good kid. I started to chafe against my brother-in-law. He was this straight-arrow, military guy, and we did not mix well.

JUDY: My husband had been a star football player in college. He was so all-American, they used his picture in Marine recruiting posters. I saw the tension between Jon and him. But since my husband flew out of a base in Keflavík, Iceland, and was gone weeks at a time, I believed their differences would be manageable.

J.R.: My brother-in-law flew planes that hunted for Russian submarines, and he thought of himself as a hero. He judged me for who I was. But I judged him, too. I looked down on people who were not on my side of the world. Unfortunately, I was not nice to my brother-in-law.

He had a silver Corvette that he loved. Before he left for Iceland, he would jack up the car in the garage so the tires would float a half inch above the floor. He explained to me, "This way my tires won't go square."

---

* When Jon is fond of someone, he often begins sentences with the improper grammatical construction "me and . . ." I preserve this when he introduces it with a particular friend, but generally correct it in subsequent uses with a given friend.

The first night he left for Iceland, I cranked his car off the jacks and drove into New Brunswick. This was a little shithole town where kids would pass the time by drag racing on the streets. Even though I didn't have a license, I was a good driver. But I wasn't experienced with the ice that Maine had in the dead of winter, and the Corvette was a lot more powerful than my Outcast Impala. My first night out, I raced some kids in another car and spun that Corvette into a snowbank.

My sister flipped. But we found a guy who filled in the mangled fiberglass body on the Corvette with Bondo putty and repainted it. By the time my brother-in-law returned, I had the car back in the garage on jacks looking cherry. The night he came home he went straight to the garage, inspected his car, and pointed to the tires like he was teaching me a lesson. "See. My tires are perfect."

The guy could supposedly catch a Russian submarine, but not me wrecking his car. What a moron.

THE ONLY thing I had connecting me to the world of normal people was basketball. That's what kept me in school. I fantasized that I would be a professional ballplayer. They put me on the varsity team in Maine, even though I was in ninth grade.

There was maybe one black kid in the school. His name was Ray Archer, and we got friendly because he was on the basketball team. Ray's dad was an officer in the military, and Ray had a lot of confidence in himself, even though he was a minority.

One day Ray got into trouble after school. There was a little café in town, with a couple of pool tables and a soda fountain, where kids hung out. There were townie kids from the high school and college kids from the nearby college, Bowdoin.

Bowdoin was a weak school in most sports except lacrosse, and the lacrosse players were very arrogant. They would come into our hangout and try to steal the high school girls. One day the Bowdoin kids got into a fight with Ray. They called him a "nigger" and beat him up.

I wasn't there for the fight, but when I saw Ray with his busted-up face the next day, I was mad. I don't care if somebody calls somebody else a "nigger" or a "wop." What made me angry was how the college kids thought they were better than us townie kids. They were like the fraternity kids in New Jersey looking down their noses at everybody. I decided to show them who's going to look down on who.

Ray wanted nothing to do with another fight, so I got another kid from school to help out. Melvin Abruzzi* was an Italian kid originally from Boston, and he was a freak of nature. He was a monster who must've weighed three hundred pounds. Once you talked to him, you realized he was a true idiotic moron. He was borderline retarded, but his parents had faked him into the classes for normal kids. Stupid as he was, he was a great guy because he would fight anybody.

I brought him with me to the hangout in town and waited for the lacrosse fucks to come in. And they did come in, and Melvin and I had a terrible fight. We picked the one day to fight them that they were carrying their lacrosse sticks from practice. They beat us bloody with those sticks. They chased us out of there. When we hit the sidewalk, I said to Melvin, "This is bullshit, man. I'm doing something else."

The lacrosse kids lived in a fraternity house by the Bowdoin campus. I waited until my brother-in-law went to Iceland and took his Corvette off the jacks. I filled a glass apple-cider jug with gasoline and drove to the fraternity house. I waited until the lights went off and gave everybody time to get into bed and start dreaming.

Then I carried my cider-jug Molotov cocktail up the lawn to the house. There was a nice big window in front. I lit the rag and tossed it. The jug was flaming before it even hit the window. It crashed in, and *boom,* the house lit up. Shit was flying everywhere. Those arrogant asshole college kids were running out in their undershorts

---

* Melvin Abruzzi is a pseudonym to protect the identity of Jon's friend.

yelling and screaming. By the time I got back to my brother-in-law's car, I was laughing my balls off.

There were no witnesses, but everybody seemed to think I did it. The cops picked me up at my sister's house. They took me down to the station. But they were small-town cops. They had no evidence. I played dumb. They let me go.*

JUDY: Jon had only been with us a short while when the incident occurred at the fraternity house. I was so mad at Jon. But when I confronted him, he told me that the boys in the fraternity house had called his friend a "nigger." Jon's explanation did not make it okay that he possibly had been involved in the firebombing, but it was more understandable. Jon was sticking up for his friend.

J.R.: I knew my sister would take my side if I played up the racial angle. I would have gone after those college kids, excuse or no excuse. I was sick of that town.

I realized one day I would never be a professional basketball player. It hit me that pro basketball was a fantasy, and I lost my only reason to stay in school. Since I was such a hairy kid, my beard grew thick and heavy. One weekend I grew a goatee and came into school with it. That was against the regulations. They sent me down to the vice principal's office. He told me, "You've got to shave the beard."

I let my beard grow all over my face. I came into school looking like I'd just climbed off a mountain. The vice principal called me into his office again. He said, "You can't play on the basketball team with a beard."

---

* Jon's tale of townie-on-frat-boy arson struck me as potentially apocryphal; however, a source I interviewed who knew Jon in Brunswick confirmed it. This source added the intriguing detail that several parents in the town "thought highly of Jon and felt sorry about his being an orphan" and arranged to hire an attorney for him when it appeared he might face criminal charges for setting the fire.

I grabbed a chair. The vice principal started yelling. I wasn't thinking. I smashed the chair over his desk. People ran in, screaming. That was my last day of school. They didn't press charges as long as I agreed never to set foot on the grounds again. That was fine with me.

JUDY: I felt sorry for Jon. In many ways, he was a normal teenage boy, trying to fit in. I could look in his eyes and see how alone he was. But Jon didn't let his setbacks slow him down. He was a hard worker, and he took several jobs.

J.R.: I pumped gas at a filling station, I painted houses, then I got a job on a lobster boat. I worked for a man named Dave Clemens, an old Maine guy with no teeth. We'd go out before dawn and haul in the traps, take the lobsters, and bait the traps. After a few weeks I proved myself, and he'd send me out alone. I enjoyed being on the water, away from everybody.

Off the coast was a place where rich people lived, called the Point. One day I was going past in my little lobster boat and I saw a beautiful girl swimming there. She had dark skin and blond hair. She looked like she'd dropped from outer space. I drifted my boat near her, and we started talking. Her name was Farah Aboud. Her father was from Lebanon and her mom was American, which is why she looked so unusual. She was beautiful, and I decided the first day I saw her that she was mine.

JUDY: Jon's relationship with Farah was a positive in his life. I had waited and hoped for Jon's first crush, because I believed that caring about another person would change him.

Farah had so much going for her. She was the sweetest girl. Her father was a respected college professor. Her mother was lovely.

They were a gracious family. They invited me and Jon to the house for international dinners where they cooked Middle Eastern food. These were such good times. When Jon looked at Farah, his eyes would light up. I hadn't seen eyes like this since he was a little boy. He truly loved her.

J.R.: Farah gave me blue balls as big as the ocean. I could not get anywhere with her. We'd lie on the couch in the living room after her parents would go to sleep, and she'd get very aggressive, then she'd stop. Even though Farah was two years older than me, she wanted to stay a virgin. She was focused on going to college.

The Abouds had a forty-two-foot sailboat, and at the end of summer the family took a trip on it. Farah's father invited me to come. Our first few days on the boat, everybody had a good time, slipping into little islands, swimming, looking at the stars at night.

Near Kennebunkport there was a storm. Mrs. Aboud got sick, so we docked the boat, and Professor Aboud took his wife to a hotel in town. He stepped off the boat and said, "I'll see you guys in the morning."

That surprised me. He was an intelligent man. I could not understand why he would leave me alone on the boat with his daughter. That night Farah and me started fooling around like we always did. This time, when she reached the point where she would normally stop me, I did not stop. I was forceful, but she did not put up a fight. We had sex all night long.

The next morning she did not talk to me. She didn't talk when her parents came back on the boat. Everybody looked at me. Finally, I reasoned it out. Farah was getting ready to go off to college, and she knew I was no college boy. She liked me enough to fool around, but she was mad I had taken her virginity because in her eyes I wasn't good enough.

It was very tense those three days until we made it back to Brunswick. As soon as we hit the dock, Farah and her mother left.

Professor Aboud came up to me and said, "Jon, there's something very strong in the air here. What happened?"

I said, "Why don't you ask your daughter."

He started to give me some attitude, and I said, "I'm not the moron who left my daughter alone on the boat."

Professor Aboud said a thing to me that made no sense. "I'm sorry, Jon. I thought of you like a son. I wish we could talk."

I realize now that maybe he did view me as a son. But I was so crazed then that his reaching out just made me angrier. I was too far gone for some do-good asshole to try to treat me like his son.

I had a terrible fight with my brother-in-law after the boat trip with the Abouds. It started over some grass clippings I had left piled in the yard. My brother-in-law came in the kitchen yelling for me to pick them up.

"Not now." I tried pushing past him.

He shoved me. The guy was a lot bigger than me, so I grabbed a frying pan and hit him on the head. He went down like a sack of shit. I leaned over him and said, "You think the frying pan hurts? I'm gonna make your insides hurt even more."

He looked at me like I was going to beat his brains out. I laughed and told him how I'd wrecked his Corvette, that it was plastered together with Bondo but he was too dumb to notice. Then I walked out of there for the last time.

I broke into the Abouds' boathouse and robbed it. I took Professor Aboud's tool kit, his outboard motors, and a couple of chain saws, and I sold it all at a shop for $400. I used the money to buy a bus ticket to New York.

I'd had my fun in Maine.

7

J.R.: When I left Maine in the summer of 1964, I was
sixteen—old enough to start working for my uncle
Sam Riccobono. He put loans on the street that needed
collecting when people fell behind. To be clear, this was
not a job that meant I was in the Mafia. It was more like
pickup work.

I took a percentage of the collections and got other
benefits, too. One guy who owed my uncle money turned
me on to a nice studio apartment by the mayor's mansion.
It was a fifth-floor walk-up, rent controlled for eighty dollars a month. I hooked up with my Outcast friends and
gave them work helping me collect from the deadbeats.

The world was changing in 1964. A couple years
earlier only street people were involved in drugs. Now
it was college kids. They were coming into Greenwich
Village to score weed. Me and Jack Buccino did a couple
of rip-offs in the Village just for fun, and we got the

idea, why not go on to college campuses? To my thinking, it seemed smarter to go after college kids than poor people. That was the problem with my dad's business. It was based on poor people. I'd go after rich kids.

In Jersey there was a school called Fairleigh Dickinson University. Jack and I went there to do our first college rip-off. It was very easy. Jack, who wanted to be an actor, started acting. We were standing around some vending machines by a lounge, and Jack told these kids I'd won a basketball scholarship and was thinking of coming, but I wanted to know about the campus social life. That was all it took for some kids to take us to a party. We saw who was passing joints around and asked where they got them, and they introduced us to the dealer kids. The first few rip-offs, Jack and I went into the dealer kids' dorm rooms and took their money with our hands. As long as they didn't have lacrosse sticks, I could beat up college kids in my sleep.

The next school we tried was Princeton. This was a very hoity-toity school. Some of the kids wore suits with bow ties. When we tried our story out—of me attending Princeton on a basketball scholarship—I felt like I was becoming an actor in a film. I had to work at gaining their trust and concentrate on being the opposite of who I was.

At Princeton they had fraternities called eating clubs. I played basketball with some kids, and they invited me to their eating club. I went alone and had a dinner, and when the kids asked about my family, I told them my father was a professor in Maine. I talked about our house on the Point and our forty-two-foot sailboat. It was easy to fit in. Finally I ended up in a room someplace smoking weed with Princeton kids. Bingo. They told me about a kid who lived off campus and was their dealer.

Jack and I came up with an idea that would make more money than just robbing the dealer alone. We would tie him up, beat him, and make him call his friends. He'd tell them to bring their money because he was going to give them a great deal on drugs. This way we'd grab rich kids coming through the door like it was Christmas.

The first time we did this, it was hilarious. My friend from the eating club took me over to the off-campus dope dealer. As we got to the front door, Jack, Petey, and Rocco drove up in another car.

"Who are these guys?" my friend asked.

"Shut the fuck up." I was no longer the kid coming to school on a scholarship. I was myself now. I enjoyed this part even more than acting.

We forced this kid into the house with the dealer. I liked seeing the surprise in these kids' faces when we came in and tied them up. We ended up doing this several times at Princeton and at a couple other schools.

When we first showed our true selves, the college kids always said the same thing. "I thought we were friends."

They didn't understand that once they got into the drug-dealing business, they were in our world. Our rules applied, not theirs.

We wouldn't tell them what we wanted at first. We'd beat them. We'd scare them. Rocco would practice his professional boxing on these kids if they gave any attitude. They'd always become willing to follow our scheme. These kids had no loyalty. They'd call every friend they had and tell them to bring all their money because they were going to sell them the best pot in the world. We'd grab every moron college kid that came through the door. We tied up so many in one house, we ran out of electrical cords.

We knew these kids would be too scared to call the cops after we left. They couldn't. They were doing an illegal thing. If any of these kids wanted to be tough, they'd never seen animals like us before.

At sixteen or seventeen I was now a very bad person. My friends were the same. Our attitude was, *You want to fight? We will break your hands, bite your ears off, whatever we need to do to make our point. We have no feelings. We are from the street.* Half the Outcasts were junkies at this point. When they saw money in front of them, their eyes blinked like pinball machines. I introduced these college kids to my way of thinking. *Evil is stronger than good. When I am alone in your house with you, you will learn this, too.*

I'm not proud of the way I acted, but I can't take it back. I did this.

A few kids tried to be brave. One kid told us he was a fifth-degree black belt in karate. Dominic, the best fighter in the Outcasts, said, "Okay. I'm going to give you the best shot you got. After that I'm going to fuck you up."

We had guns, so we knew if the kid by some miracle actually knew karate and hurt Dominic, we'd shoot him. We let the kid loose. He asked if he could warm up. We sat back and watched as he did some kicks and stretches, like he's giving a class in Princeton karate. Finally Dominic walks up to him and says, "Okay."

The kid gives Dominic his best kick to the chin and misses.

"That's your Princeton karate?" Dominic asks.

Dominic gives him some Jersey karate—he kicks him in the balls. He throws the kid through a door, beats him down, stomps him. I'm laughing my ass off when I feel my shoe crunch on the floor. Dominic had knocked the kid's teeth out of his head. Dominic got so crazed with beating him, he broke the kid's arms, his legs. He fucked him up to the point where I'm sure he never told anybody ever again he was a fifth degree in anything.

We had an incident where a college kid pulled a gun. He was so excited, he shot himself in the leg. We took the gun from him and shot him in his other leg. When it comes to defending himself, the average college kid isn't worth three dead flies.

There are not a lot of tough people in normal society. Many guys will act brave for a few seconds, but as soon as you hurt them, all that bravery goes out the window. You bite someone's ear off, you break his fingers, shoot his legs, and he will come around. A guy who fights every day of his life reacts differently. This guy, when you hurt him, he fights harder. Very few men react like this. And those who do are dangerous people.

For me, robberies were my amusement. Jack Buccino was as sick as me. Since he fancied himself an actor, his enjoyment was the acting we did to befriend our victims. Jack always thought he was on stage. After we were done, he was so out of his mind, we'd be in the attic of his mother's house counting the money, and Jack would ask me, "You think I played the part good?"

Sometimes, just to eat his guts out, I'd tell him, "You didn't do a good job acting today."

When Jack and I went out to set up different kids, we would have contests to see who got bigger rip-offs. That was our game. Most kids our age were competing in things like "Hey, I got six home runs."

With Jack it was "I stole $2,200."

"I got $3,000."

"You won, motherfucker."

That was our fun.

MY SISTER did not give up on me. When I was seventeen, she came down to New York. She saw my apartment, the nice clothes I had, and she knew I was not doing things legally. She begged me to get a real job. She actually believed I could go into the straight world. That's how good my sister was. Good people can't understand how truly bad a bad person can be. Good people are good, but they're also a little bit stupid. That's why my sister never lost hope in me. She was good.

JUDY: There was a boy I had dated in high school, Walter Hutter,* who had gone on to work at E. F. Hutton as a stock trader. I called him up and asked him, "Please, can you find a job for my little brother?"

J.R.: Walter Hutter had always been in love with my sister. He had been a great athlete in high school. He was signed to play pro baseball, but he fucked up his arm and went into the stock business.

---

* Walter Hutter is a pseudonym to protect Judy's friend.

When he agreed to hire me, my sister begged me, "Do me this one favor, Jon. Go in and work for Walter. Try it."

I said, "Judy, I love you. You're my sister. I'll do it for you."

I thought it would be interesting to get inside a brokerage house and see how they made money. I bought a suit and tie and nice shoes to look proper. I went down to Wall Street the next morning. I find the building, ride up the elevator, and there's Walter. He's in his suit. I'm in mine.

"Hey, Walter."

"Jon, I'm going to teach you how to chart stocks." He led me into his office.

"Okay, what do I do?"

"Take this blank paper and read these numbers. Write this into a chart."

I charted stocks all morning. By lunchtime I was getting uptight with this bullshit work. I thought, *God Almighty, when do I start to make money? I'm not going to sit here for a fucking month and make charts.*

Walter invited me to have a sandwich with him in the lunchroom, but I went down to the street to smoke a joint so I could relax. I came back to the office lit out of my mind. But I was calm.

Walter said, "Jon, I made some transactions this morning. You're going to post them in the book. When you finish, I'll explain to you what we just did."

"Walter, I'm not stupid. I can figure out what we're doing."

He told me to watch myself.

I tried to calm things down by explaining myself. "Walter, I want you to teach me how to buy stocks and make money. Don't make me do this shit-ass paperwork, man."

Walter told me I had no choice. The walls were becoming tighter. My pot wore off. I was starting to lose it. I was not on the level. I was feeling violent. I said, "Walter, I don't feel good. I better go home."

"On your first day of work?"

"Walter, listen to me. For your sake and my sake, let me leave early."

Lucky for him, he agreed.

I went home. I told my sister, "Judy, I don't think a stockbroker job is a wise thing."

"Please, give it a chance."

"All right, Judy. I'll give it a chance."

I went in for a whole week, maybe two. Finally, I can't take it. I go one morning, and Walter says, "Okay, Jon. Here's the paper. Chart ten stocks."

"I'll tell you what, Walter. Here's your paper. Use it as toilet paper. Shove it up your fucking ass."

Walter stands up.

"Walter, sit down, please," I tell him. "You're my sister's friend. Don't do this. Sit down and let me walk the fuck out the door."

He steps in front of me. I grab an adding machine and knock him on the head. His friends run in. I bang them with the machine. A security guard comes in. I run the fuck away, get on the elevator, and I'm gone. That was my stockbroker experience.

A couple days later Walter called my sister. "Your brother almost killed me. How could you send that maniac into my office?"

JUDY: I became so angry when Walter called Jon a "maniac." I told him, "How dare you call my brother a maniac." I was overprotective, but Jon was my baby brother.

J.R.: My Outcast friends got more wacked out on heroin. Petey, Jack Buccino, and Dominic Fiore were needle-in-the-arm junkies. Their minds were gone, but their muscles could still destroy anybody on the street. When they did rip-offs, it wasn't for fun anymore, it was because they had to.

My uncle Sam knew something was up. I came around a few times with my Outcast friends, and he told me maybe I should stop using my friends to help with collections. He said, "Jon, take my meat guys."

The "meat guys" weren't Mafia. They were actual meatpackers in the union my uncles controlled. The union thugs were loyal to my family. But I was loyal to the Outcasts. This caused me some aggravation in the spring of 1965.

My uncle Sam had a dry cleaner who got behind on a loan. Dominic and I grabbed him off the street and took him into an apartment I kept off of Lexington and 48th. Obviously, you couldn't beat people on the streets of Manhattan, so I had an apartment for collections work. We developed a method. We'd strip the guy naked, tie him to a chair, gag him, and beat him. I didn't say a word. Just beat, beat, beat. We'd beat a person on and off for hours. It was like marinating a piece of meat. Everybody softens over time. When we'd finally pull the electrical cord from his mouth and tell him to get money, he'd be grateful he was being talked to like a human. I'd hand him a phone and tell him to call somebody—his wife, his in-laws, his rabbi, anybody—and get the money he owed. That person would deliver the money to one of my guys at a coffee shop. We'd let the guy go, and everybody'd be happy.

This time I stepped out during our beating to meet a girl I was seeing. While I was out, Dominic shot up a load of heroin and nodded off. He fell on the floor like a dead man. The guy managed to escape—crawl down the stairs and roll onto the street—still naked, and tied to the chair. Some asshole Good Samaritan called the cops. They came into the apartment and found Dominic on the floor. He was comatose, and they actually drew a chalk outline around his body before they realized he wasn't dead. They took him to the hospital, and when I walked back in, two cops threw me on the floor. I saw the chalk outline of a body, and I said a very stupid thing. "Where's Dominic?"

The cops had Dominic's name from the ID in his wallet. If I had been wise, I would have said I'd walked into the wrong apartment. But I'd let them know I knew Dominic. My own mouth gave them the evidence they needed to arrest me. Every cop in the room laughed at me.

I fucked up. Evil is stronger than good, but it don't beat stupid. I was young. Young people make mistakes. Mistakes can help you learn. As long as you don't do it a second time, anybody's entitled to a mistake. Because of my mistake, I was charged as an adult for kidnapping and attempted murder.

8

J.R.: They took me to the Manhattan Detention Center on White Street, the "Tombs." In 1965 the Tombs was made of stone and iron, like a jail in medieval times. The cells had metal shelves on the walls for inmates to sleep on. Two guys had to sleep on the floor. It was overrun with rodents. You'd wake up with a rat tail dragging across your mouth. We slept with our shoes in our hands to fight the rats.

The Tombs exposed me to new things. There were hippies in there who were part of a movement headed by Timothy Leary. He got all these kids to take acid, and they'd trip out on the streets and get arrested. The hippies believed in revolution, but some of them were so blown in their minds, they could hardly put two words together. There were also Black Muslims in jail. I had never been aware of the Muslim situation until then. They weren't friendly to white people, but they didn't look to pick fights. They would preach, "You whiteys are going to get it because it's all going to come back around. You're all going to kill yourselves."

What the Muslims and hippies had in common was they all talked about overthrowing "the man" and the Vietnam War. I had never heard about this war before. A few years earlier I was bored because everybody in America was into the Beach Boys and was squeaky clean. Now it was like the whole country was flipping out.

My legal case got complicated. The bail bondsman decided not to write my bond, and my uncles had somebody beat him up. The attack made the TV news, and the prosecutors decided to come down harder on me.

My family sent a lawyer to see me. He sat me down and said, "You're dead here. They got you cold. In the State of New York, kidnapping's a serious offense. You're also going to get charged with usury. And you had a gun on you. On top of this, you have an outstanding gun charge in New Jersey.* They're not offering any deals."

The army sent recruiters to the Tombs every week. They didn't bother talking to the hippie acid cases. They came to violent guys like me and said, "If you join the army, we'll erase your criminal record."

At first I told them to get lost. But I saw that the Black Muslims, even though they hated whitey, they were signing up. I watched twenty of them get on a bus one day to go join the white man's army. After my talk with my uncle's lawyer, I had a change of heart.

I told the recruiters I was interested in their offer. A few days later, they did a physical exam right in the jail. Next thing I knew, I was walking out the gate to a bus. They didn't put chains on us when we got on the bus, and I respected them for that. I'd thought we'd be treated like prisoners. But we were on our way to being soldiers.

• • •

---

* In 1965 Jon was also arrested after an assault in New Jersey and convicted of carrying a concealed weapon. He was on probation for this at the time of his kidnapping arrest in New York.

I DID my basic training at Fort Benning in Georgia. A military base is like a low-level security prison. There's fences and people telling you what to do. One guy from the Tombs wound up in my training company. He told me, "I had the perfect crime going when I was outside."

"It must have been genius for you to end up here," I told him.

This moron told me he'd robbed a supermarket by walking unarmed into the manager's office and telling him his partner was holding the manager's wife and kids hostage. He told the manager if he did not open the safe, he would never see his family again. The only problem was, the manager wasn't married. The manager beat him up and called the cops. "Next time," this idiot told me, "I'll make it work."

These were the kinds of morons I met in the army. But basic training was a breeze. I was in good shape. At the end of two months they separated us. Some guys they sent to school for trades like truck repair. Some, they said, "You're going to Vietnam."

I was in a different group. They told us we could volunteer to go to "advanced school" and get more training. I didn't see the advantage of it. I wanted to go to Vietnam quick and get it over.

But the night before we had to make up our minds, they let us go out in the town and get drunk. There was a club where you brought carry-in booze in paper sacks. I was sitting there with these guys with a few weeks' training, and I thought, "I'd be stupid to go into a war with these dopes."

I signed up for advanced school. Only after I signed up did they tell me that advanced school meant jumping out of a plane. I told them, "Are you crazy? I'm from New York. I don't jump out of airplanes."

THEY MOVED us to a different area of the base where they had steel towers to practice jumping. My first time jumping, they had to push me off the tower. I did not like heights.

In the offices by our barracks I'd overhear officers talking about how bad Vietnam was. They'd told us this in boot camp, and I'd assumed they were trying to scare us. I started to wonder if they were telling us the truth. I became serious about training. I'd been focused when I played basketball in school. Now I focused my mind on the army.

They put us in a plane for our first real jump. On the inside it was like a boxcar. When we got in the sky, we formed up along a cable leading to the door and they started pushing us toward it. The guys in front were already jumping out.

Each guy was supposed to jump when a red light by the door blinked, but a guy ahead of me wouldn't jump. The instructors told him, "Here's your choice: if you want to be in airborne, we're throwing you out of the plane. If you don't want to be in airborne, sit down and you're done. You've failed."

The guy screamed, "You push me out, I'll sue you!"

What a moron. Sue the army? That's like suing the Mafia. They sat that asshole down. When my time got closer, I was shaking. The guy directly in front of me said, "Don't worry. I've jumped before. If you jump immediately after me, I'll watch you."

I trusted this guy so much, when he jumped, I rushed after him ahead of the blinking light. An instructor held me back. When they finally let me out, I couldn't see where the guy was who was watching me, but he made me feel confident. After I hit the ground, I saw the guy. I said, "Thank you."

He fell over laughing. "I never jumped in my fucking life, man."

He was fucking with me to build up his own courage. But he gave me the balls to do my first jump. After that I was excited to get in the air. Jumping is euphoric.

They sent us to Kentucky for more training—from living on berries in the woods to knife-throwing. With knife-throwing, I never got consistent results. In Vietnam I worked with a guy who could throw a knife from twenty feet and put it in someone's chest. I would throw a knife, and the wrong end would hit the guy. I tried once on a Vietnamese. Dinged my knife right off his chest. Luckily, my buddy was able to shoot him.

Through the army training I learned that running around on

the streets of New York hadn't given me much advantage. I was not as good as I thought I was. The farm boys shot rifles better than me. The only advantage I had was that I was mentally prepared. The people who recruited me knew my history. They knew I hurt people. My emotional responses were different. I could withstand pain better than other people. I could inflict it. That's something many people can't do. The army recruiters had been smart about me. When I got to Vietnam, they put me with some guys as bad as me, and God Almighty, we went fucking crazy over there. The sickest part of it was, we enjoyed it.

9

E.W.: A hard rain falls outside. The windows in the living room thump as raindrops as big as marbles hit them. The surface of the lake out back looks like it's boiling.

Jon approaches the couch where we do our morning interviews. His hair, normally meticulously combed, is disheveled. He says he barely slept last night. We have the following dialogue:

JON: Noemi had to leave our bed. Many times she can't sleep through the night with me. She says I move around and I sweat. It's very bad some nights.

EVAN: Do you have any idea why?

JON: Because I dream. They're not really dreams. I relive bad things I've done. How can I explain it to you?

EVAN: You say you never had a problem sleeping no matter what you did to people.

JON: My dreams aren't like I'm picturing things. I wake up, and my heart pounds. If I could associate it with anything, it'd be the times in Vietnam when I had to hide in the mud to wait for people we were ambushing. I dream of the adrenaline. I don't dream about specific bad things I did, like "Oh my God, I skinned that guy in Vietnam. I hung him from a tree. I took off his skin and watched him suffer."

EVAN: Wait, did you actually skin somebody alive?

JON: Oh, yeah, bro. Not one person. We used to do it all the time.

J.R.: I flew into Danang with a bunch of guys I didn't know. The way the army ran things was, your platoon was already in Vietnam. It stayed there forever. They brought in replacements like me as other guys in the platoon died or finished their tour. So we all came in as replacements. Our flight landed at a time when they were moving the dead soldiers in body bags onto planes for the trip back home. The military was so coarse and stupid, they had us walk past the body bags. I turned to a soldier waiting to load them and said, "Jesus. Bad day?"

"It's like this every fucking day," he said.

After all the training and buildup to the war, they had me wait in a hut by the airport for ten days. We played cards and drank Cokes until one day someone said, "You got five minutes to grab your shit and get on the bird."

They flew me to Hau Nghia,* a province by the border with Cambodia. It was only fifty miles from Saigon, but in a primitive country fifty miles can take you back a thousand years. There were

---

* In 1976, after the fall of Saigon, the Communist leadership dissolved Hau Nghia and absorbed it into its neighboring provinces.

paddies and woods everywhere. People said you could see tigers at night, but I never saw one. Since I like cats, I would have liked to see a tiger in Vietnam.

I was put in an LRRPs platoon.* LRRPs didn't do a normal one-year tour. Guys in my unit were already in their second or third tour. One of them was an E-5 named Steve Corker.† He came up to me and said, "I heard you came from jail. Guess what, bro? Everything you thought you knew don't mean shit out here. There are Communists out in the trees who want to kill you. You got that, Little Mafioso?"

"Little Mafioso" was what Steve called me. He was a few years older than me and had grown up out in the woods in New Hampshire. Normally I wouldn't take a person talking to me the way he did, but I'm out in the fucking woods with armed Communists and tigers. Steve obviously knew how to survive.

A Green Beret who was training our unit saw me talking to Steve. He came up to me later on and said, "I'd avoid Steve if I was you."

"Why?"

"He's out of his mind. When you see him go into a village, he leaves a trail of bodies."

My thought process was *I want to be with the person leaving that trail of bodies, because that's the most evil motherfucker in the woods.* I followed Steve from then on. Steve taught me the basics. We had to patrol through high grass, and they gave us machetes to cut through it. Steve taught me don't just slash your machete like an idiot. It's a fine tool. Maintain a razor edge on it. Make it an extension of your hand. Use it to feel the trail as you cut. Most important, always move very slow. Take your time. You can't hear when you're moving too fast. The slower you move, the more you see, the more you understand, the better you control the situation.

---

* LRRP stands for Long Range Reconnaissance Patrol. Soldiers in LRRP units were organized in companies but worked in small teams similar to Special Forces.
† An E-5 is a sergeant. Steve Corker is a pseudonym to protect the identity of Jon's friend.

The other thing Steve taught me was, stay low. You get very sore and uncomfortable crawling on your belly, but you need to be low to see trip wires and one-step snakes. Steve was the one who told me about the one-step snake.

"What the fuck is a one-step?"

"That motherfucker bites you, you take one step, and then you're history. That's all you need to know, Little Mafioso."

Hau Nghia was pretty quiet when I got there. One of the jobs we did in LRRPs was screen regular army companies. When they moved into a village, we would go ahead of them off the main trail and look for enemy—Viet Cong [VC] or North Vietnamese Army [NVA]. The VC were the sneakier ones who wore the black pajamas, and the NVA were like a regular army. We called them all gooks, but that wasn't a racist term to us. It was like calling Germans krauts. Americans respected gooks—how persistently they fought. I later started to believe the Americans overrated the gooks.

Our patrols lasted a couple days to a week. The first few we did, I didn't see a single enemy gook. All I saw was mud. Even if there was two inches of water on the ground, we carried reeds to breathe through. That way you didn't suck mud into your mouth. From being wet all the time, your skin would shrivel up and peel off.

A few months into this, we're in the slime one day, and I hear *splash splash splash*—footsteps. Steve could count the number of people by listening to the splashes. He holds up his fingers—it's five to ten gooks. Our tactic was to wait until they moved past—then when they got their backs to us, we would start shooting. That was the plan.

I'm lying there waiting, and suddenly I can't get enough air from the reed I'm breathing through. I want to spit it out, but I don't want to raise my head or make bubbles in the mud. I feel like I'm choking. My heart is pounding. And even though I'm in slime, I'm sweating my balls off. The sweat's running in my eyes, so my vision is blurry. I don't give a fuck how brave you are, your heart pounds like a maniac when you're waiting to attack someone. When I actually see the first gook maybe twenty-five yards away, the splash he makes sounds like a *boom* to my ears.

The gooks don't see us. When they get so their backs are to us, Steve shoots one guy in the middle of their column. Me and the other guys working with us do our best to pick off the soldiers on either end as they scatter. We shoot the motherfuckers in the back. I've never done anything easier.

I can't say we killed all ten NVA. We put them down and scattered them, then radioed the army platoon following us. They spent an hour firing machine guns and LAWs* rockets—everything they carried—at the gooks. Then we pulled back and called in artillery strikes. Steve laughed. "What do you think about this now, Little Mafioso?"

I will admit, that first firefight was the biggest kick I'd ever had in my life. I was pretty sure I killed at least one of the guys I shot at—meaning the first time I killed someone, I was paid by the government to do it. That's a kick, isn't it?

Before I got to Vietnam, I heard guys talk about how good the North Vietnamese could fight. But a lot of their infantry did stupid shit. Their platoons didn't always have guys looking behind them. When we moved, we looked in all 360 degrees. The gooks would march straight ahead, never look back. We shot a lot of them in their backs because of this. Some of the gooks were very good, but we saw many who were more like coolies than soldiers.

I was lucky that Steve was like a real-life Rambo. He didn't look like a Rambo. He looked like a normal person. Nothing stood out about him physically, but he was fucking crazy. This shit was fun to him. He loved using his knife.

It's much harder to stab a person than shoot him. When you stab, you get close enough to smell and hear the person you're killing. You stick a knife into someone, and you feel their skin tearing.

---

* The M72 Light Anti-tank Weapon (LAW) was a small, powerful rocket sometimes carried by infantry in Vietnam and used against a variety of targets.

Skin makes a sound like *vishhh* when you cut it. You get their blood on you. You feel their gristle on your blade. It's very personal.

Steve enjoyed it when we caught a straggler—a lone gook on the trail—that he could knife. For me, stabbing a guy to death was a whole new world. My first was a little VC in pajamas who came at us on a trail. Because there were others nearby, we didn't want to make noise by shooting him. I couldn't reach high enough to get his neck, so I grabbed a leg and sliced his Achilles tendon. I nearly cut my hand when I brought him down, and he screamed his head off. So much for silence. Even after I sliced his neck, he was rasping and gurgling so loud, I drove my knife into his eyeball to shut him up. Even then, the little fucker was flopping around, trying to throw me off. Steve crawled over, laughing. The man was long dead. I was so jumpy, I was the one flopping. I did not like killing with a knife. I'd rather shoot somebody. That's just me.

The other guy who worked with us was a guy named George,* a Greek kid from New York. George was an orphan raised by his aunt in Lower Manhattan, not far from Little Italy. But George grew up the opposite of me. He had been a straight kid. He'd been a New York Boy Scout. All that merit-badge thinking went out the window in Vietnam. George was not wacked out of his mind like Steve, but he did whatever it took to live another day. The three of us were always together. Sometimes we worked with other guys, but we were the core. We were a wrecking machine.

The first time we went into a village together, I had my eyes opened. We came in with a regular infantry unit. We walked into the village without a shot being fired. As we approached the first hut, Steve said, "Hey, Little Mafioso, we're gonna kill everybody in the room."

I still thought this was a normal war. You kill gooks if they got guns. Not kids and old ladies. But I was trying to build trust with

---

* George's surname has been removed. He is no longer alive and so is not able to counter Jon's depiction of the unit's actions. He is honored on the Vietnam Veterans Memorial Wall.

Steve and George, so I didn't say nothing. The first hut we went into, they shot everybody in the room—a couple women and some kids. Steve trained me, when you clear a room, to make sure somebody isn't faking being dead, you step on their eye socket. If they're alive, they will definitely squirm, and if they do, you pull your foot back and put a bullet in their brain. I walked through that hut putting my boot in the eyes of these little dead kids, old ladies. I'll tell you the truth, I felt nothing. There was no shock to me the first time we killed a hut full of normal people.

Many army units we worked with had rules against shooting villagers. Even if they found tunnels or radios or weapons in the village, they wouldn't shoot women and children. They'd get uptight if we acted too aggressive. Steve would find other ways to fuck with the villagers. He'd blow up their pig with a grenade or set their rice on fire. Steve was a wacko. One time we went into a hut, and he pulled his dick out and pissed on the women. He wanted to rile them up so they would rebel and we could shoot them. But they just cowered.

When we left, George asked Steve, "Why'd you do that shit?"

"Well, you got to change things up," Steve said. "It gets boring doing everything the same way."

"Let it get fucking boring, then," George said.

George acted disgusted, but when he got his chance to leave Vietnam, he signed for another tour. Normal soldiers had to go home after a year. Not us. As LRRPs, we could sign up as many times as we wanted. I re-signed, too, when my year came up. I forgot what the outer world looked like. None of us smoked weed out there like other soldiers, but my whole body went numb. I felt nothing in a gunfight. Adrenaline still pumped in me, but there was no fear left. We spent days together with nobody talking, just crawling in the mud. My first couple months there I still thought about things back home—girls, friends, nice cars, movies. But that went away. My brain shrank until all I could think about was whatever was in front of me. If I got a leech on my ankle, that would be the focus of my mind: burning the leech, shooting the gook, taking a crap—whatever I did, that was my universe. Because I couldn't imagine the real world anymore, it became the unknown, and Vietnam became the normal, familiar thing.

Once you go into a room and shoot a grandmother, a teenage girl a few times, it's not like you feel worse and worse. You feel the same nothing every time. I did not want to go home anymore. What the fuck was I going to do? Be a maniac in the street? After living like we did, you become uncivilized. You become an animal, I guess. A person like me could stay in Vietnam forever.

10

J.R.: I was nineteen on my second tour in Vietnam. I felt a hundred years old. Steve and George and I had become very good. They attached a Green Beret to us and a gook translator so we could do something new. The American government got it in its mind that the best thing we could do to beat the Communists was to assassinate the military leaders in the field. The idea was if you took away a major or colonel, the men under them would be like chickens without a head.

Instead of ambushing gooks, our job was to hang back and watch when other American army units got into fights. Then we'd try to follow any gooks who survived. We'd grab one of these fuckers and make him talk. Or we'd take the radio and try to listen in with our translator. We'd try to find out where the leaders were—their base camps, tunnels, their weapons and ammunition caches, and destroy these by calling artillery or air strikes.

We'd wait at our base camp until they'd come to us and say something very basic like "A hundred ten degrees west, ten clicks out, we got two platoons engaging NVA." They'd put us in a helo and drop us off to the side of the fight. Nine out of ten times, when the NVA fought our army, they would break off and sneak back to a rear camp. They would start to move their guys out even while they had other guys up front still fighting.

We'd follow the guys who were leaving first. Some would be in uniforms, others in the pajamas and hats. Some would be dragging out wounded, or carrying baskets with shell casings they picked up. They'd clean up everything from their fights and reuse it. We'd focus in on any stragglers carrying shit, and grab as many as two or three at once. We'd kill one or two of them right away and keep one to talk.

For us this was a game, like when Jack Buccino and I competed to rob college kids. In Vietnam we'd call first dibs on who got to kill which guy. It was like, Steve will get the coolie dragging the wounded guy. George will finish off the guy on the stretcher. I'd have to grab the guy we wanted to keep alive. We'd get into arguments over who would get to kill someone. "You went last time! It's my turn to kill!"

To us, we were just killing the boredom. But the tactics worked. The guy we kept alive would show us where their camps and tunnels were and who was in charge. Sometimes, we'd keep him alive for a few days. We'd set up an observation point and call in artillery strikes. We'd have our captive tell us what they were saying about the strikes on the radios, so we could adjust the targeting of the artillery and hit them again. Then, when we got everything we could, we'd kill him.

The Green Beret we worked with was a half-Jew from Chicago named Lou. He thought we were out of our minds. He wasn't against killing gooks. We succeeded in our missions, which made him look good. But he acted like he was above our mentality. If you laugh when you kill somebody, or cry, it makes no difference to the guy you're killing. So why not have fun? But Lou thought he was superior because he didn't laugh when he killed a gook. Plus, he was a Green Beret, and they looked down on everybody.

The Vietnamese interpreter we had, he was as sick as we were. He'd giggle and egg us on in his high-pitched squeaky voice. When we'd capture a guy who didn't want to cooperate, our interpreter would be the first one cutting him with a knife, or burning him. Forget lit cigarettes, our interpreter would take a Zippo and burn the guy's ears and nose and eyelids with the flame. He'd be giggling and squealing like a teenybopper on *American Bandstand*.

When we got a guy who lied to us and gave us attitude, he would pay. Our interpreter called these guys "snaky tongues." They'd say they were innocent, and we'd find maps on them. A few times we listened in on their radios as the gooks talked about how stupid the Americans were, how they captured an American kid and had done this or that to him. When we ended up grabbing guys from one of those units, our thought was, *We can't just kill him. If you shoot somebody four times, and then another guy a hundred times, what fucking difference does it make?*

Our amusement was finding new ways to make the bad ones suffer. Our interpreter would cut their tongues or sometimes their dicks. There was a gook we picked up who made Lou really angry. He hid a blade and jabbed Lou in his thigh next to his dick. Lou snapped. He pulled out the guy's dick and tried to cut it off. But he didn't do it right. It was flopping around, bleeding.

"He a snaky tongue!" our interpreter said, pointing and laughing in his squealy voice. "Snaky tongue. *Tee-hee.*"

I shot the captive gook just to put his misery out of my face.

Sick as we were, the gooks would do the same to us if they could. The VC skinned people alive. They did it to villagers they didn't like. They did it to Americans.* We spent weeks following

---

* While the specifics of Jon's accounts of prisoner abuse cannot be confirmed, in *The Valley of Death*, published by Random House in 2010, author Ted Morgan notes that from its start the Vietnamese conflict was notable for the grotesque atrocities committed on captive soldiers by the Vietminh and later the Vietcong. As Morgan writes on page 93: "Captured soldiers were impaled, sawed up, emasculated, drowned, buried alive."

a company of VC who on their radios had bragged about torturing Americans, saying what morons Americans were. We picked off stragglers, and instead of shooting them when we were done, we started skinning them. Steve had done it before. We stripped them naked and hung them upside down from a tree. When you hang a person upside down, it makes his heart pump faster. All the blood flows into the person's head. It makes everything much more painful when you start skinning him.

We'd start with little slices in the guy's scalp. You cut his chest, his back, his stomach. Let his intestines pop out and hang in his face. You work your way up. This could take hours. Eventually, the whole body slides out from the skin. Even with his ankle tied to the tree, everything starts to slip out from the skin. People will stay alive for hours like this. Their eyes would be moving even if there's no skin left anywhere. Steve would lean over that fucker, look into his crazy eyes, and say, "You think I'm a moron? Who's the moron now. I took your skin."

Our evil was as strong as theirs. There were dozens of teams like ours roaming around in the woods. Not everybody would act the same as us. But we killed a lot of gook officers. We called many strikes on tunnels and weapons caches. The government needed people like me and Steve and George. They didn't want to know we were out there skinning people, but we were all cogs in the same machine. You can't expect to fight a war and not use evil on your side if you want to win.

In Vietnam I came to dislike the American government. They got their power in the war by using people like us, but the officers looked down on us. They were like the Green Beret who worked with us. He'd always tell us how sick we were, but he was out doing the same things. He told himself he was better than us because he didn't enjoy what he did, as if having a conscience made him superior. When a country goes into a war, it acts like a sociopath. It sends people like me out in the woods to do the most evil things we can think of, but everybody else pretends like they're on the side of the angels. The reality is, if the angels want to win, it takes the devil to succeed.

WE SPENT so much time in the woods that Steve went out of his mind. You couldn't take him back into civilized places. We were in Saigon once. George and I saw him walk up to a man in the street and slice off his ear. We had no clue what started it. It's the middle of the day. We're outside a restaurant. Suddenly, people are screaming bloody murder, running everywhere. Steve had his knife out and an ear in his hand. He was laughing. George and I hustled his ass out of there so he wouldn't get arrested.

They sent us to Thailand for R&R. They had very nice hotels. Can you imagine how good a bed feels after you've been living in the mud? Our last trip to Thailand, Steve had gotten so wacko, me and him and George check into the hotel and Steve kept saying, "I don't know if I can handle this."

I said, "Shut up and fucking enjoy it, man. Look at the nice beds we got."

We'd always get two or three Thai girls. They'd bathe you, massage you, and take care of you. I'm in my room getting my brains fucked out by these two girls, and I hear a commotion in Steve's room.

I go in, and the place is destroyed. There's blood on the wall. Steve's on the bed fucking one girl, and the other girl is in the bathtub, drowned.

"What is this?" I ask.

Steve says, "I didn't like her. I like this one." Steve is screwing this girl. A few feet away her friend is floating dead in the bathtub.

I'm not judging anybody, but this was awful. I mean I was fucked up on that shit. It's not easy to talk about these things.*

---

* At this point in the interview, Jon had me stop the recorder as he appeared to struggle with emotions. Given that Jon often describes himself as a "sociopath," I am never certain if his emotional displays are genuine or part of an effort to manipulate his audience, but here and at other points in his interviews on Vietnam, Jon stopped to cry.

Sometimes after I tell you something, today it doesn't make sense anymore. Why would you kill a girl who was giving you a bath? Those guys we skinned. I wonder about some of the things our interpreter told us about the gooks we grabbed. Did he make things up, like tell us the guy we grabbed was a colonel when he was really a cook, so he'd look good? A lot of the craziness that made sense to me then doesn't make sense anymore.

Steve was my brother. But when I saw him in the hotel with the dead girl, I knew he was totally gone. He was a psycho. I'm not saying I wasn't psycho, but I knew I was. Steve didn't know what he was anymore.

George and I helped clean up the mess. We paid off the one whore to tell the hotel her friend got drunk and drowned. We left. Nobody ever questioned us.

AFTER THE incident in Thailand they sent a bunch of us for jump training in Okinawa and Korea. I had never jumped in Vietnam. Now they trained us for a new kind of jumping—High Altitude, Low Opening, or HALO, where they fly you 35,000 feet in the sky and you jump. It's so high, you have to breathe pure oxygen before you jump to adjust your blood, and when you go out, you carry an oxygen can because the air is so thin up there. You don't open your chute for a long time. You fly in the air. If the plane is going 200 miles an hour when you jump, that's how fast you're flying. This way they can drop you one place, and you fly another 20 or 40 miles before you open your chute and land.

The idea of a HALO jump was, the plane could go to the border of a country and let us out to fly in ourselves. That way if anybody asked, America could say, "No, we never flew our plane into your country." That was technically correct. The plane didn't fly in, but me and Steve and George did.

Many times we'd crawled across the border into Cambodia when we were looking for arms caches. This time they wanted us to go in farther to a river town south of Cambodia's border with Laos. There was a specific group of guys they wanted us to kill who met every week at the back of a restaurant. What made this operation different was, these guys were all civilians. The main guy we were after was the mayor of the town. That's why they wanted us to jump in from a distance.

There were six of us who jumped, Steve and George and three other guys. They dropped us at just under 20,000 feet, which meant it was technically not a HALO jump but an extremely high free-fall. The effects from falling from that height were the same as HALO. It's so cold you become frozen. You turn blue. As you come down into the warmer atmosphere, your brain starts to rush like you got high on the best drug in the world. When you land, you're so cold you don't feel nothing. You touch the ground, and it's like, where are my feet? It takes twenty minutes to thaw out. But it isn't a bad feeling at all. I felt high when we hit the ground in Cambodia. I remember thinking, *I can't believe I get to go kill a bunch of guys with this rush on.*

It took us a day to sneak into position. It was a nothing town, a few buildings around a small bridge on a river. There were no soldiers or police. The place we hit was a bar that was up on stilts. There was a dry canal on one side where two of our guys stayed to watch our backs. George and another guy took out a guard on the stairs at the rear entrance of the bar. The mayor's meeting was in a room at the back of the building. Steve and I climbed up the stilts by the side of the building and waited by a window. As soon as George dropped the guard, we went in.

The room was a dining area with one table and a bunch of chairs. There was a Chinese girl with a microphone who couldn't sing singing an American song, a couple waitresses or whores in silk dresses, and three or four guys in suits. These weren't straw-hat-and-pajama guys. The mayor and his friends looked like businessmen. I have no idea why we had to kill them.

We had a system for killing a bunch of people in one room. Steve and I would divide the room in half. We'd each kill everybody on our half of the room, moving in opposite directions until we met on the other side. You face the person you're shooting to make sure none of your guys are behind him. Always move forward. You shoot and move. You can roll toward the people you want to kill, but you got to be careful you don't lose your orientation and turn your gun in the wrong direction when you come up to shoot.

There were eight or ten people in the room, and we killed them all in under half a minute. We killed the guards, the waitresses, the singer, and the guys in the suits. *Click click click*. Everybody was dead. We made sure with shots to the head. There could be no witnesses to say the shooting had been done by Americans. We even used short-barreled Chinese AKs carried by the Communists so nothing would be linked to us. It was like a Mafia hit, but done by the United States government.

When we were done, we crawled through a dry canal to the edge of the town and walked into the woods. It took us a couple days to walk back to the border with Vietnam.

That was the high point of Vietnam for me. We did a couple more jumps, but we could not find the actual people we were supposed to kill, so we had to walk back empty-handed. But I loved jumps so much, I still had fun.

IN 1968 they sent me and Steve and George back to Hau Nghia Province. Our first time out we found an underground storehouse for weapons and called in the coordinates for an artillery strike. We climbed into a tree to wait for the strike. We'd seen no people near the targets, but sometimes after a strike, gooks would run out of holes we hadn't seen and they would lead us to a new set of tunnels.

Standard U.S. military training is that at least one man stays up on watch at night. But when it was just the three of us, we would all sleep. Our reasoning was that if we found a good hiding place up in a tree, the enemy would have to have one-in-a-million luck to find us. And if he had that much luck on his side, we'd be done anyway. To our thinking, we were more effective out in the woods if we could sleep a little bit, which you can't do if everybody's taking turns on watch.

Our way of doing things never let us down. The enemy never

surprised us. It was the U.S. Army that got us. We were set up in our tree one night, waiting for a fire mission we called, when we got blown up by an off-course American artillery round.

I never heard the explosion. One moment I'm up in the tree at night. The next moment I'm waking up on the ground in the daylight. My clothes were shredded. I had no weapon. There was blood on my arms and stomach. I ran my fingers over my body but didn't find any deep wounds. I didn't touch my head right away because I thought, *If I'm thinking, my head must be okay.*

But when I touched my face, I felt clots of blood. I moved my hands up past my ears, and at the top of my head there was a mushy hole. I put my fingers in and they went in my fucking head. I thought, *There's a hole in my head.*

It was in the crown of my head. The hole was as wide as a baseball. I poked my finger in and felt tissue inside. First I thought, *How the fuck am I alive?*

Then I thought, *Am I alive?*

I didn't have a mirror. I couldn't look inside my head. I had to deal with it. I took green leaves off the ground and pressed them into the opening. I tore off my pant leg and wrapped it around my head to hold the leaves in place.

Then I saw the chunks of meat on the ground. That was George. His head was sitting by a pile of intestines. I saw Steve in one piece, sleeping on the ground a few feet away. His foot was moving on the ground like he was pedaling a bicycle. I rolled him over and saw the side of his face was gone. His nose and half his jaw were missing. He had one eye, and it looked at me, like he might be awake.

I wasn't sure if he could hear, but I said, "You've got no face left."

He put his hand to his head and made it like a gun, motioning for me to finish him off. I said, "If you can't stand up, I will blow your head off. But if you can stand and walk, you're coming with me."

I pulled him onto his legs, and he was okay. I'm not telling you he could catch a ball and run down a field, but he held his own weight. I tied a T-shirt over his head and cut a hole in it for his one eye and his mouth—what was left of it. We started to walk. That's when I felt the pain. With every step, it felt like somebody hitting my head with a hammer.

It took us a day to find an army patrol. We scared the shit out of them. Can you imagine seeing me with fucking leaves on my head and Steve with one eye sticking out of his shirt? When they got us into a camp and lifted Steve's shirt, one of the soldiers puked. They wouldn't give me morphine because they were worried about my blood pressure dropping. I wanted to kill them. "I got a hole in my head. Blood pressure is not high on my list of worries."

Steve and I went out on separate medevacs. I went to Japan, then to Long Beach Navy Hospital in California. I was out of it for a couple of weeks because of a bad infection. Finally they put a metal plate in my head. When I got good enough to talk, I asked about Steve. They told me he was at a rehab hospital somewhere else.

They let me send him a note. He wrote back weeks later, "You should have blown my brains out."

I didn't see Steve until a year later. They had remade his jaw and given him a mouth, but he could barely form words. They couldn't fix his nose, so they gave him a plastic thing with snaps that covered half his face. He looked disgusting. But his attitude had changed. He was planning to live in the woods in New Hampshire, and that made him happy.

I loved Steve, and he loved me. I would never judge him. I did say to him, "Maybe what happened to us is payback for all the things we did to people out there."

"It's possible," Steve said. "But so what? We enjoyed every second of it."

11

J.R.: I had problems getting out of the hospital. I got more infections in my head. When I would stand, I would fall over. Weak as I was, I went crazy one night and beat up a male attendant. They moved me into a locked ward. They tied me to a table. I tried to chew through the restraints. They sent a new doctor, who pointed to chew marks on my restraints and asked, "What's this?"

I said, "There's a fucking rat. He comes in every night and chews and chews."

The doctor cracked up. He became the first human I formed a relationship with after I came back. He untied me. He gave me his arm and helped me walk to a toilet, so I could pee standing up for once.

Other doctors came. They gave me the psychological test where you pretend to be driving a car and you have to choose between running over a woman or a dog. They asked, "What would you do?"

"I'd run the bitch over. It's her fault for being in the road," I said. "The dog don't know any better. He's innocent."

When they gave me crayons and asked me to draw something pleasant, I drew the woods, with stick-figure people in pajamas. I said, "This is my pleasant thing."

It was obvious I was thinking of gooks in the woods, and I wanted to kill the gooks in the woods. They sent in a priest. I had no strong feelings about priests. I'd never interacted with one. He said, "None of your thoughts are in the right place."

"Are they going to keep me locked up here forever?"

The priest said something very strange to me: "Your body is overrun with evil."

I found this very unhelpful. "Why don't you put your ass where I was, and then tell me what's in my body? You fucking moron."

"I just want to help you," he said. "I apologize."

The fact that this man apologized got my attention. The next day he returned and talked to me, without any mumbo jumbo. He said, "The powers that be are scared to let you go. They think you have not been rehabilitated to go among the general population. I want to help you get out."

This priest came every day. We'd shoot the shit, but without any God crap. The man did help. I'm not saying he showed me the light, because I certainly didn't go to church afterward. But he explained to me I needed to change my thinking when I answered the doctors' tests.

A day came when the doctors gave me a new round of tests. Again, they asked me to draw something pleasant. I gave them a sunset. When they asked about my views on life, I became a flower child. I said, "I realize how important peace is. War is really bad."

Their whole attitude changed. It's funny, because these were army doctors. The army recruited me in jail after I was charged with attempted homicide. They trained me in better ways to murder and let me loose in the woods for a killing spree. They trained me to fly in the air so I could kill people that were hard to reach, and to use Chinese guns so nobody could finger America for the murders. But to go home I had to pretend I liked sunsets and rainbows.

Once I understood the game, I played it. The doctors knew I'd killed a bunch of people, but they didn't know my actual personality. If they did, they never would've let me out of the room.

I left the army in late 1968. My army service cleaned my record.* I wasn't a criminal no more. I was twenty years old and free. My mind wasn't completely proper, but I was better off than most guys returning from Vietnam. I had a future. I knew I wasn't going to be flipping burgers at McDonald's.

---

* In response to my Freedom of Information Act request for Jon's military records, the National Archives and Records Administration replied that its technicians were unable to locate his records. I interviewed one person by phone, identified in the book as Steve Corker, who claimed to be the man who served with Jon in Vietnam, and I found records of the soldier identified in the book as George, who died from friendly fire as Jon described. I have viewed Jon's medical records, and he does have a metal plate in his head. I have viewed records indicating that one of his associates was arrested in connection with the kidnapping and attempted murder case that Jon claims resulted in his entering the army. Jon's sister, Judy, recalls his entering the military and returning from Vietnam. Police involved with Jon's arrest in 1986 were told by informants on the street that Jon was known as a "psycho Vietnam vet." Jon is an avid and skilled sky diver. Previously, as a reporter on military matters, I have encountered rare cases where records have been misplaced by the National Archives, but until Jon's government records can be produced, his recollections of military service in Vietnam cannot be independently verified.

12

E.W.: Jon emerges from his session with a therapist at a Broward County mental health center. A few months earlier, Jon's previous wife, the mother of his son Julian, filed a motion to alter their custody agreement so she could have more time with Julian. Jon counter-sued, and a judge ordered Jon and his ex-wife to undergo psychological evaluation. Now Jon meets the therapist, a woman in her thirties, two times a week. I watch from the waiting area as Jon shakes her hand good-bye. She is attractive in a slightly disheveled grad-student way. Jon smiles broadly and, as he releases her hand, says something that makes her laugh. As we walk out to his car, he says, "She's completely on my side, bro."

Jon tells me he has shared everything with the therapist, including highlights of his tour in Vietnam.

J.R.: She asked me, "Do you ever think you'll be at peace with yourself?"

I said, "How could I ever be at peace with myself? I just want to make myself calmer for my son's sake."

E.W.: What did you talk about today?

J.R.: Self-esteem. She asked me how I define self-esteem. I told her it's the values you have of yourself, and what others think of your values.

E.W.: Was that the right answer?

J.R.: Who the fuck knows, bro? She seemed happy. She likes me. Obviously, I don't tell her everything. I didn't tell her about skinning people in Vietnam or beating that guy who hurt Julian.

E.W.: What guy hurt Julian?

J.R.: Two years ago Julian came back from his mother's with bruises on his leg. It wasn't his mother who hurt him. He told me a man who visited her house had kicked him for making too much noise. I knew who this man was. I had some guys pick him up off the street.

E.W.: What guys?

J.R.: Two kids who work as bouncers at Scarlett's. They do odd jobs for me. They threw this piece of shit in the trunk of a car and drove him on I-75. Every half hour they'd pull over, open the trunk, and hit him on his leg with a hammer. They did this many times but never said a word. Finally the dumb fuck got it. "I understand," he said. "I'll never hit the boy again."*

They threw him in the weeds by the road, and that was that. He has not touched Julian since. So the doctors have their ways of doing things, and I got mine.

That's one thing I learned in the mental ward after Vietnam. You need to get along with people. However much force you have, sometimes you need to play somebody else's game. Other times force works best. You need to be smart about how to balance those things. I took that with me when I came back to the civilian world from Vietnam.

---

* Scarlett's Cabaret is a strip club in Broward County frequented by Jon.

13

J.R.: New York was a different city when I came back in 1968. Girls on the streets wore flowers. The squares who worked on Wall Street were growing their hair out. The beatniks had taken over. Even Dominic Fiore had joined the hippie movement. After his overdose that got us arrested and me sent to Vietnam, he did no time in prison, because when they sent me into the army and expunged my criminal record, the case against him was ruined. While I was off fighting gooks, Dominic started wearing tie-dyed shirts and took up the flute. He'd sit in Washington Square playing his flute, preaching love. But anyone who gave him shit, he would knock their teeth out. He was the same guy underneath the flowers in his hair. When he needed money for dope, he'd rob some hippies.

My uncles didn't give a shit that I'd gone to Vietnam. To them, going to the army was the same as going to prison. What mattered was, I hadn't ratted anybody out when I was arrested. My second day back in New York, my uncle Sam had me out collecting debts. Instead of a gook in front of me, now it's a white guy or a black guy who owes money. I wasn't ecstatic going back to collections, but I needed the work.

Rocco Ciofani put me up at his apartment in Teaneck. While I was away, he had joined the Mafia as a soldier for the Bonannos, but he was still friendly with the Outcasts. Of those guys, Petey Gallione was such a bad junkie, he was always getting arrested for stupid things, and Jack Buccino was still living at his parents' house, scheming and scamming.

Jack knew a guy who booked musical acts. He got the idea to go into the concert business. His idea was we would rent the old Fox Theater in Hackensack and bring in a band that was popular back then, Ten Years After.*

Jack got me involved, because he thought it would help clear my mind up from being in the army. The concert business turned out to be very easy. After we paid a radio station to make the ads for the show, we sold every ticket. This gave me an idea. I said to Jack, "You know what? Why don't we print up an extra thousand tickets and sell these, too?"

Jack and me brainstormed it out. We had two shows booked for the band, one after the other on the same night. We decided to oversell only the second show, so any problems would only happen later in the night. We put an ad on the radio that said, "Due to printer error, we found extra tickets which are on sale now."

We sold all of them. At the first show we had the time of our lives. Alvin Lee was a phenomenal guitar player. The crowd went crazy. After we started to let the people in for the second show, we knew the shit was going to hit the fan. It was obvious there was no way you could fit an extra thousand people in there.

We went and got Petey, who we'd hired to be in charge of security, and said, "Let's get the fuck out of here."

---

* The British blues band, featuring Alvin Lee, that would perform at Woodstock.

We ran. The fire marshal closed down the show. There was may-hem outside the theater, with angry kids, fire engines, police cars. We drove away, laughing our asses off.

Later, the city sent lawyers after us. They said, "You'll never again put on a concert in Hackensack."

As if we cared.

ABOUT THAT time I ran into a kid I knew from New Jersey named Howie Tannenbaum. He wasn't an Outcast, but he was interested in different illegal things. After the Ten Years After concert, Howie asked me if I would help him set up some hippies to buy weed and then rip them off. Howie was a good kid. Later, he got caught in a bad case, and I guess he was afraid of going to prison, so he ended up locking himself in a hotel room and killing his girlfriend and then himself. But when I worked with him, he was good. We did a couple of rip-offs together in Manhattan, and Howie brought in a friend of his to help out, Junior Sirico,* who became an actor on *The Sopranos*.

Junior was a nut even then. If you see on *The Sopranos* how Junior played a wacked-out wiseguy who wore his hair slicked back on the sides, that's exactly how Junior really was on the streets. Junior was very good. He was a knife guy, not a gun guy. He always had switchblades, and he knew how to use them.

Junior was a soldier for a guy named Fat Anthony.† I mean no disrespect, but Fat Anthony was not good to the guys who worked for him. He'd slap the piss out of his own people for no reason. Junior could really take care of himself, but he couldn't raise a hand to Fat Anthony. He was the boss. I felt terrible for Junior.

As I got friendlier with Junior, I saw that Fat Anthony had a very nice business going. Fat Anthony controlled a bunch of fag

---

* Anthony "Junior" Sirico, after an arrest in 1971 for armed robbery, became in-terested in acting and played Paulie on *The Sopranos* from 1999 to 2007.
† Anthony "Fat Anthony" Rabito, reputed Bonanno family soldier, was convicted in the Donnie Brasco case, later fictionalized in the 1997 movie *Donnie Brasco*.

bars in New York. In the late 1960s, the fag joints were changing. They weren't just for fags anymore. They were turning into discos. The fags still went, but so did all the normal people. Discos were a big business. They were growing up and down Manhattan so fast, a lot of them didn't have any Mafia control.

I went to my uncle Sam and told him I wanted to get into the nightclub business. My uncle Sam talked it over with my uncle Joe, and he went to Carlo Gambino. They all agreed I should work in the nightclub side of the business. Collecting debts for my uncle had been part-time work. When my uncles talked to Gambino, this was different. I had shown ambition. I'd come up with an idea. It was a pretty big idea, too. I couldn't be one guy taking over a club. I had to work with the family. Within months after leaving the army, I became a soldier for the Mafia.

14

J.R.: Carlo Gambino and my uncle Joe were both in their seventies. To me, these men were ancient, like statues in the park. I met Carlo Gambino the first time when I was fourteen or fifteen. My uncle Joe took me to his house in Queens after my mother died. When we went in, I had to shake Gambino's hand, and Carlo Gambino told me I had grown. I guess he had seen me before when I was very little. Or maybe that's what he always said when he met kids of the guys who worked for him. My memory of that meeting was mostly of how stuffy his house was.

When I came up with the idea of getting into the nightclub business, Gambino gave me one of his top young guys to work with, Andy Benfante. Andy was a very trusted guy. For six years he had worked as Carlo Gambino's personal driver and bodyguard. Now we were cut loose to find good businesses to take a piece of.

There were dozens of soldiers running around putting the squeeze on different establishments. Andy and I were given free rein as long as we didn't take over any place that was already controlled by somebody else and start a war.

Andy was nearly thirty when we started. I was not yet twenty-one, but I had seen him around for years. When I was a kid, I looked up to him like a big brother. Now he was my partner. That gave me confidence, like having Steve watching over me in Vietnam. The first day Andy and I talked about working together, he said, "Jon, I know you're strong because of who your father is, but everybody knows I got Carlo Gambino. So whatever the fuck you want to do, don't worry about it."

If anybody on the street had a problem with me, they had to take it to Andy. And from Andy it went to Gambino. Everybody knew that. There was a flip side to the deal, too. The family wasn't going to let me run on the streets for free anymore. From now on, anything I did, even a drug rip-off, when I made a score, I had to pay a cut to Andy, who pushed this up the ladder. You pay the tax up to the family because kicking some money into the bucket now will buy protection for any problem that might come down the road later on.

My uncles were glad I was with Andy because in their minds Andy was going to look after me and keep me out of trouble. But what nobody understood was, Andy was a wild guy.

Andy called himself the "new breed of Italian." He didn't dress like other soldiers in the family. He wore open silk shirts, expensive shoes, gold chains, nice watches. He was into getting high, partying in the clubs, and fucking a young blonde one day, a young brunette the next. He liked Motown music and rock, the same as I did. I could relate to Andy.

The first night we really hung out together, he said, "Let's do some coke."

This freaked me out, because I still thought of him as the older guy I'd see with my uncles. Their generation—what we called "mustache Italians"—would all be sitting in Little Italy sipping coffee, and if you mentioned drugs, they'd smack you. That's how straight the Mafia was. It didn't matter that they'd been importing heroin from France since my father's time—soldiers were not supposed to get high.

So when Andy brought up coke, I worried he was trying to trick me. I said, "Drugs? No way."

Andy laughed at me. "Fuck that shit, man. Let's get high."

Andy was unique. He was completely loyal to Gambino, but he didn't give a fuck what anybody thought of him. I loved that about Andy. He drove a big Lincoln Continental, pimped out with extra chrome and the fake spare tire in the back, not because he thought it was a good car but because it was a ridiculous car. He did a lot of shit just to make himself laugh.

As soon as we started working together, Andy said, "We need to get you some nice clothes, man."

He took me to a shop called Granny Takes a Trip.* It was a crazy place where rock stars went to get dressed. They sold everything—wild, psychedelic silk pullovers, cashmere sweaters, velvet pants. Andy turned me on to a guy in the store who made custom boots by measuring your whole leg. The boots he made you were skintight and went up past your knees. That was the style. The leather was in patches of different colors, like yellow, white, green, and orange. The heels must have been four inches high.

Normal wiseguys looked at Andy and me like we were nuts. We went to a restaurant dressed like this with Gambino and my uncle Joe, and my uncle Joe got uptight. He made a comment to me about my boots. Andy said, "Jon and me have to dress like this. We're in the nightclub business. We need to blend in. We can't dress like hicks from New Jersey."

Andy would always stick up for me. When I got into trouble with older wiseguys, Andy would always say. "Jon, don't worry

---

* Granny Takes a Trip "revived the British mod movement in the late 1960s for young, fashionable people entranced with finery . . . A notable design is a colorful snakeskin boot patchworked like Joseph's coat." *New York Times*, February 24, 1970.

about it. When the sit-down comes, I'll lie through my fucking teeth for you, bro."

When Andy defended me to the family, he'd always say, "What do you want me to do about Jon? The kid's crazy."

The reality was, Andy was the one always putting shit up his nose, waking up every day with a new scheme. That's what made him ideal for the nightclub business. In the late 1960s, the owners, promoters, and in clubs were changing so fast, the family needed guys like me and Andy out roaming around, looking for opportunities.

THE FIRST thing me and Andy did together was start hanging out at Maxwell's Plum. This was a restaurant on the Upper East Side where all the beautiful people went before and after hitting the nightclubs.* The owners of Maxwell's Plum were already paying a cut of their money to someone else in the Gambino family, so Andy and I could not take it over. But we went there to learn. We spent a little money and got friendly with the people who worked there. You could learn a lot from the people who worked at bars and restaurants. A maître d' at Maxwell's was a degenerate gambler. We helped him out with some loans. He turned us on to Alice's, a restaurant on the East Side that was doing good business but didn't have any Mafia control.

Alice's was a joint with great hamburgers. It looked like a nothing place, but it got the same crowd as Maxwell's. It was owned by a man named Hampton Smith.† Andy and I offered Hampton a down payment of $10,000 to buy him out. He didn't want to sell because we'd offered a ridiculous deal, but he had no choice.

---

* Maxwell's Plum was created by Warner LeRoy, whose grandfather, Harry Warner, founded Warner Bros. Studios. In a 1971 *Esquire* profile, LeRoy described Maxwell's Plum as "a kind of living theater in which diners are the most important members of the cast. The regulars who come—Bill Blass, Barbra Streisand, Warren Beatty and Julie Christie—are players with our other clientele."
† Hampton Smith is a pseudonym to protect the identity of the owner.

That was the power of working with Andy. Our first month out, we bought a restaurant.

As soon as we bought it, one of our waiters came to us and said, "There's rats in the basement."

We went down there, and the rats were the size of small dogs. We told the waiter, "After we close tonight, bring some chairs down here. Bring a bunch of cheese."

Me and Andy had the waiter throw the cheese all over the floor and put the lights out. We all sat in the dark, listening. When we heard the rats going *eek eek eek,* we told the waiter, "Flip the light switch."

As soon as he does, Andy and I take pistols and shotguns and blast the rats. There's bullets, pieces of rat flying everywhere. The surviving rats scurry away. We stop shooting. The waiter is standing there in the smoke, nearly pissing himself. We tell him, "Okay, asshole. Turn off the lights. We're doing it again."

Me and Andy loved that shit. Anytime we got bored, we'd take a waiter down there with us for rat patrol. That's how we'd amuse ourselves.

At Alice's I'd get friendly with the customers. In the late 1960s, you couldn't tell if a kid in dirty dungarees was a millionaire or a bum. Everybody dressed the same. I met some kids with long hair and jean jackets who wanted to buy some pot. I told them I knew someone who could help them out. Then I set them up for a rip-off with Jack Buccino.

When I ran this past Andy, he had no problem with it. "As long as I get my cut."

So we ran the scheme. I introduced the hippies to Jack Buccino. He ripped them off. I gave a cut to Andy. Everybody was happy.

Then the hippies returned to the restaurant and told me to give back their money. I said, "Fuck you."

As they left, I noticed these hippies had come on motorcycles. Back then, I didn't know much about the Hell's Angels. I'd seen them in movies. But I didn't know the hippies I'd set up were Hell's Angels.

A few nights later, after I closed the restaurant, the Hell's Angels rolled up. They started banging on the door. I'm not scared to fight anybody, but not twenty fucking guys. This was a losing situation. I called Andy. He said, "Let them bang on the doors. I'll take care of it."

Half an hour later two refrigerator trucks pulled up outside. My whole life my uncles bragged about their "meat guys"—the union meatpackers loyal to the family. This night I finally saw them in action. These guys piled off the trucks. These were three-, four-hundred-pound men who spent their lives throwing around dead cows. These were people who I didn't believe really existed. They were like an army of pro wrestlers. They wore bloody coveralls. They carried meat hooks and baseball bats. They surrounded the Hell's Angels.

The fight wasn't even close. The meat guys rioted on the Hell's Angels. They clubbed the Angels. They fucked up their bikes with their meat hooks. For them, it was probably less work fucking up a Hell's Angel than it was throwing around a frozen cow.

That night I truly understood the logic of working with the family. I watched the Hell's Angels get their asses stomped and thought, *There's nobody I can't do something to.*

I HAD enjoyed smoking weed since I was a kid. Andy did too, but he had a special kind he smoked. He got weed with elephant tranquilizers mixed in. Now they call it PCP. We smoked it twenty-four hours a day, and I guarantee you, it made us lose our fucking minds.

Sometimes we did things under the influence of PCP that were not the brightest things to do. We had a little problem with Hampton, the man we'd bought Alice's from. We were supposed to pay him off in installments for the restaurant. But as soon as we got the papers from him, Andy said, "Fuck this guy. He's nothing. We ain't going to pay him another dime."

Hampton had a friendship with John Gotti* that we didn't know about. Back then John Gotti was not yet prevalent. People knew who he was, but there were ten guys like him.

When Hampton went crying to Gotti about how we stole his restaurant, Gotti decided to take his side against us. His end of it would be to get a cut of what we would pay Hampton, or maybe he'd take over Alice's from us.

Gotti and Andy and I were all part of the Gambino family. Normally, to settle a dispute between guys like us, we would go to the old mustache guys, and they would have a sit-down. But when Gotti came to talk to me and Andy, we were wacked out on PCP. We told him, "Fuck bringing this to the family. We'll settle this ourselves."

Since Gotti was young and crazy like us, he agreed. A few days later he told me and Andy to meet him at a metal shop in Brooklyn. The day of the meeting Andy and me smoked a bunch of PCP. Andy had a sunroof in his Lincoln. I remember driving through midtown Manhattan looking up at the buildings and telling him, "Drive faster, bro. Come on, before the buildings tilt down and melt on us."

We had shotguns, pistols, machine guns in the car, and I thought the city was melting.

The building Gotti picked to meet us in was a metal shop. There were workers grinding steel rods, sparks flying. I'm tripping out on the lights. At the end of the main room was a big metal door that opened onto a staircase to the basement. Gotti had a guy at the door. He says, "Down here."

---

* John Gotti, eight years older than Jon, became boss of the Gambino crime family in 1985, when he had Paul Castellano murdered. Castellano had run the family since Gambino's death in 1976. (Indicating how small a world the Mafia was, when Jon's uncle Joe Riccobono was arrested at Apalachin in 1957, he was in a car with Castellano.) Gotti's reign as top boss was turbulent and short. He was convicted in 1992 of racketeering and died ten years later in prison.

Andy and I brought some Outcasts for backup—Petey and Dominic and a couple more. We go in the metal door, down a metal staircase. There's nothing in the basement. No windows. A couple of boxes. Gotti's got six of his guys. Me and Andy got ours. We're dressed in our velvet shirts from Granny Takes a Trip. Dominic's got on his tie-dyed hippie shit. Andy and I are wacked out on elephant tranquilizers. Dominic and Petey are strung out on heroin. What a gang we are.

But all of us have guns. And all of Gotti's guys got guns, too. Gotti comes up to Andy and says, "What do you got?"

"What do you mean, what do we got?" Andy says.

"You owe Hampton for the restaurant, and Hampton is my friend," Gotti says.

We stand there facing Gotti and his guys. There's no rules in the basement. We all have guns, but our sides are even. If one side shoots, everybody's dead. This balance is what keeps everybody reasonable.

Then the door at the top of the stairs opens, and twenty guys come down. They are all there to back up Gotti.

PETEY: I was right behind Jon in that basement. I was calm because I was on heroin, but I was cognizant. I had no worries that we controlled the situation. But when I saw the door open and all the meatheads pile into the basement, I thought, *This is going to turn out really bad.*

J.R.: It turned out Gotti had his meat guys, too. He set us up. Now, it's us against twenty of Gotti's guys. After all the shit I survived in Vietnam, the last place I want to die is a basement in Brooklyn. A basement is a terrible place to die in.

Fear starts to clear my mind. I reason if Andy and I back down and agree to pay money for the restaurant, we'll be finished on the streets. We have to say no to Gotti. It would be crazy of him to kill us, but we don't know him very well. When people get their backs up, they can do stupid things. If we make him look weak in front of his guys, he might lose all his reason.

Andy doesn't even look at all the meat guys. He steps closer to Gotti and says, "Your friend Hampton is a piece of shit. He's a rat. He ain't getting a dime from us."

"He's a rat?" Gotti says.

"Ask around," Andy says.

Gotti's face doesn't show if he believes Andy or not. But by telling him that he is defending a rat—a man who is snitching to the cops—Andy has given Gotti an out. He can let us walk out of there without giving him a dime, but his face will be saved.

I say, "Thanks for having us out here so we could clear the air. See you later."

We walk out past Gotti's meat guys. When we get in the car, I ask Andy if Hampton is really a rat. He laughs and says, "He looks like a rat, don't he?"

A few weeks later Gotti came to Andy and me and said, "You guys were right. Hampton is bad."

It turned out Hampton really was working as an informant. Andy's hunch that he pulled out of his ass while we were tripping on PCP proved to be exactly correct.

Gotti ended up doing a short stretch in prison. We never had a problem again. Our run-in with him taught me a lesson. We should have settled our dispute through the family. That's what the Mafia was made for. It kept mad dogs like Andy and me and Gotti from wiping each other out. We were wild Indians. The old mustache guys like Gambino and my uncles could impose enough rules on us to keep us from killing each other. Without them, we would have had constant war, and we'd all be dead in a few weeks. That's when I started to respect the wisdom of my father's generation. Back in the twenties they were all wild Indians, too. But men like Luciano and Lansky were able to make order out of the madness. Once I became a part of the Mafia that my dad's generation had made, I got respect for my father that I'd never had before.

ANDY AND I moved more carefully after our run-in with Gotti. From now on, when we found a club or a restaurant we wanted to take over, we'd make sure the owners had no connection with anybody else in the family.

Most of the times we took over a club, we kept the same owners. All we asked was they give us a cut, buy booze from the suppliers we chose, put our guys on the door for security.

Taking over a nightclub was easy. Andy and I would send a bunch of our friends to go as paying customers, and then they'd pick fights. Sometimes the clubs got wise to this. They wouldn't let a group of eight knuckle-dragging goons come in all together. So we'd tell our friends to get beautiful girls and take them in as dates. Some of the guys we used were Outcasts. Others were half-assed soldiers like Mikey Shits from Little Italy. Mikey was a terrible fighter, but if he had something in his hand, he was okay. So he always carried a can of Campbell's soup in his pocket. He'd use the can of soup to beat people. They called him Mikey Shits because he used to sit at the bar and get so fucked up he'd shit himself. He always smelled bad. But if we put a pretty girl on his arm, they'd let him in the nightclub.

Once we got a bunch of our guys inside the club, they'd start fighting. They'd beat up everybody. When the bouncers tried to stop them, my guys would take out their pieces. *Click. Click. Click.* Just the threat of a shooting and most bouncers would quit, and everybody would lose confidence in their safety. Then Andy and I would go to the owner and say, "We hear you have a problem in your club. Give us a piece, and we can help you out."

This was too easy. Andy and I took a piece of half a dozen nightclubs before I even turned twenty-one in 1969. The problem we had was, a lot of clubs we took over died after we got them. What we didn't understand at first was that the business was based on people, not locations. Clubs were only successful if they could

bring the right crowd. There were a few promoters in New York—
literally two or three people in the whole city—who could make a
club a success. We could take over the clubs, but if we didn't get one
of these guys on our side, we were dead.

One of the top promoters was a guy named Bradley Pierce.* We
made Bradley our partner. When that happened, Andy and I were
able to take over the most successful clubs in New York. I'm not
saying this to brag. Once we started working with Bradley, me and
Andy became part of what they used to call the jet set. Not that we
belonged, but nobody could say no to us. Beautiful people bleed like
anybody else.

---

* Bradley Pierce was a legendary scene maker in the New York nightclub world of
the late 1960s and early 1970s.

15

Arthur, the East Side discotheque, whose psychedelic lighting, frenetic music, and chic informality attracted the young and the restless, is closing. The discotheque was opened on May 5, 1965, by Mrs. Jordan Christopher, formerly Mrs. Richard Burton . . .

Arthur was owned by a corporation of which Edward Villella, star of the New York City Ballet, was president; Roddy McDowall, vice president. Backers included Rex Harrison, Julie Andrews, Leonard Bernstein, Mike Nichols and Lee Remick . . .

Arthur will be converted into a supper club, under a new name, by a group headed by Bradley Pierce.

—Louis Calta, "Party to Mark Closing of Discotheque," *New York Times*, June 21, 1969

J.R.: Arthur was one of the clubs Andy and I destroyed. It was run by some real morons. We sent our guys in to wreck the place, and the owners would not cut us in.

We drove them out of business and took over with our new partner, Bradley Pierce.

We had found Bradley at a club called Salvation.* Salvation was a terrific club. The dance floor was sunk into the floor, with tables around it in tiers. When you sat, you could look down at the girls dancing. It was sensational.

It was run by Bradley Pierce and a man named Bobby Wood. Bobby was the money guy. Andy and I came on strong to Bobby Wood, and he made us partners.† We treated Bradley with kid gloves. Bradley was a special guy. I mean unusual. He had long curly blond hair and walked around like Jesus spouting peace and love. Bradley believed in all that crap. He was not a phony. Bradley could get along with anybody, from Mikey Shits to the king of Siam.‡ He was the guy who could make clubs happen. He was a genius at getting the right look, the right music, and he was tied in to all the beautiful people—models, actors, rock stars—who made the clubs go. Nobody had a better mailing list of guests than Bradley, and the list was everything.

BRADLEY PIERCE: I entered "café society"—as they used to refer to the world of nightclubs—in the late 1950s, when I was a student at Columbia University, and I began working nights at the

---

* Located at the site of a former jazz club at One Sheridan Square.
† Describing the business relationship between Wood and Jon (who is referred to by his birth name, "John Riccobono") on page 394 of *Jimi Hendrix, Electric Gypsy,* published by St. Martin's Press in 1991, Harry Shapiro and Caesar Glebbeek write, "Things took a more serious turn when Wood was persuaded to take on as club manager John Riccobono, a relative of 'Staten Island' Joe Riccobono, a key figure in the Carlo Gambino family . . . Mafia associates were put on the payroll, large sums of money were going out of the club while Wood tried rather foolhardily to resist this take-over."
‡ Pierce was profiled in Albert Goldman's *Disco,* a history of nightclubs in New York, published by Hawthorn Books in 1978. In it Goldman writes, "Bradley's stock-in-trade was his great personal charm. It was said that when a mobster would come into one of his clubs and start waving around his gun, Bradley would take the piece out of the hood's hand, make him laugh, and end up with the killer kissing him."

Stork Club. The Stork Club epitomized New York glamour.* In the 1960s café society began to change. It started with the bohemian folk-music scene in the Village. Café society embraced a new social informality. It turned slummy. P.J. Clarke's,† a divey Irish bar with sawdust on the floor, became the in place. After John Glenn became the first American to orbit the earth, his ticker-tape parade ended at a party at P.J. Clarke's, where I had begun working. About that time Olivier Coquelin‡ opened Le Club in a warehouse on the Upper East Side. Instead of a band, he had deejays spinning records. He made his club difficult to find. Entry was often invitation-only. Inside he brought together an eclectic mix of old-money blue bloods with movie stars and artists. Le Club became the first real scene in New York.

It took a creative celebrity guest list to make a club, and I had been building contacts since my time at the Stork Club. In the mid-1960s I started working with Jerry Schatzberg, who was a partner in Ondine's. When Jerry's partner in Ondine's, Michael Butler, left to produce *Hair,* he brought me in as his manager.§ I booked musical acts that shocked people—Jimi Hendrix, when he was still known as Jimi James, and the Doors.** Ondine's was avant-garde.

---

* The Stork Club was the place for everyone from the Duke of Windsor to Marilyn Monroe to Groucho Marx.

† P.J. Clarke's is still located at 915 Third Avenue.

‡ Coquelin is credited with being the originator of the disco in the United States. His Le Club was modeled after the Whiskey au Go-Go in Cannes.

§ Schatzberg was a top fashion photographer of the 1960s. The Beatles, the Rolling Stones, and Bob Dylan used his photos for their album covers. In the 1970s Schatzberg became a leading film director, known for his gritty, realist style, starting with *Panic in Needle Park*. That film, written by Joan Didion, launched the career of Al Pacino. Ondine's was a club that blended deejays with live music at 308 East 59th Street. Michael Butler was heir to a Chicago industrial fortune, theater producer, and confidant of John F. Kennedy, who at one point made him a special adviser on the Middle East.

** According to deejay Terry Noel in an interview published on djhistory.com, Pierce gave Hendrix work as a busboy at Ondine's. When Hendrix asked to perform and demonstrated his ability to play the guitar with his teeth, Pierce told him, "I don't know what to do with you. You're like a freak act." But Pierce did let him play, giving Hendrix his first significant show in New York. Pierce had the Doors perform for a month at Ondine's in 1966, before their first album was released.

Andy Warhol and his crowd would come. But we still brought in old café society people like Louis Auchincloss,* Frank Sinatra, Judy Garland, and Jack Warner.†

A new spirituality was coming alive in the country. In my clubs I wanted everybody to love and respect everybody. I wanted to get rid of that snob factor that predominated in the Stork Club. My secret was to treat everybody like a celebrity, and nobody was above anyone else. When a member of the Rolling Stones called my doorman a "nigger," I banned the group. If you can imagine it, we sought an atmosphere that was egalitarian and exclusive.

Jon and Andy came into my life after Jerry Schatzberg and I launched Salvation.‡ We were very successful, but Jerry left to pursue making movies. I took on Bobby Wood as a partner, and he in turn introduced me to Jon and Andy.

When I first met Jon and Andy, I didn't believe they were part of the mob. Neither of them looked like a guido from Jersey. They were hip. They were very likable. I could see there was a toughness in them, but they were very sweet to me.

J.R.: Bradley could not judge people properly. He did not understand us. He did not understand his other partner, Bobby Wood. Bobby Wood was a guy who came out of the used-car business on Jerome Avenue in the Bronx. Jerome Avenue was nothing but hustlers. They knew every trick in the world. If they were selling a car that rattled, they'd have you test-drive it on a rainy day, because the rain drowns out the rattles. If the engine ran rough, they'd stuff bananas in the exhaust pipes to make it sound smooth. That was Bobby Wood. He was a piece of shit.

But he was smart enough to get into nightclubs with Bradley.

---

* Auchincloss, the writer known for chronicling the rich, was related to both Franklin D. Roosevelt and Jacqueline Onassis.
† Jack Warner was head of Warner Bros. Studios and son of the founder.
‡ When they launched Salvation actress Faye Dunaway, who was very close with Schatzberg, served on the board of directors.

And through him, Andy and I took a piece of Salvation. Imagine a guy like Bradley who knew the most famous people in the world, and now he's working with me and Andy.

BRADLEY: Eventually I figured out that Jon and Andy were with the mob. But I believed in the spirit of the time. I didn't believe in labels. I saw Jon as a human being. I believed when you reached out with love to people—no matter who they were—you got such beautiful things back.

After Jon and Andy arrived on the scene, we relaunched Salvation. It was a fantastic event. We remade it as a theater in the round. I had everybody sit on pillows because I wanted to get people into very relaxed positions. It was an Eastern thing I had in mind. We got rid of the abrasive strobe lights, and I hired Joshua White* to create a unique mood through lighting. Jimi Hendrix, who had just played Woodstock and was huge, agreed to play as a favor to me.†

J.R.: At the reopening we had movie stars, models, and one of the Kennedys all waiting to get in. Andy was always a funny guy. He pulled me aside and said, "Jon, let's spike the punch. Let them all freak out at our party."

---

* In the 1960s Joshua White Light Shows, featured at concerts by the Jefferson Airplane, pioneered psychedelic lighting. White is now considered a fine artist of light.
† In *Jimi Hendrix, Electric Gypsy,* Harry Shapiro and Caesar Glebbeek describe negotiations to get Hendrix to play at Salvation differently. "Knowing Jimi was a regular in the club, [Bobby Wood's] associates suggested Jimi perform the opening night. Jimi didn't want to do it." The authors claim that Hendrix only changed his mind after a bizarre incident in which a mafioso arrived at his temporary house in upstate New York and began firing a gun at a tree outside his window. I asked Jon about this story and he said, "Andy and me used to shoot guns off all the time just playing around. It's possible we went up there and did that, but I don't remember needing to shoot a gun to make Jimi Hendrix play for us. He liked Salvation because he could get drugs there."

We put handfuls of Quaaludes in the punch. People used to call Quaaludes "leg-openers" because of the effects they had on women. Our party was unbelievable. People that had probably never been high on a drug in their life were taking their clothes off. I saw an older lady in a fancy dress bent over a pillow in the middle of the club getting nailed by a guy in a suit. It was like Rome. Jimi Hendrix tried to get me to shoot speed with him, but I wasn't into needles. He went out and played like crazy.* We had beautiful models walking around naked. But nobody caused any trouble. If anybody was looking for a fight, I had guys who would drag them into the back room and beat them within an inch of their life. That's how I kept the spirit of peace and love going.

BRADLEY: Salvation became such a sensation that one of the airlines ran an ad in *Life* magazine that said, "When you're in Rome, visit the Vatican. When you're in Paris, see Notre Dame. And when you're in New York, find Salvation." And there was a picture of our club.

As well as we were doing, I was starting to see the dark side of Jon and Andy. There was a shooting outside the club, and I was pretty certain they were involved. Yet there was always something playful about them.

I once offended Andy. I hadn't included him in a social event. Jon showed up at the club without Andy a few nights later. I asked him, "Where's Andy?"

"He's upset. His feelings are hurt," Jon said.

Andy was at home sulking, so I phoned him. I said, "Andy,

---

* Here is how the show was described on page 395 of the previously cited *Electric Gypsy*: "Jimi came onto the stage at around 12:15 a.m. with the Woodstock band and, although the crowd was expecting Hendrix pyrotechnics, he stood there calmly, the band working pretty well, Jimi trading solos with Larry Lee, who according to a reviewer from *Rock* magazine was 'wonderful'. "

please come out to the club. Jon's here. We're having a wonderful time."

Andy said, "I'll only come if you put on 'My Way,' by Frank Sinatra. I want the deejay to play it, so I can hear it over the phone."

We played it on the dance floor so Andy could hear, and he came. Jon and Andy were both like that. They were playful, and they were sensitive. There was a little boy inside each of them. Of course, they were tough boys, too.

J.R.: My father's only belief was that evil is strong. But I was learning I could go further if I reached out to people like Bradley who had abilities I lacked. We never fucked over Bradley because without Bradley, we would've had nothing. He was friends with Jimi Hendrix, not us. People loved Bradley, not us. To other celebrities, he was their celebrity. They'd beg to come to his parties.

Bradley used to say that our business was about putting more love in the world. Can you believe this shit? He was taking six hits of LSD a day, so he was gone. He was blind to us. Bradley was half business genius, half out of his mind. He did not understand what the Mafia meant. We started to teach him.

Because Andy and I were a part of the Gambino family, there were wiseguys we could not keep out of our clubs—friends of the family we could not say no to. As we got more successful, more of them came to our clubs. They would not come to fight. They would bring dates. They came with respect.

But wiseguys, even when they're out for fun, will always start fights. And once the wiseguys start fighting, wiseguy girlfriends always do the same thing: they stand on chairs, scream at the top of their lungs, and throw bottles. It's in the genes of Italian girls.

If wiseguys hurt other wiseguys, that was not a problem. None of them would call the cops. But when you mix wiseguys with society people, you end up with people calling the cops. The cops would come, but Andy and I wouldn't deal with the cops. It was not good for the cops to see us as involved in the business of the clubs.

Bradley would deal with the cops. Bradley would have to clean up the mess.

It must have been hard on Bradley as he got more exposed to my kind of people. He started to see who we were. But he got over it. Bradley stayed our partner as we expanded control of New York's discos for the Gambino family.

16

J.R.: After Salvation we took over Directoire.* Andy and I put up $100,000 of our own money to redecorate it, and Bradley went to town.

BRADLEY: Directoire was named after the Directoire period of France, and the club was all about that style.† When we redesigned Directoire, we didn't change the theme but we made it fresh. I brought in Jackie Kennedy's designer, Oleg Cassini, to supervise the redesign, and, of course, he made it even more fabulous.

J.R.: When Bradley introduced me to Oleg Cassini, I had my doubts about this little half-a-fag Frenchman. He cost us a lot of money. But his work was top-notch.

---

* The original Directoire was on 48th Street between Third and Lexington.
† Directoire fashions rose out of the French Revolution and emphasized a classless informality that influenced the styles of the 1970s.

They put in big fly chairs, with cushions all around. Bradley always liked cushions for people to lie on. It was very tasteful. There was no club like it. Even the bouncers we got were celebrities. We had Ray Robinson, Jr., whose father, Sugar Ray Robinson, was one of the greatest boxers of all time, and Richard Roundtree* working the door. Backing them up were my guys.

Petey, when he was not in prison, always worked as a bouncer for me, and so did Jack Buccino. With his desire to be in show business, Jack loved working the nightclubs, but he was always a problem. At Directoire, Jack nearly shot a customer. Jack was checking the ID on a kid, and Jack's own gun fell out of his pocket and fired when it hit the ground. The bullet went straight up and into Jack's leg. Petey and my other guys all took their guns out to shoot the kid. They didn't realize Jack got shot by his own gun. But doped up as Jack was, he had the presence of mind to say, "It was my gun. He didn't shoot me."

Poor Bradley. He came out to everybody screaming, my guys with their guns out, and Jack on the ground with blood pouring out of his body. Bradley was beside himself.

WHEN WE had parties at the clubs, Andy and I started spiking the punch with LSD. We'd have the old mustache Italians show up, and we thought it was hilarious to get them high on acid and lose their minds without knowing what was up. At one of these parties at Directoire, we dumped handfuls of LSD blotter paper into the punch.

"This is going to be the funniest shit ever," Andy said.

No old wiseguys came like we expected, but Ed Sullivan did.† He came in looking like he did on TV, like a corpse in a suit. First thing he did was take a cup of LSD punch from the bowl. Andy and I followed him while he walked around, talking with the models and singers hoping to get on his TV show. He held the cup the whole

---

* An aspiring actor in the late 1960s, Roundtree found fame in 1971 playing Shaft in the film of the same name.
† Ed Sullivan was host of *The Ed Sullivan Show,* which ran for twenty-three years on CBS and introduced America to such performers as Elvis and the Beatles.

time, without taking a drink. Andy and I were going nuts watching him. Finally Sullivan remembered he was thirsty and drank the cup.

Andy and I continued following him around, watching him like he was a science experiment. He was known to be very against drugs,* and we wanted to see the effect LSD could have on Mr. Clean. He walked around chatting like normal. Then his face got a wild look. He grabbed at something in the air that didn't exist and began holding the walls with his hands.

Andy and I always stocked our parties with whores. We sent a whore girl over to Ed Sullivan to ask what he was feeling. He went paranoid on her. He yelled, "Who are you?"

She smiled at him and calmed him down. Sullivan lost his paranoia. He stepped closer and put his hand on her tit. He started twisting it like a doorknob. Andy and I got a brainstorm. What if we could get Sullivan to take his clothes off and fuck the whore in a back room? If we got it on film, we could blackmail him. I told the girl to take Sullivan into the back. Andy and I asked around for a camera. But who had a camera in a discotheque? There were no security cameras back then. We sent a guy out to find one.

Andy and I peeked through the door to the back room on Sullivan and the whore. She took her tits out of her shirt so he could play with them better, but when she tried to get him undressed, he freaked. He went into the corner and started crying.

Andy and I got worried. We couldn't have Ed Sullivan lose his mind in our club. We sent for Sullivan's driver and brought him into the back room. We told him, "We don't know what happened to your boss, but he attacked a girl in there. You've got to get him out of here."

The driver said, "Mr. Sullivan has never acted like this in his life."

We hustled him out a side door, and a few days later I called his

---

* Sullivan banned the Doors from his show after Jim Morrison sang "Girl, we couldn't get much higher," from the song "Light My Fire."

driver to find out how he was doing. "Mr. Sullivan has been locked up in his apartment for three days," he said.

Andy and I did not think this was good news. What if we had destroyed Ed Sullivan's brain? This could be a scandal. It could bring heat into our club. Sullivan's driver told me a doctor had seen Mr. Sullivan in his home. I got the doctor's name from him and called my uncle Sam to see if he knew a way to get to this guy. My uncle didn't even ask why. Two hours later he called back. He had a guy I should take with me to talk to the doctor. He explained that if I took my uncle's guy, the doctor would talk to me.

The next morning I met my uncle's guy. He was a very tall man. His face was all pockmarked and scarred. Maybe he was somebody the doctor malpracticed on. Whoever he was, when we called on the doctor at the office, he saw us right away.

I'm wearing my platform boots and velvet pants with a gun in the waistband. Next to me is this scarred freak. The doctor looked from him to me, took a deep breath, and asked how he could help.

I said I wanted to know how Ed Sullivan was doing.

The doctor told me Ed Sullivan had called him and told him he had been drugged. When he went to his house, he found Mr. Sullivan barricaded in his bedroom.

"My God, is he all right now?" I asked.

"He's thinking about filing a complaint with the police. He thinks he was drugged at a nightclub."

"Did you run any tests to make sure Mr. Sullivan's cock is all right?" I asked.

"What are you saying?" the doctor asked.

"Mr. Sullivan attacked a girl. He got her alone, and she was screaming her guts out. We had to pull him off of her," I said.

"Does the girl want anything from Mr. Sullivan?" the doctor asked.

"This girl would rather everybody forget about the whole thing," I said.

The doctor promised me he would explain the situation to Ed

Sullivan. Two days later he called me and said, "I talked to Mr. Sullivan. He's much better now, and he'd rather forget the whole incident."

A week later my uncle Joe tells me to meet him at La Luna in Little Italy.* He had heard from my uncle Sam about my seeing Ed Sullivan's doctor. When I sat down in the restaurant, he said, "What the fuck is this shit about?"

I told him we'd drugged Ed Sullivan as part of a plan to blackmail him. I didn't say that we'd originally done it just for kicks. When I got to the part about the whore trying to take Ed Sullivan's dick out and him going bananas, my uncle slammed his drink on the table. "You fucking young kids, you've got to do every fucking thing in the world. Stick to your business. Leave Ed Sullivan alone. I watch his show."

Who knew my uncle Joe's favorite program was *The Ed Sullivan Show*?

MY UNCLE was right about sticking to the business. Between Directoire and Salvation, Andy and I were making good money. We went to Bradley and Bobby Wood and said, "Let's go get another club." And that's what we did. We turned The Envoy East restaurant on 44th Street into a club. We opened a place called the Boathouse in midtown and Salvation Two near Central Park West. We took over another place called the Church, which was an actual church. We named it Sanctuary.† We took cuts of other clubs up and down Manhattan.

Everybody came to our clubs—Mick Jagger, Teddy Kennedy, Johnny Carson. I met people I never imagined existed, like that freak artist Andy Warhol, who used to come to our clubs all the

---

* Not the same Luna restaurant in the Bronx below Jon's parents' apartment. La Luna was a classic Neapolitan eatery off Mulberry Street in Manhattan's Little Italy.
† Sanctuary, located in an old Baptist church on West 43rd Street, featured a mural with fornicating angels. It billed itself as the "most decadent discotheque in the history of the world."

time. He tried to get Andy to pose as a model. I gave Andy a lot of shit for that because Warhol was obviously very gay for him. Bruce Lee was one of the nicest people I met in our clubs. He wasn't famous yet, and he was small, but you could see from the way he carried himself that he was in phenomenal condition. I used to joke that I was going to fight him. I'm glad I never fought Bruce Lee. After I saw his movies, I realized I probably couldn't have taken that guy with a baseball bat. Another man I found interesting in our clubs was John Cassavetes.* He'd ask a lot of questions about how Andy and I ran the clubs, what we did for fun. Even though he was in the movies, he did not put on airs.

None of these people would have given me the time of day if it weren't for Bradley Pierce. If we didn't have Bradley, we'd have been out of business in a week. As much as he was into peace and love, Bradley was shrewd. One of his tricks was getting certain girls to follow him—a group of fashion models who went wherever he told them to go. He would tell them, "Come to this club for a week or two and drink your brains out." If a club was dying a little, he'd send his army of models, and it would get hot again.

Bradley had other tricks, too. He told us, "Always keep a line of people outside on the street. I don't care if the club is empty inside. I want people outside dying to get in."

No matter how much LSD he took, Bradley knew his business better than anybody.

ONCE WE were in the club world, in the summer we did what everybody else did. We left the city. Everybody went to the Hamptons or Fire Island. Andy and I rented houses in both places at different times, but on Fire Island we found an incredible old farmhouse on the water that we got for nothing because the owner was a degenerate gambler who owed my uncle. I bought my first nice boat, a

---

* The actor, director, and screenwriter who died in 1989.
† The Donzi was a premier small racing boat made by legendary boat racer and builder Don Aronow.

Donzi† that we used for water-skiing. Both Andy and I had dogs, and they wouldn't let you take dogs on the ferry to the island, so we'd hire a helicopter or a seaplane.

The seaplanes picked us up by the East River. One time Andy and I got in the plane wacked out on PCP. The thing that fascinated me about flying over New York was the bridges. That day we got up in the air, and I told Andy, "I'm going to force this motherfucker to fly our plane under a bridge."

Andy laughed. "He ain't gonna do it, Jon."

"Oh, I'm going to make him do it."

"What do you mean you're going to 'make him do it'?"

I pulled my piece out. "Andy, I'm going to put this up that pilot's ass if he don't do it."

"Don't do that to the pilot, Jon. He's flying us."

But I'm tripping hard. Everything is becoming out of proportion in my mind. I'm going crazy because I want to fly under a bridge. My dog, a beautiful Doberman named Brady, could feel my aggression.

Brady gets uptight and lunges at the pilot.

The pilot screams, "Control your dog."

I say, "Look, man. I communicate with my dog. My dog wants to fly under the bridges. He's scared to go over the bridges at this point in time."

Andy starts laughing his ass off. He takes his gun out, aims it at the pilot, and says, "Do what the dog says."

This poor pilot. He flies under every bridge for us.

The next week when we called his company for another plane, the owner apologized for the pilot. "He should not have argued with you," he said.

This man knew who we were. I was barely twenty-one, and Andy and I lived like kings—if you can imagine kings who smoke PCP every day.

17

JUDY: Of course I went to Jon's clubs. I loved to dance. Everybody loved Directoire. It was such a wonderful time to be in New York.

When Jon first came back from Vietnam, I worried so much for him. He was so withdrawn. I was living in Boston then. I'd divorced my husband and was finishing my degree at Emerson College. I moved to New York a year later.

What a difference that year made. Jon was so successful in the nightclub-management business. He was on top of the world. He had impeccable clothes. Everything was tailored. He wore custom boots and carried a cane. He had the craziest collection of canes.

I got to know Jon's friend Andy. They were inseparable. Andy was a very nice guy. I was not clueless. I knew Andy was not a nice, nice guy. Maybe he was a bad guy. But he was a nice bad guy. To me, he was a man of his word. I could look in Andy's eyes and see he wasn't all bad. He was a caring person. He was a genuine person. I believed he was a good influence on my brother.

J.R.: Andy woke up every day with a new scheme. Andy had a guy in the main U.S. post office. When the credit card companies sent out new cards, they'd arrive in duffel bags at the post office. Every few weeks Andy's mailman would steal a duffel bag of new credit cards and sell them to Andy. He'd roll up to my apartment in his Lincoln and yell, "Come on, Jon. Let's go burn some cards."

We'd buy thousands of dollars of merchandise up and down Manhattan. We made money from the scheme, but we did it mostly for kicks.

Any information we found, we'd figure out a way to use it.

We had that maître d' at Maxwell's Plum who was a degenerate gambler. When he fell behind on his debts, he earned his way out by telling us where they kept the safe at Maxwell's Plum. We sent guys in to rob it.

When I worked those two weeks at E. F. Hutton, I made friends with a stockbroker about my age. We met again after I was into the nightclubs. He had moved to Merrill Lynch and had an idea as to how to steal bearer bonds. This scheme was so big, I took it to my uncle Joe. He brought in a kid from another family, Vincent Pacelli,* who had done broker-firm rip-offs before. They stole a million in bearer bonds. Everybody made out, though later on that scheme ended up causing some problems for my uncle.†

Every day Andy and I were like sharks looking for more people we could swallow.

• • •

---

* A member of the Genovese family, allied with Gambino.
† The theft of the bearer bonds from Merrill Lynch provoked a scandal and resulted in Jon's uncle Joe being ordered to testify before a hearing by the New York State Legislature. He refused to testify and no charges were filed against him. See Richard Phalon, "Hooded Informer Reveals Stock Theft," *New York Times*, December 12, 1969.

ANDY AND I both loved dogs. He had a little bitch Doberman named Nicky, and she was best friends with my Doberman, Brady. We used to train our dogs together. You have to work to keep your dog aggressive. If the dog doesn't bite somebody occasionally, the dog will get rusty.

What we used to do with our dogs was not very nice, but I was not a nice person back then, and this is what we did: We would drive down to the Lower East Side. There was an area where all the bums would build fires in trash cans and stand around drinking. We'd pull up. I'd get out of the car with a twenty-dollar bill and say, "Hey, man. Here's twenty."

"Twenty dollars?" The bum would be all happy.

"In a few seconds you're going to do me a favor," I'd explain.

Andy would let out one of our dogs from the car and yell, "Get him!"

His dog or my dog would go after the bum. The dog would knock these bums to the ground and bite them all over. When the dog got his senses resharpened by attacking a person, we'd pull him off. If the bums were really bitten bad, I'd throw them an extra twenty.

Andy, with his sense of humor, would laugh his ass off. As many times as we'd do it, it was always a little different. You'd watch a guy's face when he saw the dog and realized it was coming for him. You cannot outrun a dog. Some guys were smart enough to hold still and get the attack over as quick as possible.

Others would try to outrun the dog, which is good for the dog because then he gets to practice chasing. We were happy when they ran. One time we had a hobo who was fast. You wouldn't have thought it, this guy dressed in rags. But he shot around the corner like lightning, and so did my dog. We jumped in the car and drove around the block. No dog.

I got out and heard the hobo screaming. He'd jumped into the entrance of a basement apartment. He was shaking the window bars, screaming for help. Every time he grabbed the bars, Brady would bite his hands. With this guy, we didn't call off my dog for a long time. We let him have fun. The motherfucker made us come around the corner after him. That's against the rules.

I used Brady in the clubs. I'd keep him in the office. If a fight broke out on the floor, I'd let him go on the brawlers. If somebody was giving me a really hard time, I would take him into my office and put the dog on him.

I drove with Brady in the car. In New York, there's always some jerk on the street wanting to get into an argument. If a stupid moron gave me the finger, I'd open the door and let Brady out. He'd jump in the guy's car window and bite his face.

BRADY WAS such a good dog because I took dog-training lessons from Joe Da Costa. Joe was a professional killer. He was also a dog breeder and a really good guy. There are all kinds of assholes who say they know how to train a dog. Joe is the only guy I ever met who really knew how. He was so good they used his dogs in the movie *The Doberman Gang.**

I spent a lot of time at his place in Jersey learning about dogs. I would put on a padded sleeve, and he'd have his dogs attack me so I could learn how to fight against a canine. He trained Brady to smell for gun oil. If somebody came to my place with a gun on him, my dog would pin him to the wall. I wouldn't tell people he was trained to sniff the gun oil.

He'd pin the asshole with a gun to the wall. "How does he know I got a gun?"

"He just knows," I'd say. "He's a good dog."

Joe showed me how to train my dogs to shit on command. In the winter when it was ten below zero, I could walk out with my dog, tell him "Shit," and he would do it. No fooling around.

Most important, Joe knew how to train a dog's heart by building his confidence, just like a boxer. When he had a new dog, he

---

* The 1973 exploitation film about criminals who use a gang of dogs to rob banks. Jon's assertion that Joe Da Costa or his dogs were involved in the making of the film could not be verified.

would get in his face and make weird noises like *sssss, sssss* to agitate the dog until he snapped at him. When the dog snapped, Joe would run away, like he was scared. This builds heart in the dog. Then Joe would fight the dog with a bamboo stick. He would hit the dog harder and harder until the dog believed in himself. If the dog was good, Joe would fight him with a rubber hose. He could beat the shit out of the dog, and that dog would not back down, because by then that dog was fearless and he thought of himself as a monster. A dog who thinks like that will attack and attack because he's got such a big heart.

All the dogs I ever owned had heart.

I wound up being a Good Samaritan because of my dog. If you wanted to get a really good slice of pie in New York—I don't care if it's apple, cherry, pecan, whatever—there was only one place to go: Better Crust Bakery, way up in Harlem by 139th Street.* They had a sweet potato pie nobody could beat, and some really unusual recipes, like a cream cheese berry pie with a crust made out of pretzel dough. It was crazy what they could do with a pie.

Better Crust was in the worst part of Harlem. You couldn't even go inside the shop. They had a Plexiglas window like at a bank. You'd slide your money into a slot, and they'd spin your pie out through a little door. Customers would line up like drug addicts, take their pies, and run.

I was up there one day in the summer getting a pie, and it was so good, I couldn't wait to get it in my car to eat it. I'm on the sidewalk chowing down a slice when a big Cadillac pimpmobile pulls up. Even though it's ninety degrees out, a black guy gets out in a fur coat. I think nothing of him. I'm happy with my pie.

I see a kid walk up the sidewalk carrying a paper bag. I assume he's a drunk, with a beer in the bag. Then I see flames coming from the bag. I think, *The bag's on fire.*

---

* The Better Crust Bakery was a fixture in Harlem since firing up its pie ovens in 1946. After a glowing profile by the *New York Times* in 1996, it shut its doors—an apparent victim of New Yorkers' waning interest in its signature sweet potato pies.

The pimp goes down before I even hear the shot. The kid had a gun in his bag and shot the pimp through the paper. Brady sees this and jumps out the back window of my car. He leaps on the shooter and knocks him over. This guy is so panicked, he drops his gun and screams.

Dobermans bite people all over. Other dogs will lock onto your arm or your neck and won't let go until you break them off. Not Dobermans. If you can take pain, you can beat a Doberman eventually in a fight because as much as they hurt, they aren't consistent in their bites. But this poor kid didn't know that. He's on the ground flailing. Brady is biting his face, his stomach, his arms.

I yell at the kid to calm down. I want my dog back before the cops come. But the more this kid screams, the more worked up Brady gets. I have to take my gun out and jam it in the kid's face. I tell him to calm the fuck down. Finally I get Brady off of him. The kid's chewed to pieces. He's a piece of meat on the sidewalk. He isn't going anywhere. Me and Brady get back in the car and drive home.

Later, they had a story on the eleven o'clock news, how a Good Samaritan helped capture a man who'd shot a "Harlem businessman"—the pimp—outside of Better Crust Bakery. Andy saw this and laughed his ass off. I'd helped the police solve a shooting.

But for all the fun I've had with dogs, I never had a situation where one actually saved my life. Great as dogs are, shooting a person in the leg is still the most effective way of making your point. Dogs are mostly just for companionship.

18

J.R.: When you run a nightclub, you will always get heat from the cops. The liquor license gives them an automatic reason to come into your place and snoop. Within a year of getting into the business, Andy and I started to draw real heat—not from New York cops, who could always be bought, but from the FBI. Two incidents made them nosy about us.

The first was the kidnapping of Jimi Hendrix. Jimi and I were never great friends. He was so far gone, I don't think he was truly friends with anybody. Jimi was a bad junkie. Jimi had people around him all the time, too. He was suffocating from these hangers-on. After we met at Salvation, he came to our house on Fire Island so he could get away from it all. We'd make sure nobody would bother him except for his real friends. Jimi really liked Leslie West,* and one night the two of them played

---

* A hard blues guitarist who fronted the band Mountain, best known for the hit "Mississippi Queen."

in our living room all night long. Jimi had to shoot speed in his arm to keep up with Leslie. That's how good Leslie West was. A few times, we took Jimi water-skiing off the back of my Donzi. He liked getting out and doing things physically, even when he was stoned.

He nearly drowned one time. Jimi's out there—no life vest on— and he falls off the skis. He's in the water thrashing around. I swing the boat past and throw him the rope. It's floating a couple feet from his hands, but he's waving his arms like crazy. Suddenly, I'm wondering if he can even swim. Andy has to jump in the water and swim the rope over to him, because Jesus Christ, if this guy dies while out with us, what a headache that would be.

I had some good times with Jimi, but he was a disaster on water skis.

I got involved in Jimi's so-called kidnapping after he was grabbed by some guys out of Salvation. Later on some people accused me of being involved in kidnapping him.* They said I was involved with kidnappers who tied Jimi to a chair and forced him to shoot heroin. Please. Nobody would have had to force Jimi to shoot anything. Just give him the heroin and he'd inject it himself. It was Jimi going out searching for drugs that got him into trouble. Andy and I were the ones who helped get him out of it.

Jimi had people who would usually buy dope for him. But sometimes he'd get so sick, he'd come into our clubs looking for drugs on his own. One night two Italian kids at our club—not Mafia but wiseguy wannabes—saw Jimi in there looking for dope and decided, "Hey, that's Jimi Hendrix. Let's grab him and see what we can get."

These guys were morons. They promised Jimi some dope and took him to a house out of the city. I don't know if they wanted

---

* In *The Jimi Hendrix Experience,* published by Arcade Publishing in 1996, rock journalist Jerry Hopkins names "John Riccobono" as a possible conspirator in the 1969 abduction of Hendrix from a New York nightclub. According to Hopkins, John Riccobono and other mafiosi kidnapped Hendrix and held him at a house in the Catskills while keeping him tied to a chair and injecting him with heroin in order to force him to sign a record contract.

money or a piece of his record contract, but they called Jimi's manager demanding something. Next thing I knew Bobby Wood called me and said Jimi had been taken from our club by some Italians.

It took me and Andy two or three phone calls to get the names of the kids who were holding Jimi. We reached out to these kids and made it clear, "You let Jimi go, or you are dead. Do not harm a hair of his Afro."

They let Jimi go. The whole thing lasted maybe two days. Jimi was so stoned, he probably didn't even know he was ever kidnapped. Andy and I waited a week or so and went after these kids. We gave them a beating they would never forget.

Here I was, the Good Samaritan—once again—in all this, but unfortunately, when Jimi was grabbed, some of his people contacted the FBI. Even after he was returned, the FBI kept poking around. My name came up, and next thing I knew I had two agents calling on me at the club. That was not good. I didn't have anything to say to them, but now I was on their radar. When the FBI contacted you, they made a new file, and once that file was made, you didn't know who would be reading it later. Because of the Jimi Hendrix incident, I had my first contact with the FBI.

OUR PARTNER Bobby Wood was involved in the second incident that brought heat on us. By 1970 he had become a real problem to our business. Any wrong thing you could think of, Bobby Wood was doing it. He was stealing money from us, picking fights with customers, shooting his mouth off. I believed it was Bobby Wood who gave my name to the FBI about the Jimi Hendrix kidnapping. The man was a mess.

BRADLEY: Bobby had developed a $1,500-a-week cocaine habit. He was acting bizarre. One night he came up to me and said, "Bradley, you're Jesus Christ to me. I know you can protect me."

He was doing funny stuff with the books, skimming money. I

told him, "Bobby, you're a fool because we have guys in this business who can be very tough. Don't be stupid. You have to be a lover of people and respect them."

But my words could not reach Bobby.

J.R.: Bobby went berserk on coke. He was one of the first people I knew who did a lot of coke where it had a negative effect on him. We could deal with him skimming a little money, even for running his mouth off to the FBI. Who was going to believe that piece of shit anyway? We weren't going to kill him for that.

But Bobby got into trouble with other wiseguys who came into our clubs. Bobby was a nobody Jewish guy from Jerome Avenue. He got so out of his mind, he hit on the girls wiseguys brought with them. When they'd comment to him that he should show respect, he'd insult them. Andy and I pulled Bobby aside many times and said, "You need to control yourself, bro."

Bobby did not listen. He disrespected the wrong people in our club. It got so bad, my uncles came to me. They told Andy and me to take care of him. Looking back, it's almost funny. There was no specific thing Bobby Wood did that made people want him killed. He was just an asshole. That was his crime. He was such an annoying asshole, he had to go.

In early 1970, on a cold winter night, somebody put several bullets in Bobby Wood and dumped his body on the street. Everybody said Andy and I did it. I have no comment regarding the truth of that rumor.

Unfortunately, prior to his demise, Bobby Wood wrote a letter to his attorney accusing me of terrible things. His piece-of-shit attorney put that letter in the hands of a newspaper reporter, and they made a story from it:

> Federal and local authorities pressed their investigations of the
> seamy side of New York's after-dark entertainment following the
> turning over of "letters from the grave" to law enforcement officials

by the attorney for Robert J. Wood, whose bullet-riddled body had
been found in a Queens street on Feb. 18.

Wood, operator of the Salvation discotheque in Greenwich
Village, left a legacy of accusations of Mafia control of bars and
nightclubs. Wood made his accusation in letters, dated Jan. 16,
which he sent to his lawyer with instructions to give them to
authorities if he was murdered. . . .

The letters relate that Wood "met a young man named John
Riccobono"* who inspired such trust that he hired him to manage
Salvation, with the option of buying 10 percent of the discotheque.
The letters say that Riccobono induced him to hire Andy B. as
doorman. . . .

John Riccobono is described in the letters as the son of one
important Mafioso and the nephew of another, Joseph [Staten
Island Joe] Riccobono, who is listed by the Department of Justice
as consigliere (counselor) of the Mafia "family" headed by Carlo
Gambino.

—Charles Grutzner, "Slain Man's Letters Give Impetus
to Local and Federal Investigations of After-Hours Clubs
Here," *New York Times*, March 23, 1970

J.R.: It was not good to have my name in the newspaper.

BRADLEY: I was there when the police came into the club and
questioned Jon and Andy the first time about the murder. When
they asked, "Do you have any idea who might've bumped off Bobby
Wood?," Andy said, "I can give you some names of people who
didn't like Bobby Wood." Andy picked up a New York telephone
directory and handed it to the police. He said, "Any person in here
might have had a reason to kill him."

---

* Although John Riccobono had his name legally changed to "Jon Pernell Roberts" when he was thirteen, many in law enforcement still referred to him as John
Riccobono, and on the streets Jon himself still went by Riccobono.

I couldn't believe Jon and Andy were laughing about it to the police like they didn't have a care in the world.

J.R.: Andy didn't give a fuck about the cops. They threw us into jail. They tried to hook us to the murder, but there was no evidence and they couldn't charge us. My dad had taught me when I was a little kid that you could kill a person and get away with it. He was right.

19

J.R.: After the Bobby Wood murder Andy and I pulled back from the clubs. We still ran them, but we moved into the background. When Bradley founded a new club, Hippopotamus,* we took a piece of the door, but we didn't keep an office there.

I was trying to settle down by then. In 1970 I got involved with my first serious girlfriend, Phyllis LaTorre.† I had met Phyllis as a result of buying my Donzi boat. One habit I got from my father was I never put my name on anything. Anything I bought, I'd give money to

---

* Hippopotamus, which opened on 54th Street then moved to 62nd Street, was arguably the most trendsetting disco in New York until the founding of Studio 54 in the mid-1970s. Hippopotamus was the setting of the Beatles' farewell party when they dissolved their legal partnership in 1974, and it was a favored hangout of an eclectic crowd that included Frank Sinatra, Mick and Bianca Jagger, and attorney Roy Cohn.

† Phyllis's legal surname was Corso. According to Jon, she adopted the name LaTorre because "it sounded artistic." Also, she wanted to avoid association with her father, Peter Corso.

somebody else, have him buy it in his name. I never wanted to have assets on paper that the government could trace to me. If it was a boat, a car, a place to live, I'd give cash to somebody I could trust or control, and he'd take care of everything. All I wanted were the keys. I bought my Donzi through a man who owned a hippie clothing boutique in Manhattan. After we did the deal on the boat, he said, "Jon, come to my shop anytime. I'll take care of you. Anything you want."

Phyllis worked as a manager in this guy's shop. She was his girlfriend. I met her when I first went in there. She was a petite Italian girl, and she was hot as shit. My friend said take anything I wanted from his shop. I took Phyllis.

I was twenty-one and Phyllis was at least thirty. The way I'd lived my life, I could not relate to girls my age. Though I enjoyed their bodies, their heads were empty. Phyllis was wise into the bottom of her eyes. She knew the things I was going to tell her before I told her. After we met, we wasted no time. Phyllis lived in a brownstone on Central Park West and 73rd Street. A few days after we met, she said, "Come on. Move in here with me."

Phyllis was the first woman who taught me anything. Not even my mother had taught me anything. I was a savage person when we met. Phyllis was definitely a teacher. She knew about restaurants and cooking. She went to movies, theaters, art shows. She had no hang-ups about showing me what she liked when we had sex. Phyllis had her own mind. She was an Italian girl, but she wasn't prejudiced like most Italians. She liked black people. She was good friends with the comedian Richard Pryor and with movie people. And it wasn't like with me and Jimi Hendrix. They were actual friends who truly liked her. She was a very interesting girl.

JUDY: Everything about Phyllis was interesting. She looked interesting. She was a classic Italian beauty, with olive skin, black hair, and such an incredible bone structure.

Phyllis was very avant-garde. She used to wear really weird outfits. Bright colors and furs. One summer she wore nothing but white. Whatever she was into, she was striking.

Jon has loved every woman he's been involved with. But Phyllis was the smartest of them all. She read. She was into politics. She was adventurous. When a friend of mine took me to Transcendental Meditation, she came. She even tried to get Jon to come to our meditation sessions to try to calm him down.

Phyllis did not take any crap from my brother. She dominated the conversations with him, but it didn't bother him a bit. He enjoyed having a strong woman in his life.

J.R.: After a few months living in her brownstone, Phyllis and I moved to a penthouse up the street. It was a gorgeous place with cathedral windows overlooking the park. Barbra Streisand was our neighbor. Not that we were friends, but this was the kind of building we were in.

Judy moved into Phyllis's old brownstone, and they were like sisters. Phyllis and I never got married, but to the people who knew us, we were a husband and wife.

JUDY: Jon finally got a family. This was a real positive. Phyllis had a big Italian family who took him in like a son. Jon was very close to Phyllis's father, her sister Fran, and their cousin Henry. Jon and Henry were like brothers.

J.R.: When I first laid eyes on Phyllis, I thought she was a hippie Jew girl. Was I wrong. Phyllis's family was all Mafia. Her father was a heroin guy out of Long Island, a real funny character who would get into a good scheme and *bang,* he'd fuck it up and end up in prison. He was in and out of prison.* When I met him, he was

---

* Phyllis's father, Peter Corso, was arrested for the last time in 1987 at age sixty-five on Long Island for cocaine dealing. "Corso—who has a felony record dating to

into a successful scheme with cocaine. He got pharmaceutical coke from a guy inside Merck.* The first good coke I ever did was the Merck stuff from my father-in-law. One sniff and your whole throat would freeze, then the freeze would spread until your brain felt like a chunk of ice. I never thought coke would end up being my future. Back then it was just a kick for Phyllis's friends, like Richard Pryor when he came to our house for parties.

My brother-in-law, Henry Borelli,† was a trip and a half. He had tried out to be a New York cop, but they wouldn't let him on the force. So he went the other way. He was with a crew of Italian kids who later got the nickname Murder Machine. All they did was kill people for hire. They had a pizza shop in Brooklyn where they'd feed the people they killed into butcher machines and take their bodies out in buckets. They must have chopped up fifty guys back there.‡ Henry was also a dependable shooter, and he did a lot of work for John Gotti. Henry and I never worked too much together, but we were good friends.

Phyllis's sister Fran was with a guy named Jack Bliss. He was Puerto Rican–Brazilian. He always wore tropical shirts with toucan birds on them. He loved music. He loved to dance. Everybody called him "Jack in the Toucan Shirt."

1938, including a two-year jail sentence for drug dealing—had several pounds of cocaine and papers detailing how the narcotics were distributed when he was arrested at home." From "29 Arrested in Dope Network Operated from Cell at Attica," the *Schenectady Gazette*, August 24, 1987. When I shared this news article with Jon, he said, "That's Phyllis's dad. What kind of moron would keep papers detailing who his distributors are in his own house?"

* Merck & Co., the pharmaceutical company based in New Jersey, sold cocaine for medical use until the late 1970s.

† Though Henry was Phyllis's cousin, she referred to him as her brother; hence Jon calls him his "brother-in-law."

‡ Henry Borelli was part of a Gambino-family crew headed by Roy DeMeo. Borelli earned the nickname "Dirty Henry"—after Clint Eastwood's .44 Magnum-toting film character—because of his reputed brutality in shooting people. The DeMeo Crew is reputed to have murdered as many as two hundred people in the 1970s and 1980s, many of whom were dismembered not in a pizza shop, as Jon states, but in an apartment next to a bar in Brooklyn. The DeMeo Crew's exploits were chronicled by Gene Mustain and Jerry Capeci in *Murder Machine*, published by Onyx in 1993.

Jack worked for my friend Vincent Pacelli. Vincent had been involved in stealing the bearer bonds from Merrill Lynch, but his main business was heroin. He and his father, Vincent Sr., ran the original "French Connection."* Jack worked for them as a courier. He drove all over the country, moving their shit in the trunk of his car.

Jack was the first guy I knew to drive a Mercedes 280 SL, the two-seater convertible. I drove a Cadillac Eldorado then, and you could practically fit Jack's Mercedes in the trunk. We used to laugh at his little car.

But Jack showed me what that Mercedes could do. One day Jack called me from Florida. He was down there to pick up some heroin but had met a guy who had twenty kilos of cocaine. This was an ungodly amount in the early 1970s. Jack asked if I knew anyone in New York who could buy that much coke. The price was a million dollars—a huge, huge sum of money then.

The old mustache Mafia guys still had the mentality that heroin was okay because they thought only the blacks used it. They didn't know Italians were junkies, too. Other drugs, like cocaine, they didn't want nobody touching. These old guys were just very set in their ways.

Through my nightclubs I knew a Jewish guy named Ray Mintner† who had a lot of money and was into different illegal things. He was a long shot, but I had nothing to lose by asking him if he was interested in twenty kilos of coke. Ray was nuts about egg rolls, so to get him in a good mood, I took him to a Chinese restaurant on Broadway, where they made the best egg rolls in New York. When I told him about my friend with twenty kilos, Ray did not bat an eyelash. He'd have the million dollars as soon as Jack brought the coke back to New York.

* The 1971 movie *The French Connection* was loosely based on a heroin-smuggling mafioso named Pasquale Fuca. The father of Jon's friend Vincent Pacelli—Vincent Pacelli Sr.—was involved in a similar French-connection heroin scheme for which he was convicted in 1965. Pacelli Sr.'s trial was notorious in its day because of his attempt to employ a Playboy Bunny to bribe a juror. See "Ex–Playboy Bunny Held in Bribe Plot," *New York Times,* July 13, 1965.

† Ray Mintner is a pseudonym to protect the identity of Jon's friend.

I phoned Jack in Florida. He put the twenty kilos in his Mercedes, and sixteen hours later he was in New York. For an investment of a few egg rolls, I made a $50,000 commission off the deal.

What impressed me wasn't the money I made from cocaine. My eyes were still not open to its potential. I was impressed by Jack's Mercedes. Until then I had always looked down on foreign cars. When I told Phyllis how fast Jack made the trip in his little Mercedes, she used this to her advantage. She said, "Since you like foreign cars now, buy me an XKE."

For as long as I could remember, Phyllis had been bugging me to buy her an XKE, the Jaguar with a twelve-cylinder engine and long hood. I went out and bought a matching pair of XKEs.

Poor Jack. He made all that money from his coke deal, and he expanded his heroin business. He hooked up with a black guy in Harlem named One-Eye Willie, who was in business with Nicky Barnes.* Jack started supplying Nicky with heroin he got from Vincent Pacelli and did very well for himself. As he got more successful, he started going around with black girls One-Eye Willie supplied him. Jack was very in the open about it. Guy wearing a toucan shirt driving around in a little Mercedes convertible stuffed full of black whores was hard to miss. Phyllis's sister Fran saw what he was up to, and she split up with him.

This turned out bad for Jack. He was not Italian. His only protection from the Mafia was Fran and Phyllis's father. When he lost their goodwill, he was nothing. Next time Jack got a big shipment of heroin, my brother-in-law Henry robbed him and fed him into the meat grinder at the pizza shop. That was the end of Jack in the Toucan Shirt. When you cross an Italian girl, you've got to be very careful how you do it.

---

* Nicky Barnes was the Harlem heroin dealer on whom Cuba Gooding, Jr.'s, character was based in the 2007 film *American Gangster*.

20

J.R.: Phyllis was always trying to teach me to be more careful. She used to tell me, "Jon, you run around like a wild Indian. You'll get shot."

I took many risks, but seeing how Phyllis's family took care of Jack in the Toucan Shirt, I was careful about seeing other women. Phyllis was wise enough to know I was a young man. I was not a monk. Her point was, I should never rub her nose in seeing other women.

When it came to women, I was crazed. It was nothing for me to fuck a woman five or six times a day. When you threw in the nightclubs, the money, and the clothes, I had a solid game. But underneath it I was still a street kid. At times the women I got surprised even me.

Phyllis turned me on to a restaurant called Serendipity 3.* It was on the first floor of a brownstone, and

---

* Still located at 225 East 60th Street, Serendipity 3 is known for some of the most extravagant ice cream sundaes sold in Manhattan.

when you walked in, they sold weird shit like espresso machines and cuckoo clocks. The restaurant part was pushed in the back of what was almost a basement. But it was where very fancy people went in New York.* They served unbelievable desserts and breakfasts. They made a French toast with cream cheese inside that was out of this world.

Since Phyllis liked to sleep late, many mornings I went to Serendipity alone. I'm sitting there one morning, eating my French toast, and seated at the next table was a girl I'd seen in the movies.† In one movie she played James Bond's girlfriend. She was a goddess. I was just a nobody twenty-two-year-old, but I decided to give it a shot.

I said, "I'm sorry to intrude, but I couldn't stand not saying hello to you, because you are absolutely gorgeous."

She smiled at that. Even though she'd been complimented a million times in her life, one more still made her happy. When she smiled, I told her I was surprised I've never seen her before at my club, Sanctuary.

"Oh, that's your club?" she says.

"Please come and be my guest sometime. Dance your brains out. Anything you want. The bar is open."

A week later she showed up at my club. I wasn't there, but my bouncer called me and said, "Jon, James Bond's girlfriend's here asking for you."

My doorman dealt with a lot of famous people, but to him, this girl was a big deal. I had him take her to a special table and bring her a bottle of wine. Not champagne. A bottle of wine and two glasses. I made her wait forty-five minutes before I came over.

"Do you like to dance?" I asked her.

"I love it."

I said, "I don't dance. So knock yourself out."

---

* Marilyn Monroe, Andy Warhol, and Jacqueline Onassis were all Serendipity regulars at different periods.
† The woman Jon is speaking of, whose name has been removed from this book at her request, was famous as a model, then as an actress.

"Let's sit and talk," she said.

I sat and talked to her. After a while I said, "I want to watch you dance."

So she got up and danced. By four in the morning, she'd danced her brains out, and she'd told me all about herself—how it's hard to be taken seriously when you're a beautiful woman, blah, blah, blah. I sat there listening, and she was very happy. She said, "What are we going to do now?"

"Whatever the fuck you want to do, we're going to do it now."

"Let's go to an after-hours club," she said.

I took her to a place downtown. It was a club where rich people and degenerates from the artistic world liked to go. That painter, Andy Warhol, had turned me on to it. I knew this would be just right for an actress. Everybody inside was wacked on cocaine. I said, "Do you like to get high?"

"I really don't know," she said.

I said, "Stop with your 'I don't know.' Do you like to get high or don't you like to get high? Obviously, I'm not a fucking cop."

She laughed, and we got high on cocaine into the morning. I drove her back to her place in my Jaguar. But I did not try to come in. When I let her off, she said, "I'm going to California to work on a movie, but you can call me here." She wrote a number on a piece of paper.

I never called. A few weeks later she came back to my club. She was angry I hadn't called. I told her to stop being like that. She brightened up. We stayed out all night again. At eight in the morning, she said, "I want to go eat."

We go to Serendipity. We order the French toast with cream cheese, and by now I'm aching for her. She takes a bite of her French toast, and the fucking cream cheese squishes out on the side of her mouth. She starts to laugh.

"That's it," I tell her. "Come with me."

"What?"

"You're a mess."

I pull her into the bathroom. As soon as I shut the door, I lift her ass up and drop her on the sink, with her legs open in front of me.

"Nobody's ever done this," she says.

"I don't give a fuck what anybody else has ever done in your whole fucking life."

We start fucking, and right away the sink busts loose from the wall. My ass is banging the door behind me. The little bathroom in Serendipity was like an airplane toilet. But this doesn't stop us. I'm not saying I was the greatest fuck in the world, but the urge of the moment was very strong in both of us. When we finish, she gets a frightened look and says, "Oh my God. The noise we made. I can't go back out there."

I leave her alone in the toilet and go back out in the restaurant. It's a really tiny place. Everybody looks up at me. I say, "I'm sorry, everybody. The restaurant is closed. You have to get the fuck out of here. Now."

The half-a-fag waiter who runs the place, he knows me. He comes up to me and says, "Jon, what are you doing?"

I explained to him there was a lady in the bathroom I'd just fucked, and because of her station in life, she did not want to step out and have a bunch of morons stare at her. I told him I'd pay whatever it cost for everybody to leave. That waiter emptied out the place.

He made up a new table for us in the middle of the restaurant, and we finished breakfast all by ourselves. I felt invincible. There I was, twenty-two, and I'd just fucked James Bond's girlfriend in the toilet.

PETEY: The movie *Super Fly* came out in the early 1970s, and working at Jon's clubs, I felt like I was living it. That movie changed everybody's look. We started dressing in Borsalino hats and tailored sharkskin suits. I was shooting so much junk, there were times I thought I was Super Fly.

Jon's club, the Boathouse, became a big hangout for the New

York Knicks. Wilt Chamberlain* would show up, and the women would line up for him. Walt Frazier† used to come in a Rolls-Royce he'd customized with whitewall tires and extra chrome like a pimp-mobile. We had real pimps that used to come to the club. There was a famous one called the Flying Dutchman. He had gold teeth, gold chains, a big watch, and a cane with diamonds on it that all the Knicks started to imitate. That bling look didn't start with rap; it started with the Flying Dutchman. Of course, when Jon and Andy saw how the black celebrities were getting into diamonds and gold, they schemed a way to rob them.

J.R.: I had admired the great basketball players since I was a kid. These guys knew what Andy and I were about, and they would ask us if we knew any deals on jewelry. Being who we were, they assumed we could get them deals on hot items. I didn't intend to rip them off, but they were asking for it.

Because my uncle Sam owned dental labs, he bought a lot of gold. Through him I had a good friend in the diamond district named Howie. Howie was a good, good guy. He was into smuggling stones from around the world. Show me any diamond guy in New York, he's got stones that don't belong to him or he's not paying taxes on. It's how their business works.

I told Howie how I got all these high-paid athletes who wanted diamond watches and rings. He said, "Send them to me. I'll take care of them."

Howie had a trick that a lot of diamond guys use. They call it "blowing out the rock." They take a piece-of-shit stone, even glass, and I don't know if they use chemicals or what, but they make it shine and feel as hard as a diamond. So Andy and I started sending

---

* A former Harlem Globetrotter, Chamberlain was an NBA champ who played for the Lakers in the early 1970s. Later, he became known for his claim of having hooked up with more than ten thousand women during his career.
†Frazier was an NBA Hall of Fame inductee who led the Knicks to two championships, in 1970 and 1973, and was famous for arriving at games in his custom Rolls-Royce.

all our wannabe-pimp basketball player friends to Howie. Even the white guys were into this. Howie robbed them blind with his junk rocks and gave us a cut. We did this for years. These athletes were happy with what they got. It wasn't our fault they didn't know they were wearing garbage.

THERE WERE many nights Andy and I went out just to have a good time. No schemes. No women. We'd just try to soak up the scene. At Hippopotamus we tried to keep very quiet, out of respect for Bradley Pierce, whose name was on the club. But there were always jerks who could make a problem out of nothing.

One time it was my Granny Takes a Trip boots that got us into trouble. I was at the bar in Hippopotamus one night talking with Andy when a couple of guidos came past. These guys were real hicks from Jersey—their hair greased back, pizza-collar shirts. It's anyone's guess how they got past the doorman. But I don't say nothing. I'm having a quiet night. As they walk by, one of these mouth-breathers makes a comment about my boots.

Andy gets very uptight. I say, "Andy, what do we care what this asshole thinks about shoes?"

Now one of the Jersey hicks says, "I told you they were nothing but a couple of faggots."

Enough is enough. I grab him by the neck, and Andy breaks a bottle on his face.

Out of respect for the club, we immediately dragged this guy out a back door to a loading area. His friend came out after us. One of our bouncers knocked him down with a baseball bat. These guys wanted to get wise about my boots, so I decided to show them my boots.

As good as my Granny Takes a Trip boots looked, they were not just for show. They were made for stomping people. One thing you should know about kicking is, never kick with the front of your foot. I don't care if you got steel-toe boots, you should never kick with your toes. Never, never, never. If you kick forcefully with your toes and hit a shin, or even ribs, you can break your toes. A rib bone is stronger than a toe bone. Even if the person you are kicking is unconscious, he can still hurt you if you kick him the wrong way. Try running away on broken toes and see how far you get.

Andy and I stomped and stomped these idiots. One guy was bleeding so much, I nearly fell on my ass. His blood was like grease under my boots. I was so intent on crushing these guys, I didn't see the cops coming at us from all directions. They grabbed me. They grabbed everybody. One of the wise-mouth hicks lying on the ground lifted his finger and pointed to me. He said, "The shoes. The shoes."

The cops shined their lights on my boots.

"So what? Everybody wears shoes," I said.

"But nobody got shoes on like you," said one cop. He must've thought he was Sherlock Holmes. He grabbed my hand to cuff me, and I got uptight.

"You're arresting me 'cause of my boots?"

"Are you wise?" the cop asked me.

"No, man. I'm not wise. I see you're a cop who likes shoes. How about I take mine off and put them up your ass?"

Right away all the cops take out their sticks and start beating me. More of our guys from the door come out. They see me getting hit, and—not thinking—they jump the cops. More cops run in from the street. We have a riot of cops. They arrest everybody.

We were two days in jail before my uncles could take care of the cops. They dropped every charge. It's America. They can't keep you in jail for the shoes you wear.

WHEN I came home with my face smashed up, stinking of jail, Phyllis nagged me. "Can't you go anywhere and just have a nice time?" she asked.

As soon as my face healed, Phyllis twisted my arm into taking her out. She wanted to go to Hippopotamus. My mind was sour when we went in there. We're standing near the bar waiting for Phyllis's cocktail, and I hear a guy talking so loud, his voice is louder than the music. I see this loud-talking clown a couple feet away—thinks he's a player in his safari jacket leisure suit, talking to a couple of stupid-looking broads. He's one of those people that has to be extra noisy to show off what a big shot he is. When he laughs, he wants everybody to hear what a good time he's having. He's really scratching my nerves. I walk over to him and politely ask him to shut the fuck up.

He turns away and gets real quiet. End of story. I parade Phyllis through the club. She dances a little. We have a few laughs with friends. A couple hours later we're ready to go. That night we had driven in my green Eldorado, which I parked a couple of blocks up from Hippopotamus on 52nd Street. I leave Phyllis in the club and walk out alone to get my car.

A half block from my car, I turn and see the jerk in the safari suit coming toward me with a pistol. He's not saying a word. I see in his eyes he's going to shoot me. There's nothing else in his mind.

In any fight, you always need to analyze the situation. If someone comes at me swinging, I'm not going to run into him and make the force of his punch stronger. I'm going to back away and weaken his punch. You should always think of how to take away the other guy's advantage.

This guy is maybe twenty feet from me. When someone comes that close to you with his gun out, your best move is to find cover. But there's no cover where I'm standing. I don't have a piece on me at that moment. Even if I did, the guy will shoot me in the time it takes to reach it.

I know I can't stay in place. Staying in place will just help him aim better at me. But if I run away, he'll shoot me in the back. Here's the truth of the situation: If a guy is a few feet from you with a gun, my belief is your best chance is to run toward him. I know that might sound crazy, but think about it. You run at him, he's only going to get one shot off before you're close enough to fight him with your hands. If you run away, he'll have time to fire every bullet in his gun. I'd rather get shot at one time than many times.

So I run at this asshole. I assume he'll hit me once. I'm not Superman. I won't be able to see the bullet spinning at me and step aside from its path. I just hope he doesn't shoot me in my heart, or my eye.

The moron hits my leg—in the meat of my thigh. He's so stupid, I grab his gun. He doesn't release it, but I'm able to jam my finger into the trigger guard. On a revolver like he has, if you jam the trigger, the hammer sticks and nobody can fire the gun. Once I have his gun, I get control of the whole situation. This guy doesn't know how to fight. I knock him down and push his head into the pavement. I take the gun from him and see it's a little popgun, a .22. I think, *I ought to just put it in his mouth and pull the trigger.*

But this asshole doesn't even deserve to get shot. I take his little gun, and I beat his brains in with it.

The important thing when you beat somebody with a gun is, always lock your finger under the trigger or under the hammer to make sure you don't accidentally shoot yourself by force of smacking the gun on the other person's body. Once you secure the trigger, always beat down with the butt of the gun on the other person's skull or teeth or whatever you're trying to break. Never hit with the barrel. Some of these guns on the street are pieces of shit. You beat somebody with the barrel, and it might fly off and hit you in the face. The other point of hitting from the underside of the gun is, most trigger guards have sharp edges, and they'll slice up the jerk's face while the gun butt is breaking his bones.

This guy in the safari suit—I would not admit to you that I beat him to death—but by the time I finished, half his brains were in the gutter.

When I finally got in my car to pick up Phyllis, I was a mess. I got pieces of the guy's brains all over my shirt. My leg was bleeding. When you get shot, it burns. By the time we got home, I felt like my leg was on fire.

Obviously, with that guy's head split open on the street, I could not go to a hospital and have people ask me how I got shot. Phyllis had a level head, and she helped fix my leg up at our place. The bullet missed the artery at the top of the thigh and circled around the bone. But I will tell you I screamed bloody murder that night. We had to cut a hole on the other side of my leg to get the bullet out.

Phyllis bitched at me for days, "I told you you'd get shot. Wild Indians get shot. Now maybe you'll listen."

But I never listened. The truth was, as bad as Phyllis thought I was, she didn't know the half of it.

21

E.W.: While sleeping in the guest room at Jon Roberts's house, I awaken at sunrise to what sounds like a gunshot. I sit up and listen for other ominous sounds but hear only the routine morning noises of the house—Jon calling his dogs, his son Julian tramping down the stairs. I go back to sleep.

At eight o'clock I find Jon in the kitchen preparing French toast with cream cheese—just like they made it at Serendipity. After he serves the French toast, Jon curses and massages his right hand. Jon's doctor has told him that the metal plate in his head is pressing on a nerve that sometimes causes his right hand to spasm and clamp into a fist—as it is doing now. Jon uses his left hand to pry open the fingers on his right hand. I have seen this scene before. In *Blade Runner*, when the combat replicant played by Rutger Hauer starts to die, his hand clamps shut, and he forces the fingers open by jamming a nail into his palm, Christ-like. Jon pulls his fingers open without stigmata, but he follows my eyes to his hand and guesses what I'm thinking.

J.R.: Yeah, I saw this in *Blade Runner* when Rutger Hauer's hand gets fucked up. Julian pointed out to me that my hand has the same problem. This is the pain I get for what I did to people all those years. See, for God or the Superior Being, this is His way of punishing me for what I did in life. I accept it. I'm going to lose this hand, and then the other, and then other parts of my body. Eventually, I'm going to lose everything. It's divine retribution.

E.W.: What was that loud noise this morning?

J.R.: You heard that?

E.W.: It sounded like a gunshot.

J.R.: I was on the deck this morning, cleaning a rug, and I looked up, and there must have been a thousand birds flying over the house. They were everywhere, like flies. One of them shit on my head.

You know it would be very bad for me to be caught firing a gun in this neighborhood.* But let's say, hypothetically, that the sound you heard was me shooting at the birds after I got angry at the one who shit on my head.

---

* As a convicted felon, Jon cannot legally own a firearm.

E.W.: That was a hypothetical gunshot I heard?

J.R.: Exactly correct. Now, this is the crazy part. After I hypothetically shot into the sky, a white bird fell at my feet. Would that not be a sign?

E.W.: What would it mean?

J.R.: A dead innocent white bird. That would be Satan throwing me a sign. That would be Him saying, "Hey, bro. This is to remind you I got my eye on you. You'll be mine soon."

Obviously, I've chosen the side of evil my whole life. Nobody could've convinced me to do things differently. I don't care if God had appeared on the highway and said to me, "Hey, Jon. I'm God. Drop your evil shit, and I'll take care of you." It was never going to happen. I've always been too loyal to Satan.

If there is a heaven and hell, I know where I'm going. But I'm not worried. They say God takes care of his people. I expect Satan will take good care of me. I've worked for Satan my whole life. I've got to be one of His best representatives.

I don't expect hell to be any different than my life on earth. I'm going to get a nice smooth job, a nice smooth bed. People think hell is filled with the whores who walked the earth. But if Satan is as nasty as they say, He wants the good girls to come to hell. Girls that have never been laid, what do you call them?

E.W.: Virgins.

J.R.: Virgins. Those are the girls Satan wants to bring into hell. When I go to hell, I bet Satan's going to put me back on the job.

He's going to send me to go find virgins so I can convert them. That's how His game works. He's the same as God. He's always got to be recruiting. Who better than me to serve Him? Satan's not going to give me bad shit in hell. Please, I'm His man.

But I anticipate that here on earth I will not have a pleasant time dying. I'm going to suffer because of what I've done to people in life. Why would whoever controls the universe let me die peacefully in bed? I'm going to have a horrible, horrible death. God will give me a good beating, His way, before I get my reward from Satan.

E.W.: Do you really believe that?

J.R.: Only the part about me having a bad death. You know me, I don't believe in nothing. Do you want some more jam for your French toast? I know you like apricot, but I swear to you, the taste is much sharper with grape.

22

J.R.: For my father evil was a tool. In the early 1970s I realized I was different than him. Evil for me was not just a tool. I liked doing the evil thing. When Phyllis used to say I was a wild Indian, she didn't have a clue what I was really doing. Forget about chasing women, or my little schemes with credit cards and fake diamonds. What I liked more than anything was to rob people, just like when I was a kid.

I was crazy about rip-offs. It made no sense. There was more money in the clubs. The robberies always had the potential to get me into a lot of trouble. As far as my uncles went, I had to keep this a secret. I had to lead a double life. But I was addicted to robberies, the same as Petey was addicted to heroin.

I liked the trick of robberies—winning people over and then turning everything upside down on them. I liked putting a gun in people's faces. I liked seeing the surprise in their eyes. When I robbed somebody, the best way I can explain it to you is like this: it's like getting your rocks off fucking a girl. Robbing somebody is the same, but it's a different tone. It's like having an orgasm in your brain.

I never set up people I met in my clubs. I'd go to somebody else's club or a restaurant, and I'd look for people who seemed hip. We'd get friendly, smoke a joint together. I'd find out if this person wanted to buy something, or sell something. It didn't matter to me. I'd rip off money or drugs.

Part of my thrill was, I never knew how a robbery would go down—how people would react when I took my gun out. One time I went into an apartment with some kids who believed they were going to sell me some hash. I pulled out my gun, and one of the idiots I was robbing put his finger in the barrel.

"Now what are you going to do?" he says.

"What am I going to do?"

Boom. I pull the trigger. Instead of the bullet cutting off his finger, like I expected, the bullet fragments and goes into his hand. His whole knuckle explodes. There's shit from his hand everywhere. He goes down screaming. Everybody in the room is in shock. I start laughing my ass off.

"Is anybody else going to do something stupid here?" I say.

His friends got very quiet. They emptied their pockets without giving me any more aggravation.

A few months later I'm robbing some stockbrokers. These are young Wall Street kids who think they can dabble in dope dealing. We meet in an office after closing. These guys actually show up in suits and white shirts. I pull out my gun. One of them says, "That's not a real gun."

I act like I believe him. "Wow. You're sure about that?" I say.

"I've seen a lot of guns. That's a fake gun."

"Okay. You caught me."

He starts to come toward me, and I shoot him in the foot. He goes down screaming his guts out.

I look at him and his friends, pissing in their suits now, and play with them. "You know what?" I say. "I thought this was a fake gun, too. I should get my money back from the guy who sold it to me."

I never ceased to be amazed. The smartest people often did the dumbest things.

SOMETIMES I was the one who fucked up. I was friends with a black guy named Herbie. Herbie was into the back-to-Africa movement. He had an Afro and dressed in African muumuus and sandals. He was a big-time hash dealer. But he came to me to set up a bunch of rich white hippies. They were college students at NYU who planned to use their college money to get into dealing. Herbie didn't want the competition. So he pretended like he was going to help them get get started in order to rip them off. He asked me to do the robbery. It had to look like Herbie was the victim in this so he could keep their trust and still do business with them.

The main hippie kid lived in an apartment near West Broadway. Herbie told the kids I would sell them hash. What I used to do was carry a suitcase that I'd fill with phone books. I'd put my gun inside the suitcase. That way, if anybody frisked me when I came in, I'd be clean. I'd take my gun out and rob them when I opened my suitcase to allegedly show them the drugs.

The minute I came in the apartment, I saw this rip-off was going to be a problem. It was a long, narrow railroad apartment. There must have been ten kids jammed in the front room. They were packed in like Puerto Ricans, sitting on cushions and crates. Herbie was sitting by the door. One of the hippie kids says, "Let's see the hash, man."

I say, "Hey, man. I don't want to be robbed. Show me the money first."

Another kid pulls a stack of money from under a pillow and holds it up. I open the suitcase and pull out my gun. I say, "Everybody stay down. I just want the money."

Out of nowhere, two guys in that room rush me. I guess they wanted to show off what great athletes they were. I didn't want to shoot anybody and turn a simple robbery into a homicide, so I tried fighting them. I hit the first kid on his head with my gun. He goes down. The other kid tries to grab my gun.

If you ever need to take somebody's gun, the first thing you should do is grab the barrel and push it back, point it at the guy who's holding it. Only when you got it pointed away from you do you then try to block the trigger or try to break it from his grip.

The kid trying to take my gun is a moron. He points my gun at his own leg and tries punching, like we're in a boxing match. He's such an idiot, he squeezes my hand and fires the gun into his own leg.

After the gunshot, it was panicsville in there. The hippie girls were screaming. Everybody started jumping around. I couldn't see where the money was anymore. I got very uptight. I worried these kids might all try to rush me.

I decide the best way to take control of the situation is to shoot another hippie. When I'm shooting somebody just to make a point, I always aim for a leg. I shot the closest hippie to me, but I was so uptight, I fired a couple of times. I ended up hitting one guy in the ass and a girl in the foot. I remember this poor girl had on white go-go boots, she was crawling around screaming. I really did not intend to hit the girl. But it's unpredictable what happens when you fire a gun.

I did get everybody's attention. I yelled, "Stop. All I came for was the money."

Finally, everybody froze. I pointed my gun at Herbie and told him to find the money. He got it from a kid and brought it to me. I didn't want to leave Herbie in there now that I'd shot three people. Even if they didn't guess we were in on it together, they might get mad that he brought me here. So I grabbed Herbie by the Afro and said, "The nigger's coming with me. Anybody calls the police, I'm killing him."

When I got on the street with Herbie, I said, "You moron. Why didn't you tell me there was ten people in there?"

"We were lucky, man," he says. "There was four or five other cats in the back room."

I couldn't believe it. This guy was supposedly street smart, and he sets up a robbery where it's me against fifteen people. If Herbie had ever made it back to Africa like he planned, he would have been eaten by a lion his first day in the jungle.

BUT I liked Herbie because he was always up for anything. One time I needed somebody to play robber in a rip-off I had set up. I was meeting two guys in an alley to sell them heroin, and since I wanted to keep them as customers, I wanted to make it look like I was robbed along with them. My plan was to drive up in my car, get out, then have a guy jump out with a gun and rob us. Herbie agreed to play the robber.

I picked an alley off of Avenue D on the Lower East Side. I drive up in a Buick I used for street work. The guys I've set up are there. I get out of my car, and Herbie jumps out from a doorway. He's got his gun out. It's perfect.

These two idiots we're trying to rob see Herbie with his gun, and instead of handing over their money, they run. This makes me mad. For all these guys know, they've left me holding the bag with Herbie. In their minds, they think they'll get away while he robs me.

I decide to give them back what they think they're giving me. I jump in my car and chase them. I have no plan to actually run them over, but as soon I got behind them, I think, *This will be a cinch*.

I punch the gas and *zoom*. I'm so close, I can see the bottoms of their shoes as they're running. I assume when I hit them, they'll go under my car. But it don't work like that, bro. What I've learned is when you run somebody over, they fly over your car. I'm going maybe forty-five miles an hour. I hit these guys, and they shoot over the top of the car. I see them flying in my rearview mirror. It's wild.

This is a kick and a half. Normally, when you punch somebody, you feel your physical strength. Hitting somebody with a machine is like, *Wow. People are nothing*. These guys flew over my car like pieces of paper.

I jam on the brakes, back up, and get out of the car. The two guys I hit are lying in the trash like mangled toys. Herbie runs over. He's upset, because he's worried I've killed them. They're not dead, just broken. As I empty their pockets, Herbie gives me attitude about how reckless I am. I say, "If you had done your job, I wouldn't have had to run them over."

After preaching to me how wrong it is to run people over, Herbie gets in the car with me and takes his cut. People love to tell you how moral they are, but they'll seldom turn down money, no matter how you got it.

IT'S MY belief people show their true colors when you put a gun in their face. In the 1960s I robbed hippies who'd look at my gun and say, "Hey, man. Your karma's gonna come back at you. You've got to love people."

Even if I didn't agree with them, I respected people who stuck to their beliefs even when they thought I might kill them. But as the 1970s rolled in, I came across more people I called "make-believe hippies." I'd take out my gun, and they'd offer to set up their friends if I'd let them keep their money. They'd sell their brothers to hold on to a dollar.

I once hooked up with a group of rich college kids who lived out in the Five Towns area of Long Island. They fancied themselves revolutionaries. They wore little Che Guevara beret hats and army boots. They were white kids who thought they were Black Panthers. They had an idea to go into hash dealing to pay for the revolution. They pooled the money they got from their parents and decided to buy $10,000 of hash from me.

When the day came for me to rob them, I brought Jack Buccino and Dominic Fiore with me. The leader of the revolutionaries lived in an apartment over the garage at his parents' house.

This guy had a girlfriend who was the one that wore the pants in the revolution. She was a tough little Jewish broad who was studying to be a lawyer.

I show up in this apartment with Jack and Dominic. The kids

bring out the $10,000, and we take our guns out and explain that there's not going to be any hash deal.

There's three guys and this girl. Everybody is very quiet, very respectful. They know me a little bit, but they never met Jack and Dominic, and these guys are very intimidating with their guns out. But this little girl, she has the balls to say, "Can I talk to you alone?"

"What do you want to talk to me about?" I asked.

"Please," she said. "I promise it will be worth it."

The girl walks me into a bathroom. As soon as I shut the door, she pulls up her top. Normally, when I'm doing a robbery, getting my rocks off is the last thing on my mind. But this girl's tits are popping at me, and I can't believe her audacity. I have my gun out, and she moves close enough to brush her tits against the backs of my fingers by the trigger. Feeling her skin on my gun hand was very distracting. If she'd known how to fight, she could have taken my gun then.

She says, "Don't take the whole ten thousand. Leave two thousand for me. That's my money. Let me keep it, and I will give you the best blow job of your life."

I couldn't believe this girl going behind her boyfriend's back like this. If she'd offered to blow me for her and her boyfriend's money, I might have respected her. But this was very sleazy.

I say, "You want to give me a two-thousand-dollar blow job?"

She kneels down and starts working on me. This revolutionary college girl puts everything she has into it. She breaks a sweat. But me, I'm used to some very fine women. Maybe what this girl is doing could impress her teachers at law school, but her technique is nothing special.

As soon as I finish coming on her, she looks up at me and says, "Well?"

"I'll tell you what. I'll give you a hundred dollars."

"I can't believe you're being such an asshole."

"I can't believe you got the balls to say that."

"My father gave me that money for law school."

"Tell your father somebody robbed you in the street."

"I can't lie to my father."

"Get the fuck out of here before I shoot you."

She had no fear, this mouthy girl. She wipes herself off, and when we get back in the room with her comrades, she says to her boyfriend, "He promised if I sucked him off, we'd get our money back."

She's some lawyer already. One sentence out of her mouth, and she's made two lies. Her boyfriend is so beaten down by this broad, he don't say nothing. But another guy in this revolutionary group gets mad at her. He says, "Did you try to suck him off for my money, too?"

It's obvious this girl's been working all these guys. They start arguing with each other while we still got our guns on them. They're entertaining to me. But Dominic is dope sick and needs a fix. He turns to me and says, "Jon, please. We got to go before I shoot these assholes."

We go out, and as I reach the door, I drop a hundred dollars on the floor and tell the girl, "Here's for the blow job."

"Fuck you, you pig," she says.

That girl, I got to hand it to her. She was a tough broad. I bet she made a good lawyer.

WHEN I ripped off people who had drugs, I ended up with shit I didn't need. Selling drugs wasn't my business. When I got twenty pounds of hash or ten thousand hits of LSD, I did something I called "reverse rip-offs."

After I robbed people, I'd save their addresses and phone numbers. If I robbed a dealer who seemed on the ball, I'd go back to his house later on and invite him to go into business with me selling drugs I stole from other people. Obviously, when I knocked on the door of a recent victim, this person was not usually happy to see me. But the smart ones understood I offered an opportunity. I'd sell them shit at cheap prices. And if they had rival dealers, I'd rob them, and we'd all profit when they sold their shit. I built up a group of college kids on Long Island who became regular dealers for me.

I found it was easier to work with college kids than street people.

Street people will always try to rip you off at some point. College kids were completely dependable. They were frightened of me, but like any other people, they were greedy, and I offered them good profits. The other benefit they got from me was, if they were hassled by other punk college kids, I'd beat the snot out of them.

I had four different kids out in Long Island who worked for me in the early 1970s. A few of them paid for college through our business. One kid even invited me to his graduation ceremony.

I'M NOT going to try to pretend I was a saint because I helped some kids through college. I was not a saint. I was a bad person. I never thought for a second about wrong things I did to get my kicks. My view of life was to take the money and laugh.

There was only one time I had a second thought about how I was to people. I was walking down the street one day in Manhattan, and I noticed a pretty girl coming toward me. What caught my eye was, she had a limp. It stood out, seeing a cute girl limping along in her miniskirt. As she got closer, she seemed to recognize me and started to hobble away in the opposite direction. At first this was comical to me, seeing this girl furiously limping away like Ratso Rizzo.*

Then I wondered, who was this girl? Why'd she run from me? It came to me. She was the hippie girl I shot in the foot when I did the robbery in the railroad apartment with Herbie. For a second or two, standing on the street watching this girl I'd crippled run away made me feel sick.

Many guys I've met, they do bad things and become afraid to look at what they've done. They pretend it wasn't them who did those bad things. Or they tell you they had a good reason to do it. I'm not afraid to look at what I've done. I can tell you I did many wrong things to people for absolutely no reason. Even that

---

* Character with a pronounced limp played by Dustin Hoffman in *Midnight Cowboy* (1969).

day on the street when I saw that little girl limping, I didn't feel bad for long.

This is why I say my real calling in life is Satan. I don't know what Satan is. Maybe Satan is just an organizing principle, like gravity. Whether Satan is a real person or something else—whatever He is—His is the side I am definitely on.

Even though I care about my son today, I still have no heart for most people. I remain evil. When I tell you about the bad things I've done, I generally don't feel bad.

I feel worse thinking of football games I lost money on.

23

J.R.: By 1972 there was tremendous pressure on the family because of the Bobby Wood murder. They never charged me or Andy, but the FBI was all over our clubs. To my uncles, heat was just a cost of doing business.

They had no idea I was running around like a maniac doing stickups in the streets. But it did get back to them when I robbed wiseguys. This was another side of how crazy I was then. Robbing hippies wasn't enough. I liked ripping off wiseguys.

I didn't invent this. Wiseguys will always rob each other if they think they can get away with it. I had a guy tell me about a wiseguy poker game in Brooklyn where they had $50,000 on the table. The information I got was, these were nothing guys to Gambino. Andy said it would be okay to rob them. The challenge was, the game was on the fourth floor of a building in Brooklyn.

They had guards on the ground floor, so nobody could get in—they thought.

I wanted to make fools of them. That was my kick. I got some guys who weren't afraid of heights, and we went onto the building next door. We put boards from the roof of one building and walked over to the other. We climbed in a window of the bathroom to the apartment where they had the game. We walked into the front room and did the stickup.

We wore ski masks, but the next day Andy told me one of the guys at the table recognized my voice. He was a friend of my uncle Sam. I had to give the money back. Nobody was mad at me. They understood I'd been given bad information about who was playing the game. People could accept an honest mistake.

Younger soldiers were going crazy in the 1970s as they saw all this money flying in the streets for pot, acid, and cocaine, while they still had these old-fashioned bosses who would not let them deal in anything except heroin. The soldiers who were stuck with bosses like this were easy to rip off. If they lost their money in a drug deal, they couldn't go whining to their bosses. So I'd approach these guys, tell them I could let them invest in a drug deal, and then make up some reason how I'd lost their investment. "Hey, bro. The cops arrested the courier at the airport. It's all gone."

I did this many, many times to wiseguys. Through Jack Buccino and his concert promotions, I found a print shop where they could make fake newspaper articles. I'd tell some guinea soldiers I was sending a guy to Mexico to buy ten kilos of cocaine. They'd give me their money, and I'd make a fake news clipping from a fake Texas newspaper about a guy busted at the border with cocaine in his car. This would be my proof. Even if they suspected I'd tricked them, they could not take it to the family.

Finally I ripped off some wiseguys who earned the name "wise." They figured out how to get their money back from me. After I took their money to make a drug score that supposedly went bad, these guys got smart. They went to their capo and said I'd ripped them off by promising to sell them stolen bearer bonds that I never delivered. Everybody knew I had helped steal the bearer bonds from Merrill Lynch, so their story was believable.

After they told their capo, he took it up to my uncle Joe.

Even Andy couldn't help me out of this one. I met my uncle Joe at a coffee shop by his house on Staten Island. By then my uncle was so old, his bodyguards had to practically carry him to the table. When he ate, it was a disgusting mess the way he drooled. Because he was half deaf, you had to lean in to his ear and shout. But when he spoke, he was as sharp as ever. When we sat at the table, he said, "Tell me the fucking truth. Did you rob those guys?"

"Yeah, I did. I pretended like I had bearer bonds to sell them."

There was no way I would tell my uncle I had set these guys up in a drug deal.

My uncle looked at me for a couple of seconds like he forgot who I was. His eyes got very dull. But then the lights flashed back on. He said, "You got to pay their money back and give me an extra ten percent for the trouble you made."

"Okay," I said.

My uncle still looked at me. He had cream cheese all over his face from the bagel he was trying to eat. But his mind was as evil as ever. He said, "Jon, something ain't right. I don't believe none of this trash about bearer bonds. Don't bullshit my ass here."

Andy and I thought we were the smart, new Italians. But the old mustache Italians, like my uncle Joe, even with his brain half gone, could not be fooled.

What could I do? I told him these guys wanted drugs, and I robbed them.

My uncle Joe actually smiled. "You're a little motherfucker. You're a cocksucking prick. You do this all time, I'm sure. And you don't give me a cut?"

I told him the truth, that anything I did I paid a cut to Andy, and he always pushed this up to the family. I did not pay the IRS, but I paid Gambino.

My uncle did not want to hear how loyal I was. He said, "Jon, next time you rip somebody off, I don't give a fuck if it's drugs, or if you take teeth out of their mouth, you bring me my fucking end, you little prick."

Then he asked, "How much money have you made in the last year robbing people like this?"

I told him I'd made $100,000 in robberies.

"That means you've made at least three hundred thousand," he said. "I'm going to teach you a lesson. From now on, you steal any money in the street, I'm your partner. I want twenty-five percent off the top."

That old prick. My uncle Joe was shaking me down. The man had no heart.

Just like the Mafia guys I ripped off couldn't tell their bosses they were into drugs, I also couldn't say nothing about my uncle shaking me down for my drug rip-offs. Drugs is what really fucked up the Mafia. They made all these idiotic rules against them, and then everybody went crazy scheming against each other. The Mafia should have known better. All the old guys got their start when the American government tried to enforce Prohibition. They saw how idiotic that was. Then they went and made a Prohibition of their own against drugs.

I've never liked rules. I am a criminal because I hate rules. But there I was sitting across from this old fucker, my uncle, telling him I'd follow his rules. I saw no choice at the time. I was a part of the family.

To live in New York, I had to be in the family. I could not imagine being in any other city. I had no concept of any other place. Within a year of my uncle shaking me down, it would become obvious to me, and to everyone, that I couldn't be in New York anymore. It would take a girl breaking my heart—if I can use that term—as well as a few more murders to make me leave the city and the family for good.

But first I would have to get shot in the ass.

24

J.R.: What I was thinking by getting involved with the wife of an older wiseguy is beyond me. I wasn't thinking with my brain, obviously.

The woman's name was Marie. Her husband had a guinea name like hers: Luigi. Luigi worked with Phyllis's father. That's how I met him and his wife. He was an older man in his fifties and she was in her forties.

I can't account for why I started fucking Marie. She was the oldest lady I'd ever been with, but I could not get enough of her. She did things I'd never imagined could be done. While we were fucking, Marie could wrap her feet behind my head and give me a toe massage. This old broad could fuck for hours—fucking me, massaging me. Marie taught me this: Some women have a great pussy, no matter how old they are.

Marie and Luigi had a little rathole apartment off of Mulberry Street. Luigi had never been a big earner. He was just a big dumb greaseball who did whatever his boss told him. I hated going to that place. It was depressing. But Marie had to stay home so she could answer the phone whenever Luigi called. I swear to you this old lady could fuck, give me a massage, talk to her husband on the phone, and smoke half a pack of Pall Malls at once. I knew in the back of my mind I should not go there. But I'd fall into that pussy of hers for hours. It felt like she had golden wheels inside her pulling me in.

Just like I knew would happen, one night I was at her place screwing my brains out when we heard the front door open. It had to be Luigi.

I wasn't afraid of Luigi. But he was a typical macho Italian guy, and if I confronted him, he would lose face and be forced by his pride to try to kill me. No matter what happened, it would be a losing situation. If he killed me, my uncles would want payback. If I killed him, he had people that would want payback. Two people like us should never try to kill each other. The best thing was for me to try to run out of there.

Luigi's footsteps came toward the bedroom door. The only way out was the window to the fire escape. But when I grabbed the window, it had burglar bars on it and was locked with a padlock. I asked Marie, "Where's the goddamn key?"

She was lying back, with her legs open showing her bush like she didn't have a care in the world. She said, "How do I know where the key is?"

When Luigi came in the room, I had nothing on but my wop T-shirt. His wife was there with her tits out like it's a normal night at the opera. Luigi pulled out his gun.

This wasn't like when the guy shot me outside Hippopotamus. I had no plan in my head. I jumped off the bed and fucking ran. Luigi started shooting.

I made it past Luigi into the living room, and a shot hit my back. The force of it knocked me down. He had shot me at the coccyx— my tailbone. Everybody has a tailbone. It's like if you're a monkey, it's the bone that you have so when you walk on all fours, your tail sticks up. It's one of the more useless things a person has on his body. I'd never thought about mine until it was shot.

This hurt so bad, I thought he'd hit my spine and paralyzed me. Normally, I could take a lot of pain, but my mind checked out. I felt like a bug stuck to the floor with a pin. I could not move. Later I found out that when Luigi hit my coccyx, the bone shattered and the splinters exploded into my intestines. The bullet tore my pancreas and part of my stomach. I had blood coming out of my asshole and my mouth. I was puking blood and bile. I nearly passed out, and if I had passed out, Luigi would have shot me again.

Luckily when I saw him coming toward me, I got enough control of my brain to try to reason with him. I said, "You know who I am. If you shoot me again, you better put a bullet in your own head, bro. Because you will pay. Everybody will talk about you."

That was one positive of dealing with a macho Italian guy. If he killed me, he would have to justify it to my family. To justify it, he would have to tell everybody I was screwing his wife. Luigi knew that, and the last thing he wanted was everybody laughing at him because of what his wife did to him with me. I saw in his eyes he had some reason in his head.

He walked closer to me and spat. He began kicking me. His natural man reaction took over. He kicked and kicked. I couldn't fight back. I put my hands over my balls and jammed my head under the couch, so it was harder for him to kick my face in.

It takes a lot of energy to beat somebody. Luigi's kicks slowed. He started to wheeze. He stopped kicking and went silent. Then he said, "Well, what do we do now?"

I looked up at him and said, "Are you a scumbag? Put me on the street and call an ambulance."

"I'm not calling you an ambulance."

I said, "You got your satisfaction. If you don't want trouble, you got to fix this."

"Okay," he said.

This asshole dragged me down I don't know how many flights of stairs. I've seen corpses rolled up in carpets that were treated more gently than me. After he dumped me on the sidewalk, the motherfucker did not keep his word. He never called the ambulance.

It was the dead of winter. I got nothing on but my T-shirt. I was on the sidewalk bleeding out my asshole, throwing up chunks of shit I'd never seen before. It took a stranger who saw me there to finally call an ambulance.

I WOKE in the hospital a day or a week later. I don't know. I felt worse pain in the hospital than when I was shot. I started to scream, it was so bad. Then I heard somebody laughing. I looked over and saw two cops.

Here's why I hate cops. I'm screaming bloody murder, pissing in a tube, and they start their typical jerk-ass shit, wanting to know who shot me. They know I'm not going to say a word, but they got to play the game.

Finally, my uncle Sam showed up with some of his goons to watch over me. With them in the room, I passed back out and slept very peacefully. When I finally woke up, my uncle Sam was leaning over me, laughing. He said, "You little motherfucker."

I saw Andy in the room with my uncle. Andy must have told him about me and Luigi's wife. My uncle said, "I'll take care of everything with the family, but you've got to think of a story for the police."

After my uncle left, one of his goons said, "Why do you want to be fucking a lady forty years old?"

"Don't knock it until you try it," I said.

"You're out of your fucking mind," Andy said.

Andy was laughing, but I could see in his eyes he was tired. People were getting worn down by the trouble I made. When a wiseguy got shot, the police made special reports for the FBI. The heat believed that if one of us was shot, it was the start of a new war, and so they would question everybody for weeks.

In the family, everybody looked down on screwing another guy's wife. When I got a little better, my uncle Sam, who normally would laugh with amusement at the things I did, came to me with a black look in his eyes. He said, "You ever screw someone's wife again, I'll cut your cock off myself."

Phyllis was another one not happy with me. As open-minded as she was, my getting shot for screwing the wife of her father's business partner was rubbing her nose in it. Phyllis had her natural woman reaction, just like Luigi had his natural man reaction. She sent her sister Fran to tell me not to come home until my wounds had healed. Phyllis did not think it was right she should nurse me back to health for the trouble I got into from screwing another woman.

I understood why Phyllis put me out, but it caused something to happen that I hadn't expected. I fell hard for another girl.

25

J.R.: Andy and I kept an apartment on the Upper East Side as a party place. We sublet it from a friend of Bradley Pierce's who had decorated it very weirdly. It looked like a spaceship inside, with plastic chairs shaped like eggs and blinking chrome lights. The walls had paintings of Chinese ladies in dresses. When we first took the place, Andy and me cut holes in the mouths of the ladies in the pictures and stuck cigarettes in them. I went there to recuperate.

For many years I'd carried a pimp cane—an oak stick with a handle shaped like a dog's head with diamonds for eyes. Now I had to use the cane for real. Every step I took hurt. Going to the toilet was agony.

One day I'm lying on the couch snarfing up some Chinese takeout when there's a knock on the door. I

---

* Vera Lucille is a pseudonym to protect the identity of Jon's former girlfriend.

limp over, open the door, and see a beautiful girl standing there, Vera Lucille.*

I had met Vera at Hippopotamus a few weeks before I was shot. I met her through Patsy Parks, who was in the group of party girls that followed Bradley Pierce to his different clubs. Patsy Parks was a half-assed model I never thought much of. She only stood out because she wore a cross on her neck like a Catholic schoolgirl. When I saw that cross, I'd usually walk in the opposite direction because she was never my cup of tea. But one night I saw her with a sensational girl, Vera. She was a French girl who was petite and dark haired like Phyllis, but with a personality that was the opposite. There was something warm about her, not hard and scheming like Phyllis. I felt it the first time I met her. But I met many cute girls, and this one fell out of my mind until the day she stood in my doorway with some crescent rolls she'd picked up at the Brasserie.*

"I heard you were hurt," she said.

It floored me that this girl had been thinking about me. When I invited her in, there was nothing I could do but lie around. Vera came every day and sat with me for hours. I was in too much pain to sleep with her. She would sit, and we would talk. She was a smart girl. She had come to New York to study at Barnard College. But she wasn't from a rich family. Her father sold fish from a cart by the road in a small town in France. She carried a picture of this man at his stand selling fish. Can you believe that? God, she was unbelievable. Vera had an innocent mind. She truly believed I was a good guy.

Even before I touched Vera's body, I started to think about how I could get away from Phyllis. Even though Phyllis had thrown me out, in her mind this was temporary. To her, we were still married.

---

* The informal yet chic French restaurant located at 100 East 53rd Street since 1959.

When I got my legs back, Vera and I kept a low profile going out. We spent a lot of time in the Village at little places like El Faro*—my favorite Spanish restaurant in New York—and out at a house in the Hamptons.

IN THE winter of 1971, Andy rented some cottages on the beach south of Acapulco, Mexico. He went with a girl of his, and Vera and I met them there. This was one of the best weeks I'd ever had. The thing to do there was ride horses. Vera loved to ride. I had ridden a couple times in Texas when I lived there with my sister. The horses in Mexico were easy because they knew the trails. We rode them along the surf. You'd see nobody for miles. The waves would roll up, and the horses had confidence in the water, so you could ride them in the ocean. When we got hungry, we'd take a boat out to an island with a shack where they cooked fresh, warm-water lobsters in hot sauce and butter.

Nobody had a care in the world down there. The other people in the cottages were all from Europe. The women walked around with no tops. But it wasn't like being at a Playboy Club. They weren't hustlers. Everybody was relaxed. Vera and I met another couple from France, and we became very friendly. We started this joke that I was going to go to France and work for her father in the fish business. It was a joke, but in my head it was a fantasy I could live in. Maybe I could get away from it all.

BUT WHEREVER I go, I meet people like me. Illegal people. One day Vera and I were at the pool, and a kid about my age came over and started talking to us. This guy looked American, but he spoke with a Spanish accent. "I'm Carlos Hill," he said. "I have a club in town called Carlos's. Please come tonight as my guests."

Carlos's was a Mexican version of a New York steak house.

* A Spanish restaurant at 823 Greenwich Street, established in 1927 and still open today. It is better known for the kitschy murals of flamenco dancers on its walls than the quality of its food.

Next door there was an illegal casino. Vera and I went with Andy and his girl. Carlos Hill hosted us the entire night. Obviously, he was a sharp kid, and he was into the same things as Andy and me. Once he broke out the cocaine, we really bonded. Andy and I told him about our nightclub business in New York, and Carlos said, "You work with Gambino?"

"Why would you say that?" I said.

Carlos said, "My mom is from the United States. She came here to hide."

"Who the hell is your mother?" Andy said.

"Virginia Hill."*

Carlos claimed he was the illegitimate son of Bugsy Siegel and Virginia Hill.† I never found out if his story was true, but he was obviously a connected guy, and I could see in his eyes he had a crazed blood in him, like me.

Vera had a great time at Carlos's restaurant and clubs. She was naïve. She really didn't understand what I was truly about. She didn't understand that her friend Patsy who had introduced us was a half-a-whore party girl. Vera was a college girl from France. She was clueless.

As we got friendlier with Carlos Hill, I got a sinking feeling. One side of me wanted to know more about what he was into, and the other side didn't want Vera involved. I wanted her to stay naïve.

Vera had classes starting at her college, so she decided to fly back to New York. Andy and his girl went with her. I stayed another week. Carlos wanted to introduce me to a friend.

The morning after Vera leaves, Carlos calls me. "Come out to the pool."

I walk out and see a little Mexican guy sitting by the pool in

---

* Hill was the longtime girlfriend of Bugsy Siegel, the gangster who worked with Meyer Lansky and Jon's uncle Joseph Riccobono in Murder Inc. and went on to develop Las Vegas. Siegel was murdered in 1947 when his Las Vegas investments on behalf of the Mafia failed to turn profits quickly enough.

† While Virginia Hill was known to have taken several trips to Mexico, there is no evidence she ever had a son there.

cowboy boots. Carlos says, "This is my friend, the mayor of Guadalajara. He's a maniac."

Carlos points to six guys sitting with the mayor. "These guys are all his killers."

Everybody smiles. The mayor doesn't speak English, but Carlos is translating. The mayor points to a skinny kid with a fuzzy mustache in his group of killers. "This one is like my son," the mayor says. "Rafa Carlo Quintero."*

The universe has funny rules. I'm on vacation with the girl of my dreams, and the next thing I know I meet a guy claiming to be Bugsy Siegel's son who introduces me to the biggest drug smuggler in Mexico. A few years later Rafa Quintero would become very important to me and Pablo Escobar.

But at that time I hung out with the mayor of Guadalajara. He was a character. He had all these young girls with him. He points to one and says, "I fucked her last night, and I found out she lied about her age. She's sixteen. My limit is fourteen."

The mayor wanted to take me to Guadalajara to show me what he promised would be the Greatest Thing in Mexico. He wanted to drive me in his car. In Mexico there were no convertibles that you could order from the factory. The mayor had taken a Ford 500 and sawed off the top. The seats were upholstered with furs from Mexican jaguars. We set off in the mayor's convertible. Outside Acapulco we get pulled over at a roadblock run by the Mexican army.

The mayor points to the trunk and says, "Footballs, footballs"— using the English word. He opens the trunk and shows the soldiers ten "footballs" inside. These are packages in brown paper shaped like soccer balls. The mayor cuts one open to show the Mexican soldiers, and the "football" is made of coke. I look at these soldiers and think, *Great. I'm going to a Mexican prison.*

But the mayor is smiling. He hands the commander of the

---

* The Mexican drug lord arrested in 1985 for torturing to death an American DEA agent. He was convicted and remains in prison in Mexico.

soldiers a "football." The commander sticks his knife into the coke and snorts. He lights up and slaps the mayor on the back for having such good coke. This football is his payoff. Next thing I know, the soldiers are standing next to the mayor taking pictures. The mayor takes one soldier's rifle and poses like he's going to shoot him in the head. Mexico was truly nuts.

We finally get to the mayor's house in Guadalajara. I had thought "mayor" was an honorary title. But my friend is the actual mayor—or at least the top political guy in town—who lives in a mansion, with police outside guarding it. They unload the footballs from his car. After we clean up and snort a bunch of lines, the mayor says, "Now. I'm going to show you the Greatest Thing in Mexico."

It turns out the Greatest Thing in Mexico is located in a Guadalajara whorehouse called Del Noche El Dia. That's where the mayor takes me. He has a special table at the bar on the first floor. The place is filled with fourteen-year-old girls in bikinis. They're coming up to him and saying, "Hello, Mr. Mayor."

Something about the mayor with these young girls turns my stomach. But the mayor is very happy. He stands up. "Now I will show you the Greatest Thing."

"Greater than this?" I say, looking at the roomful of teenybopper whores.

The mayor is giggling as he pulls me into a theater. At the front is a stage with a band. There's a singer in a blond wig, and a magician pretending to saw a girl in half.

The mayor points to the stage. "Here it comes," he says.

A curtain opens. There's a donkey with three whores standing around him. Have you ever seen a donkey cock? It's not a small thing. These whores start touching it. They are dressed in French lace, but the whores must have come straight from the farm. They know exactly how to handle that donkey. He gets hard, and one of the whores slides under him on a table so he can fuck her.

I know I'm a freak for sex, but this is disgusting. Enough is enough. I really am not enjoying the Greatest Thing in Mexico. This poor donkey has enough problems pulling a plow, or whatever he does for a living, without these whores making a spectacle of him. I know I'm fucked up, but this sickens me.

The mayor opened my eyes to why I dislike politicians. People like me, people on the streets, we know we're bad. Politicians do the same things we do, but they act like they're such good people, giving speeches, handing out medals to crooked cops. Politicians are the worst scumbags I've dealt with.

I left Mexico with a bad feeling. Vera showed me the differences between our lives. Her life was riding horses on the ocean. Mine was sitting with a dirty mayor at a donkey show. For the only time in my life—until I had my son—I got the idea of trying to go to the other side. On the plane ride back to New York, I thought about trying to get more serious with Vera.

26

J.R.: When I returned to New York, I had a problem. My friend Vincent Pacelli was getting married. Vincent was expanding his heroin business into Chicago, and he was marrying the daughter of one of Sam Giancana's* top bosses from Chicago. The marriage was like a business deal. This is what I hated about the Mafia. Everything people did was decided according to what was best for the families.

My problem was that Phyllis and Vera were going to the wedding. Vera was going because her friend Patsy Parks knew Vincent. Phyllis was going because her dad was in the heroin business with Vincent. Plus, the wed-

---

* Sam Giancana, head of the Chicago Mafia, was a close friend of Frank Sinatra's and of Sammy Davis Jr.'s, and is believed to have helped secure votes in Cook County for John F. Kennedy's election in 1960. Also an alleged CIA operative, he had turned secret government informant by the time of the wedding Jon refers to. Giancana was murdered in his home in 1975, a few days before he was to testify to the U.S. Senate about his ties to the CIA.

ding was a big event on the social calendar of the New York Mafia. The reception was going to be held at the Pierre.* They were going to have several orchestras playing, a rock band, belly dancers. What a guinea wedding. No way was Phyllis missing this.

Phyllis wanted me to go with her. In her mind, it was time for us to start up our marriage again. Vera knew about me and Phyllis, and she did not pressure me. I hadn't figured out how to deal with Phyllis yet. If I broke up the wrong way, I could have Henry and his crew trying to feed me into a meat grinder at their pizza shop. I hadn't resolved this in my mind.

I went to the wedding with Phyllis, and Vera went with her friend Patsy. The wedding was a real guinea party. There were old mustache Italians at the tables with walkers and oxygen tanks. The young guys are all sneaking into the bathrooms putting shit up their noses so the old guys didn't see. Everybody was stuffing money in the belly dancers' bikinis. Half the waiters were undercover FBI agents.

I snuck off to talk to Vera. We stood there watching all these drunk greaseballs, and she asked, "Is this a normal American wedding?"

"Ours will be different," I said.

Without thinking it, I'd just told her my plan. My way out from Phyllis and her family was, I would go to France with Vera. I'd meet her family and ask her dad, the fish seller, if I could marry his daughter. I'd stay in France as long as it took for Phyllis to get over her anger at me. If it took a couple years, so be it. I really wanted to be with Vera. I was wild about her.

JUDY: Vera was so special. Phyllis was like my sister. I love Phyllis, but she was a very hard person. Vera was like Jon's high school sweetheart, Farah Aboud, but she was a mature young woman. What an effect Vera had on him. Jon's face became soft around her. His voice changed. He was gentle.

---

* The landmark hotel on Central Park at 61st Street and Fifth Avenue.

I was so happy for him. And then one day, she was gone. To this moment, I don't know what happened to Vera. One day Jon said, "Vera's gone. You'll never see her again."

J.R.: What happened to Vera was, she saw me as I truly was. She stopped being naïve. Her eyes were opened by something that happened to her friend Patsy Parks.

Patsy claimed to be a model, but she was really a club girl who followed Bradley Pierce around. People called her Park Avenue Patsy because she acted like she had a lot of money. The truth was, she supported herself as a courier for Vincent Pacelli's heroin—just like Jack in the Toucan Shirt used to. I was not involved in Vincent's heroin business, but I knew that Patsy would drive heroin to Boston. She worked with a kid named Barry Lipsky. Barry was always in our clubs. He looked like a college boy from Princeton. The idea was Patsy, who always wore the cross on her neck, and a straight-looking guy like Barry could drive heroin around without looking suspicious.

But as normal as Barry Lipsky looked, as soon as you talked to him, you realized he was a goon. He was always talking about horror movies. He would come up to people and make faces, imitating screams and monsters. He was not right in his mind.

Vincent Pacelli and his father had always used odd people to move heroin for them. They once used Playboy Bunnies as couriers.* Patsy and Barry did okay for about a year, and then, around the time of Vincent's wedding, she was busted. Vincent had an informant in the New York prosecutor's office who told him Patsy was going to testify against him. The girl was stupid because she bonded out. People knew she was a rat, and she was running around being a party girl.

---

* Jon may be confusing his facts regarding Playboy Bunnies used as drug couriers with the 1965 heroin trial in which Pacelli's father attempted to use a Playboy Bunny to bribe a juror. It could also be that the Pacellis had a myriad of nefarious uses for which they employed Playboy Bunnies.

Even though my business was different from Vincent's, we were part of the Gambino family. He came to me and said, "Patsy's got to disappear."

I knew this was a problem. Patsy was Vera's best friend. Vera did not understand the Mafia. She had figured out that Andy and I weren't normal businessmen. She'd been to a Mafia wedding. But she didn't know what the Mafia truly meant.

I was superstitious about Vera. I believed if I took care of Patsy for Vincent, Vera would know what I did by looking into my eyes. So for one time in my life, I chose not to do the evil thing. I took the good side. I went to Andy and I said, "Andy, Patsy's best friends with my girl. This is really fucked up here. I don't want to do this."

Andy did not blink. "Nobody's going to force you to do nothing, Jon."

Andy went to the family and said I should not be involved with Vincent's problem. He pointed out there was still heat on me from the Bobby Wood murder. Everybody agreed I should stay away from this one.

Vincent made an impulsive choice. He decided to take care of Patsy using Barry Lipsky, the moron, to help him. This turned into an absolute disaster. They killed her fine, but when they set her body on fire, they left a matchbook from Hippopotamus next to her burned car. They had witnesses who saw them buying the gasoline. The papers made it a big story that Patsy's cross supposedly didn't melt in the fire. Vincent was a good guy, but he screwed up, big time.

BRADLEY PIERCE: I would see Vincent Pacelli in the clubs with Jon and Andy. They could pass as nice guys. Vincent looked mean. One just knew he was savage. When Patsy told me she was working for him as a "broker"—moving drugs for him—I knew this was bad news. What happened to her was terrible. Before they killed her, they tortured her. She was a nice girl who came to my clubs. But she took a trip into the Devil's territory. When you take a trip down a dark alley, you don't know what demons you're going to meet. I began to wonder if the journey I'd started in café society had turned into a dark alley. By the 1970s many of us were staring at demons.

J.R.: When Bobby Wood died, everybody knew he was scum. When Patsy died, the papers played her up as "Park Avenue Patsy." They wrote about her burned up with her cross like she was an angel.

Patsy was also a government witness. If you ever have to kill a government witness, never leave the body. That's like waving a red flag at the cops. Always make rats disappear. If I'd taken care of Patsy like I'd been asked to, nobody would have heard about it. Making somebody disappear is the easiest thing in the world.

Forget about "cement shoes" and all the garbage in movies. If you need to get rid of a body, the simplest way is to drive it out on the water in your boat, smash the teeth out with a hammer, and sprinkle these in the water. Then take a sharp knife—like a fillet knife for fish—and cut the body from asshole up to the solar plexus. The guts will pop out like Jiffy Pop. The fish will eat this right away, and everything else will sink. The reason bodies float is because the juices inside the guts make gases. Cut out the guts, you don't have a problem. If it's warm weather, you can drop the body in the water next to your boat and jump in to do the filleting. You won't get a single drip of blood on your boat. If it's colder, you want to push the body right up to the edge of the gunwale so there's less to clean up when you're done. Either way, any idiot who knows the basics can make a body disappear forever.

If Patsy had just disappeared, nobody would have noticed. She was the type of girl about whom people would have said, "Maybe she ran away. Maybe she went hitchhiking and met a bad person."

But Patsy became an even bigger news story after Barry Lipsky confessed and ratted out Vincent Pacelli.* Now Vera's eyes were opened. She knew Vincent and I were friendly. We'd just been to his wedding together a few weeks earlier. There was no hiding what I was about. Vera was wise to me.

She would not look me in the eye. I'd catch her in my apartment sitting across the room, staring at me like I was a monster. She cried all the time. Then she accused me of being involved in killing Patsy.

"That's crazy," I told her. "Why would I do that to Patsy? She's your friend."

"Maybe they're going to kill me next?"

"They're not going to kill you. Trust me."

"How do you know they're not going to kill me?"

There was no bringing her back around. People also filled Vera's head with stories about how I must have killed Bobby Wood. I didn't touch a hair on Patsy's head, but all of a sudden I'm the bad guy. If I had done the right thing and taken care of Patsy, none of this would have happened. This is what I got for turning away from my father's philosophy. If the most evil thing in the situation was to take care of my girlfriend's best friend—and do it right—everything would have turned out better. I was a kid. I had gotten so twisted around by this girl, I forgot who I was. I would never make that mistake again.

WHEN VERA came over to my place and said she couldn't see me anymore, I felt cold to her, but I asked her if we could have one last time together. She said yes, but the way she said it sickened me. I watched her eyes as she took off her clothes. I could see there was

---

* As reported in the *News and Courier*, June 2, 1973: "Vincent Pacelli, Jr., a convicted dope dealer, was sentenced to life imprisonment Friday for the slaying last year of Patricia 'Park Avenue Patsy' Parks, scheduled to be a witness at his narcotics trial." In the trial, as summarized in the findings of the United States Circuit Court of Appeals, Second Appeals, ruling on an unsuccessful appeal filed by Pacelli on November 1, 1973, "Lipsky testified . . . that arriving at Hippopotamus at approximately 2:00 p.m., they picked up Parks and proceeded to Massapequa, Long Island . . . Almost immediately thereafter Pacelli stabbed Parks in the throat. Parks pleaded not to hurt her since she was a mother, but he said, 'Die, you bitch,' and stabbed her several more times in the throat until she was dead."

nothing in them. She was throwing me a fuck to get rid of me. This filled me with poison.

Vera had liked to play silly games when we had sex where we'd tie each other up with scarves. I decided to show her what I was truly about. She wanted to look down on me now because she was such a good person and I was such a bad guy, so I would show her the bad guy I was. I tied her wrists up with the silk scarves she liked, but instead of love taps, I turned her every which way on the bed and belt-whipped her. This was not play. I wanted to leave scars. I made her hurt. I wanted to stamp out anything that was left between us. I whipped her for a long time.

Finally all the poisons were out of me. I untied her. This girl was spent. She looked up at me in shock. I said, "Take your shit and get the fuck out of here. Go to the airport, get the fuck out of my country. If you ever say a word, I will skin you. You understand?"

She nodded. Her eyes moved in her head, but there was nothing left. I had Andy come over and take her bloody ass to the airport.

After she left, I felt good. She hurt me, and I got my revenge. But then I didn't feel good. I went crazy. I started calling her parents' house in France. They didn't speak English, but I called every day and shouted at them. They would not put their daughter on the phone.

I went to Andy and told him, "You've got to help me find her."

I drove Andy crazy. Finally he got a guy who worked with Vincent Pacelli's father—importing the heroin from France—to get some of their guys to look for her. They found Vera at her parents' house and took her. They did not treat her rough. They were told not to harm her. They took her to a phone and made her talk to me. I just wanted to explain to her that I knew what I did was wrong.

As soon as I heard her voice, it tore me apart. I begged her, "Please come back. Please let me come and see you. Anything you want."

She wanted nothing to do with me. She was terrified. I heard it in her voice. I'd made things worse by having those guys grab her. I didn't do it the right way. I told the guys who were holding her to let her go. That was it. I knew she wasn't coming back, ever.

I'm sure I damaged Vera. Physically, she probably healed, but mentally, I'm sure this girl was fucked up for the rest of her life. I regretted my mistakes with her. This was not like the time I saw that girl limping on the street and I felt a little bad for a second. I became very dark inside. Why did I have to abuse her physically like I did? I ruined all the good memories I had. If I'd told her to leave when she wanted to, I could have at least remembered the good things. Instead, I felt sick anytime I thought of her.

Certain things get burned into your mind. Vera is burned into mine. The pain I inflicted on her was inflicted back on me a thousand times over. I'm not claiming my mind hurt more than her body hurt when I whipped her. But she comes into my mind every day, and it hurts. That girl is never going away.

There are many days I picture her from the top of her hair to her toes. She comes into my mind exactly the way she looked when we had good times. I picture her on the horse running in the waves, and it breaks my heart. If I could change one thing, I wish I'd not touched a hair on her body.

Don't misunderstand me. I don't have a conscience. I've felt a small amount of pain about this one thing I did. If you add up all the things I did to everybody in my life and compare this to the pain I felt for Vera, my suffering has been nothing.

27

J.R.: I went back to Phyllis. I crawled into our penthouse, and I told myself I was back to normal. But my mind did not focus properly. Little things tripped me up.

I had stopped doing drug rip-offs when I was with Vera. When I picked these up again to try to have some fun, I made stupid mistakes. I got arrested for assault after I beat up some kids near a house where a cop lived. I got into a ridiculous shoot-out while chasing some guys on the street in Fort Lee and was arrested for discharging a firearm. I got arrested on an illegal gun charge when I was pulled over in my Jaguar and mouthed off to the cop—after I'd forgotten about a gun I had in the glove box. Andy and I also got arrested when we went to a friend's house who made porno movies. We'd gone for stupid kicks but happened to go on the one day the cops raided the place. These were not the actions of a very wise wiseguy.

While all this was going on, the family was having trouble with a bad cop, Detective Joe Nunziata. He'd been on the payroll for years and years. He'd been helping out with the so-called "French Connection."* There were two things the movie left out about that case. First, the cops never stopped the French Connection. They stopped a few loads from a couple of smugglers. That's all. The funnier part is, what heroin the cops did get, the Gambino family stole back from them. They took hundreds of pounds from the New York police evidence locker, and Nunziata was one of the cops who helped.† Nunziata had made many promises to people in the family,‡ but he turned into a rat.

No matter how much you pay one off, you can never totally trust a cop. I knew Nunziata very well, and he was the worst kind. He was crooked, but he would bust people, too. That was the bad in him. He went both ways. A cop is much better off if he is all one way or another. You can't take my payoffs, then try to be a good cop and arrest me. That's wrong.

Because I knew Nunziata, some people in the family came to me and asked me to deal with him. It was a big deal to kill a cop. It was not normal. But Nunziata was the exception. Not only was he ratting on the family, he was ratting on other cops. Even the cops don't like a cop who's that dirty.

I had turned down helping Vincent Pacelli take care of Patsy Parks, but I learned my lesson about picking and choosing what I did. So it happened that Detective Nunziata committed suicide.

---

* Jon is referring to the film *The French Connection* as well as to several Mafia rings smuggling heroin that were not actually the subject of the movie.
† The Gambinos "set up the looting" of the evidence locker and "pushed 169 lbs. of the stolen drugs in Harlem . . . Thus far the only suspected police link that has surfaced is Narcotics Detective Joseph Nunziata, whose signature was on the form with which 24 lbs. were signed out." From "Coffins and Corruptions," *Time*, January 1, 1973.
‡ In the Patsy Parks murder trial, Vincent Pacelli attempted unsuccessfully to introduce testimony from Nunziata that he was involved in a drug deal in a New York café at the time of Parks's murder. See opinion of United States Court of Appeals, Second Circuit, *United States v. Vincent Pacelli*, July 24, 1975.

I have no direct knowledge of how this happened, but I can tell you it was someone Nunziata knew, a crazed Italian kid. Maybe he was talking to the Italian kid in his car, and in the middle of their discussion the kid was able to take his gun and blow his fucking head off.* Who knows? One thing you can know for sure is, Nunziata was a real asshole who deserved to die. Trust me on that one.

As if things weren't hot enough then, Andy and I got into another problem with the nightclubs. It started when we were introduced to a man at Hippopotamus named Shamsher Wadud. Shamsher was from Bangladesh, and he had a curry restaurant on Central Park called Nirvana.† When we met him, we were told Shamsher wanted to get into the nightclub business.

People came to us all the time to talk about nightclubs. They knew if they were serious, they would have to deal with us one way or another. After we met Shamsher, I checked him out and found he ran his restaurant very well and even had his own little celebrity following.‡ Shamsher also had a liquor license, and his record was clean. Andy and I believed he could be a very useful partner. We sent some guys to Shamsher who offered to sell him our old club Salvation.

But he decided to stiff us. He went behind our backs and opened a nightclub without our help. Obviously, we had to send in our guys to bust things up and shut it down, which we did. We went back to Shamsher and gave him a second chance to work with us. But he was a proud man and a stubborn man. He told us no.

At some point in the negotiations, we sent our friend Mikey Shits to talk some sense into Shamsher. Mikey Shits was the guy we had who carried a soup can that he used for beating on people,

---

* Nunziata "died of gunshot wounds inflicted by his own revolver. The death was labeled a suicide, but that verdict was challenged by Nunziata's widow . . . Mob sources have been saying that Nunziata's death was a 'hit,' ordered by the Gambinos." From "Coffins and Corruptions," *Time,* January 1, 1973.

† Nirvana is still located at 30 West 59th Street.

‡ Nirvana was a favorite hangout of John Lennon, who used to display his drawings there, using the restaurant as an informal gallery.

and when he was talking to Shamsher, one thing led to another, and Mikey beat him so bad, Shamsher had to go to the hospital. If that's not bad enough, this idiot talks to the reporters, and they make a big story about it.*

WHY WAS this man such a problem? Andy and I had been running the clubs for nearly five years. On the street, five years is a lifetime. You meet very few criminals who do any one thing for more than five years. Any illegal operation is a finite thing. The bigger your numbers, and the more things you do, the bigger the chances that you'll have a problem with the law. Smart people can usually get away with an illegal business for maybe two years before they run into a problem. If you make it to two years, you've done very well. The really smart guys go a couple years at one thing, wash their hands of it, and move on to something new. I wasn't like that. I've always pushed things as far as I can.

By 1974 all the heat knew I was into wrong things. When the Gambino family put Andy and me on point to take over clubs, they knew we'd draw heat. If you are in the club scene, the police automatically know something is wrong with you. Nightclubs are not based on lawful people. Except on the weekends, lawful people are not in a club until three or four in the morning because they have to get up and go to work in the morning. During weeknights, any club is going to be filled with illegal people—gangsters, drug dealers, hustlers, pimps. The lifeblood of nightclubs is criminals. The police know this, and you can't pay off every single cop. When you're involved in nightclubs, eventually you will get heat.

I don't know how I made it five years in the nightclubs. But after all the problems with Hendrix, Bobby Wood, Patsy Parks, Nunziata, and Shamsher, I didn't see good times no more. I just saw heat coming and coming.

---

* The *New York Times* later ran a front-page, above-the-fold feature about Shamsher's ordeal, "A Nightclub Owner Says He Has Woes—The Mafia," by Nicholas Gage, *New York Times,* October 10, 1974.

By then my old Outcast friends had started to fade. Petey got arrested on heroin charges for the millionth time, and he ended up going to prison for a couple years. Big Dominic Fiore kicked heroin by leaving the city. He moved to Connecticut and started a rendering business—which he still has today—where he drives a truck to all the McDonald's and Burger Kings and picks up their grease. Rocco Ciofani became a very hardworking soldier in the Bonanno family and got promoted to capo. Jack Buccino started hanging out in Asbury Park following around Bruce Springsteen. He had learned the guitar and was finally going to do his own stage act. He married a beautiful blond girl from Teaneck, and after the wedding he was driving her across the George Washington Bridge when he hit a concrete stanchion at a hundred miles an hour. It squashed Jack, dead as a bug. His wife survived, but she was left a cripple and a vegetable who didn't even know her own name.

Even Bradley Pierce was affected. After Patsy Parks got whacked, he went crazy and ran away to a monastery.

BRADLEY PIERCE: I'd started out in the 1960s believing I was spreading a new spiritualism. The murder of my friend Patsy Parks was an awakening. My spiritual interests changed. I was baptized at St. Patrick's Cathedral, and I entered a Trappist monastery. After I went to seminary, I became a priest.*

I have contemplated my time with Jon and have prayed about it. I have good memories. But I came to understand the evil in him. Everybody has a dignity given to them by God. Jesus Christ is in Jon. I know Jon struggles within himself. I pray for his soul. We have kept in touch over the years, and I share my love with him every time we speak. I believe Jesus can give anyone a second life.

---

* Father Pierce is now director of field education at the Holy Apostles College and Seminary in Cromwell, Connecticut.

I was born again through Him. We all are given the chance to be born again, even Jon.

J.R.: My end in New York came when an informant told the cops that I was involved in the murder of Nunziata. He said that if they searched the apartment I kept with Andy, they'd find evidence.

When they raided the place, they found no evidence linking me to the murder of Nunziata, but they did get about a dozen illegal guns and some pills. In normal times, this would be a nothing arrest. But when I bonded out, my uncles sent a lawyer who told me, "Your family wants you gone. Get the fuck out of New York. They don't want you to exist anymore."

I believe the family made a deal with the New York police. I believe someone in the family told them I was involved in killing Nunziata. If I died, or disappeared off the face of New York, the family could go to the cops and say, "Okay, we got rid of your problem."

And the cops could say, "Okay, we did our best to catch the cop killer."

That way everybody could save face and go back to doing business. I was the logical choice to go because there was so much heat on me. I saw this coming before I was popped on the weapons charges. When I bonded out of jail, I called Andy, and he said, "You're my brother, Jon, but I can't see you no more."

For all I knew, Andy was supposed to whack me. I didn't think this was the case, but I didn't want to put him in that position. I hung up the phone, and I ran to Phyllis's place to grab my dog, Brady. I kept an old Buick Le Sabre parked on the street for emergencies. It was a junk car. I jumped in with my dog and left. I didn't take nothing. Not my boots, not the clothes in my closet. I was busted out. I had my dog, six hundred dollars in my pocket, and a Beretta .38 pistol. That was it, bro. I got on my horse and split.

I lost everything, but I wasn't worried. Tomorrow was another day. At twenty-six, I was dead in New York. But I would live again.

I'd go to Miami to escape the heat.

28

It's the happy meeting of ocean and shore that has made Miami one of the world's premier destinations.

—*Fodor's Miami Travel Guide*, 1985 edition

I heard that my little brother had moved to Miami. Jon became a dog trainer there. He started a very successful business training dogs.

—Jon's sister, Judy

J.R.: I drove straight to Miami. I had no plan. I had no vision, but I had a good feeling about Florida. When I was seventeen, Rocco Ciofani and I once made a big score in a robbery and decided, "Let's go to the sun and swim and have fun in the Miami paradise." We had good times on Miami Beach, chasing the girls in bikinis, and when we needed money, we robbed some college kids using only our fists. We didn't need guns in paradise. That was Miami in my mind.

Miami was the last big city on I-95, the farthest I could get from New York and stay on the East Coast. If I completely disappeared from New York, the heat would assume I was dead and move on. They didn't need a death certificate. It was a simpler time. In the 1970s your driver's license was just a piece of paper. Nobody had Internet computers tracking you from one state to the next. If you used cash, and didn't get arrested, you were gone, bro.

My one worry was phone taps. I always assumed in New York that the feds tapped my phones and the phones of people who knew me. If every phone they listened to had people saying I'd disappeared, that would reinforce the idea I was gone for good. I would not contact anybody for many months—and when I did, it would be indirectly.

When I left New York, I was wearing a "monsignor ring," a ruby ring I'd gotten when I was running my club Sanctuary and carrying my pimp stick cane with diamonds on the head. (Later, when I pried the diamonds out of my pimp stick and tried to pawn them, I found out Howie, my diamond guy who'd sold them to me, had used blown-out glass like he'd sold to my friends on the Knicks. He'd scammed me like I'd scammed them. You live and learn.) I must have been quite a sight. At a rest stop in the Carolinas, I got out—with my cane, in my velvet pants—to let Brady run, and people stared like I was the Devil. Little kids with a family pointed at me and ran. My New York look did not cut it beyond the tristate area.

I reached Miami early in the morning. The sun was coming up like a fireball. Biscayne Bay was liquid gold. I've always liked being by the ocean at sunrise. I pulled over, walked into the sand, pulled off my shirt, and let the sun soak into my skin.

I checked into the Castaways, a Hawaiian motel on Miami Beach that had a corner room I could sneak Brady into.* With my limited funds I could barely afford a week there. My new wardrobe consisted of swim trunks, a tropical shirt, and flip-flops I bought

---

* The Castaways Island Motel billed itself as "America's Most *Funderful* Resort-Motel." It was an iconic tiki-theme motel designed by Charles Foster McKirahan. It was torn down in 1981.

from a dime store. Across from the motel there was an Arby's, where I lived the next few days on roast beef sandwiches.

My first full day in Miami, I decided to get some tail. There was nothing at the motel pool but tourist families from nothing places like Ohio—kids and the sunburned parents who were stuck with them. I walked to the beach, and ten steps from the motel there was a very hot girl in the sand. I put my towel next to hers and lay down. She had on white plastic sunglasses that she lifted to look at me, like she was angry I had sat by her. She had the most beautiful green eyes. They were a shock because she had dark hair and olive skin. Finding a girl so beautiful was a sign that my luck was good.

I started giving her some bullshit New York lines, and *ba ba ba*, she went from angry to very receptive. Time passed. I said, "You hungry?"

"You go ahead and eat," she said. "I love to lie on the beach."

I couldn't understand why she'd brushed me off. I went in the motel pool and swam. Ten minutes later the girl walked past—limping. She had a clubfoot. It was bad, but I had to smile. That was why she gave me the cold shoulder.

Her bum foot didn't bother me a bit. Maybe she was payback for making that girl walk like Ratso Rizzo in New York. Besides, it wasn't like her foot would be the centerpiece of screwing her. I got out of the pool and walked up to her. She said, "I guess you can see now."

"Your foot don't bother me a bit. Let's have dinner."

She agreed to meet later. But she never showed up. I'm sure she just had a bad complex about how she looked. But to me, being blown off was a sign. It was like, *I'm new in town. I'm broke. And the girl with a clubfoot won't even have dinner with me.*

NORMALLY, TO make cash I could do a quick drug rip-off. But I didn't know the lay of the land down here. I could not risk being arrested at that time with the heat on me in New York. I had to get a square job.

One of the kids in Long Island who worked for me selling drugs used to tell me about a family that his family knew in Miami.

This kid had rich parents, and they knew a family in Miami named the Gendens who owned a big landscaping company. The kid had told me I should meet them someday because the father, Dave Genden, was a character who liked gangsters and had known Al Capone.*

I looked up the Gendens. If I had to work, I liked being outdoors and using my hands. Why not landscaping? I drove over to meet them at their nursery. On the streets in New York many people knew me by my old family name Riccobono. In Miami, Riccobono was dead. From now on I used the legal name I'd adopted when I was a kid, Jon Pernell Roberts. That's how I introduced myself to the Gendens.

Dave Genden was about sixty. He had a son, Bobby, who helped run his company, and another son who became a judge. Dave had been around enough to see I was wise, but he didn't ask questions. He offered me an honest job.

They put me on a crew to plant trees, sod, and flower beds at high-end developments. My main job was planting trees. The Gendens took their time to show me the proper way. Other landscapers would dig a hole and throw a tree in it, and that was that. The right way, which they taught me, is you should always dig the hole twice as deep as the roots of the tree you are planting. That way, when you refill the hole, there's a nice bed of loose soil for the baby roots to grow into. The next thing, which some people neglect, is the first time you water it, soak the soil. Just shove your hose in the hole and let the water run fifteen minutes or more. If you do this, you will grow a successful tree. I don't care if you're planting a tree or a shrub or a little flower, it's the same principle.

I enjoyed working in the landscaping industry. I like plants. It's

---

* "David 'Dave' Genden, landscaper to the wealthy, pool hall impresario, world traveler and social rebel, died Sunday morning in hospice care in Pembroke Pines. He was 97. While landscaping was his longest-running business venture, it wasn't Dave Genden's first. In the 1930s, he served gangsters and literary figures alike in the pool hall he opened on South Beach." From Dave Genden's obituary, written by Christina Vieira in the *Miami Herald,* January 18, 2010.

interesting to watch how they grow. All they eat is air, sunlight, and water. My pay was not much more than that—two dollars an hour. It was enough for a small apartment in North Miami Beach.

I had to be careful because North Miami Beach was crawling with wiseguys, and I didn't want some jerk blabbing to someone in New York he'd seen me. I even had to watch out for my uncle Jerry Chilli—from my mother's side of the family—who was a capo and controlled the neighborhood around the Thunderbird Hotel.* I didn't know him very well, and I stayed away from him. I stayed away from all the wiseguy hangouts.

Outside of Miami Beach, Dade County was a backwoods. A mile inland from Collins Avenue, there were rednecks in pickup trucks with gun racks. People had rebel flags on their houses. They sold gator meat sausages in the shops. Between the rednecks and the tourists, nobody had a clue to what life was really like in Miami. Even the black people—who were called "coloreds"—were backward. They weren't like the Super Fly'd–out black dudes you saw in New York. They were zippity-doo-dah black people, like from Old South times, who put on big smiles and called you "sir."

In my job I saw how the people with money lived—the doctors, the lawyers, the real estate assholes. I was in their lawns every day. Rich people were very relaxed in Miami. We'd be working, and they'd be by their pools smoking weed. Even then I'd see people sniffing coke. Girls would be lying around with no tops. You know how stiff rich people are in New York? Miami was the opposite. I was working in a rich guy's yard, and he invited me to smoke a

---

* Gerard "Jerry" Chilli has a lifetime of convictions for racketeering, conspiracy, forgery, and attempted manslaughter. He has also been linked—but never charged—with the 1989 murder of an undercover DEA agent in New York. His most recent arrest came in Florida in 2005 for his alleged involvement in running illegal gambling machines, loan-sharking, stock market scams, offshore sports betting, dealing in stolen property, the distributing of narcotics, and orchestrating the theft of more than $300,000 worth of veal, liquor, and smoked salmon. In 2009, while awaiting trial for his 2005 arrest, he was indicted on separate racketeering charges in New York. He is currently awaiting trial in the Eastern District of New York.

joint. It turned out he was a local judge named Howie Gross,* and we got to be friends. Everybody called him Mouse, because he loved mice. He had a collection of them in his house and his pool was shaped like a mouse. Mouse was the biggest pothead I ever met. He could always party, because judges don't work long hours and they have every fucking holiday off. You learn this if you ever go on trial. While you rot in jail, the judge is probably out at his pool having a party. But Mouse was a good guy. When I first met him, he blew my mind. I'm on the run, and a judge invites me to get high with him. If only all judges were this good.

Miami was a little town. People were so friendly and stupid. I remember thinking, *Boy, this is an easy place to make a fresh start. I'll get in on this city before everybody else finds out about it.*

WHILE I was still working for the Gendens, I tried to start a legitimate business. Everywhere I'd go with Brady, people would notice what an amazing dog he was. They'd ask me, "How can I get my dog trained so good?"

I got the idea, *Fuck it. I'll train people's dogs for them.* I knew what I was doing from working with Joe Da Costa, the hit man in Jersey who trained Brady. I could start up a real business. I could build up a client list, get some trainers working under me, and sit back and run it—like when I had the college kids selling drugs for me. Only this would be legit. None of the stress of wiretaps, paying off cops, shooting people. Just a nice little business, catering to select clients. What would it cost to have a nice place, a decent car, a little boat, and keep a couple of decent broads going? In 1974 Miami not much. You could almost live off the air and sunlight like a plant.

I named my company Dogs Unlimited. I had business cards printed and hired an answering service. Back then people didn't have cell phones. You'd pay a company twenty dollars a month, and

---

* Dade County circuit court judge Howard Gross was arrested in 1987 for accepting a bribe, but was acquitted of all charges against him in a 1988 trial. Five years later he was disbarred by the Florida Supreme Court.

they'd answer your calls. I put an ad in the paper that said, "Dogs Unlimited. Experienced trainer will come to your house."

I got customers right away. I'd bring Brady to people's homes. I'd show what he could do, and I'd say, "Okay, let's train your dog to be like my dog."

The problem was actually making someone's dog act like my dog. The key to training a dog is training the owner. But the average dog owner didn't want to invest the time. People expected me to sit in their homes drinking coffee and listening to their stupid bullshit. When it came to the work, they either dropped out or they were too dumb to follow my simple directions.

What I learned is there are a lot of homes with very smart dogs, but the owners are stupid. There are more people who are morons than dogs. I'd be in an owner's backyard running my ass off with the dog, and the idiot owner would go into his house and watch from the window. Your dog will not learn properly unless you learn with him. When he sees you're not putting in the effort, he's not going to do it to either.

I decided, *Fuck it. These people are so dumb, the best thing is to hustle them.*

I'd say, "You want me to train your dog? I need a two-hundred-dollar deposit."

I'd take the money and never show up again. If they wanted to call me, all they were going to get was my answering service. One customer did find where I lived and came to my front door. He wanted his money back. I had to beat him up and throw him in the bushes. Now I knew why my father always burned down the legit businesses he owned. The average customer is a jerk.

29

J.R.: I was tired of being a ghost. After weeks of sweating my balls off in Miami, I contacted Phyllis in New York. Hearing from me was no big deal to her. She understood, when I disappeared, why I did it. She never thought I was dead. That was Phyllis's good part. You never had to explain anything. She already understood.

Phyllis told me I was out of everybody's minds in New York. I had some breathing room. It was time to put some feelers out in Miami. I wanted to start earning again.

If you want to do illegal things, you need other people. You rob a bank, you need a driver. You deal drugs, you need a supplier. There are very few criminal fields where one guy works by himself. Even a counterfeiter needs help getting special inks. When you need other guys to do something illegal, you got to trust each other.

Trust is in short supply on the street. Obviously street people got to be careful of each other. We're all criminals. The other problem we got is snitches. How do I know the other guy is not setting me up? How do I know he's not going to rat me out if we get heat? Does he got balls, or does he shit his pants when we got a problem? You need to know all these things before you start working with somebody.

To build trust takes time. You need to get high with a guy, joke with him, chase women with him, get into fights with him to see how he carries himself in different situations. It can take months and months to figure out who the other guy is.

The Mafia was many things. It was paying taxes and rules and old mustache guys telling you what you couldn't do. The Mafia was also a trust organization. If someone in the Mafia you knew pointed to a complete stranger and said, "He's a good guy," you could take that to the bank and rob it. You didn't need to spend months with the guy. You and he could immediately focus on making money together.

I'm sure the legitimate world works the same way. If you were in the stereo business starting off in a new city, it would probably help if you had a friend to introduce you to a big stereo seller in your new place and say, "This guy is okay. He knows a lot about stereos."

That was me. But I didn't sell no stereos.

Phyllis understood I wanted to reach out to wiseguys in Miami but I needed to keep it quiet. Phyllis had the idea I should talk to a friend of her father's named Two Fingers. Two Fingers got his name because he had fired a gun one day to shoot somebody, and the gun blew up and burned his fingers off. He lived in New York, but he had worked in Miami with a man named Patsy Erra.* Patsy had run casinos in Cuba before Castro kicked everybody out. Now he ran some of the biggest hotels and clubs in Miami, including the Dream Bar, which was a famous gangster hangout.†

---

* Pasquale "Patsy" Erra was a top boss in the Bonanno family. He was also affiliated with Sam Giancana, Santo Trafficante, Jr., and Meyer Lansky.
† Erra is alleged to have had an interest in Miami's iconic Fontainebleau Hotel, as well as in numerous nightclubs in Miami Beach's entertainment district. He was a significant figure in illegal gambling. He died in 1976. The Dream Bar, also called the Dream Lounge, occupied a few different locations in its time. It was a popular

Phyllis called Two Fingers and asked him if he knew any good guys I could meet in Miami who would keep quiet about me because of my trouble in New York. A few days later Two Fingers called me. He told me I should meet Patsy Erra's son, Bobby. He said, "Bobby's a crazy kid like you, and he's a good guy."

Bobby Erra was very friendly when I called him. He said, "I'll meet you tonight. I'll take you to a club, a restaurant, whatever you want to do. Meet me at the Dream Bar."

Going to the main gangster bar made me a little uptight. If that wasn't bad enough, the Dream Bar was in the heart of "79th Street"—a ten-block area in North Miami Beach where all the nightclubs were. It had been wiseguy paradise since the 1930s. Bobby assured me, if we met early enough, there'd be nobody in the bar.

I had to laugh when I walked into the Dream Bar. It was your classic guinea shithole. It was gaudy as shit. Golden chandeliers. A giant sphinx on one wall. The place was dead inside. I guess the old generation of mustache wiseguys were getting too old and infirm to go out. I'd barely reached the bar when three guys dressed like college kids walked over to me: Bobby Erra and the brothers Gary and Craig Teriaca. They were dressed in shorts, Izod shirts, and Gucci slip-ons. I could not believe these were wiseguys.

But the fact was the fact. Bobby was Patsy Erra's son. His friend Gary was the son of Vincent Teriaca,* who worked for Patsy. Bobby and Gary were both wiseguys. The exception was Gary's little brother, Craig. He partied as much as anybody, but he was not wise. Craig worked as a golf and tennis pro. He was a straight kid.

Me and Bobby and Gary were all about the same age. Once I got over the surprise of how these guys looked, we became very

music spot where Dean Martin and Frank Sinatra frequently performed. Jazz great Buddy Rich cut an album there. A late-1950s cabaret guide described it: "Make with the jazz, and dance music, in this highly-modern, dark club. Gander the waitresses here (they wear sheer, sheer negligee-type gowns). Open from 9 pm to 5 am." From *Cabaret Quarterly,* Special Resort Number, vol. 5, p. 74, 1956.
* Vincent Teriaca was the longtime manager of the Dream Bar and reputed underboss to Patsy Erra.

comfortable. We'd all grown up with fathers who were in the Mafia. They were "new Italians," like Andy Benfante and I had been, but even more so. Bobby and Gary had gone to the University of Miami and had been in fraternities. Imagine that. College-educated wiseguys.

Both of them played golf and tennis. They hobnobbed with upper-crust people. They always dressed "country'd out." That's what Gary Teriaca called his look, like he was ready at any time to play tennis at a country club. They always wore sweaters over their backs, but without their arms in the sleeves. If it was warm or cold, it didn't matter. The sweaters were on their backs. All they talked about was golf, tennis, boats, nice cars. Everything with them was "Relax. Don't you worry about it."

That first night they took me around 79th Street. Bobby's father had a piece of another club down the street called Jilly's Top Drawer, which was guinea heaven. Jilly was hooked up with Frank Sinatra,* and Jilly was very high on himself because of this. I went there a few times to see Frank Sinatra, but that was it.

One thing that stuck out about 79th Street was all the Cubans working the doors at Italian clubs. Cubans were bouncers. Cubans were car parkers. In New York Italians did not put anybody on the door but Italians. Andy and I used black guys at our clubs, but that was not normal. In Miami, Italians and Cubans were very close. Italians had run the nightclubs in Cuba, and when Castro kicked out the Mafia, the Italians brought the Cubans who'd worked for them in Cuba over to Miami. It worked out good because Cubans and Italians are good at doing wrong things together. It's the same with Jews and Italians. By themselves, Jewish people are no more

---

* Jilly Rizzo was a restaurateur who operated nightclubs in Manhattan and Miami. Through his friendship with Frank Sinatra, Jilly achieved minor celebrity status. He became a regular on the 1960s comedy show *Rowan and Martin's Laugh-In* and made a cameo appearance in Frank Sinatra's 1968 film *Lady in Cement,* which also features Jilly's Miami nightclub. Jilly was convicted on federal fraud charges in 1990 and died two years later in a car crash outside Sinatra's Rancho Mirage, California, home.

criminal than anybody else. But you put a Jew and an Italian together, a crime is going to happen.

The best place Bobby and Gary turned me on to was Sammy's Eastside. Sammy's was where younger wiseguys went. On the outside it looked like a pisshole. But they had a doorman out front, and if he didn't know you, you did not come in.

The inside of Sammy's was even worse than the outside. The front room was nothing but an old bar and a few tables. It was always packed. This place was madness. There were gangsters with machine guns on the tables. There were Miami Dolphins. Jimmy the Greek and Hank Goldberg hung out there.* In the back Sammy's had a room where professional girls from the bar would fuck the customers. Sammy's was the kind of place you'd walk into at ten at night, and you'd be stumbling out, blinking your eyes, at ten in the morning, wondering what happened. I loved Sammy's.

That first night I went in there with Bobby and Gary, Gary pulled me aside and asked me, "Do you want to do a line?"

Now I knew Gary was my kind of people. When we did lines together—that night or any time—Gary hid it from Bobby. He and Bobby had grown up together, and Bobby was like his older brother. As close as they were, they were very different guys. Gary was a wiry, slick-looking Italian kid. He was a good athlete, but he was not a fighter. He was a pretty boy. Everything he did had extra class to it. He was a natural ladies' man. When I met him, he was just starting to get involved with Carol Belcher. Her family owned the Belcher Oil Company† and islands in the Bahamas.‡ Not only was she rich, she was married to a wealthy man in Beverly

---

* James "Jimmy the Greek" Snyder was a sports commentator and oddsmaker who died in 1996. Hank Goldberg was a protégé of Jimmy the Greek and a Miami radio personality. He now works as a commentator for ESPN.

† A Florida oil transport and pipeline construction company that merged with a Texas firm in 1977.

‡ The Belcher family owned the northern half of Great Stirrup Cay, a private island in the Bahamas. They sold it to the Norwegian Cruise Line in 1977 to be developed into a resort.

Hills, California, when Gary first met her. Gary stole her from her husband.*

Gary was wacked out on coke from the day I met him. I don't know why he hid it from Bobby. Bobby did not do coke, but he didn't give a shit what Gary was into. I believed Gary had a complex about his father finding out. So he pretended he never did coke, which was ridiculous. His nose always ran. He sniffed constantly. Later, after he lost his mind on coke, he still pretended like he didn't touch it. But *sniff sniff sniff*, that's all you heard from him. Gary was a guy who was, as they say, not true to himself.

Bobby Erra was the opposite. He was who he was. Bobby carried himself like a man. He ran his father's gambling business. He wasn't just a bookie, he was a layoff guy—a banker for other bookies. Bobby was nationwide. He worked with bookies from New York to Las Vegas to Los Angeles. You could put $200,000 or $300,000 on a game with him, and he would not blink. He was the bookie to the rich and powerful. Bobby was in the top, Waspiest country clubs of Miami—the Palm Bay and La Gorce Country Club. Bobby also had a piece of the Jockey Club with a guy named Armand Surmani.† If you were a rich person, a celebrity, or a politician, and you gambled, the odds were good you knew Bobby Erra.

Bobby was not an outgoing person like Gary. But he was good

---

* According to statements she later made to federal investigators, Carol Belcher met Gary Teriaca in Miami when they were both in high school. She married a man named Kattleman and moved to Los Angeles. In 1974, while her marriage to Kattleman was already rocky, Gary Teriaca visited her in California. They began an intimate relationship, and Teriaca persuaded her to move back to Miami, where her father purchased a home for the two of them in the exclusive, gated community of Bay Point Estates.

† The Palm Bay was a club and private hotel that catered to celebrities visiting Miami. Robert Duvall, James Caan, Peter Ustinov, Oleg Cassini, and painter Frank Stella were frequent guests. In John Platero's profile of the club, "You Can't Buy Your Way In at Palm Bay Club," published by the AP on July 7, 1982, he wrote, "The late Greek shipping magnate Aristotle Onassis was once almost turned away. Spiro Agnew—when he was vice president of the United States—also was left cooling his heels outside. But for those who get past the guarded entrance to the Palm Bay Club, they'll find the essence of old Florida." Noting such ameni-

at cards and backgammon and used to play all hours at the club-house at La Gorce. One of his good friends was Raymond Floyd, the PGA champion.* Bobby was not a ladies' man like Gary, but he was hooked into rich women. He married Marcia Ludwig, a very wealthy girl who was friends with the governor of Florida.† He used to brag to me that he took bets from the governor.‡

Bobby dressed in nice clothes, but no matter what he wore, he

---

ties as boat slips that can accommodate 130-foot yachts, a floating heliport, and a pond stocked with $400-a-piece Japanese koi, Platero quoted the daughter of the club's founder, Gayonne Dinkler: "People here are not nouveau riche. They have innate class and the majority of them have been that way for generations." La Gorce was founded by real estate and railroad barons in the 1920s and has been a playground to Miami's old-money elites, as well as several American presidents, ever since. The Jockey Club was a residential tower, with tennis courts and a complex of private bars, restaurants, and discos, at 11111 Biscayne Boulevard. It was a favored haunt of former vice president Hubert Humphrey, comedian Jackie Gleason, and actress Eva Gabor. Surmani was a manager of one of the Jockey Club's bars. At the time Jon met Bobby Erra, he was facing charges for an assault in Las Vegas where he severely beat a man in his hotel room with a water pitcher. The man whom Erra assaulted was due to testify against Surmani in a tax-evasion case.

* Floyd won the PGA Championship in 1969 and 1982, as well as the 1976 Masters Tournament and the U.S. Open in 1986. In a 1990 federal organized crime investigation into Erra's activities, investigators found there was no evidence of impropriety stemming from Floyd's friendship with Erra. In addition to his friendship with Floyd, investigators discovered that Erra had a business relationship with legendary race car driver Mario Andretti, with whom he attempted to open a chain of pizza restaurants.

† Erra and Ludwig were never legally married, though they maintained a residence together and Ludwig described herself as his "wife" in testimony she gave in 1991 to a federal grand jury regarding her relationship with Erra. A former Orange Bowl queen, Ludwig was from an old Miami family. She was a close friend of Adele Graham's, wife of Bob Graham, a former governor of Florida and U.S. senator, and most recently President Obama's handpicked co-chair of the National Commission on the BP Deepwater Horizon Oil Spill and Offshore Drilling.

‡ In 1986 then-governor Graham endured the biggest political scandal of his career after state troopers discovered that his wife had taped a note to the mirror of his bathroom in the governor's mansion urging him to pardon Albert San Pedro, a criminal associate of Erra's. Graham did not issue the pardon. But according to Mike Fisten, a former Miami Dade Police Department detective who, while serving on a federal task force, investigated Erra's gambling operations in the early 1990s, numerous calls were placed between a phone used by Erra's organization to take illegal bets and a private line at the governor's personal home in Miami. Fisten says his request for a subpoena to tap Erra's phone line and record calls to the governor's private phone line was denied by his superiors.

had no style. For instance, he cut his hair in the shape of a football helmet. He had thick, bushy hair, and it looked like the barber just put a helmet on his head and clipped around it. Everything he did was off. We made a big score once, and I decided to buy Bobby an Audi 100, a top car in the 1970s. I sent him to a dealer to pick one out, and a week later Bobby rolls up in a bright orange Audi. It's the most disgusting color I've ever seen on a car. That was Bobby. Even when he got the right car, he made it look weird.

Don't get me wrong. Bobby was a tough, tough guy. He flipped a race boat when he was a teenager, and when the boat came down it cut off a bunch of fingers on his hand. Who knows, maybe that's why Two Fingers liked him? They both had fucked-up hands. But Bobby didn't let that stop him. He became a great golf player, and because of that mangled hand, he could hustle the fuck out of people. He'd say, "Look at my hand, you've got to give me a few shots here." And he would beat them for big money. Afterward they'd be like, "Motherfucker." Bobby was unbelievable that way. He used that stump to his advantage. He was not the type of guy who moaned about it.

Bobby had a brother who was blind. I don't know what caused it. Bobby would always talk about his brother—how he had to pick him up or do this or that for him. But all the years I knew Bobby, I only met his brother one time. We had to take him to the bank to sign something because Bobby used to put property in his brother's name to hide assets.* Bobby's brother was like a shadow he didn't let you see.

THE FIRST night I partied with Gary at Sammy's Eastside, he tapped the mirror we were snorting lines off of, and said, "This is it. Coke is the thing, man."

I'll never forget that. Gary, wacked out as he was, he was intelligent. He saw the big picture. Everybody and his brother smuggled

---

* Erra's financial dealings with his blind brother were exposed in a 1990 federal racketeering investigation into his activities, which resulted in his entering a plea of guilty. His brother avoided prosecution.

pot in Florida. Prices were dropping. Bales of weed lost by smugglers used to wash up on the beaches. They called them "square grouper fish." Coke was a different story. There was a permanent shortage. People could not get enough. A kilo wholesaled for $50,000 and sold for two or three times that on the street. Coke was such a concentrated drug that $100,000 worth could fit in a shoebox. The same value of weed, you'd practically need a dump truck to carry it.

Gary also talked about another advantage coke had. It was classy. Heroin addicts were filthy pigs who walked around like zombies. It was a ghetto drug. The main customers for cocaine were upper-class society. Coke was the opposite of most Mafia businesses, which, like my father's numbers game, were based on making money off of poor people. Coke was about supplying rich people with something they wanted.

Gary Teriaca had a vision of the future, but he was in a bind. Like other young wiseguys, his father would kill him if he caught him dealing coke. The other problem Gary had was, coke was not easy to get steadily. He was selling coke to his rich country club friends, but this was small-time. His main business was real estate scams, like selling shares in make-believe condos, but he was aching to grow the coke business.

As I hung out more with Gary and Bobby, I tried to think about things we could do together that would build a bond between us. The only thing I had to offer them was kicks. Neither of them had ever done a drug rip-off. When I told them stories about robberies I did in New York, their eyes lit up like kids at Christmas. I planted the idea in their minds that if they had real wiseguy balls, we should do a robbery together.

30

J.R.: I was not thrilled to do a drug rip-off. Since all the chaos in New York, my appetite for stickups had gone away. But in the position I was in, even making a thousand dollars would be a big score. And it gave me a way to bond more with Bobby and Gary.

Bobby and Gary had a country club friend who was into coke. Gary told the guy I was a new connection. I would bring coke to his house. He lived in an apartment off Sunset Drive in South Miami. They told me he might want to frisk me for a gun. Since coke is so small, I couldn't carry a package big enough to hold a gun. I used an old trick. Before I went in the victim's apartment, I hid my gun in a fire extinguisher box by his door. I'd put him at ease, make an excuse to step out, and get my gun.

I walked into the victim's apartment clean. I had bought an Izod shirt and Sperry Top-Siders like country club people wore. I had a sweater on my back. The victim didn't even search me. Bobby and Gary were already there. We acted like we'd never met before in person. The victim had a nice pad. One wall had shelves with a quadraphonic stereo and big speakers in tall wooden cabinets. The victim offered me a drink. We sat on his nice chrome and leather couches, talked about the Dolphins, his quadraphonic sound system, *blah blah blah*. Then I say, "You got the money?"

"What about what you got?"

"No offense," I say, "but there's three of you and one of me. I didn't carry nothing in here. You show me the money, and I'll get my product."

I'm supposedly selling him four ounces of blow for $8,500. The victim walks into his laundry room. I hear him open his washing machine. That's the moron's hiding place. He comes out and shows me his cash.

"Thanks, bro," I say. "I'll get the shit from my car."

I step in the hall, take my gun from the fire extinguisher box, and go back in the apartment. When I push my gun in the guy's face, he almost pisses his little tennis shorts.

Bobby and Gary put their hands up. I push everybody against the wall. I tell Bobby and Gary I want the money from their pockets. I see in their eyes, they're almost pissing their pants, too, but from trying not to laugh. I decide to give them something even funnier. I say, "Now, take off your pants and get on the ground."

Bobby says, "What do you mean, take off my pants?"

"I don't want you assholes running after me."

Bobby's angry now. I look in his eyes and let him see now I'm the one laughing inside. Then I leave them all ass-naked on the floor.

When we met up at Sammy's Eastside to divide up the money, Bobby said, "You motherfucker! Take my pants down?"

We laughed, but I wanted Bobby to know I didn't give a fuck who he was or who his father was. Now he knew I wasn't like Gary. I wasn't his little brother asking for approval.

• • •

NOW THAT we'd had our fun, I told Gary I liked the coke business. I wanted to hang out with rich people at country clubs and supply them, like he did. Gary didn't see it the same way. He didn't want a partner, but he'd figured out by now I wasn't the kind of person he could brush off.

He told me if I found customers, he'd supply me. Obviously, Gary wasn't going to tell me where he got his coke from. He mentioned it was from a Cuban, but that was all. Every few weeks Gary would get a hundred grams* from the Cuban, and that's what he sold to me and to his customers. That's how small the business was in 1974.

The only rich degenerates I knew in Miami were people I met when I did landscaping. One was a man named Judge Alcee Hastings.† I bought a quarter ounce of coke from Gary and went to Judge Hastings and asked him if he'd like to buy some.

"Are you kidding me?" he said. "I'll take the whole quarter."

He was a happy judge.

That proved it to me. When you got into the coke business, you were promoted in the social world. Selling coke, now I was best friends with a judge.

I then made contact with my uncle Jerry Chilli. We met at the coffee shop at the Thunderbird Hotel on Collins Avenue, which was his unofficial main office. My uncle Jerry was in the old mustache

---

* A hundred grams is roughly four ounces, or a quarter pound. Jon, like most drug dealers, freely mixes his use of the metric and English systems for weights.
† Judge Alcee Hastings was a Miami circuit judge when President Carter appointed him to the federal court in the Southern District of Florida. In 1981 he was indicted for taking a $150,000 bribe from a reputed mafioso. In 1988 the U.S. Congress impeached him, and the Senate convicted him of bribery and perjury—making him only the sixth federal judge in history to have been so removed. Disbarred and seemingly unfit for decent society, he found refuge in the United States House of Representatives in 1992. He persuaded the voters of Florida's 23rd District to elect him to Congress, where he serves today. Still a complete dirtbag in the estimation of many, on August 31, 2010, the *Wall Street Journal* identified Representative Hastings as one of the most profligate and possibly unethical spenders of junket money in Congress, and on March 8, 2011, in the article "Alcee Hastings' Scandals Collide in Sexual Harassment Lawsuit," Bob Norman reported for the *Broward Palm Beach New Times* that Representative Hastings was the subject of a sexual harassment suit.

generation, but guys in his crew were moving coke. If I could obtain coke in quantity, his guys would move it.

I was in a sweet spot with the Mafia. In New York people had forgotten about me. In Miami people were coming to know me. But I wasn't in anyone's crew. I had the benefit of being connected to wiseguys, but none of the downside of being in the Mafia.

SEVERAL MONTHS after Gary, Bobby, and I ripped off his friend with the nice quadrophonic hi-fi, Gary found out the same guy had got his hands on a kilo of coke. I said, "Gary, we got to get that kilo."

Our plan was, Gary would go visit his friend, and I'd pretend that I'd followed him, then rob the two of them. The victim recognized me as soon as I kicked open the door. He tried running, and I knocked him down and gave him a few kicks. He whimpered like a girl.

I said, "Gary, how do you put up with this?"

The victim looked at Gary and said, "You mean, you're in on this?"

I said, "You idiot. He was in on the first one."

The victim said the strangest thing: "Now I've got nobody."

He started to physically cry. He was shaking. He was bawling his eyes out. He wasn't psychologically fit to be a criminal.

Gary said to me, "He knows who I am now."

Just to put some fear into the victim, I said, "Let's put him in the dirt."

"Please, don't kill me!" The victim started to cry so hard, he vomited.

I said to Gary, "Does this weepy bitch have a mother?"

"What about my mom?" the victim said.

"I will let you live, but if you ever give me or Gary any trouble, I will skin your mother alive."

I knelt down and put my gun in his mouth and made him listen to the details of how you skin somebody, based on my experience. He shit his pants. It was disgusting, but I knew he was never going to be a problem for me or anybody.

After I joined the Palm Bay Club, I started to run into the guy, who was a member, and we got friendly. His mother was a member, too. But he never introduced us.

GARY GOT pissy with me about ruining his friendship with his Palm Bay friend. I was irritated that even though I'd taught Gary how to rob people, whenever he sold out his coke to his customers, he left me high and dry. But things worked out in a funny way. I found some wacked-out hippies selling coke in Coral Gables, and they led me to Gary's Cuban supplier.

The hippies lived in a commune house. They had Indian guru pictures on the walls. The guys walked around in swami diapers. The girls had dots on their foreheads. People would go nude in the house. They didn't care who walked in. They'd sit on the floor nude and meditate. They'd fuck in the bedrooms with the doors open. They were real freaks. They actually preached that nudism was mentally healthy. It takes all kinds to make the world go.

The nudist I dealt with was a skinny guy. When I first met him, he wore the guru diapers like the other hippies, but as he relaxed he got more open. I'd meet him in a side room, where he'd sit on a pillow with a poncho over his lap. Then he'd start talking and the poncho would fall off. Please. I do not want to do a business deal with some freak with his dick hanging out. This was not my scene.

I made a few buys from this kid and hinted that maybe we could all do business together, if he turned me on to his supplier. The kid would only tell me he got his shit from a Cuban. I was tired of that game. On my next visit, I put my gun on the kid and said, "Give me all your shit."

"Be cool, man," he said. "This coke is from Albert San Pedro."

"I don't care if it's from Ricky Ricardo."

"You don't want to piss off Albert. He's a crazy Cuban. He'll kill you."

The nudist kid did not lack confidence. He stayed calm with my gun on him. He obviously thought the Cuban was such a bad guy, I should be afraid. That was his error.

"Fuck you. You're a jerk-off sitting there with your dick hanging out. I'm fed up with your hippie bullshit." I kicked the kid so hard on his dumb little pillow, he flipped back and his head went into the plaster of the wall. The nudist kid had balls. He said, "Fuck you."

I laughed. "I did you a favor. Now when you show your busted-up face to the Cuban, he'll believe you when you say you got robbed."

As a favor, I kicked him again on the way out.

It wasn't two hours later that I got a call from Gary Teriaca. "Did you take coke from some kids in Coral Gables?"

"What if I did?"

"They went to the Cuban and told him what you did."

"What's it to you?"

"Their Cuban is the guy I get coke from. He says he wants to kill you."

"Fuck him."

"He's willing to meet you."

"He wants to meet me or kill me?"

"Probably both."

31

J.R.: I met Albert at the Fun Fair in North Bay Village.*
The Fun Fair was a hot dog stand with an arcade of
amusements behind it. I'd just ordered my hot dog—no
mustard, extra kraut—when I saw a big pockmarked
Cuban with really strange white-blond hair approach
me. He was Albert's main bodyguard, El Rubio—which
is Spanish for "Blondie." Later Rubio and I got to be
friends. He was a really good heavyweight boxer. Not
that he was going to win the title or anything, but he
knew how to punch. After Rubio checked me out, Albert
stepped out of a black Corvette by the curb.

I judge a person by how he carries himself. Albert
was short, but he had a big upper body like a weight
lifter. He was twenty-five years old, but he had the face
of a man. He dressed nice, but not in country club Izod
shit. He wore a suit, like you'd picture John Gotti after

---

* North Bay Village is a small municipality on three islands connected by a causeway to Miami Beach.

he got famous, only Albert had a tropical look, with a bright shirt. He didn't have any kind of Spanish accent. He sounded more like a New York wiseguy than me.

Albert wore sunglasses, but you could see that one of his eyes was not right. A few months before we met, he was ambushed outside his house and shot five times.* Albert said he had taken cover behind his Corvette and when the guys who were trying to kill him shot his Corvette, pieces of the fiberglass body splintered off and took out his eye.† He was blinded by his own Corvette. They put in a piece-of-crap plastic eye, and it never looked right. No matter how much money he got, Albert's eye was a piece of shit. It looked like an eye from a cheap doll a kid would have, and it wandered around in his head. Trust me, you did not want to look at Albert when he had his sunglasses off. With his eyes going in different directions, it always looked like he might be staring at you. And once you figured out how crazy Albert was, being stared at by him—even if it was from a plastic eyeball—would make you feel uptight.

The fact that Albert was walking around a few months after he got shot five times showed he was a tough guy. No matter how disgusting his eye looked, you couldn't take that toughness away from him. There was no bullshit at our meeting. He said, "I know you took the coke from that kid. He can't pay me my money because you robbed him."

"Did you know this kid you got helping you, he walks around in his house with his dick flopping out? He's a fucking nudist."

Rubio nodded. Obviously, he was the one who dealt with the naked commune bullshit.

---

* San Pedro was shot outside his house in 1975.
† According to his ex-wife, Lourdes Valdez, San Pedro was born with a birth defect that made him cross-eyed. She claims San Pedro made up the story of his eye being injured in the shoot-out because he thought it sounded better than being born with a birth defect. One of Albert's childhood friends told me that in grade school kids taunted him by calling him Bizco—a derogatory Spanish term for "cross-eyed." To hide his eyes, young Albert squinted, earning a somewhat improved nickname, El Chino—"The Chinese."

"I don't care if these kids got cocks growing off their faces, they work for me."

"I don't want to have a gun battle with you," I said.

"Let's work it out the best way for both of us."

Albert and me decided that the most fair way for him to get his money back was for me to start supplying the nudists with his coke. I became Albert's distributor. I'd charge them twice the normal price until Albert got his money back, plus interest on his loss. That was their punishment for being stupid enough to get robbed. What did they need money for? They lived in a commune and didn't wear pants.

THAT'S HOW it started with Albert and me. We worked together for more than a decade. He was a good guy. He'd been into wrong stuff his whole life. He was born in Cuba, but his parents took him to Miami when he was in diapers. His father had been a horse trainer at a track in Cuba controlled by Patsy Erra. In Miami, Albert's father got a job as a milkman, and he did odd jobs for Patsy Erra. When Albert grew up, he was loyal to Italians, but he didn't want to be a gofer parking cars at the Dream Bar and breaking knees for pocket money.

Albert did some collections for Bobby Erra, but he also built up his own power in the Cuban community. He'd been running around with guns since he was a kid, getting his reputation as strongman.* By the time I met him, people called him "the Fixer" because he

---

* According to former Miami-Dade detectives I interviewed, San Pedro's first significant run-in with the law occurred in 1969 when he discharged an antique Thompson submachine gun toward members of an opposing football team in a park after his team lost a pickup game. Nobody was injured, and according to police, San Pedro disposed of the weapon and evaded prosecution. In 1971, after shooting at two undercover cops making a drug buy, San Pedro was convicted of conspiracy to commit murder and received probation. Anger management problems persisted. Police say San Pedro was arrested for beating a motorist with a tire iron following a traffic dispute. Later, San Pedro was arrested for pimping, assault, and robbery revolving around a scheme in which he used hookers to lure tricks to motel rooms where he would then rob them. Other assaults were connected to a freelance business San Pedro ran in which he offered to beat the crap out of anybody for $50. In 1988 he was convicted of cocaine trafficking and of bribing public officials in Dade County, for which he served three years in prison.

could make any problem go away. He was a genius at working the system.*

From the time I knew him, Albert lived in Hialeah,† in a house

---

* San Pedro was later dubbed "The Great Corrupter" by the Miami press. From his earliest arrests, he skillfully evaded punishment by intimidating witnesses, destroying evidence, and paying off police, judges, and at least one mayor. By the late 1970s, he employed two professional state lobbyists to manage his political contributions. He is alleged to have paid reporters from the *Miami News* to write articles favorable to the politicians he supported. He also cultivated a friendship with local TV news reporter Rick Sanchez, who later went to work for CNN until he was fired in 2010 for making anti-Semitic comments. Years before that scandal, Sanchez was put on leave from a Miami TV station when police wiretaps revealed that Sanchez, a frequent guest in San Pedro's home, had introduced San Pedro to officers of a local bank in return for unspecified favors. San Pedro's efforts at community outreach paid off. He developed a close relationship with U.S. Representative Claude Pepper, who lobbied the state to pardon San Pedro for his 1971 felony conviction. In a letter to the state parole board, Representative Pepper described San Pedro as a "friend, a conscientious young man, and a very responsible businessman." San Pedro received similar help from the state's attorney general, Robert Shevin, who filed a letter with the parole board stating that he found San Pedro's "integrity, character, and personal conduct to be irreproachable." After his 1988 cocaine trafficking and bribery conviction, San Pedro cut a deal with U.S. Attorney Dexter Lehtenin to provide evidence for a federal corruption case against Hialeah mayor Raul Martinez. At the time of this deal, Martinez was the leading opponent of Lehtinen's wife, Ileana Ros-Lehtinen, in a congressional race. Lehtinen's corruption case against Martinez damaged his credibility as a candidate in the race that Lehtinen's wife subsequently won. Representative Ileana Ros-Lehtinen is today the chairman of the House Committee on Foreign Affairs. The corruption case against Raul Martinez was later thrown out because, in the words of San Pedro's own attorney, "They had nothing on Martinez, because San Pedro gave them nothing. He tricked Dexter Lehtinen and the entire federal government." Lehtinen resigned his position as U.S. Attorney after the Justice Department investigated him for ethical violations unrelated to the San Pedro case. The immunity deal Lehtinen gave to San Pedro was so extraordinarily broad, it protected him from a subsequent 1991 federal racketeering case that tied him to drug trafficking, money laundering, and murder. San Pedro, one of the most significant crime figures of Miami in the '70s and '80s, went free in 1996. But he never received American citizenship, and in 1996 he was brought before an immigration court. During the hearing, San Pedro's stepdaughter testified that he began raping her at age thirteen. Her allegations of child molestation—supported by the fact that San Pedro fathered two sons by her—were deemed credible enough by the judge to issue a deportation order. Yet because the U.S. government does not have normal diplomatic relations with Cuba, the deportation has not been enforced. San Pedro still lives as a free man, and according to his attorney, currently he is a significant player in the outdoor advertising business in Miami.

† Hialeah is a working-class community near Miami International Airport that became almost entirely Cuban in the 1970s.

by a water-treatment plant. When I first went there in 1975, it was a little cinder-block working-man's house. As Albert grew more successful, he took over the lots next to his and built his house bigger and bigger. He turned it into a truly fucked-up mansion that looks more like a prison than a home that a normal human being would want to live in.* You would have to be a deranged maniac to live in a house like the one Albert built. Plus, even if he made it nice, it was still next to the water-treatment plant.

Because Albert was paranoid, he built walls and guardhouses around his house. He put in cameras. He made his windows with bulletproof glass. He kept a weapons armory, hidden in secret closets behind his bookshelves. He paid off the police to keep a squad car parked outside the house.† He owned his own detective agency so the thugs who worked for him could be licensed professionals and legally carry concealed weapons.‡ His inner-circle enforcers, who lived at his house, were all Cubans he'd grown up with. They'd started off in high school playing football and bodybuilding at the gym together. Rubio was the one I got along with best, but he went away after he got in some trouble.§ Albert also had another big Cuban named El Oso, which means "The Bear." El Oso was a tough kid,** and his job, in addition to collections and burning down buildings, was to start up Albert's cars and make sure they didn't blow up. Albert's most trusted guy was Ricky Prado. He was a shorter person like Albert, but he was into martial arts and had served in the military in Special Forces. Ricky did not come off like

---

* In the federal racketeering case against San Pedro, one of his former bodyguards testified that San Pedro ordered him to burn down his aunt's home on the adjacent lot after she refused to sell it to him. The house in Hialeah, which San Pedro still inhabits, is a multi-story structure of approximately 8,000 square feet, surrounded by walls and occupying several adjacent lots. The rest of the street is occupied by single-story, 1,100-square-foot homes.

† San Pedro's younger brother, John, was a police officer in Hialeah. In 1986 San Pedro was caught bribing several officers in the department—but not his brother, who continues to serve today.

‡ In 1975 San Pedro purchased Transworld Detective Agency.

§ El Rubio was convicted of manslaughter shortly after Jon met him.

** In 1989 Miguel "El Oso" Ramirez was convicted of shooting and beheading undercover DEA informant Larry Nash.

a thug. He was quiet and professional. He was so good that after he worked for Albert, Ricky was hired by the CIA.*

Albert was his own one-man mafia. Even as a twenty-five-year-old kid when I met him, he thought of himself as the Cuban god-father.† He was into many, many schemes. He put money in the street, ran card games and betting. He operated a *bolita*—a Cuban numbers game. He ran whores at airport hotels. He set buildings on fire all over Miami. He was a famous arsonist. He did it to take over properties or just to instill fear in people he didn't like. My father would have understood Albert.

But even as he rose up in his neighborhood, he stayed loyal to Bobby Erra. Anything he did that might be in competition with the Italians—like betting and the vig—he kept it inside Hialeah, where the Mafia didn't give a shit.

The cocaine business was ideal for Albert because of the Mafia hypocrisy about not dealing most drugs. The old Mafia bosses left cocaine wide open for the Latins.

When I started buying from Albert, he kept his source secret from me. I knew he got it from Colombians running it through the Bahamas, because everyone did back then. Every couple of weeks he was getting maybe two to five kilos. Between my uncle Jerry and the country club people I was selling to, I could move half a kilo in a good week.

Once I met Albert, Gary Teriaca was actually kind of relieved. Gary was not a street kid, and Albert scared him. So now I started picking up the coke from Albert, but we'd store it at Gary's house. That made Gary feel like he was still in control. I did not sell to Gary's customers, and he didn't sell to mine. We got along fine.

---

* Enrique "Ricky" Prado served in the air force from 1971 to 1973. In 1974 he joined the Miami-Dade Fire Department. While working as a fireman and para-medic, he also became a corporate officer in San Pedro's Transworld Detective Agency. When Prado worked at the fire department, his personnel records indi-cated he periodically lived at San Pedro's house. In 1981 Prado was hired by the CIA, and he was stationed in Central America until the mid-1980s, where he is believed to have been involved in training Contra paramilitaries.
† San Pedro kept a copy of Mario Puzo's *The Godfather* in his bathroom and Al Capone's biography on his office desk.

...

BESIDES BEING tough, Albert was just a really strange guy. Even though he acted Italian, he always had a stupid-ass Cuban cigar in his face. He was truly the king of the Cubans in Hialeah. Albert's big cause was San Lazaro. Do you know who San Lazaro is? San Lazaro was a guy who got wounds all over his body and was left in the street to die, but some dogs licked his sores, and instead of dying he got better. I'm not saying this is a true story. It's what they say is true in the Catholic Church,* and Albert really believed it. San Lazaro was his protective saint. He was nuts about his saint, because he thought San Lazaro kept him alive when he got ambushed behind his Corvette.

Albert paid off the priests at the local churches in San Lazaro's name. When he started buying racing horses, Albert named his stables San Lazaro. Inside his house it got even nuttier. Albert lived with his parents, and his mom, a very devout lady, was always shouting blessings to San Lazaro when she'd serve us food. To please his mom, Albert filled the house with life-size San Lazaro statues. They were made of porcelain and painted like living people. His mom put human-hair wigs on them. Albert bought a robe made by monks that was supposedly spun from gold. He told me it cost $30,000, and he kept it on his favorite San Lazaro statue.

When you get friendly with most guys, they want to show you their sports cars, or their illegal machine guns, or they got women on the couch that will flash their tits and go down on each other when you snap your fingers. Not Albert. You got friendly with him, and he and his mom would take you into the special room to show you his robe of San Lazaro. His house was a madhouse.

Every year Albert held a party for his patron saint. In the early days he would put a San Lazaro statue on the back of a truck and parade it through the streets of Hialeah. Then his crew would drive

* In Cuban Santeria, San Lazaro—Saint Lazarus—is a key figure. But the Santeria version of Saint Lazarus combines elements of two different Lazarus characters who appear in the Bible and melds them into a single narrative.

it to a vacant lot and feed everybody roast pork. Later it got fancier. He started renting the rooftop ballroom at the Doral Hotel for his San Lazaro dinners, and he invited all the judges and politicians he was bribing.*

As Albert and I did more work together, he introduced me to his other religion: Cuban voodoo Santeria. That was some crazy shit, bro. His mother would make witches' brews in the back of his house, and he had African Cubans who would come over dressed in white suits and cut the heads off of chickens and goats. One time Albert and I were involved in a murder together,† and he had his voodoo priests come over to cut the heads off of chickens to make sure it went right.

You can imagine how his house was decorated. I'm not saying Albert didn't have taste, but the way he was brought up, he liked things that were disgusting. There were these giant disgusting couches and gold shit everywhere, mixed in with his crazy San Lazaro statues. In one room he kept a voodoo caldron, filled with voodoo dolls and crosses. His house was like mixing together the gaudiest Italian restaurant with a horror movie.

Albert had no sense of humor. He didn't laugh or play jokes. Me, Gary Teriaca, Bobby Erra, we all had boats. But Albert never wanted to go on anybody's boat. He was not into chasing women like a normal guy. When I first met him, he had one wife. Then he moved a much younger girl into his house, his second wife.‡ Albert

---

* "The last two of [San Pedro's] $50,000 parties were held at the posh Doral Hotel in Miami Beach, and among the guests were Hialeah mayor Raul Marti-nez, Representative Claude Pepper, Miami Beach mayor Alex Daoud, WSVN-Channel 7 weekend anchor and reporter Rick Sanchez, Miami police major Jack Sullivan, ordinary cops, political fund-raisers, lawyers, various right-wing bra-vos, and a load of judges. San Pedro brought along a nine-foot statue of the saint, dressed himself in a tuxedo, was flanked by bodyguards, and posed with the as-sembled celebrities." This account is from page 82 of Pete Hamill's book *Piece-work: Writings on Men & Women, Fools and Heroes, Lost Cities, Vanished Calamities and How the Weather Was,* New York: Back Bay Books, 1997.
† Jon discusses this in chapter 38.
‡ San Pedro's stepdaughter Jenny Cartaya began living with him as a "wife" when she was fourteen or fifteen. Cartaya, whose testimony in 1996 led to San Pedro's pending deportation order, described the house to me much as Jon did. She alleges

prided himself on being a family man. For the guys that worked for him, he went to their weddings, christenings, all that. He was a devout guy, with the Catholic Church and with voodoo.

Did you ever see *Goodfellas*? Albert was like Joe Pesci's character when he starts whacking everybody around him. When Albert would get paranoid, he would have to kill somebody. Without a doubt, he was nuts. He was gone. I mean, there was nothing to figure out. He was out of his mind. He was a psycho, and everybody knew he was a psycho. One day, you'd be with him, and everything was great. The next day he'd be screaming, "This motherfucker has got to get killed."

One time it was the poor Cuban kid who washed his cars. All of a sudden he had to be killed.

"Albert," I said, "he's barely eighteen. What did he do?"

"He was looking around under my car. What the fuck was he looking at?"

"Albert, this kid is very thorough. He was probably looking for more dirt to clean."

"I'm telling you, man. There's something very wrong with him."

When Albert got something in his mind, that was it. The next day, or even the next hour, that person would be gone. There'd be somebody new out there washing his car.

They never proved anything,* but this one disappeared and that

---

that San Pedro first raped her under a statue of San Lazaro at age thirteen and used to beat her regularly with his leather weight-lifting belts. She became his wife after, according to her, San Pedro set up her mother in a cocaine bust and sent her to prison. Cartaya gave birth to two sons by San Pedro, whom she raised along with her mother's son. The sons were raised as brothers, though they were simultaneously half brothers and uncle-nephew—a family situation right out of the film *Chinatown*. When Cartaya was nineteen, San Pedro had the Hialeah Police Department arrest her for being a danger to herself and attempted to confine her to a mental hospital. Cartaya eventually fled the state.

* The 1991 racketeering case against San Pedro was to include an indictment for four predicate act murders until it was struck down on the basis of the immunity deal U.S. Attorney Dexter Lehtinen provided him. In addition to the slack the U.S. government cut San Pedro to commit mayhem, even the Mafia gave him a wide berth. In 1984 San Pedro shot reputed mobster Carmine Scarfone in the arm while having drinks with him at Capra's Italian restaurant in Hallandale. A couple of days later, Scarfone's home was riddled with machine-gun fire and set ablaze

one disappeared. He called it "feeding the swamps." That's how everybody got rid of bodies in Florida. Whack the guy, chop him into chunks with a chain saw, throw the parts into the swamps, and let the gators do the rest. In the movie *Scarface* they showed the Colombians killing people with chain saws. They didn't invent that shit.

Everybody around Albert was petrified of him. He burned so much shit down, he corrupted so many mayors, so many police. If he couldn't buy you with money, he burned your house down. That was it. There was nothing to talk about. "You don't want to sell me your thing? Okay, nice meeting you."

Next day everything you have is burned to ashes. No maybes about it. He got mad one time because they ran out of his favorite sweet rolls at the bakery. That night his guys poured gasoline down the bakery air shafts, and *boom,* problem solved. No more bakery.*

Albert did not take drugs that I saw. He was straight as a motherfucker, and he went to church, but he was completely gone.

As far as we went, I never had a problem with Albert. He made my life a lot easier. When I started working with the Colombians, I always had Albert to back me up. After Mariel,† Miami filled up with the guys that came over on the boats and didn't give a fuck about nothing. They were wild Indians. There were a few situations where I'd come across one of these guys, and I'd think, *I'm going to have a problem with this asshole.*

I'd go visit Albert and say, "I've got a problem with these Cubans over there."

---

with Molotov cocktails. Despite there being witnesses, Scarfone declined to testify against San Pedro for shooting him.

* According to San Pedro's former bodyguard Miguel Ramirez, on orders from their boss in 1975, he and future CIA officer Rick Prado burned down San Bernardo Bakery on Flagler Street, using so much gasoline that the initial flash burned their eyebrows off.

† During the Mariel boatlift in 1980, Cuban dictator Fidel Castro allowed a hundred thousand Cubans to leave for Florida, declaring, "I have flushed the toilets of Cuba on the United States." Many were violent inmates released from Cuban prisons.

Within a matter of two, three hours, those Cubans would be walking into Albert's house with their heads bowed, apologizing to me. Albert controlled the Cubans. Hialeah was his own world. Nobody could touch him there.

Now, as soon as Albert crossed the little bridge from Hialeah into Miami, he went from being king to just another crazy Cuban in a piece-of-shit Corvette. Upper-class society had gotten liberal enough in the 1970s that wops like Bobby Erra and Gary Teriaca could go join the top golf courses and clubs, but not an insane cross-eyed Cuban like Albert. Please. To the upper-crust people, Albert was, pardon the expression, the same as a nigger.

That boxed Albert out of the main part of the coke market. It wasn't poor Cubans in Hialeah that were buying it. It was rich ass-holes. Albert needed people like Gary and me to move the cocaine he was getting, because the people who wanted to buy it wouldn't let Albert in their clubs.

That's why I always felt reasonably safe around Albert. He needed me. And with him backing me up, I was able to grow my distribution business.

32

J.R.: You remember Bernie Levine, the fat little Jewish kid from Jersey who turned on the Outcasts to heroin in his mom's basement? By the early 1970s, Bernie had moved to San Francisco and was managing a recording studio that the Grateful Dead used. We got in touch, and he told me people were crazy about coke in San Francisco. He could sell anything I could get him for an outrageous amount because he was hooked in with celebrity blowheads like Jerry Garcia.*

I said, "Bernie, come to Miami."

Bernie got on the next plane. He had gone from being a pudgy kid to a fat fuck of a man. He must have weighed three hundred pounds. I knew a Chinese restaurant in Coral Gables that was sensational. They had duck that was so tender, you could touch it with a spoon and the meat fell off the bones. Bernie inhaled two whole ducks and became a very happy fat man. We went to his

---

* Garcia was lead singer for the Grateful Dead.

hotel, and I showed him some coke I was getting from Albert. Bernie did a line and said, "Your coke is no good for San Francisco."

Bernie explained that people in California had their noses up in the air and only did the finest cocaine. He showed me some tricks about cocaine. I believed that if coke had more rocks than powder, it was pure. Bernie explained that rocks are bullshit. Anybody can press shitty coke into rocks, just as guys can blow out glass to make it look like diamonds. A good test for coke purity that Bernie showed me involved buying a hot plate from an appliance store. You put your coke on the hot plate and slowly turn up the heat. Any shit that starts to melt below 180 degrees is not coke but the junk it's cut with. Good coke should melt at about 180 degrees. Later, people found shit to mix with coke that also melts at 180 degrees, so melting will not always tell you the truth, but back then what Bernie showed me gave me an edge.

I took my hotplate over to Albert's and showed him how he could test his coke scientifically. Albert thought I was a genius. He used what I showed him to demand better coke from the people supplying him. Within a month I had a quality half-kilo to sell Bernie. He flew down again and picked it up. Two days after he got back, he told me he'd sold the entire half-key.* Jerry Garcia was one happy blowhead.

Bernie and I began building our business. Our problem was transporting the coke to California. Miami was filled with stewardesses in the 1970s. Because of the warm weather, the airlines had stewardess training centers in Miami, and these girls were everywhere—at the beaches, in the bars and clubs. I got friendly with a stewardess named Susie who worked for National Airlines—and later for Pan Am—and flew the route to San Francisco. I asked her how easy it would be to carry a small package onto the plane.

She said, "There's no security for me. I put on my little outfit, carry my little bag, and nobody even asks to see an ID."

I paid her a hundred dollars the first time. I gave her a half-kilo

---

* *Key* is shorthand for "kilo."

that fit in her flight bag. Bernie met her at a hotel near San Francisco airport, and the next day she brought back my money. This was too easy.

Within a few months Bernie was taking a few kilos from me every week. Sony had started selling Betamax videotapes, and I discovered that a half-kilo of coke fit perfectly in a tape container. In her roll-on luggage, Susie could fit a box of twenty Betamax tapes holding ten kilos of coke. She did this for years, and she never got questioned.

The only problem I ever had was one time Susie got drunk on the plane to San Francisco and was picked up by a passenger. When she landed, instead of meeting Bernie with the coke, she went with the guy from the plane and got fucked silly for two days. Ten kilos of coke, gone.

People were freaking out. Susie had a boyfriend in Miami. This poor kid, not only did his girlfriend fuck this guy behind his back, but me and Albert's guy Rubio picked him up and broke his arm, then held him in the trunk of a car until Susie turned up. But it ended well. Susie showed up with all the coke a couple days later. She brought back the money to me so I could pay Albert. Her boyfriend got to live.

THE WAY I worked it with Bernie was, I marked up his price 10 to 30 percent over what I paid Albert. The price Albert charged me per kilo changed week to week, going anywhere from $18,000 to $50,000. In the early days coke was usually at the higher end because nobody could ever get enough. Sometimes the cops or Customs Service would get lucky and bust a smuggler. Then the politicians would go on the news and announce, "We got all this dope, and we're winning the fight against drugs."

Were they really that stupid? When they made a bust, it sent prices higher. Even when everybody like Albert or me was holding coke, and our prices hadn't gone up, we'd raise them anyway. After a big bust, I'd add on a surcharge and tell Bernie, "Look at the news. They're arresting everybody. You're lucky I got this. I want five thousand dollars more."

I was always happy when they caught some dumb fuck with a boatload of coke. That meant more money for me. Thank you, cops.

Once Bernie got up to five or ten kilos a week, I had a hundred grand a month rolling in easy. I did very little work compared to running clubs in New York. I paid no tax to my uncles. Once a week Albert would have Rubio or Ricky Prado leave a car with cocaine in the trunk at a market. I'd have Susie's boyfriend pick it up and pack it into Betamax cases. After we broke his arm, this kid was very dependable.

MY BUSINESS was like any other business. You meet people. You build connections. I was constantly looking for bigger customers and bigger suppliers than Albert. I wasn't going to sell grams of coke to some jerk in a disco, but if I met interesting people who amused me, I'd sell them smaller amounts. I liked rich people. They were into the same things I liked—beautiful women, boats, horses, cars.

The thrills I used to get from drug rip-offs I now got from meeting different, strange people. For example, I liked to run on the beach. One day out running, I met a wealthy Jewish kid, Lev Davis.* We got to talking, and I found out he was hooked up with models and Playboy Bunnies. He had a beautiful boat that he used to take them on. Lev was a real cocksman. He and I wound up partying together with many ladies. All his friends were doctors, lawyers, and dentists, and they all wanted coke. In that day—1975—normal, wealthy Americans just wanted to live the good life. People didn't have hang-ups. They had money. They had nice houses on the water. They had boats, and coke made all these things even more enjoyable. Nobody was thinking about cops, or is this person an addict? None of that existed. This was just good times.

One day Lev called me and said, "Jon, I'm bringing you to a

---

* Lev Davis is a pseudonym to protect the identity of Jon's friend.

party. I'm going to turn you on to more beautiful girls than you've ever seen. We're going to my friend's house. He's going to love you, but I want you to bring him an ounce of coke."

"What's so special about your friend?"

"Jon, he's the greatest tit doctor in the world. Every model, stripper, and beautiful woman who wants to take care of herself is dying to get a pair of tits from him. He's got women flying in from Hollywood just to get his tits."

I'll tell you the truth. I did not see my first pair of fake tits until after I got to Miami. It was a girl I picked up at Sammy's Eastside, maybe a year before I met Lev. I had her at my place, spinning her around, turning her this way and that, and those tits stuck up like rockets. I had to ask her about them. I thought I was seeing things. She explained they weren't the breasts she was born with. They had been given to her by a special kind of doctor. I'd never heard of such a thing. It was like putting a man on the moon. You can make big, beautiful tits from nothing?

Obviously, I was intrigued when Lev invited me to a party at a prestigious tit doctor's house.

The doctor had a sensational three-level place on the water. There were gorgeous women everywhere. Half were flat-chested. Half had big racks. These were the doctor's Before and After girls.

Lev introduces me to the doc. I toss him an ounce. The doctor says, "Come up to my bedroom, and we'll try it out."

There are people doing lines everywhere. *Why hide out upstairs?* I think. But I go upstairs with him. We throw some lines on a mirror and get high. The doc says, "This shit's great, but usually I don't like to put it in my nose."

He gives me this funny look, like he wants me to ask where he normally puts it. But I don't need to know. Whatever people do, that's their business.

I spent the rest of the night partying with the After girls. As I was leaving, the doctor said, "Come to my office sometime. I'll show you pictures of all the women I gave tits to in Miami."

I never took him up on that. I didn't want to go to some doctor's office and look at surgical pictures, even if they were of tits.

I went to more parties at the doc's house, and I saw he always went off alone to get high. It didn't make sense.

One day Lev and I go out on a boat with the doctor and five or six girls. They all have their tops off and are swimming, having a good time, and the doc pulls me aside and asks, "Is it okay if I go down by the head and shut the door for a moment?"

"What are you going to do? Fuck somebody?" I ask.

"No, no, no."

"Look, doc. You always disappear at your house. What do you do? Do you jerk off before you fuck someone, so you don't have to come quick? Are you a gay? I'm not judging you. I just want to know."

The doctor walks me behind the cabin and pulls out a little bag with a syringe in it. Instead of a needle, the syringe has a plastic thing on the end. "Don't tell anybody," he says. "This goes up my rectum. I mix the coke into a solution, and I shoot it up my ass."

"What the fuck are you talking about?"

"I'm a doctor. If you looked into the ass of a person, you'd see there are more connections to your blood system than anywhere. When I shoot the coke up my ass, it gives me the most explosive high you could ever imagine. Then I run and I fuck somebody, and it's the greatest high in the world."

"You swear you're not bullshitting me?"

"You want me to do it to you?"

I laugh at him. "Get the fuck away from me. I'm not a faggot, okay? But go ahead and knock yourself out."

These wealthy people, you never knew what they were going to do or say next. They were not uptight people at all, and they didn't look down on me. I fit in. Not that I was putting shit up my ass. Between Gary Teriaca and me, we were probably moving another five to ten keys of Albert's blow just to Miami's upper classes every month. This was not a world Albert could enter so easily. Politicians would take Albert's money, but nobody was going to invite that crazy-eyed Cuban to a fun party. He'd have been a disaster. If a doctor had offered to put a syringe up Albert's ass, he would be dead. Everybody on the boat would be dead. The whole party would be chum on the water.

33

J.R.: Cocaine put me back in the good life. I got a beautiful new dog, a Doberman, to keep Brady company. I named him Chulo, which is Spanish for "pimp." I got a nice wardrobe, but with a Miami flavor. Sneakers were in. The more sneakers you had, the better you were. Everybody wore white Adidas, with the stripes on the side. To me, Puma Bananas were the end-all of sneakers. I loved my Bananas. The Puma Banana was a yellow sneaker with black on the side. They lasted maybe a month, and then you had to throw them out and get a new pair. I went crazy with Bananas. Then it was saddle shoes. I couldn't get enough saddle shoes.

People in Miami had a casual but classy look, Armani jackets and jeans. When *Miami Vice* came on TV, people said Don Johnson invented the Miami casual look. Not true, bro. He was copying us. Not me personally, but everybody I knew.

One thing I liked about Miami was the weed. I

personally smoked weed all the time. In New York there was a prejudice against wiseguys smoking weed. People looked funny at Andy
and me when we smoked out. In Miami nobody cared. I could be
myself. I was lucky with pot. It never dulled my senses. I was never so
high that I couldn't shoot somebody or beat him when I needed to.

My friend Mouse, the pothead judge, turned me on to a nice
little Spanish house up the street from him on North Bay Drive. I
planted gardenias in the front and bougainvillea along the sunny
side of the house. I love the explosion of red and purple in a bougainvillea, and to me the fragrance of the gardenia is un-fucking-
real. In my backyard I had a little pool. Beyond that I had all of
Biscayne Bay.

I put in a dock and a boatlift and got my first Cigarette racing
boat—a beautiful maroon and gold 28, with twin engines. I got
into diving for conch and for lobsters. Some mornings I'd wake up
before the sun and drive my boat to the Bahamas. If the sea was
flat, I could make it there in ninety minutes. In Bimini there was a
bakery where they made bread that was out of this fucking world.
Because of how the air is down there, you could taste the sea in the
bread. It went perfect with lobster. That was my life. I'd drive to
Bimini to pick up a loaf of bread.

The first club I got active in was the Palm Bay. It was built on
pillars over the water, and you would dock your boat at the club
by driving it through a tunnel underneath. All the celebrities visiting Florida played tennis at the Palm Bay. I went because it was the
easiest place to get to by boat from my house, and they served a
fantastic lunch.

Gary Teriaca was into Porsches, and he turned me on to the
911. I fell in love with that car. My first was champagne with a
black interior and a turbocharger. We had a terrific Porsche-Audi
dealer in town who never had a problem accepting a shopping bag
of cash for payment. Over the years I probably bought a hundred
Porsches. Many I gave away to different women.

Bobby Erra knew a lot about boats and boat engines, and he
turned me on to a custom shop run by Butch Stokes, who'd been

the racing-team mechanic for Porsche.* I told Butch, "I want my Porsche to be faster than any other Porsche on the road."

Two weeks later I picked up my Porsche. Everything looked the same except Butch had put in a little dial on the dashboard. The dial had numbers on it, from one to fourteen. Butch explained the dial was to set the air boost in the turbo. A factory Porsche comes with a turbo boost of six.† Now I had boost that I could dial up to fourteen. My cylinders were bored out. I got special oil coolers. Butch said, "I'm going to have to teach you how to drive this car because, honest to God, this car is ridiculous."

"Okay, bro."

We drove it out to I-95, and I stopped it in the middle of the highway. We had all these cars honking and pulling over to the side. But fuck those assholes, I needed to see what my car could do. I turned my dial up to fourteen and punched the gas. The front tires rose off the fucking ground. I did a wheelie down the highway like my car was a motorcycle. Butch started yelling, because a car doing a wheelie you can't control, so I let off the gas, and *boom,* the front wheels smacked the ground. We easily hit 160 or 180. Butch did not lie. That car was ridiculous.

I got thirty-six speeding tickets in the next four months. I had more legal trouble from tickets than I ever got from doing a murder. That's a fact.

GARY TERIACA was becoming a high-flyer. He and his girlfriend Carol Belcher moved into a $400,000 house on Sabal Palm Drive, in Bay Point Estates.‡ Carol was close friends with a state attorney, Dick Gerstein,§ who lived nearby. When I first went to Gary's

---

* Abner "Butch" Stokes is better known as the racing boat engine mechanic who founded Stokes Porsche of Hollywood, Florida, in 1973 and is still in business today.
† Boost numbers refer to pounds per square inch of air pressure above normal atmospheric levels.
‡ Sabal Palm Drive was among the most exclusive addresses in Miami in the 1970s. Bay Point Estates was among the first gated communities on Biscayne Bay.
§ Richard Gerstein was Florida state prosecutor for Dade County and served six terms from 1956 to 1980.

house and he invited me to have drinks with his new best friend, the top crime fighter in the county, I was a little bent out of shape. Gary would have Dick Gerstein downstairs laughing at the bar, and upstairs in the study was where we kept the cocaine we got from Albert. Gary felt his house was a safe place to hold coke because Bay Point was a gated community. But it made me uptight. I remember sitting in the kitchen once holding five keys of coke in a gym bag while I chatted with State Attorney Gerstein. It was not a comfortable feeling. Gary always said Gerstein was a good guy. Later I found out Gerstein was a degenerate gambler who placed bets with Bobby Erra, so maybe he was right.*

NEXT TO cocaine and pussy, tennis was Gary's favorite thing. He was always trying to get me to play. One time he insisted I bring my racket.

"Okay, okay."

I show up and see some very attractive girls hopping around the court in their little tennis whites. Then this guy skips over with a sweater over his shoulders. He's a pretty boy like Gary, an old friend from college. His name is Steven Grabow.

Gary says, "Why don't you and Steven partner up?"

We knock the ball around for a couple hours, do some lines, have a few laughs. Later that day I bang one of the tennis girls in a little clubhouse by the court, which Gary's friend Steven thinks is

---

* Aside from Jon's assertion, there is no evidence that Gerstein placed illegal bets through Robert Erra, but Miami-Dade police intelligence reports from the 1970s noted personal ties Gerstein had with organized crime figures like Meyer Lansky. Gerstein is best known for his role in exposing money laundering in the 1972 Nixon reelection campaign, which helped to break open the Watergate scandal. Ironically, Gerstein was ensnared in a financial scandal after he and defense attorney F. Lee Bailey became directors of CenTrust bank, which in 1990 was linked to a massive money-laundering scheme involving BCCI bank, General Noriega of Panama, the Medellín Cartel, and Middle Eastern arms dealers. Gerstein avoided criminal prosecution but was reprimanded for "ethical violations," and his partner, F. Lee Bailey, was disbarred. Gerstein's final public role was to serve as Pee Wee Herman actor Paul Ruben's defense attorney after his arrest in a Florida adult movie theater for masturbating. Today, Dade County's Miami county court complex bears his name in stately letters: The Richard E. Gerstein Justice Center.

comical. He's a total pussy hound. We're all joking about this later, and Gary says, "My friend Steven has been living in Aspen, Colorado, the past couple years working as a ski instructor."

"What's it like out there in the mountains?"

"It's like Miami, except nobody can get any coke." That's how Gary's friend Steven put it.

Gary knew I was working with Bernie Levine to supply San Francisco. He wanted to run the same kind of setup with his friend Steven in Aspen. But the airport was small in Colorado, and there were rumors that the heat watched it. We decided the best way to move kilos to Aspen was to have guys drive it out. I helped Gary get started—got him cars to run the coke, and later hooked him up with a good customer out there. Gary would move a billion dollars of coke through that Grabow kid. It started with a tennis game. That's how the business was sprouting up then.

FOR A couple of years, me and Gary and Bobby had good times in Miami. Bobby stayed away from the coke business and from Albert San Pedro for a couple years, but we all partied together. The old nightclubs around 79th Street were dying.* Cubans were moving into the neighborhood. It was one thing for them to park your car at a club. Nobody wanted to sit next to them in a club.

Everybody moved to new hot spots—the Jockey Club, the Coconut Grove, the Bombay, and later the Cricket Club, the disco in the Quayside Towers.† People called the Quayside Towers the "Quaalude Towers." Quaaludes were the other great drug that people were taking along with coke. Quaaludes were more underground when Andy and I snuck them into the punch in our New York discos. In Miami you'd go out for drinks with a broad, and she'd bring her own Quaaludes. It wasn't like today, where a guy will sneak roofies into some poor broad's drinks so he can have his

---

* In 1981 the Dream Bar shut its doors and was turned into a punk rock club.
† Quayside Towers are premier condo high-rises in North Miami, built in the early 1980s, where units today go for several million dollars.

way with her. Back then broads would knock themselves out on purpose.

Me, Bobby, and Gary all had boats. We'd get six or seven girls, take them out on the ocean, tie our boats together, get the girls fucked up on Quaaludes and coke, and have a party. We had a girl get so wasted one time, she passed out, rolled off the deck, and fell into the water. Her girlfriends were so fucked up, they didn't even notice that she'd fallen off the boat. Finally I saw this stupid girl floating facedown in the water. Me and Bobby panicked. With all the shit we were into, a girl drowning from our boat could be very bad.

Gary swam out and dragged the girl back onto the boat. She was gone. Gary started pumping her, and water shot out of her mouth. He pushed on her chest and blew air into her mouth, and finally she started puking and coughing. She was a mess, but thank God she lived. This could've been an absolute fucking disaster.

I saw the oddest thing in Gary that day—something that really showed me he was different. After this girl came back to life, he went down in the boat and started crying. His reaction was very strange.

BOBBY ERRA liked to drink and party with women, but he was not a showy person like Gary. Bobby was understated. In that way he reminded me of Carlo Gambino. With his rich wife, Marcia Ludwig, Bobby led a more quiet life than we did.

Bobby was such a weirdo, his idea of a wild time was running his dogs on the golf course at the La Gorce Country Club. Bobby and Marcia had Airedales, and at night when the club shut down, we'd take his dogs out with my dog and run them on the grass. Bobby had paid off the greenskeepers to give him keys to everything. He kept a special cart that was souped up to go thirty-five miles an hour, and we'd run our dogs off it while we talked about business.

If Bobby hadn't been a gangster, he would probably have made a name for himself as a sportfisherman. He taught me more about fishing than anybody—flatfishing in the Keys, game fishing for humpback tuna in the Bahamas. Bobby had a Merritt boat,* and we'd go together for five-day tournaments. What makes the tuna a strong opponent is that not only is it a monster fish, but a tuna never stops swimming. If you want tuna, you wait until the water gets choppy, then throw out bait while you run your boat. A tuna will fight you for hours. I once caught a 426-pound fish, but Bobby routinely brought in fish over 700 pounds, which was incredible with that mutant hand of his. But every year we went to the contest, these same assholes in a beat-up yellow boat used to win. That's life.

Bobby was a cheap bastard. His Merritt boat was no good for taking women out on. Instead of buying his own Cigarette, he'd borrow mine.

I kept my boat raised on a lift above the water. If you kept it in the water, there was always some asshole speeding past in his boat, which could damage your boat if it wasn't on a lift. One day Bobby came over to borrow my boat and crashed it off the lift and sank it. He claimed the lift malfunctioned. I got the insurance company to pay for the boat, but this didn't help how I felt inside.

I was crazy for that boat. It was my first nice boat in Miami. I ended up buying a new Cigarette 35 that I named *Mistress*. She was a great boat, and I owned several more afterward, but I never loved a boat as much as my first Miami Cigarette. I was heartbroken when Bobby sank her. Absolutely heartbroken.

---

* Merritt is a manufacturer of premier sportfishing boats.

34

J.R.: Our coke business was picking up around the time the old generation of wiseguys was dropping like flies. My uncle Joe Riccobono died in 1975. Carlo Gambino died a year later. Bobby Erra lost his father the same month Gambino went. I had no fond memories of these people. I did not mourn the end of the good old days. I was already making more money with coke than I ever had working for the family.

For Bobby Erra, the death of his father gave him the go-ahead to get into coke. He saw the money me and Gary were making, and he jumped in with Gary to move Albert's coke out to Gary's friend in Aspen.

By the end of 1976 I was moving fifty kilos of coke worth half a million dollars or more a month and 10 to 30 percent of that was my profit. So much cash was a problem. Not every car dealer would accept grocery bags of cash for a car. It's challenging to buy a house for cash. When you have millions of illegal dollars coming in, it creates a new risk. If you spend it or put it in the bank, it can be just as bad for you legally as getting caught with a trunkload of coke. A pile of coke money is just as dangerous as a pile of coke.

One thing the Mafia did very good was launder money. Gambino had Andy and me take over nightclubs in New York to launder his money. Before everybody started using credit cards, you could take a bar or restaurant, put all your illegal cash through it, and pretend it came from customers. That's how you cleaned up your money and put it in the bank and paid taxes on it. You ran it through a cash business.

When it comes to criminality, money laundering is almost its own specialty. To me, it wasn't fun like robbing people, so I never paid much attention to it. In New York, if I needed to buy something expensive, I'd find a crooked businessman to take my cash and buy what I wanted in his name. He'd keep the title, so it looked to the bank like it was his, but I would use it.

In Miami I bought a couple of houses like that. And the way I partied and went through cars, I could burn a couple hundred thousand dollars a month. But it got to the point where no matter how crazy I went, I had boxes of money left over. I was choking on cash. I'd stuff it in cans or bags and bury it on pieces of land near where I lived. The dirt was my bank.

Bobby Erra still owned pieces of clubs, restaurants, and hotels that his father had controlled, and he ran money from his gambling business through these. He had a problem, though, when he tried to wash coke money through his Mafia businesses. The Mafia would want to know how he made that money. Was it drugs? They were just as bad as the IRS.

So Bobby started working with Albert San Pedro to launder his money. Bobby and Albert went in on a strip club together, the Pink Pussycat,* in Hialeah. Titty bars, because of all the cash that runs through them, were a great way to launder money. They still are.

---

* A strip club just over the Hialeah side of the border with Miami, still in operation today.

Another scam Bobby and Albert got into was the Puerto Rican lottery. Albert found a guy in the government office of the Puerto Rico lottery who he paid off to tell him when someone came in with a winning ticket. If the winner hadn't announced his winning ticket yet, Albert's guy would buy the ticket from him with Albert's dirty cash. The guy who sold the winning ticket would get a bag full of cash. Spending that money without paying taxes or getting caught would be his problem. Albert and Bobby would get a legitimate winning ticket. They would give it to a relative, or trusted associate, and that person would cash it in. They'd pay taxes, but the money they kept was now clean. Millions of dollars got washed through the Puerto Rican lottery that way. That's how Albert and Bobby paid people off. They'd give them a winning Puerto Rican lottery ticket.*

I'm only explaining this so you understand how much work it is to launder money. It's harder laundering illegal money than making it, in my view. Not having smart guys like my uncles to help me with laundering money was the one thing I missed about the Mafia.

THERE WERE other things I missed, too. In New York my uncles could take care of almost any legal problem up to attempted murder. Above that, they could help, but it was iffy. In Miami I was getting killed by traffic tickets. I'd throw the tickets out the window like I normally did in New York, but soon Florida cops started impounding my cars, threatening me with jail. I couldn't believe it.

I went to my friend Mouse, the pothead judge, and told him my problem. He said, "Don't worry. I'll work it so you appear in my court, and I'll fix everything."

---

* The Puerto Rican lottery-ticket-laundering scheme was probed in the early 1990s racketeering investigations of San Pedro and Erra. Erra's common-law wife, Marcia Ludwig—the longtime friend of Florida governor Graham's wife, Adele—testified to a grand jury that on a visit to Puerto Rico she obtained a winning lottery ticket worth a quarter million dollars. She denied that there was any impropriety in her purchase of the ticket. Investigators noted that Ludwig won the lucky ticket about the time of the scandal when she had enlisted Governor Graham's wife to help persuade him to pardon Albert San Pedro for his 1971 felony conviction.

And he did. Mouse almost cracked up when I stood up in front of him in his courtroom. But after he got me out of the first jam, I got many more tickets. Mouse came to me and said, "Jon, I love you, but there's only so far I can push it."

I didn't get mad. Mouse was a stand-up guy. But without him, I was facing real aggravation. I told Gary Teriaca about my problems. He said, "Don't worry, Jon. I know a lawyer who can fix anything. His name is Danny Mones."

Danny Mones was of the Jewish persuasion. He was about my age, and he'd grown up in Miami. Danny was not in the Mafia, but he was connected to a group of guys who were raised by Meyer Lansky.* Not like he fathered them, but he helped them go to law school and learn about illegal businesses. Danny's father, Al Mones,† was an old-time crook who'd worked for Lansky.

Meyer Lansky was very much alive in Miami in the late 1970s. He was a walking dinosaur like my uncles, and like them, he was out doing illegal things until his last breath. The place you'd see him was the Forge Restaurant, one of the finest eating spots in Miami.‡ Gary Teriaca and his little brother, Craig, practically lived there. It was the main spot for wiseguys and Jewish crooks because it was

---

* Meyer Lansky worked with Lucky Luciano to forge an Italian-Jewish alliance that dominated organized crime in America through the twentieth century. Lansky's financial schemes laundered billions of Mafia dollars and helped finance Las Vegas, and he worked closely with Cuban dictator Fulgencio Batista to build an Italian-Jewish crime empire in Cuba. With the fall of the Batista regime in 1959, Lansky joined the diaspora of American gangsters who fled the island. To evade prosecution in American courts, he sought asylum in Israel but was kicked out in 1972. After reaching a legal stalemate with U.S. authorities, he came to Miami, where it's believed he remained a shot-caller in the Mafia's vast financial dealings. When he died peacefully in 1983, his known assets consisted of little more than suits in the closet of the rented apartment he shared with his wife of more than thirty years, Thelma.

† Al Mones was an organized-crime partner of Meyer Lansky.

‡ The Forge, still popular today, opened in 1969 and defined Miami chic in the 1970s: "Lavishly decorated to resemble a San Francisco restaurant circa the turn of the century, the Forge has food and service that is equally lavish, making it one of South Florida's truly great restaurants. If you're seeking a fine piece of beef, accompanied by a bottle of 1947 Cheval Blanc or 1959 Lafite, served with efficient elegance, this is the place to find it." From page 84 of Harvey Steiman's *Guide to Restaurants of Greater Miami*, Los Angeles: Brooke House, 1977.

owned by Al Malnik, who was a half-assed Jewish wiseguy and social climber.*

The Forge had a terrific bar, where we all used to hang out.† One night I'm in there, and Gary Teriaca says, "There's somebody you got to meet."

He takes me into the private dining room behind the bar, and I see an old Jewish guy, Meyer Lansky. He's got a nice head of hair, and he's wearing a suit with a bow tie. He looks like an appliance store salesman. Gary introduces me as Jon Roberts.

Lansky tilts his head back and says in his thick, old Jewish-guy accent, "What was your father's name?"

"Nat Riccobono."

He looks at me like he's seen a ghost. He grabs my shoulder and says, "I knew your father forty years ago. He was with Lucky Luciano all the time."

I wouldn't know if that was true or not, since my father barely talked. Lansky asked about my father. I told him he went back to Italy, and I hadn't heard from him since. Lansky said, "If you ever need anything, ask me."

Hearing those words, Gary Teriaca believed I had a favored relationship with Lansky. There was nothing between Lansky and me, but because Gary and other people now believed there was, it caused some problems for me later on.

---

* Alvin "Al" Malnik was rumored, but never proved, to be a front man for Lansky. After Lansky's death in 1983, it was alleged that Malnik was heir to Lansky's criminal organization, though Malnik denied any connection with organized crime. In 1982 a valet was nearly killed when a bomb planted in Malnik's Rolls-Royce exploded outside the Cricket Club. The crime has never been solved. Malnik, who is seventy-nine years old today, is best known for his relationship with singer Michael Jackson. In 2003, when Jackson was facing trial for child molestation in California, he stayed at Malnik's home in Miami and named Malnik godfather of his child, Prince Michael Jackson II, aka "Blanket." Jackson later had a falling-out with Malnik and accused him of scheming to take control of his multimillion-dollar music catalog. After Jackson's death Malnik claimed that Jackson had named him as executor of his estate. The validity of his assertions have been vigorously disputed by some legal experts.
† "The big negative point [of the Forge] is the cocktail lounge, from which raucous rock music sometimes emanates, to be heard throughout the restaurant, which is

. . .

ITALIANS HAD a holy reverence for Lansky. They talked about him like he was the pope. Obviously, he was more important than the pope because he helped them hide their money. When I met Danny Mones, he had none of that holy reverence for Lansky. "I heard you know the old cocksucker," he said.

Danny Mones knew him better than anyone because of his father. Danny's business partner, Ronnie Bloom, was the son of Yiddy Bloom, another famous old-time gangster.* Danny knew every trick there was.

Danny did more than fix tickets for me. He did everything. He was like my mafia. He was the guy who helped me launder millions of dollars. He became my partner in real estate, buying horses, and running dummy companies. He was so good at crooked things, he ended up becoming Albert San Pedro's lawyer. We were his two main clients.

Danny was a funny guy. He was very short, maybe five-five. He was fat and had a small face with squinty eyes like a rodent. He truly had the face of a rat. Sometimes he'd talk tough, but when the shit hit the fan, he'd run with his arms flailing. He was a pure coward, but with a big mouth.

Danny didn't know how to argue in court. He had another lawyer who did that. The one thing Danny knew was how to buy off judges. He was like the Albert Einstein of bribery, a genius. After I turned Albert San Pedro on to Danny, those two practically competed to see who could bribe more politicians in the county.

Albert held his San Lazaro dinners where he paid off judges. Danny held "honorary" dinners, where he'd honor the achievements

---

not conducive to elegant dining." From the previously cited *Guide to Restaurants of Greater Miami*.

* Ronnie Bloom's father, Harry "Yiddy Bloom" Blumenfeld, was the brother of Isadore "Kid Cann" Blumenfeld, a Minneapolis mobster convicted of murder and running a prostitution ring. Both brothers moved to Miami in the 1960s and worked closely with Meyer Lansky.

of a judge or some other crooked official. Danny would come to me and say, "I'm holding a party to honor Judge So-and-so for ending youth crime"—or some other noble bullshit—"and I need a hundred thousand dollars."

The dinners cost only a fraction of that. The rest was for the payoffs. Danny held the dinners either at the Coral Gables Biltmore or at a club at the University of Miami, also in Coral Gables. Coral Gables was good because many judges and public officials lived there. They could drink their brains out and not have far to drive home.

We could use the University of Miami because Danny's little brother went there. It seemed to me that that guy went there for ten years. He must have been a real scholar. Danny sponsored him at the university and made himself a big shot at the school by donating money. Using the university made his dinners look clean. Sometimes Danny would give a big check, with my money, to a charity at the dinner. But what the politicians came for were the party favors. Danny knew the special things each crooked judge liked—Cohiba cigars, Jim Beam, shirts from London. He would give the judge his little gift, and there'd be cash in an envelope with it. Danny was unbelievable. He got state judges, circuit judges, county commissioners. The only thing Danny couldn't get was a federal judge. Because they're appointed and they don't have to pay for campaigns, they're tougher to bribe. But all the rest, even if they were too clean for cash, they all took campaign contributions. I helped a lot of judges get elected in the 1970s and 1980s.

Once Danny and I owned the judges, the trick was working the prosecutors. From a legal perspective, even if you own the judge, you're much better off if you don't go to trial. Plus, that adds court costs to your bribery expenses.

What Danny would do is go to the prosecutor before a trial. He could not tell the prosecutor he'd bribed the judge. He'd say, "What's the sense in you knocking your brains prosecuting this case, when you know we're going before Judge So-and-so. We all know what a liberal judge he is."

"Liberal judge" was a code Danny used that meant this judge

was in his pocket. Most of the time Danny could talk the prosecutor into throwing out a case before it ever went to trial.

As good as Danny was at bribery, he was a moron of a lawyer. For arguing cases in the court, he had a partner, Frank Marks.

FRANK MARKS: Danny and I practiced in the same office for seventeen years. Danny didn't have many friends. He was a very bad lawyer, and he would insult the other lawyers. He'd get a case and tell the other lawyer, "I'm going to take your ass and wipe the sidewalk up with you. You don't know shit."

Then he'd run into my office and say, "Frank, you need to take the case."

I was the litigator. I met Danny after he had a case against me in court, and I won. He insulted me in the hallway, and I punched him. Somehow that led to me sharing an office with him.

I was very stupid when I started with Danny, because I didn't know he was greasing the palms of the judges. I learned of this after I took a case for Danny. I won the case, I thought, because I'd argued it so eloquently. A week later I was walking down Flagler Street and I saw the judge. He brought up the case I'd won in his court, and he said, "Danny is the tightest wad I ever saw. I thought the case was worth a better tip."

I went back to the office and told Danny what the judge said, and Danny said, "That son of a bitch! I gave him ten grand."

I'd been practicing law for more than ten years in Miami, and until that day I didn't know it was possible to grease a judge's palm. I was scared to death to offer somebody a bribe. But Danny had a gift.* He'd hint to a judge, "I'm available if you need a favor." Or

---

* In 1989 Danny Mones's lawful contributions to judges sparked a statewide controversy, as reported by David Lyons in "Court: Campaign Gift Was Conflict for Judge" in the *Miami Herald*'s September 21, 1989, edition. Mones's help in financing judges' campaigns led to a battle in the appellate courts and a call for reform that was subsequently abandoned at the urging of judges and lawyers who preferred the corrupt campaign finance system as it was—and remains.

he'd give the judge a legitimate campaign contribution after a ruling, so it couldn't be tied to a specific act.

Danny had funny arms that did not fit in off-the-rack shirts, so all his shirts were custom made. If a judge complimented him on his shirt, Danny would say, "I'll get you one." Then he'd send a young lady to the judge's office. Her job was to take his measurements and do anything else that pleased the judge in his chambers. We had a senior state court judge who used to come into our offices all the time to pick up his shirts. Other judges would come by with requests: "My son is going to get married to a wonderful girl. The newlyweds need a twenty-five-inch color TV."

It was unbelievable what went on. I knew of at least a half-dozen judges he paid off. Only a few were ever caught. A couple are still on the bench.

Of all of Danny's clients, there were two he never spoke to on the office phone, Jon Roberts and Albert San Pedro. Danny would run to a pay phone whenever he needed to call them. He said, "With these clients, we have to be careful of the FBI." Danny later got an office with Jon so they could meet and talk in person. That's how paranoid he was of speaking on the phone with him.

Because Danny was a pathological coward, he liked to brag about what a tough guy his friend Jon was. When I met Jon, I was surprised. He didn't talk about what a big shot he was or act tough. I found Jon to be a warm person. I'm several years older than he is. To me, he was a kid who was going places. He was a nice-looking kid. His hair was a little woolly, but that was the way young men looked then. I liked him. He was a one-hundred-percent up-front man. My biggest job with Jon was keeping him out of jail for his speeding tickets. He had a terrible problem speeding. He was compulsive.

Danny ran a lot of businesses with Jon, but I stayed out of those. I wasn't born yesterday.

J.R.: Danny and I started buying property in Coral Gables. We bought a hundred-unit building, a sixty-unit building, a bunch of smaller buildings. Later we got into developing Aventura. We had several companies together—J.P. Roberts Investments, Straight Arrow Investments, Good Deal Autos, Prestige Automotive, Mephisto Stables. We ran all our companies out of an office on Biscayne Boulevard.

We got into car leasing and trading because the car business was a good way to launder my money. We brought in a professional manager from a Ford dealer in New Jersey to run our car businesses. We also partnered with Ron Tobachnik.* Ron was a hit man out of Chicago, but he also had a car business in Miami. He was a very bad guy, with a lot of balls, but unfortunately he was very stupid. He ran a car-rental company out of the Holiday Inn at Fort Lauderdale Airport that I took a piece of.

When it came to growing my legitimate businesses, I never had a vision like "Let's build a factory and produce lightbulbs and make something useful." I just wanted simple, easy ways to launder money.

The great thing about the car business was that, as I started moving more coke around the country, I could draw from the business and use plenty of vehicles. I'd give my drivers different rental cars, so they were harder to follow in any kind of pattern. Plus, if, God forbid, one of my drivers was stopped and they found dope in the trunk, he'd then have a defense that it wasn't his car. How did he know there was dope in the trunk?

·IN MY first few years in Miami, I only had one non-driving-related problem with the law. My business was growing. I tried to keep my nose clean. But one time in about 1977 I was in the Palm Bay Club with Gary Teriaca. A big-shot jerk at the bar made an obnoxious comment to Gary about something. Gary said something back, and the guy hit him. Gary was a wiseguy who could not fight. I reacted out of instinct to defend him. Gary always drank Johnnie Walker, with the bottle and a shot glass on the bar in front of him. I picked

---

* Ron Tobachnik is a pseudonym to protect the identity of Jon's former business partner.

up his Johnnie Walker bottle and broke it on the guy's head. My mistake was, after the guy went down, I got on top of him and shoved the broken bottle in his face.

People in the club, they did not want to see that. They weren't used to seeing how people fight in the real world. They started screaming. Some idiot called the cops. Next thing, I'm being led out of the Palm Bay in handcuffs. It was very awkward for me.

I was going to be charged with assault with a deadly weapon. The guy I'd hit just about had his nose cut off his face. The prosecutor told Danny Mones, "This one is going to court."

But I was so confident in Danny's bribery skills that the night before the trial, I partied my guts out. The next morning I phoned the clerk of the court and said, "Tell the judge I ain't coming."

Danny paid a doctor to write a note saying I was too sick to go to court. Frank Marks argued some bullshit to the judge. Meanwhile, the guy I allegedly assaulted moved out of the state and refused to testify. I made sure of that. The judge realized he had a difficult election coming up, and it would be even worse if we started contributing money to his opponent, so he threw out the case.

When I was younger, I used to believe that the Mafia got all its power from brute force. But as I got more in the world and analyzed how to run my business, I realized that force only goes so far. There's more power in paying off the right politicians. When I looked back at what my uncles accomplished with Gambino, they got much more done with lawyers and payoffs than by killing people. This is true at any level of illegal work. If you're going to commit crimes, don't be a jerk and wait to get a good lawyer. Get your lawyer first, and pay off all the judges and politicians before you do illegal things. If you follow my advice, you'll thank me.

35

J.R.: I never smoked a cigarette in my life. I was always into fitness. I ran at least five miles on Miami Beach every day. Running was how I made friends, too. The 1970s weren't just about coke and Quaaludes. Fitness was a big craze in Miami. It was how I met Harvey Klug.* He was a runner on the beach. Harvey's relatives owned a Nathan's Hot Dog store in New York, and he was one of those nice, straight-arrow kids who grew up without a care in the world. Unfortunately, he got interested in betting, and after I hooked him with Bobby Erra, he ended up owing some money. The truth is, if you were hanging out with me, you weren't ever a completely straight arrow. But everybody liked Harvey. He was such a good runner, he worked out with some of the top athletes. One day Harvey said to me, "I've got to turn you on to my friend."

---

* Harvey Klug is a pseudonym to protect the identity of Jon's friend.

"Who's your friend?"

"Mercury Morris."*

Merc was an amazing runner, ballplayer, you name it. I used to play basketball with him and some of his NFL friends, and these guys were so good, they could have played in the NBA. They would kick my ass up and down, but it was worth it just to play top athletes in the world. Merc was also one of the first spokesmen for Nautilus workout equipment. He'd travel around the country promoting fitness.

Merc also loved smoking weed and doing lines. One time we were at a club doing lines right at a table. Some asshole fan came up to him and said, "You're a professional athlete. You can't be getting high."

Merc laughed, "Hey, man. Watch me play on TV. You'll see how high I am."

It was a little sad, because Merc was traded, then retired from the NFL right around the time he made that boast. By then I'd started hooking him up with kilos of coke that he was selling to his friends in the NFL with Randy Crowder,† another football great.

I'll be honest. I probably sold them coke because I liked hanging out with these guys. Movie stars don't impress me. Athletes do, and one of the magical things coke did was bring these heroes into my world. Merc was a special guy. Not just a great athlete—he had a heart. He went through some troubles. At one point he came to me needing money really bad, and he offered to sell me his Ferrari Daytona. He was so desperate, I gave him a ridiculous amount for the car, like fifteen grand. When they arrested him in 1982 for drug trafficking, he was not caught with my coke, but he could have given up my name anyway, and he didn't. He was such a good guy,

---

* Eugene "Mercury," or "Merc," Morris is the former Miami Dolphins running back who helped lead the Dolphins to two Super Bowl victories. In 1982 he was convicted of cocaine trafficking. After serving four years in prison, his conviction was overturned on appeal. Today he is a motivational speaker.

† Crowder is a former Penn State All-American player. As a defensive lineman for the Dolphins, he was arrested in 1977 for selling a pound of coke to an undercover cop. He is the father of current NFL player Channing Crowder.

I felt a little bad for being so rotten to him with his Ferrari. But I'm not the good guy. That's not my role.

As MUCH as coke brought me up in the world, sometimes it did bring me down.

One day the Buffalo Bills were coming in to play Miami, and Merc called me up. He said, "Jon, I'm going to bring a guy by your house."

"Merc, you're my man. Bring anybody you want to bring."

I'm in my house on Bay Drive, and in walks Merc with O.J. Simpson. I was taken aback. Here was O.J. Simpson—Juice,* one of the best running backs in history—in my house. We sat down and started putting shit up our noses, and everybody's high as a motherfucker, and everybody's laughing. O.J. turns to me and says, "Hey, man, if you're ever in Buffalo, look me up."

I said, " 'Ever in Buffalo'? Juice, are you out of your fucking mind? I ain't never going to be in Buffalo unless they blow it up and put the pieces on a barge and bring it down here where it's nice. What the fuck is wrong with you?"

I don't know what came over me. I guess O.J. rubbed me the wrong way. After an hour in my house, it was tiring to be around him. Even though all of us were doing coke, O.J. went beyond. He was a coke fiend. He was crazed.

Talking to O.J., the other impression I got was that he was very fortunate he had his talent as a running back. Without that, he would have been lucky to work flipping burgers. I'm not saying O.J. was a dummy. He told a lot of funny stories. But he was very stuck on himself, and I didn't see that he had the brains to back that up.

When O.J. left my house that first night, I was glad.

A FEW weeks later he showed up again with Merc. After a few hours Merc had to go home to see his kids. Like I say, Merc was a good guy.

Now I'm alone with O.J. He came on a Thursday night, and the

---

* Juice was a popular nickname for Simpson in the 1970s.

next day he's still in my living room, blasted out of his mind, doing more lines. Suddenly I'm his babysitter. Outside of doing my coke, O.J.'s only other interest was, he wanted to fuck any white girl there was. But he was too crazed to leave the house. The easiest thing was to put him in the guest room and bring in a bunch of hookers. They could be ugly, as long as they had bleach-blond hair and were white. He'd party with one or two girls for a couple hours, then he'd want the next ones. I kept a small herd of whores in my living room, feeding them booze and blow, so they could be on call for O.J.

Saturday night I go into O.J.'s room and say, "Look, man, don't you got to practice with your team? Isn't there a curfew?"

"Curfew?" he says. "I'm O.J. I do anything I want."

"Juice, you got a game tomorrow in Buffalo."

"As long as you get me on the first plane in the morning, I'll be fine."

By Sunday morning the man is totally, totally gone. He's burned through so much blow, so many whores, his eyes don't even focus no more. He's awake, but his head is rolling on his chest.

I call a friend to help me carry him to my car. By the time we get to the airport, O.J.'s in another world. I slap him in the face and shout, "Juice, I'm going to give you a big fucking line." I spoon-feed a mountain of shit up his nose. I thought it would wake him up, but it works the opposite way. He goes out cold.

He's almost in a coma when we carry him out of the car. A sky-cap gets us a wheelchair, and we roll him into the airport. O.J. was famous then for that commercial where he jumps over hurdles at the airport.* As he rolls him through the airport, my friend is goofing on the ad, shouting, "Go, O.J.! Go!"

We push him right up to the gate. I find a stewardess and say, "Ma'am, Mr. Simpson drank a little too much last night. Can you pour some coffee down his throat and make sure he gets on the flight to Buffalo?"

---

* A Hertz ad that ran in the 1970s featured O.J. leaping over obstacles in an airport while an old lady shouts, "Go, O.J.! Go!"

O.J. finally opens his eyes. "Hey, man. Where am I?"

"You're getting into an airplane."

"Jon, I left my rental car at your house."

"Don't worry, Juice. I'll return it."

"Just leave it until next weekend."

"What do you mean, 'next weekend'?" I say.

"I'll be back, man. We'll party some more."

"Juice, man, I'm going to be out of town."

Obviously, I was lying. Next weekend I was going to take some quiet runs at the beach and work on my fitness.

36

J.R.: Phyllis started flying down to Miami to visit me after I got set up in the coke business in 1975. Italian girls are like ticks. Once they stick under your skin, it's hard to burn them out. I had mixed feelings for her. There were times still, like when she gave wise advice, that I was glad I had Phyllis in my life. Other times her voice made my stomach twist in knots. The one saving grace I had when Phyllis moved down was that she disliked my Bay Harbor house. It was too small for her. I gave her a condo in one of the buildings I owned in Coral Gables. The idea was, we would move in together when Phyllis found a decent place for us. Most nights I was free of her. Phyllis was happy if I kept her supplied with money for her shopping. I was happy if I could chase other girls.

One night I'm out at Sammy's Eastside with Hank Goldberg and Jimmy the Greek—another person who became my best friend because of my coke—when

Hank sees a beautiful girl at the bar. Hank goes over to her, starts laying some shit on her about what a big deal he is, and she says, "I don't give a fuck. You're too ugly for me. Introduce me to your friend."

Jimmy the Greek stands up and says, "Me?"

She says, "You're even uglier."

She points to me. That's how I met Lee Sweet.* Lee was involved with a guy who owned Chevrolet dealerships across the country. He paid for her to live in the Charter Club, which was a new building on the bay,† where all the girls lived who had somebody else paying for them. Even after Lee and I got together, she hung on to this old car dealer to pay her way.

Lee was just an average blond girl, but she was easy to spend time with because she liked boating. She'd stay over, and we'd swim in the ocean in the morning, and cruise around Miami in my boat, looking for good places to eat. One day Lee and I pulled up to the Palm Bay for lunch. I was salty from swimming in the ocean, so I told Lee I was going to shower by the pool, then meet her in the restaurant.

I decide to take a lap in the pool, and when I reach the other side, I see a knockout redhead sitting at the edge. I swim right over to her. *Bippity bop,* I make some jokes, tell her my name.

"I'm Betty Collins," she says.‡

"Do you like boats, Betty?"

"No."

"I know you like to spend money because you hang out here."

"Who says it's my money?"

"Whoever's taking care of you must be loaded, because you got a smile worth a million dollars."

"Well, Donny Soffer takes care of me."

---

* Lee Sweet is a pseudonym to protect the identity of Jon's lady friend.
† The Charter Club, built in 1973, is a twenty-three-story tower at 600 N.E. 36th Street in Miami.
‡ Betty Collins is a pseudonym for Jon's friend, who at the time he met her was a featured nude model in a popular gentlemen's magazine.

I knew Donny Soffer. He was a big-time developer in Miami who built Aventura.* He was one of the developers Danny Mones and I lent money to when he had problems with normal banks.

I say, "That old fuck takes care of you? Why don't you come on my boat tomorrow?"

"Okay," she says.

"I'll pick you up. Where do you live?"

"The Charter Club."

"Get out of here," I say. "I got a friend who lives in the Charter Club."

"What's her name?"

"Why do you think my friend is a she?"

"I'm pretty sure you have a she-friend who lives in the Charter Club, not a he-friend. But that doesn't bother me. We're adults."

I liked this girl's attitude.

In less than ten minutes I'd rinsed off the salt water, had a swim, and made a date. I had a nice lunch with the other girl, Lee Sweet, and got rid of her that afternoon.

The next morning I took Betty out on my boat, and she gave me the fuck of my life. We saw each other like that for a couple of weeks. Even though she had Donny, Betty had hit that point where she wanted to get more serious.

Betty invited me for dinner at her place in the Charter Club. She was preparing a nice veal piccata when I came in. I'm waiting for her to finish, and I decide to check my answering service. There's an urgent message from Lee Sweet, who also lives in the Charter Club. I go into Betty's bedroom and call Lee. She says, "I know you're in the building."

---

* "Donald Soffer's ingenious plan to transform a mosquito-infested swamp in North Dade County, Florida, into an upscale, planned community began more than 50 years ago when he purchased a 785-acre tract of marshland and sketched his vision on a cocktail napkin. Today, that parcel of land stands in the heart of the City of Aventura, one of Florida's most prestigious addresses." From a Turnberry Associates corporate profile posted in 2011. Despite Jon's assertions of having provided investment money to Donald Soffer, he has offered no paperwork to support the claims.

Stupid me, I drove to the Charter in my gold Porsche. It's a unique car, and the valet left it in front of the building. This is how Lee knows I'm here, and now she's going crazy.

I tell Betty I need to get something from my car, and I go up to the floor where Lee lives. Soon as I step in the door, Lee pulls my slacks off and starts sucking my cock. She tears off my shirt, my underwear, and I can't stop her because, I'll tell you the truth, nobody sucked a cock like Lee. I could not defend myself. She's licking my legs, sucking on my toes, putting her tongue God knows where. This girl was insane the way she gave head. She says, "Stand over here. I know you like to look out the window and watch the boats while I finish sucking your cock."

She knew I had a thing where I liked to watch the boats on the water when I was coming. It was my weakness. She moves me to the balcony window, and *boom,* I explode, watching the boats glide past. Next, I see Lee throw my pants, my shirt, my underwear, and my saddle shoes out the window. The whole blow job has been a trick.

"You're not leaving until you tell me who that other girl is," she says.

"Let me wash up, and we'll talk." I go in the bathroom, grab a towel, and run out the door. There's no reasoning with a girl when she goes crazy with jealousy. By now my appetite is really worked up for Betty's veal piccata, and strange as it sounds, Lee's blow job had me even hornier to fuck Betty. I'm thinking, *One girl gives the greatest head, and the other is the best fuck. I'll combine them in one night.*

I go to Betty's floor and knock on her door. She opens it, sees my towel, and I say, "I decided to jump in the pool, and some asshole stole my clothes from the changing room."

Unfortunately, Betty is not stupid. "You saw your other girl-friend, didn't you?"

"Betty, it was only a blow job."

I can see in Betty's face I've said the wrong thing. She says, "I'm going to shut the door now. Let's have lunch tomorrow. But nothing's happening tonight."

I get the message. I walk down to the elevator, and as I'm getting in, Lee Sweet comes bombing in. She's stalked me.

There's other people in the elevator. A family with their grandma, taking her out to dinner. The fact I'm in a towel is not a problem. It's Miami. I look like I came from the pool. But Lee starts laughing. She says, "What's under the towel?"

The other people in the elevator look at this crazy bitch and press against the wall. Lee tries to yank off my towel. I grab her hands, and she starts fighting me. "You motherfucker," she says. "I want you to walk out of here bare-ass nude."

She gets a surge of crazy-bitch strength, breaks free from my grip, and pulls off my towel. I'm standing there, no clothes on, no shoes, nothing. The family in the elevator, they are freaked out. The mother turns her kids' heads away. The grandma glares at me like this is my fault. I look at Lee and say, "You know what? Go fuck yourself."

The doors open, and I walk out bare-ass nude into the lobby. I go out the front doors. The valets all know me. They don't say nothing. The main valet runs to my car and screeches it up in front of me. He gets out, holds the door for me, and I just say, "Obviously, I'll tip you later."

I never saw crazy Lee Sweet again. I saw Betty, but it wasn't the same. These were semiprofessional girls. They dated guys for money, but the reality is, even whores have feelings. The truth is, whores have hearts the same as so-called regular women. That was one experience that made me consider trying to give domestic life with Phyllis another shot. I could have been arrested walking through the lobby with no clothes on. That's one risk I could not take. I needed to settle down.

37

J.R.: When my sister finally came down to visit, I told her I'd gone from my dog-training business into real estate, where I'd gotten lucky on some investments. Thanks to Danny Mones, this was partway true. We had an actual office* and I barely spent any time involved in moving coke. To my sister, it looked like I was in a new world.

By then she was head of personnel at a large company in New York, and she was as straight as could be. She was very happy for my seeming success as an investor.

My sister was worried about our grandfather, Poppy. Our grandmother had passed away, and Poppy was alone in Teaneck. I decided to bring him to Miami. I got him a place in South Beach, which was where all the old

---

* Jon's office with Danny Mones was located in a handsome neo-colonial building at 12700 Biscayne Boulevard, which is now home to the Transatlantic Bank.

people lived back then. After I got him set up, I'd take Poppy out in my boat and we'd fish. When he got too weak for the boat, I moved him to an apartment by a bridge where old people could stand and drop their fishing lines in the water. Later I moved Poppy to an assisted-living apartment. He even found an old broad who used to come by and hustle him—bake him pies and cook him dinner— because she figured he must have money from the way I helped him live.

JUDY: Poppy was very proud. Jon put him into a place that was way more than Poppy could afford on his Social Security. Jon told the landlord to lie about the rent to Poppy, and he secretly paid the difference. When Jon took Poppy shopping for clothes, he would tell the man in the store, "Don't tell my grandfather what the price really is." It was very touching to see Jon and Poppy together.

J.R.: What I did when I got Poppy down in Miami was, I used his apartments as stash houses for the coke I was getting from Albert. Who would ever think an old geezer in an assisted-living home was holding twenty keys of coke? I'm not saying I didn't enjoy seeing the old guy, but he served a purpose, too.

The other person from the past that came back into my life was my old Outcast friend Petey. Around the time I fled New York, he'd gone down on a drug charge that got him locked up for a couple years. When I heard he got out, I invited him down.

PETEY: I was happy to see Jon. I heard he was dead, but there he was. His life in Miami was beyond anything I would have imagined. He had six servants. He lived in a beautiful house, but it wasn't that big. *Six servants, Jon?* I had to laugh.

I had gone straight. My last year in prison I had joined a drug program to fake out the parole board, but after a while the things they said on the program started to make sense. When I visited Jon I was trying to clean up my life, and I wanted to tell him about it. I wanted him to know he was still my brother, even though I was leaving our world behind.

J.R.: Petey had got religion. He kept me up one night telling me we'd been living in hell our whole lives and he was getting out. He wanted me to join him. No thanks.

But I understood. He didn't want to be a bad guy anymore. He was trying to walk away from the evil side.

I left him alone one day, and when I came back, Petey had his face buried in a pile of coke. He'd broken into my party stash and snorted it like a pig. Being in my house, unfortunately, made him feel safe to go back to his old ways.

PETEY: The last time I ever got high was on Jon's coke. When I relapsed, Jon told me not to worry, he'd take care of me. I had another friend who offered me a job managing a porno bookstore in Miami. But something inside said, *Leave.* I could see Jon was going far with his cocaine schemes. But I was done. I checked into a rehab in Jersey and started walking in a new direction. My heart is with people from the street. Where I got my happiness after I cleaned up was working with guys in prison and helping any who wanted to escape from hell like I did.*

---

* Peter "Petey" Gallione became a drug counselor and then a senior director of New Jersey's statewide prison rehabilitation program. As a sworn officer of the Department of Corrections, he carried a badge, like any other cop. Upon his retirement in 2009, he bought a house in South Florida and moved into a home a few blocks from Jon's. Unaware that they lived so close, the two met by accident in 2010 and quickly rekindled their friendship, though not their criminal partnership.

J.R.: Normally, I don't trust people who go into the straight world, but I was proud when Petey left my house to get clean. I'm happy for him that he was able to leave my world.

THE LIE I told my sister about being in a totally legit line of work almost seemed true. Cocaine had elevated me above the streets. I did business in exclusive clubs. My lawyer was probably more valuable to me than a gun. But as straight as my life seemed, my existence had fewer limits than ever. I went to extremes to amuse myself.

When I look back on what happened with Princess the cat, I have to admit what I did was slightly insane. Princess was my cat. I always liked cats. There's people that say they're "dog people" or "cat people," but I don't agree you to have to choose one way. A dog is more able physically and mentally to do things with you, but cats have a lot of heart for their size. The way they stalk and hunt shows they have sharp minds. I respect cats as much as I respect dogs.

My yard on Bay Drive was a hangout for stray cats. The vacant lot next door, where I buried my cans of money, was where they played and hunted. Of all the cats there, a calico female rose to the top. She would come into my house and didn't have any fear with my dogs. They were killers, but this little sassy bitch walked among them. I named her Princess.

One day I found Princess hiding in the corner. She must have been out hunting or fighting another cat, and she got a stick in her eye. She wasn't complaining, but when she looked at me with that one good eye, it broke my heart.

I put her in my Porsche and drove 120 miles an hour to get her to the vet. Her vital signs were stable, but the vet could not fix her little eye. He turned me on to a lady vet who was a specialist. She couldn't save the eye, but she stitched it closed, and Princess had a full recovery. Within days she was running around like she still had two eyes.

Not a month later Princess disappeared. I got very uptight. I searched up and down the street to see if she'd been squished by a car. But no Princess. I had Albert's enforcer, Rubio, come over, and we went down the block banging on doors, asking people if they'd seen Princess. The last house we knocked on had a nosy broad living in it. She and her husband used to stand in their yard looking at me when I drove past. I always had a bad feeling about them. They claimed they were very successful wine merchants, and they looked down on everybody.

When this broad opened her door, she told me she didn't know anything about a cat with one eye. No sooner did she speak than Princess ran out from under her legs. I picked up my cat and said, "Thank you very much, you lying snob."

I went straight to Albert. I said, "Albert, I got these people on my street. I want you to burn their fucking house out of my life."

Albert said, "You want to buy the property? Is it a good investment?"

I explained to Albert that I wanted their house burned because they stole my cat.

"Are you out of your fucking mind, man?"

"Albert, I want those thieves out of that house. I don't ever ask you favors, do I?"

Albert waited until my neighbors went out to dinner one night, and he burned their house down. Albert kept his word, and Princess was safe from being kidnapped by my wacko neighbors.

I admit when I saw the smoked-out house a week later, even I thought maybe that was a little extreme.

I was moving from the neighborhood anyway.

PHYLLIS WAS on the warpath about finding a home for us. After my experience being chased naked from the Charter Club by that madwoman, I was open to the idea of settling down.

Phyllis teamed up with Danny Mones to find a house. Danny lived over on La Gorce Island* in a wild house where he made a dome over the bedroom that he'd painted like the Sistine Chapel, but with angels that looked like Playboy Bunnies. Phyllis had more respect for his financial advice than for his taste in painted angels.

---

* La Gorce Island is among the most expensive areas in Miami Beach.

She fell in love with a mansion on South Beach. They wanted $180,000, and I thought that was a steal. It was a grand Venetian palace. I could picture myself in it. But I showed it to Danny, and he said, "The neighborhood is shit. Never buy in South Beach."

Danny was wrong about the neighborhood and the house. Years later Versace bought that mansion.* I was a moron for listening to Danny.

As it happened, Danny Mones and I had some business with Donny Soffer, the guy whose girlfriend was cooking me dinner when I was chased out of the Charter Club. Donny was looking to borrow some money for his development in Aventura, and while we were talking about that, he turned me on to a house rental on Indian Creek Island.† It wasn't the biggest house on the island, but it was built almost over the water. From the dining room it looked like you were on a boat. I paid an ungodly amount to live there, $30,000 a month, but that's what I made from two or three kilos. Phyllis was satisfied. We tried having a domestic life. We'd have parties. We socialized with the neighbors. I'd take Poppy out of his rest home and have him over for dinners and sleepovers. He loved the dining room because of it being on the water.

But almost as soon as we moved in, Phyllis found another place she liked better, the estate at 121 Palm Avenue on Palm Island.‡ The main house was a big Spanish place, and it was next door to where Al Capone retired after prison. Capone used to fish out in the back, and they say he died there fishing, which is a nice way for a gangster to go.

---

* Gianni Versace, the Italian fashion mogul, was murdered outside the house in 1997. The home is now a hotel and club called the Villa.
† Indian Creek Island is sort of like the Liechtenstein of American municipalities. It is connected to Miami Beach but is an independent community of twenty-three homes. It has the eighth-highest per capita income of any community in America. When Jon lived there with Phyllis, his neighbors included Julio Iglesias, corporate raider Carl Icahn, Don Shula, and retired U.S. senator George Smathers.
‡ Another island enclave with a few dozen homes that today are commonly listed for more than $10 million each.

Phyllis talked me into buying it for $275,000.* Her life project became decorating the place. I dumped hundreds of thousands of dollars into that house, but the cost was nothing—a couple of buckets of cash I dug out of the ground. Most contractors in Florida back then took cash.

ANYTHING WAS possible in my world. I went to every club and knew everybody. First it was because I had the cocaine. Then it was because I had the money. I was happier not bringing cocaine to a club. I made more money off of bulk distribution. I went from being the coke guy to the rich coke guy to just the rich guy.

Money was a different kind of power than being a gangster in New York. I watched rich people and saw they can do anything. They get their power because top politicians in America suck their dicks just for a chance to ride on their yachts or sleep in their mansions. And when the top politicians are your friends, you've got it made. Truly rich people make the Mafia look like losers.

I saw how it worked when I was living on Indian Creek. One of my neighbors was a retired politician named George Smathers.† Phyllis and I went to a cocktail party at Smathers's house, and there I met a guy named Bebe Rebozo.‡

Bebe and I became very friendly. We went fishing together many times. He was a major crook, as big as Carlo Gambino, but he owned banks. Bebe helped me launder my money for a couple years.

---

* Records indicate the home on Palm Island was not purchased by Jon but by an individual whose name does appear on corporations Jon formed with his attorney, Daniel Mones. Jon says this person was a front employed to help him hide assets.

† Former U.S. senator George Smathers, who died in 2007, was originally a segregationist Democrat but changed his views. He forged close relationships with both John F. Kennedy and Richard Nixon. He sold Nixon the property on Key Biscayne that served as the Florida White House during his presidency.

‡ Charles "Bebe" Rebozo, who died in 1998, founded the Key Biscayne Bank and was among Richard Nixon's closest friends. Rebozo lived next door to Nixon's Florida White House residence. Rebozo was implicated in numerous underworld laundering and finance schemes but was never convicted.

Everybody said Bebe was Nixon's main man, but I didn't understand the power of this until a little thing happened.

One of my favorite spots to eat was Joe's Stone Crab in South Beach.* There is nothing like Joe's, because a stone crab is not like a Maryland crab, where you eat the meat off the body. A stone crab, you eat the legs and feet. You won't find the kind they serve at Joe's anywhere else. Joe's has always had their own boats to catch the crabs. Their crabs are colossal, and they serve them with the finest mustard sauce. I turned Bernie Levine on to Joe's when he visited from San Francisco, and he went nuts for them.

One day I went to Joe's with Bebe Rebozo. I told him about my friend in California wishing he could eat stone crabs, and Bebe said, "I can take care of it, Jon. You want to send him crabs tomorrow?"

The next day I went to Joe's and had Calvin, a black guy who worked in the kitchen, cook me a batch of crabs. Bebe told me to load them into a cooler chest. I drove the cooler out to Homestead Air Force Base† and asked to meet a colonel whose name Bebe gave me. This colonel takes the cooler, has his guys strap it into a fighter jet, and they fly it out to California.

A couple hours later Bernie called me. He told me when he got home from the Air Force Base in California and opened the cooler, the crabs were still hot. "How the fuck did you do this?"

"Don't worry, bro. The government took care of it for me."

I'm sure that fat slob almost choked himself eating them.

That night Bebe had me come over to his house, and he gave me two cases of Coors beer.‡ These they flew back on the jet from San Francisco. Bebe explained, "They started flying things for me when Nixon stayed at my house."§

---

* Opened in 1918, Joe's Stone Crab has been a favorite of generations of customers from Al Capone to J. Edgar Hoover to George and Barbara Bush.

† Homestead Air Force Base is about forty miles south of Miami.

‡ In the 1970s, Coors beer was not sold east of the Rockies and was highly sought after on the East Coast.

§ After he resigned the presidency and sold his Florida White House residence, Nixon was a frequent houseguest of Rebozo's.

"What? He forgets his slippers in California, they fly them out here on a jet?"

"That's how it works, Jon."

Think of all the people paying their taxes to support this nonsense. They train these guys to be the best fighter pilots in the world, and they're flying crab legs and Coors beer. That's the power Bebe had. Even though Nixon was a bum, thrown out of office, he still had enough pull that Bebe could use the air force as a delivery service for his friends. The square, normal people in this world don't have a clue.

EVERYBODY I knew in Miami was constantly seeking new amusements. I wasn't finding as much domestic bliss with Phyllis as she'd promised we'd have, so I was up for any excuse to leave the house. Me and Gary Teriaca and Bobby Erra started regular dinners at the Forge restaurant that turned into orgies. This began when a friend of ours, Leonard Codomo,* got the idea to hold a dinner with only us and Playboy Bunnies. The Playboy Club was big in Miami then, and Bunnies, or wannabe Bunnies, were everywhere. The orgies started by accident. The first time we held our all-Bunny dinner, they put us in the main dining room. Some of the Bunnies downed too many Quaaludes and got rambunctious. They started flashing the normal people out for dinner with Grandma or whatever, and Al Malnik, the owner of the Forge, told us next time he'd seat us in a secluded area.

The next week we showed up for another Bunny dinner, and they put us in a private room. It was the same room where I'd met Meyer Lansky. It had one big table where eighteen people could sit. The walls were covered in colored fabrics. There were chandeliers, oriental rugs. It was an unbelievable room. Once the champagne and Quaaludes started to flow, the Bunnies went wild.

---

* Leonard Codomo is a South Florida entrepreneur. His father was a Miami hotel developer who in 1951 was arrested for allowing members of the Bonanno crime family to use his hotels for "boiler rooms" where they peddled fake stocks and fraudulent real estate schemes over the phone and also took illegal bets. Codomo Sr. negotiated a plea allowing him to avoid prison.

One of them was actually not a Bunny, but a boat-show model named Monique. She had come to Miami to go to college, but she turned into a model and a freak. I had been with her once many months before this dinner, and she was the first girl I ever met who had pierced rings—like for ears—but in her pussy. Everybody starts partying, and I see Monique is missing. I look for her in the main dining room. I send a girl into the bathroom to search for her. No Monique.

I go back in the private room and see under the dining table, there's Monique. Bobby's fucking her with a piece of asparagus. Normally, if you think of fucking a girl with a vegetable, you think of a cucumber or a zucchini, but Bobby's got this little asparagus going in and out. Bobby was a traditional guy, not a freak. What an effect Monique had on him. Her freakiness was contagious. He's laughing. She's laughing.

I said, "Bobby, why can't we all enjoy this shit?"

Bobby says, "You're right." He decides to put Monique on the floor in the middle of the room so everybody can watch. Bobby wants to spread the tablecloth on the floor for her to lie on, and to show off his magician skills, he grabs the tablecloth with his claw-hand and yanks it. His idea was, he could pull it and all the bottles and plates would stay on it like when you see this done in the movies. Instead, everything spills over. He reaches out and pushes everything that's left onto the floor.

That's how the room started to get destroyed.

The Bunnies now got food and wine all over their clothes, so they start tearing them off. Monique climbs on the table. Bobby picks up the asparagus to fuck her some more, and Leonard Codomo says, "Hey, Bobby, is your dick bigger than the asparagus?"

I couldn't believe Codomo's balls in fucking with Bobby. Leonard was not a tough guy at all, and Bobby was someone, if you made fun of him, he would not forget.*

---

* Perhaps he did not forget. Police discovered during a 1990 rackateering investigation into Erra that throughout the 1980s he apparently strong-armed large amounts of cash from Codomo by threatening him with bodily injury and death.

But Bobby just laughed. He pulls his dick out, which was really disgusting to see because he's holding it with his claw fingers, and he says, "My dick's bigger than the asparagus, you motherfucker."

Bobby starts fucking Monique on the table. Then he takes his dick out and pushes the spout of a wine bottle into her. He must have filled her with red wine, because when he pushes his cock back in, wine comes shooting out from her pussy.

I'm so fucked up, I think, *Oh my God, she's bleeding.*

But another Bunny starts licking Monique's pussy, and I realize it's wine.

On the other side of the room I hear *slap slap slap*. Gary Teriaca has another Bunny bent over the table. He's fucking her from behind, and in each hand he has chunks of prime rib, and he's slapping the shit out of her ass with the beef. While he's slapping her, he keeps saying, "It looks like we're in hell now, doesn't it, Bobby?"

Gary, with the beef, was out of his mind.

As it progresses, we have a contest where we have the Bunnies kneel on the floor in a row with their asses in the air. We stick cherries in their cracks, like teeing up golf balls, and smack them. We bounce the cherries off the wall, and any girl that can catch a flying cherry in her mouth, she gets five hundred dollars. As you can imagine, the girls are leaping like trained seals to catch the cherries.

At some point Gary starts nailing these girls, moving down the line, poking each one. Me and Bobby and Gary and Leonard follow. We're fucking the shit out of these Bunnies, when *boom boom boom*—some poor waiter knocks on the doors. Bobby goes so crazy, he picks up his gun and shoots at the ceiling.

Bobby's gun fills the room with smoke. Now everybody's coughing and laughing. I stumble over to the door and open it a crack. There's two waiters on the ground, taking cover.

I tell them, "Do not come in here."

I go back in, and it's hours until we are all fucked out. The room is destroyed. The Bunnies are a mess—covered in garbage, food, wine, cum. They start digging through the trash looking for their clothes, combing their hair, putting on makeup—like that will help.

Monique gets upset because she can't find a gold earring that fell out of her pussy, and she accuses another girl of stealing it.

When we finally open the doors, the restaurant is closed. The waiters who stayed on looked shell-shocked. The maître d' comes over to say something. I shove a wad of wet money into his hand and say, "I'm too fucked up to talk. Just have Al send a bill. Whatever the fuck it is, I'll take care of it."

A few days later I go into my office with Danny Mones. He got the bill from Al Malnik. Danny says, "Al says you destroyed his restaurant. He's got construction workers coming in to rebuild it."

"What does he want?"

"Forty-six thousand dollars. Al says the fabric on the walls was very special. So were the rugs. It's a classy place, Jon."

Bobby and Gary and me gave Al the money, and he rebuilt the room. We came back and had more orgies and wrecked it again and again. We always paid Al for the damages. To spend fifty grand in a night was worth the amusement we got from it. Hell is expensive.

38

J.R.: Unfortunately, we weren't the only ones looking for crazed amusements at the Forge. One night in 1977 Gary Teriaca's little brother, Craig, was shot to death in the bar there.* This was tragic for the Teriacas. Even though Gary and his father, Vincent, were wiseguys, they had a special thing for Craig. They didn't want him in the business. They wanted him to be a normal Miami kid having fun on the golf course, chasing girls, whatever. Craig was a nice kid. He would come out with us sometimes, and he truly didn't have a wrong bone in his body. I always thought Gary was a little bit like him, and that's why he had trouble being comfortable with himself and tried to hide his cocaine use from Bobby. Both those brothers were a little soft.

For some idiotic reason, Craig used to sometimes drink with a guy named Richard Schwartz at the Forge.

---

* Craig Teriaca was killed at the Forge on June 30, 1977.

On his own, Richard Schwartz was what I call a "make-believe wiseguy." He was a nothing guy who owned a hamburger shop on Bay Harbor Island.* But because his mother was married to Meyer Lansky—making him Meyer Lansky's stepson—Richard thought he could do anything. If Meyer Lanskey is your stepfather, that is mostly correct.

Nobody really knows why Richard shot Craig Teriaca. They weren't close friends. They didn't have any business together. All anybody knows is, Richard was standing by Craig at the bar. Richard went to the bathroom to piss. When he came back, he accused Craig of stealing ten dollars he'd left at the bar. He screamed, "You piece of shit. You stole my ten dollars," and he shot Craig in the face. My belief is, Richard Schwartz was so drunk and fucked up on coke, his amusement was to shoot his friend.†

Gary wasn't there when his brother got shot, but he found out within minutes. Craig was still alive when they got him to the hospital. Gary had all of us come down to give blood. All of us—me, Bobby, Albert San Pedro, even Albert's bodyguard Ricky Prado—went to St. Francis Hospital that night.‡ This turned out to be a waste. By the time we filled out the papers to donate blood, the kid was dead. He died in Gary's arms. It broke Gary. He was sobbing like a baby. I'm not judging him. Anyone has a right to act like that if his little brother dies in front of him.

They arrested Richard Schwartz, but with his stepfather being Meyer Lansky, no way would the politicians let him go down for

---

* Bay Harbor Island was and is a fashionable shopping, nightlife, and residential district by Miami Beach. It is a series of islands connected by causeways and bridges to the wealthy residential islands where Jon and his friends congregated.

† Though witnesses differ as to whether the shooting stemmed from gunplay gone bad or from a serious argument, most agree that Schwartz appeared under the influence and out of control.

‡ Prado, who was a full-time Miami-Dade fireman at the time he was moonlighting for San Pedro, has a note in his employment files with the fire department that on the night of the shooting he took time off "for an emergency to give blood."

murder.* Don't be ridiculous. Think of all the judges Danny Mones and I owned, and we were little guys compared to Lansky. Judges in that city would rather shoot themselves in the head than put his stepson on trial for murder.

Knowing he was going to be freed put everybody in a difficult situation. This was a Jew-on-Italian murder. Every Italian likes revenge, but Lansky was the Mafia's top financial guy. He gave them Las Vegas. It's not that he owned it himself, but he knew who really did. He knew where all the secret bank accounts were.

And something Gary had to face was the fact that his little brother was no wiseguy. Would the Mafia risk pissing off Lansky over the shooting of a nothing kid? Their father Vincent was no big guy. He was a soldier who worked his whole life for Bobby Erra's father, Patsy, and Patsy was dead. Bobby was running things now, and he didn't want to start a war.

Italians like honor, but if you compare it to money, they like money even more.

People said that Lansky himself had no feeling for his stepson, but Lansky was crazy about Schwartz's mother. He'd been with her for years and years, and tough as he was, she led him by the balls.†

What most people hoped was, everybody would do nothing. But Richard Schwartz did a dumb thing. Instead of sitting in jail and waiting for people's emotions to calm down, he bonded out. The moron walked out of jail a couple weeks after the shooting and went back to work at his hamburger shop.

This made Gary's mind crazed. His father, Vincent, was crazed, too.‡ Gary came to me and said, "Jon, we got to take care of this."

---

* Not long after Schwartz's arrest, recordings of emergency calls from the bar to the police—which would have been helpful to the prosecution—were mysteriously destroyed in the evidence room.
† Schwartz's mother, Thelma, had been with Lansky since the late 1940s, and he was, by some accounts, devoted to her.
‡ Miami-Dade police investigators have speculated that the attempted car bombing of Forge owner Al Malnik in 1982 was carried out on the order of Vincent Teriaca, who held Malnik personally responsible for the shooting of his son. This theory was never proved.

I said, "Gary, forget about it, man. Obviously, you have the right to kill a person who kills your brother, but this is Meyer Lansky's stepson."

"Fuck this shit. I'm going to do what I want to do, and I don't give a fuck."

Gary was beyond reason. I didn't give a fuck about this personally. Couple of drunk guys get into a gunfight at a bar. Big deal. My worry was our coke business. Me and Gary were not partners exactly, but if he started a war and brought heat down, that could affect me. I'd learned my lesson from all the shootings that went down in New York. I told Gary, "If I can't talk you out of this, we will work on this together and do it the proper way."

Bobby, who was getting more involved in the coke business with Gary, saw things the same way. We'd help Gary, so getting rid of Richard would go as smooth as possible.

IF YOU'RE going to kill somebody connected to a guy like Lansky, you've got to ask permission. If you don't ask and you just kill a person—even if it's a guy like Richard, who you have a right to kill because he shot somebody for no reason—then a Lansky-type guy has every right to do whatever he wants to you. That's how wars get started for no reason.

In normal times the Mafia would have gotten involved. But the shooting happened right in that period when all the old guys were dropping dead. The old Mafia families were in chaos. So me and Bobby and Gary had to take care of this situation on our own.

They stuck me with the job of approaching Lansky to get permission to kill his stepson. Gary had seen how Lansky had talked about my father when we met, so in Gary's mind Lansky and I had a deep connection. In my mind, I wasn't so sure. Lansky's story about knowing my father was just words from an old man in the back of a restaurant. But Gary was too involved to make the approach to Lansky. And Bobby, because of his gambling business, definitely wanted to stay in the background. It was up to me.

Left: Before Jon was a cocaine cowboy, his mother took this photo (1956) when he was a child obsessed with conventional cowboys. Jon later changed his name to Jon Pernell Roberts after Pernell Roberts, star of *Bonanza*.

JON ROBERTS

Right: Jon's mother, Edie, was cursed with a beauty that seemed to attract only bad men.

JON ROBERTS

Jon *(third from left)* at a 1973 wedding in New York. It was his last wiseguy party before he fled to Miami. PETER GALLIONE

Left: Jon with his common-law wife, Phyllis LaTorre Corso, whose colorful family background made her the perfect mate—and a formidable enemy.
JON ROBERTS

Right: Albert San Pedro saw himself as a Cuban Al Capone. He was one of Jon's earliest Miami coke connections and allegedly helped Jon plan the murder of Meyer Lansky's stepson in 1977.
LOURDES VALDEZ

Max Mermelstein was the top American in the Medellín Cartel when Jon became his partner. Max's deal to supply car magnate John DeLorean with cocaine proved to be his undoing. JON ROBERTS

Rafa Cardona-Salazar was Pablo Escobar's top lieutenant, famous for his coke-fueled rages and who worked with Jon in Miami.
JON ROBERTS

Left: Mickey Munday, Jon's smuggling partner, was a technical wizard who didn't swear or take drugs. JON ROBERTS

Below: Rafa Cardona-Salazar, Mickey Munday, Rafa's wife, Odelia, a bodyguard named El Negro, and Max Mermelstein clowning around as old-fashioned gangsters at a county fair photo booth. SHARK BLUE

Fabito Ochoa, whose father ran the Medellín Cartel, recruited Jon to serve as the Cartel's "American representative." JON ROBERTS

Don Ochoa, the Godfather of the Medellín Cartel, would entertain Jon in Colombia by showing off his skills as a Paso Fino rider. JON ROBERTS

Jon called Henry Borelli his brother-in-law even after Borelli tried murdering him in 1979. Borelli is in prison for his role in the "Murder Machine" gang. SHARK BLUE

Jon's loyal and murderous bodyguard Bryan Carrera moonlit as the popular professional wrestler named The Thing. JON ROBERTS

Griselda Blanco's gang murdered as many as one hundred people while moving thousands of kilos of cocaine. Jon helped her hide out when the Cartel turned on her. JON ROBERTS

"FLORIDA BREEDERS' SALES FUTURITY
CHAMPIONSHIP - 1st Div.

MEPHISTO STABLE INC.'s "*Best Game*"
Judge Supreme - second
Ishudahadthat - third
Six furlongs 1:13:3

JOCKEY KEVIN WHITLEY up
JUAN SANCHEZ - TRAINER
TAMPA BAY DOWNS, FLORIDA
December 18th, 1982

When Jon owned Mephisto Stables, many of his horses made it to the winner's circle, as Best Game did at Tampa Bay Downs in 1982. JON ROBERTS

Meyer Lansky, the legendary Jewish gangster, whom Jon met with in 1977 to obtain permission to murder his stepson. SHARK BLUE

Jon's longtime girlfriend Toni Moon was the poster girl for the Ryan O'Neal movie *So Fine*. Jon and Toni later reenacted the photo with Jon in the place of O'Neal. BILLY CORBEN

Jon's mugshot taken after his arrest in the 1986 cocaine bust that unravelled his empire. JON ROBERTS

Barry Seal was a former commercial airline pilot hired by Jon to fly cocaine and later weapons. When he turned snitch, Jon helped the Cartel murder him. MDPD FILE

Detective Mike Fisten, a lead investigator on the organized-crime squad, tracked Jon in the mid-1980s, when Jon was known to the police only as the "Bearded Gringo." MIKE FISTEN

Jon enjoying his pool at his home in Hollywood, Florida.
EVAN WRIGHT

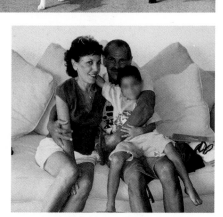

Jon walking his beloved dogs Sassy and Shooter near his Hollywood, Florida, home. EVAN WRIGHT

Jon's wife, Noemi, shortly after they met in 2003. JON ROBERTS

Jon with his son, Julian, and his sister, Judy. JON ROBERTS

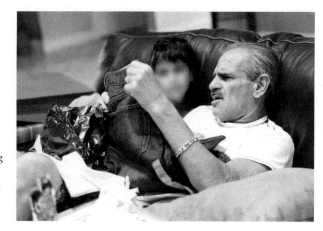

Jon receiving a birthday gift from his son, Julian. EVAN WRIGHT

In our circle, my lawyer Danny Mones knew Lansky the best. Danny told me the best way to approach him was to go to the beach by the Imperial House where Lansky lived.* His wife had a pair of little yappy dogs that he walked every morning on the beach. That was how the last giant of the old generation lived.

I went there a couple mornings but just missed him both times. Finally, I saw him come down on the beach. I will hand it to the guy, he walked around with no bodyguards. He was just an old man walking his toy dogs. After the life he'd lived, to be alone on the beach without a worry in his head showed his true power.

When I walked up to him, he looked like he was expecting me. I said, "My friend is very upset."

He said, "My stepson is very stupid, but I told his mother I would do the best I could for him. She wants nothing less. That's all I can do."

Even though he said he was doing his best, the way he spoke sounded the opposite of that—like he'd given up and was washing his hands of the matter.

I said, "What else can you do? People are upset."

"They have a right to be." Then he said, "You're a gentleman for coming here while I walk my dog. Let's talk again sometime."

A few days later Danny Mones told me I should go to Pumpernick's,† where Lansky liked to eat breakfast. I went in the next morning after I spoke to Danny, and Lansky was at a table eating his nova lox. When I walked up to him, he nodded and said, "You've got a free hand. God bless you."

He knew his stepson was a fucking moron. The poor kid he shot never did nothing to nobody, and we handled this the right way. We asked his permission. He gave us a pass to kill Richard Schwartz.

ALBERT SAN PEDRO was hot to help us. He liked killing people, and as crazy as he was, he was loyal. He was also smart. He was

---

* The building where Lansky lived is still located at 5255 Collins Avenue.
† A Miami Beach deli that closed down in the 1980s.

building his empire inside Hialeah, but he always looked for ways to prove his worth to Italians.

Albert being Cuban was an advantage. The cops were so stupid, they did not imagine Italians and Cubans could work so closely together. Anyone could see the Cubans parking cars at Italian nightclubs, but the idea that they could also be partners in a high-level hit did not occur to the cops. They still looked at Cubans like they were monkeys.

Albert said he would give us his best shooter, Ricky Prado. Ricky was clean. He'd never been arrested. He had his day job at the fire department, and he worked at the detective agency Albert ran. He was above suspicion.

I worked with Ricky when he delivered cars to us with Albert's coke. He was very dependable, and he was a quiet, clean-cut kid.* But I didn't have confidence in him to commit murder. Ricky had embarrassed me a few months earlier. It was a little incident, but since I was getting involved in a murder with the guy, it stuck in my mind.

Albert had asked for my help in getting him a dog. I called my friend Joe Da Costa in New Jersey, and I said, "Joe, I need a very bad dog."

Joe came to Miami with Sarge, a monster German shepherd. As you know, if you want your dog trained good, you need to be trained with him. Albert understood this and had Joe stay for a week in his house to work with him. Joe was a monster of a guy, and he brought a couple of his guys, who were also monsters, with him. I'm over there one day, and Ricky's sitting with me, Joe, and his monster guys. Ricky's a little guy, and I guess he wants to show how big he is, because he starts talking about the special training he has to kill people, the karate he knows.† It's odd, because Ricky almost never talks. Suddenly, he's telling these guys his hands are lethal weapons and garbage like that. He's such a joke that when

---

* Prado was twenty-seven at the time.
† During this period Prado was involved in a martial arts training gym in Miami with another of San Pedro's enforcers, Miguel "El Oso" Ramirez.

Ricky turns to leave, one of Da Costa's guys points to Ricky's gun and says, "Should we steal his lollipop?"

They laughed about that for days. I was not at all happy that Albert wanted Ricky to be the shooter. But I couldn't say to him, "Albert, I lack confidence in your hit man." He would have taken that as a personal affront.

When I met with Ricky, he was very excited about the job. He told me he was going to dress up in disguises for the hit—put on a tourist shirt, wear a fake beard—and I got a sinking feeling. I thought, *This kid has watched too many spy movies.*

Of course, I was proved wrong. Ricky did an excellent job killing Richard Schwartz.

39

E.W.: Jon and I step out of his Cadillac near the murder scene at East Bay Harbor Drive and 96th Street. The summer heat is softened by a breeze from Biscayne Bay. Jon wears shorts and a festive blue-and-white-striped shirt that looks like something Simon Le Bon could have worn in a 1980s Duran Duran video. He gestures to a footpath by the nearby Seascape Club apartments. The path leads to a small dock, but we can't see it because it's hidden by dense, flowering bushes. "That's where I waited in my boat the morning Ricky shotgunned Richard Schwartz," Jon says.

We cross the street to a row of shops along a brick, tree-lined sidewalk. We pass a real estate office and a pet-grooming clinic, then reach Asia Bay Restaurant. In 1977 this was Richard Schwartz's gourmet hamburger shop, the Inside Restaurant. "He came in to work here every morning," Jon says.

We walk to the parking lot behind the restaurant.

Jon stops by a parking space near the rear entrance. Jon says, "This is where Richard Schwartz would park his car. This was the place to get him."

From where we stand, it's about seventy-five feet to East Bay Drive and the footpath to the dock on the other side of the flowering bushes. Jon says, "After Ricky shot him, all he had to do was walk to the dock where I was with my boat. My job was to dump the murder weapon in the ocean."

J.R.: In an ideal world, you would murder somebody in private. It's safer that way. You can take your time and make sure there are no witnesses. But Richard Schwartz must have at least suspected somebody was going to kill him, and when a person's expecting to be murdered, it's harder to get close to him in a private place.

It's not easy to shoot somebody on the street. You've got witnesses. Unexpected things can go wrong. Bay Harbor only has a couple bridges to get on and off. But one advantage of shooting somebody in the open is that's where they least expect it.

What made the parking lot by Richard Schwartz's restaurant good was that the dock was close, so Ricky could give me the gun after he used it. The first thing you want to do when you shoot somebody is get rid of your weapon. I can't emphasize this enough. Separate the shooter from his gun. If they catch the shooter, they don't got the weapon. If they don't got a weapon, it's much harder to make a case. Always eliminate the gun, and your life will be a lot easier.

Me and Ricky rehearsed the murder on many different days. When we first started watching the hamburger shop, we couldn't believe that Richard, after he bonded out, came in to work every morning. He lived in an apartment with his family a couple blocks away, but the lazy fuck always drove to work in his blue Cadillac. Maybe he felt safer driving. Sometimes he came at nine. Sometimes later. But he always came.

Ricky timed everything. He was going to carry a sawed-off

shotgun in a Bal Harbor Mall shopping bag. He was going to use a double-barrel, break-action gun because it wouldn't eject shells. He didn't want to leave nothing behind. It would take less than a minute to walk from the parking lot to the dock. The dock had bushes by it, so nobody could see Ricky hand the gun off to me. Then Ricky would walk through a half-empty lot to 96th Street and East Bay Harbor Drive. Albert or one of his guys would pick him up and drive him off the island.

I have to say, Ricky impressed me. When he first talked to me about using disguises, I thought he was out of his mind. But when we practiced, he always looked different, but normal, not like a freak you'd point at or remember.

Gary and Bobby decided they were going to come on my Cigarette boat with me. Gary obviously wasn't going to miss this. Bobby came along to keep an eye on Gary. We had to talk Gary out of doing the actual shooting. Then he wanted to take his boat to dispose of the weapon. He wanted to have that connection to the murder. What good is revenge if it's not personal? But Gary's boat only had one engine. If, God forbid, it threw a rod or blew a gas line when we were making the getaway, we'd be sunk. We went with my boat, because I had twin engines.

We killed Richard on a weekday.* Me and Gary and Bobby docked my boat before nine. We brought some fishing gear and goofed around on the boat, like we were getting ready for an outing. Gary was clowning around. He snorted spoonfuls of coke whenever he thought Bobby wasn't looking. Both of them were laughing. Then *boom boom*. Not thirty seconds later Ricky came down the path. He had on a tourist shirt and a Panama hat. He carried the shopping bag from the Bal Harbor Mall. When he got a few steps from my boat, I saw a little smile on his face. And why not? He'd done his part correctly.

When Ricky pulled the sawed-off gun from his shopping bag, Gary stuck his arm up and waved, like he wanted Ricky to throw it.

---

* Tuesday, October 11, 1977.

He was almost close enough to hand it over, but Ricky threw it. He was done. He walked off and caught his ride out.

Gary was so high, he dropped the gun into the water. Bobby was pissed. The water's not deep, but he had to push the boat back from the dock so Gary could dive in and get it. While we were doing our *Three Stooges* act on the boat, we started to hear sirens and then this god-awful screaming. Some girl was just yelling her guts out in the parking lot. At least we knew Ricky must have hit the mark.*

---

* Prado's employment records at the Miami-Dade fire department indicate that the Schwartz murder occurred on one of his days off. In 1991 Prado became the target of the same federal task force that was investigating Albert San Pedro for racketeering. Witnesses and forensic evidence linked Prado to arsons, assaults, and three murders allegedly carried out on San Pedro's orders, in addition to that of Richard Schwartz. In July 1991 federal investigators interviewed Prado at CIA headquarters in Langley, Virginia, about his relationship with San Pedro. He admitted having worked for him in the 1970s but denied any involvement in or knowledge of criminal wrongdoing carried out by San Pedro. Following the intervention of E. Page Moffett, a top CIA attorney who later became the general counsel for the National Security Agency, the investigation into Prado's alleged activities with San Pedro was abruptly dropped. Moffett made at least one visit to Miami and lobbied the U.S. Attorney's office there. Sources I interviewed who were involved in the matter say that Moffett argued that prosecution of Prado jeopardized "national security." The CIA also refused to provide Prado's major case prints to help FBI investigators match them to partial prints, believed to be Prado's, found at a scene of another murder. But Prado received his greatest protection from the prior immunity deal U.S. Attorney Dexter Lehtinen negotiated with San Pedro. When a judge determined in 1992 that San Pedro's prior immunity deal shielded him from prosecution in the racketeering case, it became difficult to pursue charges against Prado. After the racketeering and murder cases against Prado disappeared in Miami, he rose through the ranks of the CIA and went on to become chief of operations at the CIA's Counter Terrorist Center, for which he was given the George H. W. Bush Award for Excellence for his service in the War on Terrorism. He retired from the Agency in 2004 as an SIS-2, the equivalent rank of a two-star general. In 2005 he became a senior officer in Blackwater, the private contracting firm now known as Xe. In 2009, after CIA director Leon Panetta informed Congress that the agency had created a possibly illegal "targeted assassination unit"—or "death squad" program as the media dubbed it—aimed at killing terrorists around the world, Prado was identified as the head of it. He was also outed as the man responsible for moving the "death squad" program to Blackwater in a no-bid contract. More recently, Prado has been the subject of an investigation into efforts he allegedly spearheaded at Blackwater to use dummy companies to procure weapons and commit other possibly illegal acts. Reporting on Prado's activities at Blackwater on September 4, in the *New York Times* article titled "30 False Fronts Won Contracts for Blackwater," James Risen and

Witnesses said they heard gunshots and ran to the rear parking area where they found Schwartz dying on the pavement next to his blue Cadillac. A passerby said he thought a man had walked up to the Cadillac just before the shooting.

—Verne Williams and Bill Gjebre, "Lansky Stepson Murdered,"
Miami News, October 12, 1977

The killer fired from about 16 inches away, and the blast went through him, shattering windows on both sides of the car.

There were no shell casings left behind and no tire marks.

Schwartz's daughter, Debbie, ran from the [family's] apartment just blocks away. "I knew this would happen," she screamed when she saw him lying in the street. "Daddy is dead."

—"Revenge Thought Murder Motive," UPI, October 13, 1977

What a bunch of knuckleheads we were. We must have spent five minutes fishing the gun from the water. By the time we got the boat going, all hell was breaking loose in the parking lot. But nobody paid any attention to us.

I drove the boat a mile south to Haulover Cut and out to Biscayne Bay. I got up to speed, and ten miles out Gary dropped the gun into the bottom of the ocean. Gary was beside himself. He got rid of the gun that killed the guy who'd killed his brother. Bobby opened a bottle of Johnnie Walker. Gary and he started whooping and high-fiving each other, like we'd won the big game.

Mark Mezzitti wrote, "Among other things, company executives are accused of obtaining large numbers of AK-47s and M-4 automatic weapons, but arranging to make it appear as if they had been bought by the sheriff's department in Camden County, N.C." They added, "It is unclear how much of Blackwater's relationship with the C.I.A. will become public during the criminal proceedings in North Carolina because the Obama administration won a court order limiting the use of classified information." For the record, Jon Roberts first told his story of murdering Richard Schwartz with Prado to FBI agents in 1992—years before Prado had been publicly outed as a CIA officer. At the time Jon made his statements regarding Prado's alleged role in the murder, investigators still hoped to bring federal racketeering or state murder charges against Prado, despite legal setbacks in their case against San Pedro. As one of those investigators, a former Miami-Dade Police Department detective and federal organized-crime-squad task force member, recently told me, "I am still hoping to put Prado away for murder."

It was strange. I got a little blue that morning. I looked at Bobby and Gary and thought, *There's been so much killing.* People disappeared all the time in Miami, and it didn't make the news. Some of the people who died deserved it. Some didn't. A few were my friends. If the swamps and the oceans ever dry up down here, I'd be curious to see what they find at the bottom.

The morning we killed Richard Schwartz, I got tired. But you shake that off. We had a nice steak dinner that night. I heard from a cop Danny Mones knew that Richard Schwartz's teenage daughter was the first to find him after he got his face blown off.* Now his little girl could feel how Gary felt when he lost his brother. Fair is fair. I wasn't glad, but I hope Richard Schwartz felt good for what he made us do.

---

* Schwartz was shot once in the torso, once in the head, and at such close range that wadding from the shotgun shells was embedded in his chest.

40

J.R.: My grandfather, Poppy, died before Christmas in 1977. He died in his bathtub. He liked to take baths. He took one, and his heart stopped. Poppy worked hard his whole life and had a good time fishing and writing his stupid poems. He was a good man. He loved water, and he died in a tub of warm water, so that was that.

Poppy kept a jar with our grandmother's ashes. He wanted my sister and me to mix them and spread them on the ocean in New York where we used to fish. He wanted to lie in the water with our grandmother by the city where they met and fell in love.

I did not want to go out and freeze my balls off in the middle of the winter in New York dumping ashes off a boat. My idea was to wait until summer, but my sister got really freaked out and made things difficult.

JUDY: I dreamed that Poppy was trapped in the ash jar and he couldn't be with our grandmother until we mixed their ashes in the water. It was a terrible dream. I called Jon and said, "Poppy wants to go into the ocean now. We can't wait."

Jon can be such a good brother. He dropped everything and flew to New York and rented a helicopter, and we went up over the water with the ashes. The pilot told us it was illegal to put ashes in the ocean where we wanted, but Jon informed the pilot the only way we were going to do it was his way.

J.R.: When my sister called and told me about her nutty dream, I said, "This is ridiculous. This ain't our grandparents no more. It's a couple of coffee cans full of ashes."

But my sister can have a very strong will, and it's easier not to battle her. So I came to New York. I got the helicopter. I argued with the pilot to let us dump the ashes where we wanted. We opened the door up to spread the ashes, and it was a mess. Freezing cold. Ashes blowing every which way. At least it got my sister off my back.

JUDY: Did Jon tell you he cried? He became very emotional when we put our grandparents' ashes in the water. Jon was so close to Poppy. I used to fly down and stay at his house on Indian Creek. As Poppy grew weaker, Jon had to carry him from the car in his arms. We had wonderful meals together. Jon can be volatile, but he was never volatile around Poppy. He was so caring around him.

I know why Jon cried after Poppy died. He let go. Jon held everything in when our mother died. With Poppy, he felt safe because he knew Poppy loved him. Once he started crying, everything came out that he'd been holding back for years. He broke down. He finally cried for our mother. My dream was right. But it wasn't just our grandfather trapped in that jar, it was Jon. His best side came out that day. I was so glad to see it. It became a joyful day.

J.R.: My sister makes that nightmare helicopter ride sound like *Gone With the Wind*. I wasn't crying. I had tears in my eyes because the wind was blowing Poppy's ashes back in my face.

41

J.R.: I was twenty-nine when Poppy died. My whole life I'd used the thought process I learned from my father to survive. To say "crime doesn't pay" is the most ridiculous thing I've ever heard. I made $400 a month digging trees and $400,000 a month moving coke.

I had so much money, I could have taken a couple of years off. But I never rested. Money was not my priority anymore. Coke dealing had become a kick for me, like the robberies I used to do in New York. Then, around the time Poppy died, the excitement I got from selling coke started to fade. I got bored. Luckily, in 1978 a new challenge came along. I shifted from being a seller to an importer. It happened when I hooked up with the Colombians.

My connection with them came through one of the sons of Don Aronow. Aronow was the greatest racer and boatbuilder of all time.* His company built the Donzi boat I had up on Fire Island that Jimi Hendrix tried to water-ski off of. Remember my maroon Cigarette boat that Bobby Erra wrecked? I bought that in 1976 after I saw it at a boat show in Miami. At the time I hadn't met Aronow. I saw the boat, fell in love with it, and when I told the salesman I wanted it, he said it wasn't for sale.

"Are you kidding me?"

"You'll have to talk to Mr. Aronow."

Aronow's showroom was also his factory. It was on Thunderboat Row, where the best racing boat companies in the world were located.† Aronow was the top guy on Thunderboat Row. When you walked in his shop, one wall showed pictures of him with famous people who bought his boats—Lyndon Johnson, Steve McQueen, the shah of Iran, George Bush.‡

Don was a phenomenal salesman. He was tall. He looked like a movie star. He came off like a man's man. When I introduced myself and told him I wanted the maroon Cigarette, he invited me upstairs to his office.

This was like a luxury apartment. It had windows looking down on the floor where you could watch your boat being made. If you were a good customer, Don would invite you to parties up there. There'd be beautiful girls left and right. All beautiful women love riding on fast boats, so they'd beg to come to his parties. You could party all afternoon with one of these girls while you watched them lay the keel on your boat. That was Don's secret to selling boats. It wasn't just the boat you were buying. You were buying

---

* "Between 1963 and 1975, Aronow won two world powerboat racing championships, 3 U.S. titles, set numerous speed records, and became known as 'the godfather of the powerboat industry.' " Elizabeth A. Ginns, "The Tale of Two Cities," *Power & Motor Yacht Magazine*, June 2003.

† Thunderboat Row, along the main channel into Biscayne Bay on 188th Street, was "a quarter mile long street once redolent with the smell of curing fiberglass and the sound of big engines." From the previously cited "The Tale of Two Cities."

‡ George H. W. Bush, then CIA director, was—like Jon—a devotee of Aronow's race boats and has owned several.

every beautiful woman you'd ever seen or ever would see, on top of the kick of driving the fastest boat in the world.

When we met, Don told me he couldn't sell me the maroon Cigarette because he'd made it for one of his girlfriends. That got me so hot for it, I offered him ridiculous money, and he finally agreed to take it.

A month after I took the boat, I went back to his shop to tell him how happy I was with it, and when I came in, he accused me of screwing his girlfriend. It was one of the few times in my life a guy said something like that to me and it wasn't true. I don't know if his girl made this up to get him jealous or what, but he came on so strong, I never had a chance to defend myself. He shouted, "You're a piece of shit. I sold you my best boat, and look what you did to me."

"Who the fuck are you, bro? A boat guy? You can take your boats and shove them up your fucking ass."

I was more hurt than angry. I'd just become friends with the best boat maker in the world, and now he wanted me out of his life. A couple days later Don asked me back to his shop. He said, "After you left, I spoke to somebody about you. I had no idea who you were. I apologize."

We never had a problem again. Don was not a bad guy. He grew up in Jersey. He did not come from money, but he married a wealthy girl whose father started him in home building. He did good with that and moved to Florida to make his name in boats.*

Don was a born hustler. He sold boats to smugglers because his engineering and design made them so fast. And he used his friendship with George Bush to sell the government boats to catch the smugglers. What made Don a genius was, he sold the government boats that were a hair slower than the ones he sold the smugglers.†

---

* Aronow moved his family to Florida in the early 1960s, after he became obsessed with the idea that New Jersey was going to be destroyed in a nuclear war. Shortly after he arrived in Miami, the Cuban Missile Crisis pushed Florida to the brink of a nuclear attack. But Aronow stayed, because by then he had taken up his new obsession, racing boats.

† There is no evidence that George H. W. Bush had improper dealings with Aronow. However, when Bush became vice president and served as President Reagan's

No way could he let the smugglers get caught. They were his best customers.*

At the same time that Aronow was helping the government fight the war on drugs, he installed a fifty-thousand-pound boatlift behind his shop that he rented to weed smugglers. The smugglers would drive up to his shop with tons of weed in their boat, and he could lift the whole boat out of the water and put it on a truck that could then be unloaded in the privacy of a warehouse. Unloading boats exposed smugglers to the greatest risk of being caught. Don's boatlift solved the problem. In the end, smuggling caused some problems for him, but he had a good run.†

I never used Don's boats for smuggling. They were strictly for pleasure. But his shop was like the main smuggler's den in Miami. Everybody in the drug business hung out there. Once in a while Don would have to clear out the shop when his buddy George Bush would visit. The rest of the time, the place was ours. Everybody got to know Don's sons. They were great kids. One got crippled in a car accident but managed to become a very good horse trainer after that. As far as I know, neither of his boys was ever involved in the coke business, but they had an idea what I was about. One day one of them came to me and said he'd met a guy at the boat shop who he thought I ought to meet.

By that time in 1978 Phyllis and I were still together, but I kept my own condo in Coral Gables for partying. I told Don's kid to send the guy he wanted me to meet over there. In walks a stocky little Colombian guy in his twenties named Pancho. He looked like

---

point man for the war on drugs, the Customs Service did award Aronow's firm a lucrative contract. He built them a fleet of trimarans, which were theoretically faster than his Cigarettes, but only on flat seas. On rougher seas the Cigarettes that Aronow sold to smugglers easily outran the boats he sold to the Customs Service. The program was widely regarded as a boondoggle, as well as an embarrassment to Bush, who had, with great fanfare, personally run vice-presidential speed trials of Aronow's boats and had pronounced them "unbeatable."

* The powerboat industry was decimated by the oil shocks of the 1970s. Purchases by drug smugglers were key to the industry's survival.

† Aronow was gunned down outside his Thunderboat Row boat shop on February 3, 1987, by a drug dealer who felt he'd been swindled by him.

a peasant who someone had bought a suit and tie that they stuffed him into even before teaching him to tie his shoes. His English was terrible. When he smiled, he showed crooked gold teeth. He was a rough guy. I liked him.

My Spanish, which I'd learned from hanging out with Cubans, was better than Pancho's English. We went out to some clubs. We chased some girls, we did some lines. After a few nights of this, he said to me, "You know, I can get coke really cheap."

I hadn't told him what my line of work was, but it was obvious enough. I asked what price his coke would be, and he named something that was way too high. I laughed at him. He said, "Okay. I'm going to bring you a friend. Maybe he can help you get a better price."

A week later Pancho shows up at my place driving a Rolls-Royce convertible. Next to him is a little kid with a face that probably couldn't grow three beard hairs. The kid has long black hair. He almost looks like a girl.

When I step up to the street, Pancho walks around and opens the door for this kid. The kid is wearing an electric blue jacket. He walks up to me, reaches his hand in, and pulls out a flask. *"Bebe, bebe, bebe"*—drink, drink, drink—he says.

I think he's amusing, so I take the flask and drink. It tastes like I've swallowed a Molotov cocktail. My whole chest is on fire. I found out they call that drink *aguardiente*,* and it's like the national drink of Colombia. They drink it like Gatorade.

I'm coughing and fucking dying, and the kid laughs. He pats my back and says, "Hey, man. I'm Fabito. Let's go have some fun."†

FABITO WAS twenty-one years old when I met him. He had recently arrived in Miami to help out with his family's business. His father

---

* *Aguardiente* is a contraction of the words meaning "water" and "fiery." In Colombia it is mainly consumed by people from the mountainous parts of the country—also where the coca leaves grow the best.

† Fabio Ochoa Vasquez. Jon refers to him as Fabito, the affectionate form of his name, which loosely translates as "Little Fabio."

was Don Ochoa, the godfather of the Medellín Cartel.* In 1978 the Cartel was getting started. There were three sons in the family, Jorge, Juan, and Fabito, the youngest. Fabito came to Miami to help grow the family's business. They were looking for people to help move their coke—to import it and distribute it. They already had Colombians in Miami and other cities moving coke. The harder part was getting it into the country. So Fabito was sending his bodyguard, Pancho, around to scout for guys to help him, and if they seemed reliable to Pancho, Fabito would meet them.

I connected with Fabito at the time the coke business was taking off. He was in Miami to build his family's empire, and I helped him make it. In this, I found my true life passion. It was beating the U.S. government. That's what smuggling was about. It got me off harder than anything I'd ever done. I was never addicted to coke, but I definitely got hooked on smuggling it.

---

* His name was Fabio Ochoa Restrepo, but he went by the honorific nickname "Don Ochoa." Ochoa, who died in 2002, was from a long line of wealthy landowners and politicians in Colombia. For his entire life he denied he had any involvement with the Medellín Cartel. His sons, Fabio, Jorge, and Juan, were all key members.

42

J.R.: Fabito's father, Don Ochoa, was a great big fat man who loved to ride those small white horses, Paso Finos. Some fat guys, when they ride horses, look ridiculous. Don Ochoa was not a ridiculous figure. He was a fine breeder of racehorses,* but his greatest accomplishment was building the Medellín Cartel. The Colombians made more money in a few years than the Mafia did in a hundred years.†

---

* In his self-published autobiography, Don Ochoa wrote of himself, "Don Fabio [Ochoa] is to Colombia's horse world what Garcia Márquez is to Colombia's world of letters."
† When Jon uses the phrase "the Colombians," he is usually referring to members of the Ochoas' Medellín Cartel, by far the biggest of the cartels based in Colombia, but there were others, such as the Cali Cartel. Comparisons between the American Mafia and the Colombian cartels are not easy. One estimate of Carlo Gambino's personal wealth at the peak of his power in the 1960s put it at $1.5 billion (adjusted for inflation), but the Mafia's influence, through its control of unions and its ability to affect the outcome of elections through civic corruption, gave Gambino an impact beyond the sheer economic scale of mob enterprises. The Medellín Cartel is estimated to

To understand what the Ochoas did, I need to break down a few things for you. Drug smuggling in Florida was invented by the Cubans. Many of the Cubans that the Mafia brought to Miami when Castro came in got recruited by the government to fight in the Bay of Pigs.* When the invasion didn't work out, they went back to working the nightclubs on 79th Street.† When American kids started smoking weed in the 1960s, the Cubans, trained by the CIA in how to use boats and planes for the Bay of Pigs invasion, decided to put their skills to use by smuggling weed.‡ That's how the smuggling business started. They'd go down to wherever the pot grew in Jamaica, Colombia, or Mexico and pick it up and take it to Miami.

---

have netted some $50 billion for its owners during a few years in the 1980s. Pablo Escobar, the number two man in the Cartel, was estimated in 1987 by *Forbes* magazine to have a net worth of $24 billion, making him the seventh-richest man in the world. Imprecise as comparisons are, one of Jon's points is undeniable: the Medellín Cartel made one of the largest fortunes in the world, and did so in the span of a decade.

* The Bay of Pigs was the failed 1961 invasion of Cuba undertaken by a CIA-trained army of Cuban exiles. Many of those exiles worked for Mafia-controlled businesses in Miami before and after the botched operation.

† A federal task force noted that as late as 1975 several of the Cuban car parks employed at the Mafia-run Dream Bar had been members of Brigade 2506, the main fighting force of the CIA-led invasion.

‡ Among the most significant CIA-connected, Cuban-exile smugglers were members of the Tabraue family, who in 1989 were convicted of importing 500,000 pounds of pot. When Guillermo Tabraue, the family patriarch, went on trial, he called a retired CIA officer to testify in his defense. As David Corn and Jefferson Morley reported in "CIA for Defense" in the April 17, 1989, edition of *The Nation*, the elder Tabraue had served as a CIA-trained mercenary in the Bay of Pigs invasion and continued to draw a $1,400-a-week paycheck from the Agency even when he was running one of the largest dope-smuggling rings in the United States. Another Cuban pot smuggler, Manuel Revuelta, started his career as a money counter in a Havana casino run by Patsy Erra, then worked as a CIA-trained pilot in the Bay of Pigs operation while holding down a day job as a cashier at the Dream Bar and at the Fontainebleau Hotel. In 1982 Revuelta was convicted of running a major pot-smuggling ring. Revuelta's FBI files, which I reviewed, note his employment history with the CIA. His first arrest was for stealing bombs from Homestead Air Force Base in 1959 that were supposed to be dropped on Havana power stations as part of a CIA scheme. When I interviewed Revuelta in 2009, he told me he got into dope smuggling after the CIA cut off his salary in the late 1960s. At the time of our interview, he had finished serving more than a decade in prison and was working as a cashier at a gourmet bagel shop in Aventura.

With pot, the easy part was growing it, and the hard part was smuggling it. Cocaine was different. Coca leaves only grow in certain parts of Colombia and Bolivia, and you can't just pick the leaf and snort it up your nose. Making cocaine is a process. It takes chemicals. It takes workers. It takes time. You need a factory to make it in.

At the end of that process you get a product that in the 1970s was worth ten times its weight in gold.* Many Colombians rose to the challenge of making cocaine. The smarter ones didn't just want to throw a $50,000 kilo onto a boat driven by a Cuban and wave good-bye. They wanted to control the whole process.

When Don Ochoa, who was based in the town of Medellín, started off, he had advantages. He was already rich. He owned ranches all over Colombia. He owned a chain of restaurants. The guy had judges and politicians in his pocket from the start. As a businessman, he knew how to run an organization.

Other Colombians weren't as smart. They'd harvest the leaves but couldn't make factories to process them properly. That was why Albert's cocaine had quality problems. His cocaine was made by half-assed Colombians.

Don Ochoa ran his business like IBM. If he sent five hundred kilos into the United States, each one was marked with a symbol. The symbol told the people smuggling it who that kilo was going to and how much money the Colombians were supposed to get for it. The symbol also told the Colombians where that kilo was made, how much the chemicals cost to make it, where the leaves came from, what kind of purity it had. Ochoa's people knew everything about every fucking kilo they ever shipped. They controlled the kilo from the time it was leaves on the tree until right before it got snorted up some idiot's nose in a bathroom in Los Angeles or Des Moines. They had their business correct.

---

* Gold hovered at around $200 per ounce in the mid-1970s, meaning a kilo of gold was worth about $7,000. With a kilo of cocaine wholesaling for up to $50,000 and going for two or three times that amount on the street, it was far more valuable than gold.

Don Ochoa was like the CEO of the business. His oldest son, Jorge, was like the president. When they started off, everybody in Colombia was fighting each other. But the Ochoas ran their business so good, when they went to their competitors in Medellín and said, "Let's band together, and we'll all make out," the other guys decided to join them. Obviously, the Ochoas had to fight a few battles to get on top, but that's basically how the Cartel started.

People in the Cartel had different skills. In the beginning Carlos Lehder was their best transport guy.* Pablo Escobar was a street guy who started off fighting the Ochoas, but they made peace and he took over running the processing labs.† Tough as Pablo was, the Ochoas always had the upper hand because they owned the leaves.

Don Ochoa sat in the background. He put everybody out in front of him. Pablo Escobar became the top enforcer for the empire. He took the limelight. But Don Ochoa was the smartest of them all. While everybody else was out fighting his wars, he sat at his ranch and let the money come to him. He rode his horses and ate great food. He was just like any other fat fucker sitting on top of a big corporation.

---

* Lehder was a Colombian of German extraction. Originally a car thief in Medellín, he pioneered use of the Bahamas as a transport hub for moving the Ochoas' cocaine into Miami. He was among the first Colombians to push aside Cuban smugglers. By the late 1970s, he fell out of favor with the Ochoas because of his megalomania—insisting he sit on an enormous gilded throne during business meetings—and because of his adoration of Adolf Hitler, which he expressed by wearing swastikas and greeting associates with Nazi salutes. In 1987 he was extradited to the United States, where he is serving a long prison sentence despite his requests to be transferred to prison in the "Fatherland"—Germany—where he believes he would be more comfortable.
† Escobar was born in 1949 and by the 1980s was by far the most notorious member of the Cartel.

43

J.R.: Fabito and me spent weeks forming a relationship. We'd meet at my Coral Gables place and do lines and go to bars and clubs. Pancho always came with us. One afternoon Fabito showed up alone. He said, "Come. You and me, we're going to go party the way I like to party."

"How do you party?"

"I'll show you."

Fabito and I get into his Rolls convertible and drive to the University of Miami. He parks by a lecture hall. He looks at his watch and says, "Five more minutes."

Five minutes pass, and all of a sudden hundreds of students pour out of the lecture hall. They must have had a class that mostly girls take, like nursing or poetry, because most of the students are female. We had dozens of eighteen- and nineteen-year-old girls streaming past our car. They're smiling at us, curious about these guys in a Rolls-Royce. Fabito looks at me and says, "Watch."

He takes a bag of Quaaludes from his glove box.

He pulls out a pill and holds it up. All these girls stop and watch. "Quaalude," he says. That's the only word in English he knows, and it's all he needs for the college girls. He throws all the pills in the air. It rains Quaaludes in our car. The girls jump in to grab them. It would be like if me and Bobby Erra went fishing and the tuna jumped into our boat. Fabito fills the car with college girls and says to me—in Spanish—"Now let's go fuck these bitches."

Fabito drives to an apartment tower near the Omni, a high-end mall they'd just built in Miami.* When he parks the car, Fabito explains he keeps different apartments around the city in different names so if he has trouble, nobody can trace anything to him. "I party hard, so I got to be careful."

The girls are already pilled out by the time we get up to his apartment. It's a nice place, high up with a view. The only furnishings are a couple couches, a stereo, and a blender in the kitchen. Fabito goes right to the blender and mixes ice, booze, and fistfuls of Quaaludes. The girls drink down the knockout cocktails while we all laugh and listen to the disco music on the stereo.

Half an hour later everybody's nude, everybody's fucking on the couches. We're really having a good time when one of these doped-up college girls opens her eyes wide and says, "I want to go back to school."

She crawls over to one of her girlfriends and says, "Let's go."

Fabito says, "I'm gonna help this girl out of here."

This girl is so stoned, she don't know where she is. Fabito picks her up and carries her out to the balcony. I think he's going to give her some fresh air, but he carries her to the railing. I watch him from the sliding door.

Fabito says, "Jon, is it okay if I throw her off?"

"Bro, are you nuts?"

"Nobody will know. I can do anything."

---

* The Omni International Mall of Miami embodied the city's aspirations for urban renewal when it opened in a declining retail corridor at 15th Street and Biscayne Boulevard in late 1976. After most major retailers in the mall abandoned it in the 1990s, it has since struggled as a low-rent "zombie mall."

"Okay, Fabito. You're the host. It's your house. If you want to throw the girl off the balcony, knock yourself out."

Fabito drops the girl onto the railing. Her naked ass is hanging over ten stories of air. The only thing keeping her from flipping backward is, her arms are holding Fabito's neck, and this girl is barely awake. Fabito gets so turned on, he opens her legs up and starts fucking her, pushing her ass farther out on the balcony. When he finished, I guess he took pity on the girl, because he yanked forward, so she fell on the terrace. She hit so hard, the floor shook. I'm sure she woke up later with a big bruise on one side of her body, not knowing how she got it, or how lucky she was to have it. It could have been her little college-educated ass hitting the concrete ten stories below.

Fabito's mind was clear. He said, "Let's go. I'll have Pancho come over and clean up the girls."

Soon as we get in Fabito's car, he said, "Jon, I like you. You understand the kind of person I am."

What happened that night built trust between us. Fabito saw I wouldn't have judged him if he'd thrown the girl off the building. I would have been uptight about being tied to a murder. But you know how I am. I had no heart for the girl. Now Fabito knew that, too. We had our trust.

For the first time we talked business. Fabito said, "I'm going to tell you who I am. I'm the guy who's going to get you all the coke you ever needed."

44

J.R.: What Fabito told me was a white lie. It was true he had all the coke in the world. But he did not have it in Miami. It was in the Bahamas. In 1978 Carlos Lehder was running his scheme to smuggle the Cartel's cocaine into Miami from the Bahamas.* Lehder got help from a local businessman named Everette Bannister, who owned hotels there. I knew about Bannister because at one point Albert, the cross-eyed Cuban, tried to open a casino in one of the hotels in the Bahamas in order to launder money, but it never got off the ground.† This guy Bannister was very connected. He owned the prime minister of the Bahamas, a corrupt black guy who gave Lehder his own island to bring in coke from Colombia.‡

* Unless otherwise stated, "the Cartel" Jon refers to is the Ochoas' Medellín Cartel.
† Albert San Pedro tried for several years to open a casino in the Bahamas, going so far as to plan the purchase of a local newspaper to influence public opinion in favor of his scheme.
‡ The "corrupt black guy" Jon refers to is Lynden Pindling, revered

The advantage of using the Bahamas was that they were less than two hours from Miami in a speedboat. You could have guys watching the Customs Service boats around Miami, and when those guys took a lunch break, they could radio to the guys in the Bahamas and have them send the speedboat up with the coke on it. It wasn't quite that easy, but it was close. The Cubans had been using the Bahamas for years.

The Colombians had an easy time getting their coke into the Bahamas because they were paying off the government there, but when I met Fabito, they were having a harder time getting their speedboats up into Florida. When they used Colombians to drive their coke boats they kept getting arrested by the Customs Service. Back in those days, the Customs Service practiced racial profiling of Latins, and it being a different era, they weren't able to complain about their rights being violated.

What the Colombians wanted was gringos to drive their boats for them. I went down to Norman Cay, the island they had in the Bahamas, to talk to Fabito's associates about driving boats for them, and when I came back, I told Fabito no.

I didn't want to race powerboats on the water. That was a flunky's job. I told Fabito that I had a much better idea. I'd give him a safe harbor in Miami.

WHEN I met Fabito, I'd already started working with dirty cops in North Bay Village. I owned the whole police department.*

---

in the Bahamas as the British colony's first prime minister following its independence in 1969. He led the nation until 1992 and died in 2000. Pindling began taking bribes from Bannister in 1977 to allow Lehder's use of an island for cocaine smuggling. He was later caught taking $56 million in bribes in one sting operation. In 1982 the U.S. government accused Pindling of turning the Bahamas into a major cocaine-shipping and money-laundering center and imposed economic sanctions on the island nation. Pindling nevertheless retired from office as a popular leader and an extremely wealthy man. The island Lehder used was Norman Cay, on which he built air and boat transport facilities. He had a staff of about forty workers to maintain planes and boats and storehouses for cocaine.

* North Bay Village, connected to Miami Beach by the 79th Street Causeway, is a separate municipality consisting of three islands. At the time Jon "owned" the police department, the entire force consisted of about two dozen officers.

I got to know North Bay Village in my earliest days of coke dealing in Miami. In 1974 when I was looking for sources of coke, I ran into an old friend of mine from Jersey named Pat Pucci. He had come down to Miami even before I did and hooked up with a local wiseguy named Ricky Cravero. Ricky was moving weed and some coke at the time, but we never did much business together. Instead, me and Ricky and Pat all became pretty good friends, and we hung out in North Bay Village because that was Ricky's home. Unfortunately, Ricky Cravero and Pat got into a business dispute, and they found Pat Pucci in a rock quarry up in Jersey. I don't know what happened. I was just friends with these guys. Even after Pat Pucci went away, I stayed friends with Ricky Cravero.

Ricky was a good guy. He was a lot of fun to be around. He reminded me of me when I was running wild in New York. He weighed maybe 160 pounds, but he was a tough kid. He would fight anybody. He was a savage. He had three or four guys with him. They were leaving bodies everywhere. Ricky Cravero was truly a bad motherfucker. He was into nothing but bad, bad shit.*

His favorite hangout was the Place for Steak, which was down from Dino's.† Ricky Cravero loved the guinea spots. One night we were in the bar, and I saw Paul Hornung, the halfback for the Green Bay Packers.‡ Compared to Ricky, Hornung was a giant. But

---

* Authorities described Richard "Ricky" Cravero as a "vicious killer" after they arrested him in the mid-1970s for running the original "Dixie Mafia" gang believed to be responsible for forty murders. Cravero was convicted of three murders and given multiple life sentences. He escaped from a maximum-security prison in 1987 and spent five months on the run. As reported by Dan Christensen in the January 28, 1988, *Miami News*, "Hiding Was Rough on Escapee," Cravero was rearrested when spotted in a 1977 Cadillac driven by a former member of his gang, Charles Grasso, who himself had been previously convicted of beating an eighteen-month-old infant to death whom his girlfriend had foolishly asked him to babysit. Cravero died in 2005 while in prison.

† The Place for Steak was a mobster hangout where in 1967 Miami gangster Thomas Altamura was executed by a rival while waiting for his table. Dino's was a nightclub owned by the entertainer Dean Martin.

‡ Jon's story about his encounter with Paul Hornung—the 1956 Heisman Trophy Winner who was once known as the "Golden Boy" of the NFL—cannot be confirmed. But in 1963 Hornung was suspended from football for his role in a

this was how Ricky Cravero was. He walks over to the bathroom, bumps Paul Hornung, and says, "Get out of my way, you fat fuck."

Paul Hornung stands up, along with two or three of his friends. I'm watching from across the bar with Ricky's crew. I say, "I guess we're going to have to help him."

One of Ricky's guys laughs. "He don't need no help from us."

I hear Paul Hornung say, "Don't you know who I am?" The words have barely left his mouth when Ricky kicks him in the balls. Hornung doubles over. He doesn't have a ball protector like they do in a football game, and I can see he's real surprised at how bad it hurts getting kicked there. He makes a squeaking noise, *Eee eee eee!*

Then Ricky takes a Heinz ketchup bottle from the bar. In those days Heinz made a solid ketchup bottle. Their bottles wouldn't break on a person's head like a normal bottle. A Heinz bottle was like a club. Ricky hits Hornung so hard in the head with the ketchup, he drops him.

Ricky turns to Hornung's friends and says, "Which one of you clowns is next?"

"No. You made your point," one of them says.

We hear sirens by the time Ricky comes back over to us. I say, "Listen, man. I think you should leave. They called the cops."

Ricky laughs. "The cops? Are you kidding me?"

By the time the cops come, Hornung's friends have him sitting up with a towel on his face to stop the bleeding, and we're sitting at our end of the bar having another round. I see a police lieutenant walk over and nod to Ricky, like they're old friends. He says, "What happened?"

"The guy attacked me," Ricky says. He adds, "You want a drink, Andy?"

---

gambling scheme, which ESPN ranks as number four on its list of the ten biggest betting scandals in American sports history. Though Hornung's suspension was for betting small amounts of money, the league was concerned about possible Mafia connections he had through the bookies he employed to place bets.

Ricky passes him a shot and says, "This is my friend Lieutenant Andy Mazzarella."

We do shots with the lieutenant as the ambulance guys come in to treat Hornung. Arresting Ricky Cravero for assault is not even a question.

After Lieutenant Mazzarella leaves, Ricky says to me, "Whatever the fuck you want to do in North Bay Village, Andy will take care of it. He's an Italian from Long Island. He knows who you are, Jon."

Maybe a year after Ricky went away to prison,* I invited Lieutenant Mazzarella to the Forge. I had Al Malnik set us up in a private room just big enough for me, Lieutenant Mazzarella, and a couple of whores. We had some drinks, ate a nice meal, and one of the girls blew the police lieutenant under the table before dessert. I left him alone with the girls for an hour or two. When I came back, I had one happy cop.

Lieutenant Mazzarella explained to me that he had a lot of leeway in his department to help friends of his. He was the number two guy in the department. He said the force was divided between cops like him and "bozos." *Bozos* was his word for clean cops. He said if I ever needed to do something illegal in his little village, he would make sure there were no bozos on the shift when I did it. Simple as that.

This was before I'd met Fabito. During that time I'd started working with my partner in the rental car business, Ron Tobachnik, to move coke up to Chicago, where he was from. I'd buy a few keys from Albert, and Tobachnik would pay some kids to run the keys up there in rental cars. To test out Lieutenant Mazzarella, I asked him if we could use a parking lot in his village to park our cars with coke in the trunks for our drivers to come and pick them up. He assigned his cops to watch our cars for us.

After I saw what a good job he did, I gave him and his cops

---

* Cravero went to prison in 1975 for the murders detailed in a previous note.

more work. By the time I met Fabito, I was paying one of Lieutenant Mazzarella's cops to use his house in North Bay Village as a stash house for my coke. This was even better than using Poppy's retirement home. There's no safer place than a cop's house for storing large amounts of drugs or cash.

ONCE I met Fabito, I had the idea to use the North Bay Village police to unload the boats coming in from the Bahamas with cocaine. Unloading drugs was where you faced the most risk. In those days, when the Customs Service and Coast Guard got suspicious of a speedboat coming into Biscayne Bay,* they often didn't stop it on the water because suspicion alone wasn't enough probable cause to search a boat. They'd wait until the boat came in to unload, then make their move.

The North Bay Village police department was ideal for unloading boats. When I tell you why, you'll fall over laughing. The department was on the water. They had their own dock just a few blocks down from the top wiseguy hangout, the Place for Steak.

When I proposed to Lieutenant Mazzarella that I had a way for him and his cops to make more money than they ever dreamed of— by helping me unload drug boats—he agreed immediately to help. He even gave me cops to physically unload the boats, put the shit in their cop cars, and deliver it to the stash house.

They were a full-service police department.

When I told Fabito I could give him a dock inside Biscayne Bay protected by the police, he thought I was an American criminal mastermind—not a guy who'd gotten friendly with a cop after my pal broke a ketchup bottle on another guy's head.

• • •

---

* The Customs Service and Coast Guard both tracked smugglers along the Florida coast. But the Customs Service, which through the 1970s and 1980s built a fleet of increasingly sophisticated boats and airplanes aimed at stopping smugglers, was more focused on the "War on Drugs." The Coast Guard, which is responsible for maritime safety, could never completely devote its resources to drug interdiction. As a result, smugglers perceived the Customs Service as a bigger threat than the Coast Guard.

INSTEAD OF being hired as a boat driver for the Colombians, I became the guy who hired drivers for them. I wouldn't hire the yahoos who hung out at Don Aronow's. I looked for guys I met in the sportfishing world, since they were more skilled with boats. I got the boats unloaded and put the product into a stash house, then I got it delivered. The Colombians had their own distributors who I brought the coke to, and I kept supplying my distributors—Bernie Levine in California, my uncle Jerry on Miami Beach, and Ron Tobachnik in Chicago. Less and less did I sell to individual blowheads.

I got a transport fee off of every kilo I moved—about 5 percent of the wholesale value. When Fabito and I started smuggling through North Bay Village, we started moving a couple hundred kilos a month and, some months, a thousand kilos or more.

I couldn't have done it without those cops. It was nuts what we did. One night I was talking to Lieutenant Mazzarella after we'd finished unloading a boat, and I happened to mention the speeding tickets I was getting in Miami. Lieutenant Mazzarella said, "Jon, are you stupid?"

I got a little uptight being called "stupid" by a dirty cop, but he explained, "Anytime you want to race, I'll close down main street so you can do it safely."

North Bay Village had two bridges on either side, and it was a straight shot through the town, perfect for drag racing. So a few days later I called Merc Morris. "Merc, let's see who's faster, your Ferrari or my Porsche."

Lieutenant Mazzarella's cops closed the street and used their radar guns to clock the winner. Anytime I wanted to race one of my friends, we'd go to North Bay Village. We'd bet bags of cash. We bet our cars. We bet women. It was really just good fun. That little town was my playground.

FABITO SAW I never ripped him off. I kept my word. It built up the bond between us. We used North Bay Village from 1978 until about 1980. We pushed thousands of kilos through the police department dock. Right down the street from the dock was the headquarters for NBC News in Miami. Reporters would drive their news vans past my cops unloading drugs. The newshounds had no clue.*

I never got caught in North Bay Village. In the years I employed Lieutenant Mazzarella, I paid him a couple million dollars. After I moved on, he started working with some real scumbags. They set him up, and down went Lieutenant Mazzarella and the North Bay Village police department.† Mazzarella never ratted on me. You won't hear me say this often about a man in blue, but he was a good cop.

---

* Until the late 1980s, the local NBC affiliate's news studios were located in North Bay Village, almost within sight of the dock used by corrupt police to smuggle drugs. Today, the studios belong to WSVN Fox 7.
† As noted in "Three Officers Charged with Protecting Cocaine Shipments," *St. Petersburg Times,* February 28, 1986.

45

J.R.: When I started my relationship with Fabito, it meant I was done buying from Albert. The Medellín coke was better quality, and they had more of it. But it would be very dangerous for me to offend Albert. I had to massage the situation.

One thing I had with Albert was personal trust. Even though Albert was a cross-eyed psycho, the man had feelings, and loyalty counted. I'd done little extra things that proved myself to him. One night Albert came to me and said, "I need you to do me a favor."

"Okay."

"I need you to let Blondie live with you for a while." By "Blondie" he meant Rubio, his enforcer.

I said, "Why does Blondie got to live with me?"

"He shot a guy in the brains and killed him. He needs to hide out."

What happened was that Rubio fell in love with a girl. Rubio was a boxer. Boxers have big hearts. It keeps them going in the ring. As physically strong as boxers are, they get their hearts broken very easily. The girl Rubio fell in love with got his heart in her fingers, and she twisted it up. She left him for another guy. Rubio loved this girl so much, he got emotional and shot her new boyfriend in the face.

Unfortunately, he did this in front of a bunch of witnesses. He walked in and did it at the dinner table where the whole family was eating. My belief is, if your woman is fucking another man, what good does it do to shoot him? It's not going to make her like you more if you kill her boyfriend. But that's my view. I'm not judging Rubio. He was a traditional man in the way he handled the situation.*

I took Rubio in at the house Phyllis and I had on Indian Creek. Nobody would think of looking there for a big blond Cuban wanted for murder. Rubio moped around the house for a couple weeks, but he couldn't take the inaction. He snuck out one night to go to the fights. The cops knew how much he loved boxing, and they were waiting for him. Rubio was a real man. He never told the cops where he'd hid out. He did his time and moved on.†

Grateful as Albert was that I'd helped Rubio, I could not count on a good vibe to make him feel better when I took away my business. Albert made at least a couple hundred thousand a month off the coke he sold me. With him, it didn't matter if it was a dollar or ten million dollars, he was a cheap motherfucker. One time I was at his house when I realized I'd left my wallet at home. I asked Albert to lend me some cash for the night. The motherfucker handed me a twenty-dollar bill.

---

* Records indicate that Roberto "El Rubio" Garcia was initially shot at by a jealous husband whose wife he was involved with. Garcia subsequently lured the husband and his father to his house and fatally shot the husband in front of his father. While Jon's version of the story garbles some of the details, he is probably correct that Garcia handled the situation in a "traditional man" way—assuming that man is a violent psychopath.

† With San Pedro providing legal help, Garcia was acquitted of murder in the shooting death of his victim Rafael Torres. He was freed and appears to have turned his back on the criminal underworld.

I reasoned the best way to handle him was to bring him a new customer to replace me. I had a friend, Joey Ippolito, who wanted to move kilos in Los Angeles. Joey was from Newark, New Jersey. His family was in the garbage business, but he got into weed smuggling and came down to Florida. Later, he bounced to L.A. and got hooked in to movie people. Going from garbage to celebrities, Joey was a big success.*

Joey told me he could move fifty or more kilos a month in L.A. My idea was that he could buy his coke from Gary Teriaca and Bobby Erra, who were buying from Albert. For Joey, buying from them made sense because they were moving coke out to Gary's friend in Aspen, Steven Grabow. He could pick it up out there, which was closer to L.A. than Miami. Obviously, it would have been simpler to sell Joey Ippolito coke directly from the Ochoas, but my aim was to keep Albert happy.

The other part of my idea was that I would go to Albert and suggest that he start buying his coke from the Ochoas. They would beat any price. Albert was a proud Cuban in some ways. But like most people, his greed was stronger than his pride, and he decided to buy from the Medellín Cartel.

By 1978 I'd traveled in a circle with Albert. I went from robbing

---

* Joey Ippolito, who died in 2002, was connected to the Bonanno family and had ties to Meyer Lansky. Ippolito, like Jon, is believed to have provided loans to developer Donny Soffer for the development of Aventura. After a conviction for transporting several tons of marijuana to Long Island, he went on to operate restaurants in Malibu and Brentwood, California. For a time O.J. Simpson's confidant Al "A.C." Cowlings worked for Ippolito as a bodyguard. Ippolito was arrested for cocaine trafficking shortly after the murders of Nicole Simpson and Ron Goldman and was the subject of rumors that he had ordered hits on the pair as a result of a drug deal gone bad. Through it all, Ippolito cultivated celebrity friends. Actor James Caan reportedly posted bail for him following a 1994 arrest. According to Eddie Trotta, a former criminal associate of Ippolito's who subsequently went straight, "Joey is the one who made up the story that he helped kill Ron and Nicole because he wanted the fame. He was my best friend, and I can tell you he was a complete nut. He once broke out of a minimum federal prison work camp by having a limousine service pick him up. He made it past the gates, but they arrested him two minutes later." Trotta was himself once arrested with Ippolito by the LAPD while the two were visiting their friend James Caan in his Los Angeles home.

him, to buying his coke, to making him into a customer of the Cartel. What I liked about this was, I earned my transport fee for the kilos I smuggled in for the Cartel. The more their business grew, the more I earned, and their business kept growing because Americans couldn't shove cocaine up their noses fast enough. Everybody wanted more and more.

46

J.R.: By 1979 my business was booming. I celebrated that year by betting a half-million dollars on the Super Bowl. The Steelers were playing the Cowboys at the Orange Bowl, and I put my money on the Steelers. Bookies took unlaundered cash, and paid unlaundered cash when you won, so it was almost play money. I bet mostly to increase my pleasure in watching the game.

When I bet, I liked to watch my games on TV. Sometimes when my team didn't do well, I'd break things, and I'd rather do that in my home or in a bar where I'm comfortable. But a couple days before the game, Merc Morris called me. "You want to go to the game?"

Even though it was my preference to watch it on TV, I wasn't going to turn him down. "Sure, Merc."

He laughed. "Then you've got to pay your dues."

That night I'm in the living room of my Coral Gables party house, and there's a knock on the door. I open it up and see Merc with a wall of monster guys behind him—several Pittsburgh Steelers. Soon as they come in, Merc says, "Break the shit out, man."

I threw down a quarter from my party stash, and everybody starts inhaling fat rails of the purest coke in the world. These guys were giants, and they snorted mountains of blow. A couple of these guys were heroes to me, and I was so interested, listening to their stories, it wasn't until dawn that I thought, *I got half a million dollars on these guys, and they're fucked up out of their minds a day before the game.*

It occurred to me that maybe I ought to call Bobby and put some money on Dallas to cover my ass. I said to one of the Steelers, "Are you guys going to crash from doing all this shit?"

I'll never forget it. One of them looked me in the eyes and said, "Listen to me, bro. This whole Pittsburgh-Dallas rivalry is hype. They make it out like Dallas could win. Dallas sucks. I don't give a fuck if I play at three-quarters of my ability and every other motherfucker here plays at half his ability. We are the better team. I promise you, bro. We are going to win. Go bet your fucking money."

"All right, bro."

Another Steeler said, "I'm going to get you on the sidelines tomorrow. You can watch us up close. We won't let you down."

"Okay, man. That's a very strong thing to say."

When I went to the Orange Bowl, I watched the Steelers win from the sidelines. It was a close game,* but they came through. The whole team went wild, but they didn't forget about me. One of them ran over to me and said, "Bro, I hope you brought some shit for us. We're having a party at the Eden Roc."†

Before I went to the game, I'd told a driver of mine to wait in a separate car outside the Bowl with a kilo of blow. I knew that win or lose, the Steelers were going to want to party. I had my coke guy follow me to the Eden Roc. Before we even got to the floor where the Steelers were having their party, the elevators reeked of weed.

---

* The Steelers won 34 to 31.
† The Eden Roc is a classic Miami Modernist hotel that opened in 1956. It's now part of the Marriott Hotel chain.

Upstairs they had a suite with a row of bedrooms filled with an endless variety of women. One of my new friends on the Steelers comes up to me and says, "I'm going to get you laid. You like black women?"

"Bro, I like women, period."

My friend points to a hot black girl, and she comes over. He says, "You're going to fuck this man so hard he's going to bleed from his dick."

This girl took me away, and she kept at me for hours. It wasn't until I was stumbling out of the Eden Roc the next morning, watching the sun rise over Biscayne Bay, that I even remembered I'd bet half a million dollars on the game and won.

47

J.R.: In early 1980 Fabito asked me to help with a new situation. His older brother Jorge had found an American pilot who was good at flying coke into the country. The Ochoas were always looking for new ways to move product. They understood that when you run something illegally, you have to always change how you do business. Over time cops get wise, snitches snitch, competitors move in. The Bahamas were getting heat from the U.S. government. On top of that, the Ochoas were leery of Carlos Lehder. I'd met him by then, and the guy was crazy. He was worse than Albert San Pedro with his voodoo. Carlos Lehder hero-worshipped Hitler. He talked about this openly. I don't care who you are, if you talk about how you want to make a Nazi state in South America and become the new Hitler, people will lose confidence in you.

This new pilot they found could pick up their coke in Colombia and fly it into the United States, but there was one problem. He would only land his plane in Baton

Rouge, Louisiana. He owned a hangar at the airport there, and at the time Baton Rouge was not being watched as a drug-smuggling center.* That was a positive. The bad part was that this pilot had no interest in moving the coke once he got it into his hangar. He wanted the Colombians to pick it up. Louisiana was all rednecks. There were blacks and Cajuns in Louisiana, but no Spanish. A Colombian in Louisiana would stick out.

Fabito asked me if I'd go with him to Louisiana to meet his pilot and figure out a way to have drivers pick up his coke. We flew on a commercial flight to Baton Rouge. On our way Fabito told me his family believed the pilot was trustworthy. But Fabito did not like him. Something about the guy rubbed him the wrong way.

The pilot's name was Barry Seal.† We met him at a coffee shop in a Ramada Inn. Barry Seal wasn't a tall guy, but he was big, maybe 220 pounds, and he made a lot of noise. He was boisterous. He looked like a braggart. When we sat down, he cracked a joke and overlaughed, so people looked at us in the coffee shop.

---

* Baton Rouge was home to a large number of small aviation transport companies that serviced the gulf oil industry. Baton Rouge–bound flights entering from the Gulf of Mexico did not typically arouse suspicion.

† Barry Seal, subject of the 1991 HBO film *Doublecrossed,* is one of the most storied figures of the early drug-smuggling era. In 1955, at age sixteen, Seal joined the Baton Rouge Civil Air Patrol, a flying club whose members included future presidential assassin Lee Harvey Oswald. By 1963 Seal had been recruited by the CIA to join Operation 40. The group, based in Mexico, included Frank Sturgis, who would later gain infamy as one of the Watergate burglars, and Porter Goss, later a Florida congressman, and then director of the CIA from 2004 to 2006. At the time Seal worked with these men, Operation 40 was a unit set up after the failure of the Bay of Pigs invasion to funnel arms to anti-Castro militants around Central America and the Caribbean. Seal was employed as an arms-smuggler pilot for Operation 40. Later Seal joined the U.S. Air Force and became a pilot for Special Forces operations in Vietnam. In 1966 Seal became an employee of TWA and was soon certified as the youngest 747 pilot in the world. While working as a TWA pilot, Seal continued his clandestine work for the CIA. In 1972 he was arrested in Mexico for smuggling two tons of C-4 explosive to a Cuban exile group that was planning terrorist attacks on the Castro government. Seal would claim that the CIA disavowed him after his 1972 arrest in Mexico. Seal was subsequently fired from TWA. He turned to drug smuggling to support himself. At the time Jon Roberts met him, Seal had recently been released from prison in Honduras, where he'd been held for marijuana smuggling.

Fabito jumped right to business. He said, "Barry, Jon's my friend. He's my *compadre*. He is me. And what you and him do, he don't have to ask me. You guys just get the shit done we need done."

I would know Barry for the next six years. He was definitely a blowhard. He drove around in an Eldorado convertible with the top down, no matter what the weather. All I ever heard him say was "I'm the best at this. I'm so good at that."

Barry could back up his bragging. He was a great pilot. He loved to fly. For smuggling, he used propeller planes. Small planes can land in more places and fly low under radar. But for fun, Barry liked to fly a Learjet.

Soon after I met Barry, he flew to Miami for a meeting. When we finished, I told him I was heading to a horse race in New Orleans. At that time the racehorse stable I'd founded to launder money was going strong, and I went to different tracks around the country to buy horses. Barry said, "I'll give you a ride."

We drove out to Opa-locka.* Barry had a little Learjet. It was a sharp-looking plane. When we got in, Barry said, "I'm going to give you the best ride you've ever had."

When we took off, he stood that plane on its tail. We went straight up, like in a rocket ship. When we get to the top of the sky, he said, "You think that was good? Wait until we go down."

That motherfucker, he turned the plane nose down. Then he turned the plane upside down. I don't normally get scared, but the motherfucker got me scared. I give him credit for that. After we landed, he said, "The Learjet is the safest plane made. The Swiss originally made this as a fighter plane. Even if we lost power, I could glide it in. It's the only jet that will do that."

That was Barry Seal. He loved flying like I loved robbing people. Some people said he was a cokehead, but I never saw him high. I never saw him chase women. He had a girlfriend, his secretary. She was in love with him. He was in love with her. When he was on

---

* Opa-locka is the large general aviation and military airfield near Miami.

the ground, they were inseparable. That was his whole life outside of flying.

Barry could fly in as much as a thousand kilos at a time—more than most pilots back then. After he landed, he'd stack the coke in his hangar. This used to drive Fabito crazy. He wouldn't even close the hangar doors. Barry didn't give a fuck. Ground work was beneath him.

That was my job—organizing the cars, the drivers, the stash houses, so Fabito's Colombian distributors in Miami and New York could get their coke.

I BECAME the guy Fabito turned to when there was a problem. I didn't have any special skills except that I was a gringo who could operate in America. When it came to the Ochoa family, my word was my bond. I was becoming almost like a straight businessman inside their organization.

The Colombians the Ochoas brought into the United States to be their soldiers—driving their cars, protecting their stash houses— were Indians from the mountains. They were peasants with gold teeth and guns, and they were the backbone of the Ochoas' U.S. distribution system. They ran coke to New York, Los Angeles, and anywhere between where they found buyers. These were the guys I delivered the Ochoas' coke to. In return, they gave me the Ochoas' money.

Whenever you have coke flowing in one direction, you get money flowing back. Cash and coke of the same value were about the same size. The only difference was cash was about half the weight. If I moved a hundred kilos of coke, I'd get about fifty kilos of money back.

These exchanges didn't go smooth at first. The Colombian soldiers tended to do things like they were in a gangster movie. They'd bring the money in one car, followed by five more cars loaded with guys carrying machine guns and knives. They were good guys, but one day they're in the jungle and the next day they're driving around Miami, heavily armed, with trunkloads of money and coke. Most were out of their minds on cocaine and *aguardiente*. It's a lucky thing they didn't have sobriety checkpoints in those days. These maniacs would have just slaughtered the police.

The first thing a Colombian mountain hick did when he landed in Miami was buy a $500 car and install a $1,000 stereo. The first exchange I did with them, I picked a quiet parking lot. These guys rolled up, drunk, heavily armed, blasting their stereos. They were going to bring the cops on a noise violation alone.

After that I met with Fabito and told him, "We got to change how your guys work. Let's have everybody relax. Keep everything low-key. Nobody needs to drive around with guns sticking out of the car. We're all on the same side here."

My way to deliver coke, or pick up money, was to keep everybody anonymous and separate. If I'm delivering coke, I have my guy drive a car with it in the trunk to a normal family restaurant like Denny's. He leaves the car in the parking lot and hides the keys in a ledge in the men's room. He walks out and gets picked up down the street by somebody else. The guys bringing money do the same thing with their car at a different restaurant. Once we get the keys to the money car, we tell them where the car with the coke is and where the keys are hidden. This way everybody is safe.

It would be very hard for cops or a do-gooder asshole citizen at one of these restaurants to see that drug deals were happening. Our activities were invisible.

As I used more and more drivers for my cars, I avoided hiring street people. I didn't need armed guys for this. I used kids trying to earn money for school, or working guys who needed a couple extra dollars for their mortgage. They were happy to earn a few bucks driving a car from point A to B. They didn't want to look in the trunk or ask stupid questions. They just wanted to earn their pay. Ninety-nine percent of the time, I never had a problem with these kids. The few times I did, they were very sorry.

I gave my drivers fake licenses. I'd found a guy whose cousin worked at the state licensing bureau. For a couple hundred bucks, I could send someone in to him, and he'd take their picture and issue a license in a fake name, and put it all in the main computer so if a cop ran the license, it came up as legit. If one of my guys got arrested, they could use the fake ID. I'd bond them out, and they could skip their bail. Obviously, once a guy was arrested, the heat took their fingerprints, but the system was so slow in those days, a guy could usually get out before they figured out who he really was.

I always tried to hire people through someone else. If I found one guy who was reliable, I'd have him hire the help he needed. When you do illegal work, you're better off to keep as much distance as you can from the guys working for you. Use your name as little as possible. Don't try to show everybody that you're a big shot. If I happened to pick up a car from one of the kids who didn't know me, I'd act like I was just another driver. That way if that guy's arrested, even if he wants to rat, he don't know who you really are.

I handled Fabito's Colombians the same as the Florida kids working for me. I got them fake licenses and had Danny Mones take care of any problems they had. These peasant Colombians were great guys but high-spirited. They were constantly getting arrested for bar fights, shootings, rapes—you name it. Soon as they got arrested, we'd bond them out and put them on a plane back to Colombia. You never want your guys sitting in a jail. That's when they get the ideas to rat people out.

My philosophy was the same as the Mafia's. Always take care of your guys.

FROM WORKING with Barry Seal, I learned there were small airports all over the United States that nobody watched. In Florida the DEA started to watch even the littlest airfields. In other states they were wide open. A small plane going from Baton Rouge to upstate New York or California could land with no problem.

Fabito had a Colombian distributor in Los Angeles whom he wanted me to supply with the coke that Barry brought into Baton Rouge. We decided to fly it to the Van Nuys airport.

My friend Joey Ippolito had his operation out there, too, with the coke he was getting from Gary and Bobby in Aspen, but the market was growing so fast, nobody worried about having more than one distributor in a city. In L.A. people snorted so much, you could carpet-bomb the city with blow and they'd ask for more. In other cities, where the Ochoas supplied more than one distributor, there were wars between them. But that was their problem, not mine.

When we flew coke into Van Nuys, we didn't want Fabito's guys driving into the airport, in case they brought heat with them. I talked to my lawyer Danny Mones about a good way to get coke out of the airport, and he helped me buy a small freight company in California. They had a little fleet of step trucks that they used to move things like furniture and office supplies. I renamed the company JF Transportation, for "Jon" and "Fabito." Looking back, it was probably stupid to use our initials, but I thought it was comical at the time.

Now, when we flew coke to Van Nuys, we put it in boxes labeled "office supplies." We had our drivers come to the airport in Van Nuys with bills of lading. Everything was proper. I started shipping coke to my friend Bernie Levine in San Francisco from Van Nuys using our trucks. He knew people with wineries up there, so our drivers would come back with wine and deliver it to restaurants in L.A.

Our delivery company actually made a profit. We sold the company after about a year, when one of our drivers drove drunk on the job and had an accident. The company got sued, and it was a nightmare. Moving coke was one thing. Dealing with lawsuits was another.

Everything I did was aimed at making things run smooth and quiet. In the late 1970s they started talking about "cocaine cowboys" overrunning the streets.* *Scarface* came out when I was at

---

* *Cocaine Cowboys* was the title of Ulli Lommel's 1979 cult film with Andy Warhol about rock stars battling the Mafia. Almost nobody saw the film except for perhaps an enterprising Miami reporter. Shortly after the movie's release, the term "cocaine cowboys" began appearing in Miami papers to describe the Latin drug gangs leading a surge in violence in South Florida.

my peak.* The mayhem of that movie was accurate, but when I saw it, I had to laugh. My goal was to run things very differently from the way Al Pacino ran his business. The backbone of my operation was American guys who did little jobs here and there, earned a few extra dollars, and kept their mouths shut.

I always tried to do my job with the opposite of violence.

That was my wish.

---

* *Scarface,* starring Al Pacino, chronicled the rise and fall of a fictitious Cuban coke dealer in Miami. It was released in 1983.

48

J.R.: I had very few upsets in my work during my first couple years with Fabito. All the chaos occurred on the personal side. Phyllis was a wicked lady, and I always went back to her. It had been like that since I was a kid in New York. No matter how much I chased other women, I'd come home to her, and out of the blue, I'd want her very badly, and she absolutely would not fuck me. When she pushed me away, it made me crazed. But Phyllis was the kind of woman, if you put a gun in her face, she'd laugh. I could rage at her to the end of the earth, and she had no fear.

When she finally made up her mind that she wanted to fuck, there was no woman who was better. That kept me on her leash. Whenever she wanted, she jerked me around the corner. I bought her houses, diamonds, horses, anything. When she told me to get her a special Mercedes 6.9 that she saw in a magazine, I had one flown over from the factory in Germany on a cargo plane.

I took care of her whole family. Every time her father

got busted, I paid for his lawyers. Her sister, Fran, was always coming to Miami for shopping trips with Phyllis. It took boatloads of cocaine to pay for the stupid shit they bought. Their cousin Henry—my "brother-in-law"—had become a top killer in New York, but he was a lousy earner. He had no mind for business. One time he got involved with some morons who sent him to Pakistan to pick up some hash. He landed and immediately got thrown in prison. Phyllis went crazy. Henry was her little angel. I spent a quarter-million dollars on lawyers to get him out. We had a welcome-home party for him in Miami, and Henry said, "Jon, if you ever need help down here, bro, we could make some real money together."

"Sure, Henry."

What else could I say? Even though Henry is the guy who turned a few pounds of hash into an international incident, he was the pride of the family. When I say Phyllis cost me, I mean I paid and paid for that whole family.

I WILL tell you something about Phyllis. She loved black guys. Most of her boyfriends before me were black. I never had a problem with that. One time they gave me a test where the doctor said I might be a "psychopath." Could be true. I might be a psychopath, but I've never been a racist.

Going back to Richard Pryor in New York, most of Phyllis's friends were black. After Phyllis came to Miami, she started spending a lot of time in California with Pryor, Herbie Hancock, and Billy Dee Williams.* She wasn't involved with these guys as boyfriends. She was godmother to Billy Dee Williams's daughter. They were her little group. As I bought houses for Phyllis and financed her decorating sprees in Miami, she'd unwind by taking off for California for weeks at a time. I'd visit now and then when I had

---

* Herbie Hancock is the Grammy-winning jazz keyboardist and composer. Billy Dee Williams is best known for costarring with James Caan in *Brian's Song* (1971) and for his role as Lando Calrissian in *The Empire Strikes Back* (1980).

business out there. The main thing Phyllis and her California friends did was play cards. They had card games that would go on for days. Billy Dee Williams wasn't a big poker player himself, but he was married to a Japanese girl named Teruko who loved cards. Herbie Hancock's sister, Jean, was another player. She was a math genius who flew all over the country fixing computers, and she was a musician.* Phyllis was very artsy, so she and Jean were close. Jean stayed at our house in Miami many times. Herbie was a down-to-earth guy. I liked him and his wife, Gigi, and his sister, Jean, and Richard Pryor best in the group. The other player in those games was Richard Dreyfuss. He liked cocaine more than cards.† I fixed up Phyllis with enough cocaine to keep the games going for days. Mostly the coke went to Dreyfuss and Pryor.

You never knew what Richard Pryor was going to say or do. He wasn't just a genius, he was insane. He used to go around introducing me to people, saying, "This is Jon, my coke-dealing friend in the Mafia."

Only Richard Pryor could say a thing like that in public and get away with it.

One time Richard didn't show up for the card game. This was nothing new. Hours later the door bangs open, and Richard walks in completely naked. He don't even got socks on his feet. "Sorry I'm late," he says.

Everybody's looking at him in shock. Someone says, "Richard, are you all right?"

"No, man. I'm not. I was raped."

This stops everybody. I notice Richard's hair is matted on one side. He's got scratches on his arm. He says, "I was crossing Sunset when a pack of black women surrounded my car at the light. They pulled me out of the car and threw me down. They tore my clothes

---

* Jean Hancock, a computer programmer, also composed music with her brother Herbie. She contributed to Earth, Wind & Fire's "Win or Lose" track for their Faces album in 1980.

† Richard Dreyfuss won the Best Actor Academy Award in 1977 for his role in The Goodbye Girl. In 1982 he was arrested for cocaine possession after passing out and driving his car into a tree.

off. One was a gorgeous lady. I reached for her, but the fattest bitch in the pack climbed on top of me. She pinned me down with her big ass, and she raped me. They all took turns. It was horrible, man."

Billy Dee Williams just looked at him. "What really happened, Richard?"

"I got in my car to drive here, and by the time I got halfway, I saw I didn't put my clothes on. I'm pretty wasted. Can I borrow some clothes, Billy?"

He was a funny guy, but he went out of his mind on drugs.*

If it weren't for my business in California, I never would have gone there. I didn't like actors. Film actors completely overrate themselves. Other celebrities have to do something—play a guitar like Jimi Hendrix or run like O.J. Simpson. Actors just talk and make faces.

PHYLLIS SPENT so much time away, it resulted in a thing happening that she never forgave me for. I ended up fucking Phyllis's sister, Fran. She was always at our house, and she looked so much like Phyllis, there were times I couldn't tell them apart. It didn't feel like cheating. Those sisters were like Coke and Pepsi. The difference was, Fran didn't play games. She was always ready to go.

I only fucked Fran in our house when Phyllis was in California. When she was home, I'd meet Fran at the International Inn, a cheap motel in Miami Beach.† It seemed to be going so well, I had the fantasy that someday I'd get the two sisters together. You know what I thought would have been interesting? If I could have convinced both sisters to lie down in front of me with their asses up, so I could do a comparison by fucking them side by side. I said this to Fran

---

* In 1981 Pryor nearly died when he accidentally set himself on fire while freebasing cocaine.

† The International Inn is still located at 2301 Normandy Drive in Miami Beach, and if the anonymous reviewers of tripadviser.com are to be believed, it remains the quintessential no-tell motel dump. As one reviewer described it recently, "Worst place on earth. Hores [sic] outside pimps looking at you. I felt I was in a *CSI* movie where I die." Or as another reviewer put it, "Views from the room were nice, but I don't expect blood, hair, and unidentifiable things on the bedsheets."

once, thinking she'd find it amusing, and she blew up. Next thing I knew, she told Phyllis, and that was it. I had to hide the guns in the house. I was sure she was going to shoot me. I could fuck a thousand women end to end, and that didn't bother Phyllis, but with her sister, she drew a line.

I had to laugh at how Phyllis decided to punish me. She'd poured hundreds of thousands of dollars into fixing up the estate I bought for her on Palm Island. She came to me and said, "You piece of shit. I'll never move into that house with you."

I told her, "Good for both of us. You can shove that house up your ass."

I sold it the next day. Phyllis and me seemed to go back to normal. But being a true Italian girl, Phyllis never forgave me. She nursed a secret grudge, and when I pushed her one more time, that poison came out of her and nearly finished me off.

49

J.R.: My end with Phyllis came when I met a woman named Toni Moon. In 1980 a friend of my sister's and his wife set me up with Toni. My sister's friend was a criminal defense attorney in New Jersey who often came down to Miami on business. He and I were friendly because I referred clients to him. On one of his trips to Miami he brought his new girlfriend, who was a model at the Ford Modeling Agency.* She was a beautiful redhead whom he later married. Back then that redhead heard how miserable I was with Phyllis, and she fixed me up with a model she knew from her agency, Toni Moon.

This couple had me over for drinks at their hotel in Miami, and in walked Toni Moon.† She was gorgeous, really striking. Did I fall in love with Toni Moon? It wasn't like I'd just smoked a hit of PCP and thought my

---

* The top modeling agency in New York and perhaps the most famous in the world at the time.

† "Toni Moon" was the stage name of Toni Mooney.

head would explode when I saw her. I was too old to swoon over a girl. But Toni got my attention.

Toni was tall. She was better looking than most movie stars. And she had brains. She'd knocked around the world. She'd lived in Paris, New York, Los Angeles. She took acting classes in New York with the top guy teaching it, Lee Strasberg.* But she wasn't a snob. She was a country girl who'd grown up in the Florida sticks. She rode horses. She knew how to hunt. I'd never met a woman like Toni before. She wasn't a phony. She was a natural woman.

As soon as I met her, I got a vision in my mind we'd make a life together.

My mistake was to tell Phyllis about this.

I BELIEVED the best way to make a clean break from Phyllis was to tell her I'd fallen in love with somebody else. I couldn't just say I was moving out or taking a break. I'd done that a million times. I had to say this was final.

I took Phyllis out to her favorite restaurant for dinner, Café Chauveron, a little place in Bay Harbor—not far from where I'd helped kill Richard Schwartz—that served a roast lamb that was out of this world. We sat down. I waited until Phyllis got some meat in her stomach, and I told her it was over. I told her she could pick one of my houses in Coral Gables to live in, she could keep her cars, keep her credit cards, but we were finished. I'd met a girl, and I was in love.

Looking back, I see my mistake. It's bad enough to break a girl's heart when she's in love with you. But if you do this to a girl who already hates your guts, it's not good, bro, especially with a wicked girl like Phyllis. You remember how I told you that back in New York her sister, Fran, got their cousin Henry Borelli to rob and kill her boyfriend Jack in the Toucan Shirt after she got jealous of him?

---

* Lee Strasberg was director of the acclaimed Actors Studio in New York and the godfather of method acting.

I told you how alike those sisters were in the sack. They were alike in more ways. Phyllis tried to get Henry to kill me.*

A couple of weeks after Phyllis and I broke up, I'm out romancing Toni Moon like a moron—riding horses on the beach, eating candlelit dinners, living in a dream—when I get a call from a guy who used to run with Ricky Cravero's gang. He tells me that my ex-brother-in-law Henry has come to town and is staying at the International Inn.

Henry was getting famous among wiseguys because of all the murders he was doing up in New York. It made no sense for him to come to town without telling me. The fact that he'd checked into a motel—the same place where I used to meet Fran—told me those two wicked sisters had brought him down to Miami for a reason.

I called my dirty cop friend, Lieutenant Mazzarella, and asked him if he could have some guys watch Henry. The motel was not in his jurisdiction, but he had brother dirty cops in Miami Beach who as a professional courtesy let him and his guys put eyes on the motel.

After a couple days Mazzarella told me Henry was sharing a room with a man. Henry certainly wasn't gay. He was lying low with the guy like they were planning something.

I went to the motel at sunrise. I brought with me a big guy who sometimes helped Bobby Erra with collections. I brought a gun with a silencer. I had my cops open the door to Henry's room, and I went in with my guy. The cops stayed outside. I put my gun on Henry. "Henry, what's going on, bro?"

Henry had balls. He sits up and looks at me with a gun in his face like it's nothing. "Hey, bro."

I say, "You know I love you, Henry. You're my family. But if

---

* I spoke to Phyllis several times by phone to confirm this and other stories Jon had told about her. Phyllis appeared to be disassociated from reality and mentally incompetent, as if suffering from senile dementia. I was told by a relative of hers that she was "very ill in her mind." Jon is the sole source of the story that Phyllis sicced Henry Borelli on him. Phyllis's sister, Fran, whom Jon implicates in the murder of her boyfriend Jack, passed away before I could interview her.

you're not straight with me, this room is where you're going to see your last piece of daylight. I want to straighten this out now. If you don't tell me what's up, that means we can't straighten this out, and we're done."

Henry tells me that Phyllis had wound him up about all the terrible things I'd done to her, and she told him I was never going to take care of her, despite all my money. So he'd decided to come down and rip me off. Henry wasn't like me. When I ripped off a person, I liked to keep them alive, so I could came back later and rip them off again. When Henry stole from a person, he'd kill that person. It's why he was so bad at making money.

After hearing Henry out, I say, "Henry, you know I would give Phyllis anything I had."

"I don't know what I was thinking, Jon."

"I wonder how we're going to solve this. You were straight with me, but I don't know what to say."

"Anything you want, Jon."

"You know what, Henry? I got a great answer. Let me do this one thing to help you out of this problem."

I go over to Henry's guy on the bed. My guy is holding him by his neck. Henry's guy has on Jockey shorts and a wife-beater. He looks like a mook you'd see twirling dough in a pizza shop. He has big muscles and gold chains. I say, "Were you going to rip me off?"

"Fuck you," he says.

"You got nothing, you piece of shit."

The dumb fuck comes into my city to rob me, then gives me attitude? What a moron. I aim my gun at his knee and *pop*. I shoot him once. The guy leaps sideways and bangs his head into the wall, like he's trying to escape through the plaster. My guy pushes him down on the bed.

"I'm only shooting your knees," I say.

My first shot had been lucky. It had gone into his knee and blown the bones apart. Normally, when you kneecap somebody, you want to press your gun to the side of the knee and feel for a bone that sticks out. If you shoot from the top, the kneecap can deflect the bullet. I once saw a guy in New York walk away after I shot him through the kneecap. He didn't go far, but it was surprising to see him take just one step. When you shoot in the bone on the side, your guy ain't going to walk after that.

After my first lucky shot, I'm more careful for the next one. I grab the good leg of Henry's guy and feel my way up it with the tip of my gun. I press my gun into the bone, and *pop*, no more knee. The guy goes limp from shock. I say, "It's very easy for me to blow your head off, but I think you got the message. Every time you try to walk for the rest of your life, you're going to remember that I let you live."

Henry's guy lost the wise mouth that he'd had thirty seconds earlier. He gasps, "Thank you."

My hand is disgusting. On the second shot, his blood and gristle had burst out and sprayed my arm. I go in the bathroom to wash it off.

When I come out, Henry has a little speech prepared for me. "Jon, I should have never thought about ripping you off. We never had a problem before. We are brothers. I was stupid. I will leave right away. I will never come back without telling you."

"Henry," I say, "it will break Phyllis's heart if you don't visit. Take a night. See your family, then go."

"You want to have dinner with us?"

"Maybe the next time, Henry."

I'M GOING to show you what kind of guy Henry is. That night he called me. He said, "Jon, I want you to see something."

We met outside the North Bay Village police station, where it's safe. Henry opened the trunk of his car, and inside there's his guy whom I kneecapped. Henry had put a bullet in his brain. He said, "Jon, I didn't want him giving you problems, and I wanted to make this right."

The guy in the trunk had been Henry's friend. But to show me how sincere he was, Henry had gone the extra distance. For all his faults, Henry was basically a good guy.

The incident had a good effect on Phyllis. Even though Henry didn't succeed in killing me, it got the poison out of her system. Phyllis and I stayed friends. I kept her in a house for years. Henry and I went back to being like brothers.

In 1985 Herbie Hancock's sister, Jean, flew down and stayed at a place I had for Phyllis in Coral Gables. Her last night there, we all had a nice dinner together. The next day Phyllis and I both drove her to the airport to see her off. We kissed her good-bye, and hours later her plane crashed. That was the end of Jean.*

It made me wonder about my father's philosophy about evil. Jean Hancock was one of the few good people I knew. And she gets in a plane that blows up. Henry, Phyllis, and I went on with our lives. If there is justice, why would guys like Henry and me get to go on in life?

Years later, after Henry went to prison,† and then I went to prison, I ran into him inside, where he was working as a barber. We laughed our asses off when we saw each other. He gave me my haircuts for months. It was great seeing him. Obviously, inmate barbers only get electric clippers, so I knew he wasn't going to slit my throat.

---

* Jean Hancock died on August 2, 1985, when the Delta Airlines jet she was taking from Miami to Los Angeles crashed in Grapevine, Texas, during an emergency landing.
† Henry Borelli was sentenced to life in prison plus 150 years in 1986. Though the presiding judge accepted evidence implicating Borelli in 70 to 200 contract killings, due to legal technicalities Borelli was convicted on 15 counts of grand theft auto.

50

J.R.: Toni Moon doesn't know the price I paid to be with her. She never knew about Henry or the guy whose knees I capped. Unlike with Phyllis, I never talked about my main business with her. When we met, I told her I was into real estate and racehorses. She was no dummy, though. Over time she saw I was involved with other lines of work.

Toni was an old-fashioned girl. She wanted a guy to build a life with. She was staying out in West Palm Beach in a little house with her mom when we met. Her work took her to New York and L.A., but Toni wanted a place with me where we could get away from it all.

We found a farm up in Delray Beach.* It was an hour's drive north from Miami. The beach side of Delray

---

* Though only about sixty miles north of Miami Beach, Delray Beach in 1980 was still largely an agricultural area and relatively undeveloped. It stretches west from the beach to the roughly four-hundred-square-mile Loxahatchee wildlife preserve in the heart of the Everglades.

was a little town of rich people, but the farm Toni found was inland by the Everglades. The area was nothing but farms and swamps and hillbillies in old trucks. The only civilization there was a Texaco station, a truck stop café, and the Hole in the Wall, a feed store for cattle.* That was it.

The property we found was in an unfinished development called Tierra Del Ray. What happened is in the 1970s some developer had decided to put in luxury estates—mini-ranches of ten or fifteen acres each. But the economy tanked, and the development never got finished. It was a gated community that ran out of money. Instead of country club people living inside, it was well-to-do rednecks. Some of the mansions were unfinished, and people lived in campers in front. There were cars up on blocks on the lawns, and people driving monster trucks. Behind the houses you'd see rednecks roaring past in airboats. They wore overalls and walked around with rifles. In that neighborhood a constant war was being waged against the alligators, who'd crawl out of the swamps and eat people's dogs, or try to grab the little hillbilly kids riding around on minibikes. It was redneck heaven.

The place Toni found was a half-finished Spanish house at the end of La Reina Road. It was on fifteen acres that backed up on the marshlands. We'd gone up there on a hot day. I got out in the hundred-degree heat, with mosquitoes trying to bite my arm off, horseflies so big they looked like birds, and I looked at this falling-down house and thought, *What the fuck is this?*

But Toni made me walk around. There were miles of horse trails in the area. There were trees and islands and canals. There were the most incredible birds and wildflowers everywhere. Ever since I was a kid, I'd wanted to have my own ranch like on *Bonanza*. Fifteen acres in Delray was no Ponderosa,† but it was enough. I bought it for $300,000. It was by far the best place I'd ever lived.

---

* The Hole in the Wall feed store is still in Delray.
† The Ponderosa was the Cartwrights' ranch on *Bonanza*.

• • •

TONI AND I turned that house into a luxury redneck palace. We added a pool, a dock in back, a skeet range, a barn, a six-car garage, a basketball court, and a guesthouse. I got so sick of driving up there from Miami, I bought a Hughes 500 helicopter. I parked it on the lawn and hired a full-time pilot, who lived in the guesthouse. For driving around town I got a Chevy Blazer with lifted suspension, so I blended in with the hicks.

I was glad to be out of Miami. The city had gotten violent in the past couple of years.* You had the Colombian peasants running around moving coke. Not just Fabito's guys from the Medellín Cartel. Up until the early 1980s Medellín was just one group of many. On top of them you had all the Marielitos overrunning the city.† Even the blacks staged an uprising in Liberty City over some guy who'd gotten a beating from the cops.‡

The problem wasn't a shortage of cocaine. Even when there was an excess of kilos on the street, gangs fought over the money to be made from it. Working with Fabito, I'd moved into what you would call management. Little subdistributors fighting over half-kilos on the street wasn't my problem. A guy who works in a motorcycle factory doesn't worry about morons driving those motorcycles he made into lampposts. I worked hard bringing in cocaine. What people did with it after they got it was up to them.

I turned our place in Delray into the ultimate getaway. I fenced off the main house. I put in mortar tubes that could launch tear-gas

---

* The homicide rate for the Metro-Dade region soared from about 50 murders per year in 1975 to more than 600 in 1981.
† The term *Marielitos* refers to the 100,000 Cubans who arrived by boat in South Florida in 1980.
‡ The 1980 Liberty City riots were sparked by the acquittal of five white police officers who beat a black motorist to death. In a retrial one of the accused officers agreed to a deal in which he provided information about corruption in the North Bay Village police department, which led to a two-year investigation of Jon's friend Lieutenant Mazzarella and his arrest.

bombs at intruders coming up the driveway. The mortars could be fired from switchpads inside the house. They'd slow down anybody coming onto our property looking for trouble, and tear gas was not against the law. I acquired a good number of hunting rifles and AKs. All the rednecks were well armed. We fit in with our neighbors.

Toni turned me on to the outdoors. I'd liked riding horses since I'd been with Vera in Mexico. We rode all the trails in Delray. Toni got me to take canoe trips around the marshes. We'd paddle around, smoke weed, drink wine, watch the animals.

I dug a pond in front of the house for ducks to live in. Toni collected exotic birds, and we built an aviary outside and connected it to the house so they could fly around inside.

We built a cage along one side of the house for our cat, Cucha.* She was a 150-pound cougar. We got her when she was a kitten from a woman who raised big cats at a farm in Broward. Cucha was a beautiful cat. We built a door from her cage so she could roam free from the house. My dogs liked cats since they'd lived for years with Princess, my little one-eyed kitty. Because we got Cucha when she was small, they acclimated to her before she grew into her full 150 pounds.

Cucha was a people cat. She followed Toni around the house and slept in the bed with us. Our only problem with Cucha was she liked to eat the exotic birds. She would get down low and make little chirping sounds to fool the bird, then she would leap. Cucha could jump ten or fifteen feet in any direction. It was a constant battle with her.

Our house was beautiful inside. It wasn't gaudy with chandeliers. It was a country house. The nicest piece was our dining room table, which I had sent to me from Italy. It was made entirely of ebony that was inlaid with ivory. People would look at my dining room table and gasp. It was the most sensational dining room table you've ever seen in your life. We had abstract paintings that I got

---

* *Cucha* is Spanish slang for "pussy."

from the painter Frank Stella, who I knew from the Palm Bay Club and was just a fun guy.* I also owned Erté paintings† and a rare series of prints showing the life of the Marquis de Sade that I kept in a velour book in my living room to show visitors.

My favorite place in the house was the glass room. I built a room off the western side of the house that was made completely of glass—walls, ceilings, even the floor. I put in a giant couch and spent more time there than any other part of the house. I felt secure in a glass room. I had my fences and tear gas and guns and dogs and my 150-pound cat. Cucha was very loyal.

I used to put a leash and chain around Cucha's neck and ride around with her in my Blazer. I'd take her into town to eat lunch with me. We'd take an outside table, and I'd tie her to a phone pole. Everybody knew Cucha.

I'd take her to the beach, too. She liked to bite the waves. One time I was driving down the beach with Cucha poking her head out the window, and I got carried away and drove into the water. *Boom.* A wave came up and sucked my truck into the sea. Cucha and me had to fight our way out. She towed me out of the water with her leash. I left my Blazer rolling in the waves.

Later, the city sent me a bill for removing it.

Those were good times up there. I give Toni credit for that. She wasn't like most lazy-ass, buying-shit-at-the-mall women I'd known. She was different.

---

* Frank Stella is one of the most acclaimed artists of the second half of the twentieth century, and in 2009 President Obama presented him with a National Medal of the Arts at a ceremony in the White House. In the 1980s he was also known for flaunting his love of racehorses and Ferrari sports cars. He frequently visited Miami and stayed at the Palm Bay Club.

† Erté, a master of Art Deco in the 1920s and 1930s, is known for his stylized paintings of women who are draped with jewels and feathers and are often accompanied by leopards.

TONI MOON: Do you know what it's like to love somebody beyond belief, to be passionately and madly in love with them? Jon was madly, passionately, wildly in love with me, and I felt exactly the same way for him. If he says anything different today, it's because of his pride. He can't admit to anything that he thinks shows weakness, and it's a shame because his capacity to love is the only worthwhile thing he's ever had, and that's what he fights the hardest to destroy.

J.R.: I'd finally learned by then that when you do illegal things, you should not get all the way close to your woman. Prisons are filled with guys ratted out by their women. I'd learned about a woman's wrath with Phyllis. When I got with Toni, I knew the best course was to have fun together but to always keep her at arm's length. Still, we had a very good life.

Have you ever seen a real Florida electric storm? In Delray the most amazing storms in the world would push out from the Everglades and swallow the house. I used to lie in the glass room with Toni, my cat, my dogs, and watch for hours. There was nothing like it. That was my life when I had my reign at the top.

51

J.R.: Without her realizing it, Toni helped introduce me to the man who put me at the top of the Medellín Cartel's operations in America. The whole time I was working with Fabito, I knew there were other Americans helping out the Cartel, but I didn't know who they were until about 1980, when I met Max Mermelstein. Max did what I did for Fabito, but he worked for Fabito's brother, Jorge, and for Pablo Escobar. They had a separate line of importation that was bigger than Fabito's. Soon enough, Max and I combined what we were doing, and our joint operation became the biggest part of the Colombians' smuggling effort.

When I met Max, it was getting more and more difficult to run boats out of the Bahamas. Everybody was turning to pilots who could haul coke from Colombia into the United States. I had Barry Seal, but I was looking for more people to fly for me. Toni knew many pilots. Being a model, she got jobs where she was flown to different places. And just being a beautiful woman, she got plenty of offers from rich assholes who wanted to fly her to a party in the Bahamas or the Keys. Before she met me, she'd become friendly with a pilot named Shelton Archer.

Shelton was actually a very bad pilot. Before I met him, he had almost killed Toni when he crashed a plane he was flying her in. But he was kind of a character, and Toni and he stayed friends despite his nearly killing her. Shelton was an Englishman, which helped him get away with being such a moron. People heard the accent and believed he was more intelligent than he was. Shelton wasn't actually an upper-class Englishman. He was the low-class kind you always meet in warm places like Florida and California. If you've ever been to those places, you know the type. Maybe the guy was a cabdriver back home in London, but in America he uses his accent to pretend he's an English lord. Shelton was true English scum. The best way to explain him is to tell you what his favorite thing was besides crashing planes. He'd take a camera, with no film in it, and go to the mall and pretend to be an English fashion photographer so he could pick up high school girls and fuck them. That was Shelton at his finest.

Shelton reminded me of Phyllis's father. He'd start off with a good idea or piece of luck, and then completely blow it. He was the type of guy who stepped in dog shit every time he put his shoes on. He'd get a scheme going, and sure enough the next week you'd hear the plane went down or his connection got busted or he fucked the wrong guy's wife or daughter. I'm amazed he wasn't killed many times over.*

The one thing Shelton had was that he knew everybody. I tolerated him because even though he was a stupid jerk, he knew

---

* Shelton Archer (who also uses the name Sheldon) was arrested and incarcerated numerous times on drug-trafficking-related charges, beginning in the mid-1980s. According to law-enforcement sources, Archer began working as a snitch after his earliest arrests, but his information often proved to be unreliable. His last conviction was at age sixty-five in 1999 for running a marijuana farm in northern Florida. After serving two years in prison, Archer relocated to Indonesia and married a woman forty-nine years his junior. As of 2011, he is running an Asian bride service at Indonesian-wife.com.

other pilots who were good. Most important, Shelton knew Max Mermelstein.

When Shelton met me, I started asking him about pilots, and soon enough he figured out that real estate wasn't my main business. He hinted around that he could fly anything I ever needed, and I put him off. Obviously, I wasn't eager to hire a guy who'd crashed my girlfriend.

So Shelton tried a different angle. He came to me one night and said, "Johnny"—the English jerk always called me Johnny—"I'm going to do you the favor of your life. You're going to owe me for this one."

"What am I going to owe you for?"

"For introducing you to the biggest smuggler in Miami."

A week later Shelton told me his guy wanted to meet me at a Howard Johnson's on Collins Avenue. That's how I first got to know Max Mermelstein.*

I MET Max over a plate of Howard Johnson's clam strips. It was disgusting food, and I'm glad that chain of restaurants went out of business, but Howard Johnson's would be Max's favorite place to meet the next several years that we worked together. The lazy slob lived down the street from it in Sunny Isles.†

Shelton had told me Max would be a large man with a mustache. I got there first and waited. In walked a guy with a mustache. He was a couple years older than me, and he wore a tweed jacket. I first thought he was another English bullshitter like Shelton. He walked up to my table in a hurry, like he was doing me a big favor by giving me his time. "You Shelton's friend?" he said.

I could hear he was American. Under his tweed coat he wore a silk shirt with a gold Jewish star around his neck. He sat down and

---

* In his interview in the documentary *Cocaine Cowboys,* Jon stated that he met a Colombian associate of Max's first. Jon now believes his encounter with Max at the Howard Johnson's was his first. In her interview with me, Toni Moon also recalled that Shelton Archer introduced Jon directly to Max.

† Sunny Isles is an upscale housing development on the western side of Sunny Isles Beach, north of Miami Beach.

puffed his cheeks out, looking at me like I should think he was a man of importance. Max was a fat fuck. He was maybe five-nine, 220 pounds. He waddled when he walked. He was very nervous, lighting cigarette after cigarette. His fingers shook. His big-shot act was not successful. To me, he was just a nervous fat guy with a mustache.

Normally, when I tried to feel out who other guys were, we'd do lines and chase broads. Max didn't do coke. He barely drank, and he chased women very quietly because he was terrified of his wife. So he ordered the clam strips and talked about Papucci, a shoe shop he owned at the Four Ambassadors Hotel.* The shop was for laundering money, but Max talked like he was the shoe king of Miami. When I talked about boats, Max made sure to tell me he had one that was bigger than mine.

That was my first meeting with Max. He told me if I ever went to Papucci, he'd give me a discount on some fine shoes imported from Spain.

I'd soon find out Max was everything Shelton said he was, and at the same time nothing at all. Inside that fat body was a very small man. Max was like the emperor's new clothes of crime bosses. He was for real, but he was also the scaredest bitch I'd ever met. He sucked on every cigarette he smoked like it was going to be his last breath.

Max's fear would be my in with him. We'd become partners because he was too chicken to be a drug lord on his own. He needed somebody to hold his hand.

---

* The hotel is still located at 801 Brickell Bay Drive in Miami.

52

J.R.: Soon as I met with Max, I had Danny Mones do a criminal record search on him through a friend in the Miami police. If a guy is a snitch, often he'll have a long record. Max came up clean.

Then I sat down with Fabito. We met in the Omni shopping center at a raw bar that served the best oysters in all of Florida. When I brought up Max, Fabito gave me a funny look and said, "I knew it had to happen."

"What do you mean?"

"He does what you do, but for my brother Jorge and for Pablo Escobar."

At that time I didn't know who Pablo Escobar was. I found out Pablo was the hands-on guy in Colombia who ran the coke factories, and Max was his guy in Miami who was running coke planes into Florida and landing them in fields outside of Miami. When Fabito and I first talked about this, Fabito's main worry was that I'd be offended that his family had another guy doing the same work as me, or that I'd see Max as a rival.

I told Fabito I didn't care about Max. I didn't have the appetite to fight my way up the organization and push guys aside. I was content doing what I was doing.

IT WAS Max who worked to bring me deeper into his organization. After our lunch at Howard Johnson's, Max invited me out to his farm in Davie.* Max on the farm was ridiculous. He wore a cowboy hat and boots and showed off his collection of Paso Finos. I didn't yet know that these high-stepping midget horses were the favorites of Fabito's father, Don Ochoa, and were a symbol of the Ochoa family. Max bragged that he got them from a "friend" in Colombia. When we were walking around his farm, Max noticed me looking at a wooden porch swing by the house. It was a very large swing for two people to sit on. Max asked me if I liked it. I said, "Sure."

A few days later, I was at my house in Delray with Toni when a truck drove up with a giant wooden porch swing on it. Max called me and said, "I thought you and your girl could enjoy the view from the swing."

"Okay, Max. Thanks for the fucking swing set."

It was comical. The guy tried to win me over with a swing set. To understand why Max was so eager to have me helping him, you need to know how Max started working for the Cartel.

MAX WAS from New York, but in the early 1970s he moved to Puerto Rico to take a job at a hotel. Max always bragged that he was an "engineer," like he was a guy who built rockets or bridges. But what I believe is, he was the kind of "engineer" they have in the hotel who comes to your room and fixes the lightbulb when it's broken, or brings a new battery for the remote.†

---

* Davie, in Broward County, was a cattle-ranching community that grew in the 1970s to include residential developments. Today it prides itself on its Old West flavor and features a main street laid out like a Wild West frontier town.

† Max Mermelstein was a mechanical engineer who claimed to have a degree from

Max's in with the Colombians came in Puerto Rico, where he met a beautiful dancer at a strip club. Her name was Cristina, and she was a few years younger than Max, but she already had two children. Max fell completely in love with her and married her. Max raised her kids like his own, and he would always tell me how lucky he was to have Cristina.

Cristina brought Max something else besides her smile and her beautiful body. She had a cousin back in Colombia named Pablo Escobar. I don't know if she was an actual cousin of Pablo's or if she just used that word, the way Henry Borelli and I used to say we were "brothers," but Cristina and Pablo were close enough that Max got special trust with Pablo Escobar. I believe Max Mermelstein is the only American who could claim he was married into the Medellín Cartel. That was his strength.

When Max married Cristina, the Cartel barely existed. Max was a mostly straight, working guy bringing lightbulbs to people in hotels. On the side he dealt a few bags of weed to make pocket money, but that was the extent of his criminal career. In 1976 he and Cristina moved to Queens, and when they got there, Max had no money.

They arrived in Queens just as a little community of Colombian immigrants was getting started in cocaine. It was small-time. Their relatives would send over a few kilos at a time in suitcases on regular commercial flights from Colombia, and these newcomers would sell it around New York. As the operation grew, Pablo Escobar sent over a street guy named Rafa who was his trusted lieutenant.* Rafa's job was to oversee the importation business. When he got to Queens, he looked up Pablo's cousin, Cristina, and that's how he met Max.

---

the New York Institute of Technology in Manhattan. If true, Max's employment history as a low-level maintenance engineer at hotels and country clubs suggests he did not maximize the career potential afforded him by his degree—at least, not until he became chief of transport operations for the Cartel.

* Rafael "Rafa" Cardona-Salazar was about twenty-two years old when Mermelstein met him in 1976. Rafael was more likely taking orders from Jorge Ochoa in 1976 than from Escobar, whose rise in the Cartel was just beginning.

From the start Max had that trust of being in Pablo's family through Cristina, and he was useful because he was a gringo. Max could drive and pick up a kilo of cocaine somewhere and not look as suspicious as a Colombian.

In 1978—the same time Fabito came to Miami and met me—Rafa decided Max and Cristina should move to Miami to build up the business. Max started helping with boats and planes and pilots and cars, just like I did. By the time I met him, he and the pilots he had working for him were moving more than me, because inside the Cartel, Pablo was more aggressive in pushing cocaine out.

Years later Max made the most ridiculous claim I've ever heard. He told people he never wanted to be in the cocaine business, but Pablo Escobar's guy, Rafa, "kidnapped" him and forced him to do everything he did.* Please. I never saw anybody put a gun to Max's head and force him to smuggle coke.

Max loved money, and he loved being *"El Jefe"*—the boss. That's what he liked to be called by the Colombians who worked for Rafa, *El Jefe*. Nobody loved being a big shot more than Max.

I'll concede that there was some element of truth in Max's story that he was kidnapped by Rafa and forced to smuggle cocaine against his will. Rafa always had a house near where Max lived, and he was always with him. Rafa would say his job was to "help" Max, but Rafa was Max's true boss. Rafa carried the orders from Pablo Escobar. Rafa had to treat Max with respect because of his marriage and the position he had for being a gringo. But Rafa was a mad dog who left bodies everywhere he went, and he terrified Max.

Underneath his *El Jefe* act, Max was a nervous fat guy who accidentally married into a job at the top of the Medellín Cartel. I believe Max sent me swing sets and brought me in to help him because

---

* In *The Man Who Made It Snow,* by Max Mermelstein as told to Robin Moore, published by Simon & Schuster in 1990, Mermelstein indeed claims that he lived in such fear of Rafa that he was his virtual prisoner for nearly a decade.

he wanted protection. He never put it like that, but I could see, as I got to know him, that he didn't want to be the only gringo surrounded by insane Colombians. If he had me with him and something went wrong on a shipment, he could blame me. That was a big help to Max. And he knew I could never fully take over his position because of his marriage, which made him royalty to the Colombians. Max was like a king who wanted somebody to help him run his country. As long as he got to be the figurehead king, he'd be happy.

WHEN YOU hung out with Max, you saw that everything he did was to show what a tough guy he was. On his ranch in Davie, he dressed in his cowboy outfit. When you went to his house in Sunny Isles, he'd show off his gun collection. He owned a full arsenal that included everything from antique rifles to machine guns. When he first showed me them, he said, "Do you like to hunt?"

"Not really my sport," I said.

Max fancied himself a big-game hunter. He used to go to a farm in Texas where some mad scientist mated cows with buffalos and made giant freak animals called beefalo. Max and a bunch of other idiots would pay to go there with their asshole rifles and hunt these ridiculous animals. To this day I don't understand what the reward could be in that. To kill an animal in a captive fucking area? It's like going to a zoo and looking over at the lion and shooting the lion in the head. Is that a joy? Does it really show how skillful you are? One time he gave me a freezer-load of beefalo meat that he'd killed. I hauled it out to the swamp and fed it to the alligators. I'd rather eat Bambi than eat a beefalo.

Later Max got into cockfighting. He'd have cockfights at his farm with all the Colombians who worked for Rafa. But the more Max tried to show how tough he was, the more I saw he was a man with a big pussy between his legs.

Much as I found Max to be distasteful, we were a good fit. He wanted to be the figurehead who did no work, and I wanted to run things but not be the boss of an organization. Max and I together became the top Americans in the Medellín Cartel.* I don't claim I put the Colombians on the map. I don't claim Max did. The Colombians put themselves on the map. But Max and I took them to a level they hadn't been able to reach before.

---

* Max and Jon would be indicted by the federal government as the Cartel's top "American representatives."

53

J.R.: The first thing I ever did with Max came at the direction of Fabito. In late 1980 I'd stopped using the cop's stash house in North Bay Village. I'd started paying some of the drivers I used to rent their garages. I'd use guys with the most boring, normal suburban homes I could find. We'd just park the coke car in the garage until we needed to deliver it. I ran into a problem when one of my drivers worried that some cops were watching his house. We had a big shipment come in, and I had no place to hold it. Fabito told me that Max's guy, Rafa, could let me use one of his stash houses.

Rafa lived around the corner from Max in Sunny Isles. Rafa was a wiry kid, and he was very hyper because he constantly smoked what the Colombians called "bazookas." A bazooka was a normal cigarette, except half the tobacco was squeezed out and replaced with cocaine. Rafa had a bodyguard named Flaco whose main job was to follow him around and roll bazookas.

When I went to see Rafa, he'd heard already that I

was coming. I'd met him a few times with Max, and he was very personable. He drove me out to his stash house in Kendall, a suburb built in the 1970s for white people fleeing Cubans in Miami. It was now being taken over by Colombians like Rafa.* It looked like the Colombians in Kendall had all used the same architect Albert had used to build his madhouse in Hialeah. In Kendall they'd buy a house on a normal suburban street, add a couple stories to it, cover the whole thing in burglar bars, and build a fifteen-foot wall around it. Rafa's stash house was a fortress.

When he took me inside, he showed me something I'd never seen, except in a movie. We walked into a normal-looking den. Rafa picked up a garage door opener and clicked it, and the wall slid open. Inside there was a stack of at least a thousand coke bricks, and bundles of cash piled to the ceiling.

"Is this good?" he asked.

"Sure, Rafa."

That's where I had my driver deliver our coke.

Later I found a redneck neighbor of mine in Delray who was a master electrician and contractor and could build hiding places like Rafa's. Unlike Rafa, I selected stash houses in anonymous neighborhoods all over Dade and Palm Beach counties. I picked houses belonging to people who worked regular jobs and didn't have criminal records.

RAFA AND I were very tight from the start. He was easier to deal with than Max. I'm not saying he was a barrel of laughs. He was like Albert in that he'd sometimes kill a person for no fucking reason. He was almost like a little kid, though. A lot of the Colombian street guys were like that. They could shoot someone one minute and the next minute be laughing or crying. If Rafa saw a sad episode of *Little House on the Prairie*—which was his favorite American TV show—he'd bawl his eyes out. Rafa's favorite fucking place

---

* Kendall was originally a white-flight enclave that in the 1980s attracted large numbers of Colombians involved in the drug trade. Police eventually nicknamed it "Doperville."

on the planet was Disney World. To me, that place is like a fucking prison, with children and the guy in the rat suit.* But Rafa and his guys loved that shit. Even Pablo Escobar, when he was the most wanted man in the world, once snuck into Florida just to visit the Magic Kingdom.

The secret to handling Rafa was knowing how coked out he was at any given time. This was easy to determine based on watching how either he or Flaco, his bodyguard, rolled bazookas. When they rolled one, they'd pinch tobacco out of it, and they'd always pile the tobacco on the table. If the pile was small, Rafa was okay. If the pile was big, he might be out of his mind.

Rafa was married to a very petite Colombian girl, Odelia. We'd be out at dinner somewhere, and she'd look at him wrong, and he'd punch her. I'd never seen anything like it. One time he broke her face and put her in the hospital. She came out with wires on her jaw to hold it together. It looked like a birdcage on her head. A month after that, she and Rafa were at Disney World laughing like kids.

Rafa was the most unstable person you'd ever meet. But he always kept some reason in his brain. He knew he couldn't touch Max because Max had Pablo Escobar on his side. Rafa understood the force that Pablo had. If someone didn't have force backing him up, Rafa would cut that guy to pieces.

I never had any problems with Rafa, except once or twice. My main problem with Rafa was partying. Since Rafa smoked coke, when you partied with him, he wanted you to smoke it. He'd be after me, *"Fume, fume, fume!"*—smoke it.

I'd say, "Rafa, I don't smoke cigarettes. It'll choke me."

"Fuck it! Smoke with me."

There were times I'd sit in his house with him, and I'd be so fucked up, I couldn't move. My arms and legs would be numb, and I'd be thinking, *What have I done to myself?*

Rafa would sit across from me covered in ashes. He'd smoke his bazookas down, not noticing as the ashes fell on his chest. I'd be

---

* Jon means Mickey Mouse.

paralyzed. I'd hear my heart beating, but I could barely move my eyeballs. Rafa would want to do more.

I'd tell him, "No more."

"Oh, no, no, no! You don't leave now," he'd say. "You sit here until I'm done."

"I'm leaving, Rafa."

"What do you want? You want a girl? You want whores?"

I once spent two days trapped at his house. I'm not sure it's medically possible, but I think the two of us smoked an entire kilo. Maybe Flaco helped. Other guys who worked for Rafa came in to ask a question, and he'd yell, "Get the fuck out," and shoot at the walls and ceiling. We'd do target practice by shooting at the chandeliers. I saw myself in the mirror, and I was covered in bazooka ashes, too. I looked like a mummy. All I could do was laugh at this crazy fucker. Rafa was wacko, wacko, wacko. The party didn't stop until Rafa passed out. Once he was out, I wouldn't even check his pulse. I'd tell Flaco, "Get me the fuck home."

Flaco and his guys would put me in a car and deliver me to Delray like a piece of beefalo meat. You wouldn't see me again for two days. Rafa was unbelievable. I'll be honest, 50 percent of my job when I started with Max was babysitting Rafa.

54

J.R.: While I was getting more friendly with Max and Rafa, I was still working with Barry Seal. One day Max asked if I could manage to get a load of coke flown from Colombia into Florida for him. Max had another guy he worked with who ran flights for him, but he wanted to try me out.

What Max wanted was different from what I did with Barry Seal. He wanted me to have a plane pick up a load of four hundred kilos from an airfield near Barranquilla* and fly it to Florida. Instead of landing the plane at an airport, he wanted me to have the pilot deliver it to an empty field. That was the method Max was using back then.

Shelton Archer, the jerk-off Englishman, was still hot for me to give him a job. In those times pilots often didn't get hired directly to smuggle. They usually had

---

* Barranquilla is a coastal city about two hundred miles from Medellín. Typically, cocaine from Barranquilla was controlled by a smaller cartel that was a rival to the Medellín operation.

somebody managing their work, like I did with Barry Seal, so the pilot could focus on flying. But I had no confidence in him, so I went to another pilot.

This pilot was a guy I'd met through Shelton, but unlike Shelton he was talented. I'd been using him to fly from Baton Rouge to Van Nuys. This guy was the best pilot I ever worked with. What made him so good? He never got caught. He flew hundreds of loads, made a fortune, and retired. That's the best smuggling pilot there is.

Today he's married, a grandparent and a pillar of his community, so I'll call him Roger. Roger was from an old Florida farm family. Dirt poor. He learned to fly by becoming a crop duster. He'd done weed smuggling before I met him. He was a big, quiet redneck.

He lived almost at the top of the state. When I called him to talk about this new job, he said, "Come up to Yeehaw Junction, and we'll talk."

I said, "Roger, come on, man. You're making this shit up. There is no place on earth called Yeehaw Junction."

"No, Jon. There is. I want you to see it. We'll meet at the restaurant."

I got in my car, and I drove a couple hours north, and there really was a Yeehaw Junction. There's only one restaurant. Inside it was decorated with dead frogs hanging on the ceiling and alligator mouths sticking out from the walls. Every fucking redneck in the world was sitting in this shithole restaurant eating, happy as fuck.

I sat down with Roger and ordered a bowl of grits. Yankees think grits are like a bowl of cereal for dumb southerners, and that you eat them by putting sugar on them. That's the wrongest thing there is. Rednecks taught me that you eat grits with butter and a little salt. That way they're very good.

To Roger I floated the idea of his picking up four hundred pieces in Barranquilla, and he said it would be no problem. He flew King Airs that could handle the load and go the distance.* But when he crossed into Florida, Roger didn't want to land, unload coke, and

---

* The King Air was a relatively large and fast turboprop made by Beechcraft.

then take off again. He wanted to do an airdrop. He brought me up to Yeehaw Junction to show me a suitable place, a farm outside the town. We drove out to a field with trees around it so nobody could see his plane from the main highway when it came low to drop the bales of coke.

Roger had a kicker from his marijuana-smuggling days who was very good. A kicker is the guy who pushes the cocaine out of the plane. He's key to an airdrop. A plane has a little door on it, and the kicker has to move fast so he doesn't scatter the load over several miles. But he can't move so fast that he falls out the door. Many times kickers got so excited throwing out the loads, they fell from the planes, or their feet would get tangled in a strap and they'd get pulled out. Of all the people it took to smuggle a load, kickers had the shortest life span. Roger's guy had smuggled weed with him for years.

Roger wanted the coke in twenty-five-kilo bales. He had a little crew of guys who'd bring ATVs up to the farm in pickup trucks. They'd park their trucks in an old barn and race out in the ATVs to grab the coke.

All I had to do was send my drivers to the barn, and they'd pick it up. Roger had never done a coke flight before, and I'd never picked up coke in a field, but he was confident, so it made me confident.

I went to Max and told him I could run the flight from Barranquilla. Max told me he had a car I should use to pick up the coke in Yeehaw Junction. I had to stop him there. One car for four hundred kilos was not right. Four hundred keys was a half-ton. The weight could bust the axle. Even if it didn't, the car would sink so low, cops would pull you over just to see what was in your trunk.

"I don't need your car, Max. I got plenty."

"Jon, you want this car."

Max took me into his garage and showed me his green Continental. It was an ugly piece-of-shit Lincoln with a landau top—vinyl over the roof—like old people drove back then. "Max, I ain't taking this Jew canoe."

Max smiled and opened the trunk. It was so deep, you could

have stood a tall midget in there and closed the lid. Max explained he had a guy who custom-made the car. He'd made the trunk deeper by taking out the gas tank underneath it. He'd put in an aluminum gas tank from a racing car that he'd hidden under the backseat. The car had special air shocks that jacked up the rear when you put a load in it. The car could carry a half-ton load and look normal. The engine was a blown-out monster, but from the outside you'd never know it was a hot rod. The guy who made this car for Max was a genius. His name was Mickey Munday. Soon I'd meet him, but not soon enough.

UNFORTUNATELY, THE Continental Mickey made for Max was so good, I got overconfident. I had a lackadaisical attitude toward the job. I thought it would be fun to watch the drop, so my plan was to go up there in the same car with my driver. I'd have him drop me at the restaurant in Yeehaw Junction and eat grits while he picked up the coke in the barn. Since I didn't like to ride in a car with coke in it, I'd send my driver back to Miami alone and have my helicopter come and get me.

I decided to use my new brother-in-law as my driver: Toni Moon's little brother, Lee, who'd recently moved into our house in Delray. Lee was a big, blond redneck kid about nineteen or twenty. He reminded me of those guys on that TV show *Dukes of Hazzard*. First time I gave him the keys to one of my cars, he pancaked it within half an hour. Somehow, after rolling it on the street, he flipped it back over and drove it back with the smashed roof. The windshield was six inches lower. "Sorry, Jon," he said.

What could I do? The kid was my brother-in-law. I decided to teach him responsibility by giving him work. I said, "Lee, can you drive without wrecking the car or getting pulled over for speeding?"

I made him my driver for the Yeehaw Junction job. The morning of the drop we left before sunrise. We pulled up by the restaurant with the dead frogs inside. I was all set to go in and eat a nice hot bowl of grits when I opened the door and heard a plane buzzing in the sky. I said, "Stay. Don't move the car."

I stepped out. I couldn't see Roger's plane, but it was so loud, it sounded like a kamikaze plane in the movies. That wasn't right. He was supposed to come in slow and quiet. The whole town was buzzing. Then I noticed that there were other sounds mixed in—a jet, helicopters, sirens.

I opened Lee's door on the driver's side of the Lincoln and said, "Move over."

I didn't want Lee doing any of his *Dukes of Hazzard* driving stunts.

"Is that cop cars?" Lee said as the sirens became louder.

"I'm going to slowly drive us the fuck out of here," I said.

Now we see cop cars driving into town with their lights on. We make it two miles out of the town. One cop car whips around and comes behind us. He puts his lights on, and I pull over.

There's nothing in the car, obviously. But I didn't know what the hell is going on in the sky, and if a cop poked around and saw the special shock absorbers and fuel tanks, that could lead to some questions.

The cop who walks over to my window is the worst kind of redneck. Sunglasses. A bushy mustache. An Adam's apple like a fist. I play it cool. Lee and I both have fake licenses. I hand mine over to the cop. He asks my name, and I tell him whatever name was on my fake license. He asks Lee a couple of questions, and being a southern boy, Lee is very good with the cop, saying, "Yes, sir. No, sir."

The cop asks what we're doing up in Yeehaw. I tell him I'm test-driving a car that a guy in Miami souped up, and I wanted to ride her on a long-distance trip.

The cop says, "Why'd you come to Yeehaw?"

"I drove past here once on my way to Disney World, and I've stopped here ever since because it's so hilarious."

The cop gets a little offended. "What's funny about it?"

"The name Yeehaw. It's like that TV show, *Hee Haw.*"

"I live in this town, and I have never compared it to the TV show," he says. Now I got a cop trying to pick a fight, so I decide to handle him very carefully.

"Officer, with all due respect, are you going to tell me Yeehaw isn't a funny name? Plus, you got a restaurant filled with dead frogs."

"You've been there?" he asks.

"I eat there all the time. You can't get grits like that in Miami."

"You eat grits?" he says.

I tell him how I'd grown up in the North, and I didn't know about grits until I moved to the South and somebody showed me the right way to put butter in them. This changes his whole attitude. He hands back my license and tells me I'm welcome anytime in Yeehaw Junction. Now that we're best friends, I'm dying to ask him what's going on with all the sirens and helicopters, but before I can ask he says, "Are you going to buy the car?"

I almost forgot my bullshit story about the test-drive. I say, "Maybe. It's fast."

The cop smiles. "I'm going to ask you a favor. When you pull back on the road, would you floor it? I want to see how fast your car goes. I'll drive behind you so you won't get in no trouble."

I look at Lee. I'm wondering if this is some kind of redneck trick, like he's going to write me a ticket after I speed. Lee just shrugs.

Fuck it. When the cop gets in his car, I drop my car in gear and floor the motherfucker. I take it right up to 110. Then I slow down, let the cop catch up in his car. He pulls alongside us and rolls down his window. We're both going 80 miles an hour down the two lanes of the road. The cop has a big, shit-eating grin. He gives a thumbs-up and shouts, *"Yeehaw!"*

Then Lee leans across me and sticks his head out the window and shouts *"Yeehaw"* back at the cop. I almost smash into the cop car. The two rednecks are laughing. The cop turns on his flashing light and gives us a redneck escort all the way to the main highway. Unbelievable.

THAT NIGHT I found out from Roger that as he was coming to Yeehaw Junction, a Customs Service jet started chasing him.* Roger

---

* The Customs Service used Cessna Citation jets to interdict smugglers.

had been chased before off the coast, and he knew what to do. Pilots called it "outslowing" the government jets. If a jet flies too slow, it'll fall out of the sky. A King Air or any plane with propellers can fly a lot slower than the jet. So when they were chased, they'd cut their speed. The Customs Service jet would then have to fly in circles to follow the slower smuggler plane. What the smuggler pilot would do, if he was good, was wait for the government jet to make its turn away from him, then slip under a low cloud and escape beneath the radar. Roger had found a cloud that morning and slipped away. He'd dumped his coke far away from the farm where his guys were waiting, and everybody got away. But the Customs Service had called in helicopters and cops, and they were searching the ground for the drugs. To us, those drugs were gone.

When I told Max I'd lost the load, he freaked. I was calm. I knew from working with Fabito that Colombians were okay if you lost coke. Their cost of making it was so cheap, they could make up the loss with no problem. The Colombians could accept you losing a load if the cops got it. A mistake was fine.

What wasn't fine was ripping them off. If you lost a load, you had to get proof that the cops had taken it from you. This was very important. If you could show them a newspaper article proving that the heat took your coke, you'd be okay.

The hard part was waiting. Since I was new to Max and Rafa, I went to Max's house every day and waited with him. But there was nothing in the news. When Max got nervous, he'd hyperventilate and get dizzy. He'd have to breathe into a paper bag to keep from passing out. Five days I spent in his dining room. On one side Max had a bag on his face, wheezing into it—then taking breaks to smoke a cigarette. On the other side Rafa was smoking bazooka after bazooka. What a fun couple these two were.

Thank God for Danny Mones. Soon as I heard from Roger, I had Danny ask some dirty cops he knew to look into police reports. One of the cops found an internal DEA report. There was no news story about kilos falling on Yeehaw Junction, because Roger had dropped them in another part of the state.

Everybody quieted down when I showed them the DEA report. Rafa was calm, and Max was able to breathe normally again. I gave my pilot Roger credit for escaping. But I was disappointed with myself. I'd run this job like a jackass.

What my mind kept going to was Max's special Lincoln Continental. I wanted to meet the guy who'd built it, Mickey Munday. Rafa told me that Mickey had brought in many flights for them. When I brought up the subject of Mickey to Max, he said, "Oh, that guy. He's just a stupid redneck."

It shows how dumb Max really was. After I paired with Mickey, that stupid redneck defeated the whole U.S. government for years and years. Mickey was the most brilliant guy I ever worked with. He was also one of the weirdest. Mickey truly lived in his own world.

55

Every kid wants to be a pirate. Look at any map of any coast in the world, and I guarantee you'll find places named "Pirate's Cove" or "Smuggler's Bay." There's a romance about it. It's a fantasy, and I got to live it.

—Mickey Munday

J.R.: After the fiasco at Yeehaw Junction, Max told me I should run a load with Shelton, the English idiot. I told Max I wanted to meet Mickey. But Max put me off. I later realized Max was trying to get me to run loads with other pilots because he wanted to push Mickey aside. Max didn't like Mickey because he was smarter than him. Mickey had a million ideas for smuggling. Max never had a useful idea in his life, except to marry Pablo Escobar's cousin. Not only did Max like being *El Jefe*, he thought of himself as the mastermind, and Mickey threatened that idea because he made Max look dumb. I told Max that if he mentioned Shelton Archer's name one more time, I'd put a bullet in the Englishman's pea brain.

The reason my pilot Roger got chased at Yeehaw Junction was that the government had stepped up its efforts to catch smugglers. We were entering a very difficult time. The government was deploying more planes and boats, escalating their "War on Drugs." The days were gone when you could pay off a few cops and hire fishermen to race speedboats in. It was a new game. Having a smart guy like Mickey became more important than ever.

I finally met Mickey one day by accident. I came to Max's farm to look at some guns he wanted to sell me, and as I pulled in, I saw a hick parking a truck. That hick was Mickey. His name was written on the patch of his mechanic's suit. Mickey was unloading ATVs that he'd souped up for one of Max's stepkids. That's what Max had this genius doing for him.

Mickey was hard to miss. He was over six feet tall, with a thick head of blond hair. Some people called him Red because of his hair color, but it looked yellow to me. I was worried about Max coming out and trying get in my way, so I immediately went over to introduce myself to Mickey.

MICKEY: The first thing I noticed about Jon was his car. It was a custom AMG that made a 450 SL look like a piece of poop because of its super-high-output engine. I believe you can never have too much horsepower, but I didn't like Jon's car. There were only three cars like his in Miami, and all of them were owned by drug dealers. Jon's car might as well have had a sign on it that said "coke dealer." That gave me a negative first impression of Jon, but when we talked, I liked him. He spoke like someone more intelligent than the car he drove.

J.R.: Right away Mickey wanted me to crawl on the ground with him so he could show me the motors he'd souped up on Max's ATVs. He ended up trying to give me a lesson on the history of the gasoline engine since the beginning of time. I found the guy annoying. He was like a hillbilly professor.

But I was intrigued by him. He told me how he made his own race boats and airplanes, which would go faster than anybody else's. He had a funny phrase that was his motto: "If it rolls, floats, or flies, I can make it go faster."

Mickey wasn't a guy I was going to bond with by taking him to the orgy room at the Forge. He was a couple years older than me, but he talked like a kid. He used Boy Scout words like "Gee whiz."

Mickey wasn't a pilot. He had a pilot friend he worked with named Ray Delmer.* But this shows you what a weirdo Mickey was. Delmer was almost Mickey's age, but Mickey called him Dad. Mickey said, "Dad knows a lot about planes." At first I thought he meant his father made planes with him, but then I found out Mickey had lost his father. Dad was his friend.

Mickey didn't belong in my world. He didn't do cocaine. He didn't swear. His favorite thing was to eat milk and cookies that his mom made. Mickey lived with his mom. He'll tell you today that he had his own apartment back then, but there was no furniture in it. He did his laundry at his mother's. He ate there. Sometimes he drove her to church on Sunday.

I'm not saying he was a freak, dressing up in a skin suit made from his mom, like in the movies.† He had girlfriends almost like a normal guy. For a while he had a little skinny girlfriend with blond hair like his who dressed in all-white-jeans outfits. Mickey got white jeans that matched. The two of them would ride up on Mickey's motorcycle and step off in their white jeans and blond hair. They looked like they might have been out hunting unicorns together.

Despite the impression he made, Mickey was no pushover. He was not a tough guy with his hands. But I never saw him afraid. He didn't like violent people, but he wasn't cowardly around them.

---

* At the request of Mickey Munday, the name of his pilot friend has been changed to the pseudonym Ray Delmer.
† A reference to Norman Bates in *Psycho*.

He was very stubborn. He was a know-it-all. He could make you mad. I was annoyed by him many times.

But Mickey and me took the Cartel to the next level. Mickey made a system where however much they tried to stop drug imports, they couldn't stop him. Mickey didn't smuggle the biggest loads, but his loads always made it through. Mickey was like the FedEx of drug smuggling. If you saw Mickey on the street, you'd never imagine this guy was the technical mastermind of the Medellín Cartel. That was part of his true genius. This guy beat the piss out of the U.S. government, and he looked like the boy next door—if the boy next door was a little freaky and still lived with his mom at the age of thirty-five.

56

President Reagan visited south Florida to highlight his
campaign against drugs today and vowed to "break the
power of the Mob in America." The president's trip was
designed to draw attention to the success of the task
force, which Reagan created last January to curb the
flow of illegal drugs. Vice President George Bush heads
the task force.

—"Reagan Pledges War on Drugs," *Daily News*,
November 15, 1982

J.R.: As soon as I met Mickey, I wanted to work with
him, because I could see he was good enough to
handle the heat that was coming down on smugglers.
I pushed Max into expanding what Mickey did. Max
called Mickey our "employee," but Mickey and I worked
side by side, like partners.* Outside of work we almost
never socialized because as people we were completely
mismatched.

* The federal indictment of Jon and Mickey described the division of labor between Max, Jon, and Mickey as follows: "Medellín

MICKEY: Kids should know I don't advocate drugs. I've never inhaled a marijuana cigarette or sniffed cocaine. The only addiction I've ever had was chewing gum. Through most of my thirties I could not work unless I had a stick of gum in my mouth. Weird, huh? I guess you could say gum was my drug.

I was raised in a good home. My mother was a schoolteacher and a deacon in the Presbyterian Church. My parents were from Ohio. My mom was a Miss Cincinnati, and my father went to college on a football scholarship. He played professional football for a couple years in Cincinnati, but that wasn't for him. In the 1940s my parents moved to Miami, and my father started a construction business. He invented a new kind of breeze block—a ventilated brick—that was common in Florida before air-conditioning was in every building. My dad's design allowed air to blow through the block, but it kept out rain and direct sunlight. The breeze blocks my father made were called Munday Blocks, and they are in hotels and schools across Florida and Latin America. My dad manufactured them at his own shop. He built the house my brother and I grew up in out of Munday Blocks.

Our house was in an ideal 1950s neighborhood. We were by a canal, and I accidentally-on-purpose fell in the water every day of the week. I made my own boat when I was in elementary school. I loved exploring the swamps. I loved maps.

My dad's shop was down the street. There were welding shops nearby, machine shops, electrical shops. I was curious about

---

Cartel and its controlling members Jorge Ochoa-Vasquez, Fabio Ochoa-Vasquez, Juan David Ochoa-Vasquez, Rafael Cardona-Salazar and Pablo Escobar-Gaviria were represented in the United States by co-conspirators Max Mermelstein and Jon Roberts. Mermelstein and Roberts would and did make arrangements with the Munday Organization [which included Mickey's friend 'Delmer'] to transport drugs from secret locations in Colombia." It further states that "Jon Roberts served as the intermediary between the owners of the cocaine in Colombia and those who were distributing the cocaine once it arrived in the United States, coordinated with the Munday Organization the transportation of the cocaine to the United States, and received the cocaine once it was brought into the United States."

everything, and I apprenticed in all the shops. I learned all the trades. Before I could drive, I was rebuilding my own cars, motorcycles, and boats.

My dad was such a neat guy. He loved horse racing. I've always wished Jon could have met my father because they both liked horses. My dad didn't bet like Jon. He bet at the two-dollar window.

My dad was honest. He was frugal because the construction business was cyclical. He'd always say, "When you have chicken, make sure you save the feathers, because you might have a day where all you have is feathers."

When I was young, my dad died from cigarette smoking. I ran his business from the time I was a teenager. But it went downhill. Munday Blocks were labor-intensive to manufacture, and by the late 1960s air-conditioning was killing off the entire breeze block industry.

I street-raced motorcycles and cars. I love piston engines. I love speed. I became friends with a black motorcycle club because I was the only white mechanic who wouldn't cheat them. From there I started a custom motor shop.

My best friend was a guy I must have drag-raced a thousand times. His name was Ray Delmer, but I called him Dad because he taught me more about engines and about life than anybody. After my dad died, I was closer to Delmer than anyone, and it was nice having someone to call Dad.

Delmer got his pilot's license about the time Jimmy Carter became president, and the economy turned to poop. My custom motor shop was barely hanging on. Delmer told me that he and other pilots were getting into smuggling. I stayed away from smuggling until one day in about 1978 when Delmer told me that a guy he knew had lost a load of marijuana from his plane. It was now sitting unclaimed in the Everglades. I decided rescuing those marijuana bales would be following my father's advice to save the feathers off the chicken. I said, "Let's go get that marijuana."

It wasn't as simple as that. The bales were thrown over a wide area of wetlands. Delmer and I flew over it for a day searching for clues. It was like a Hardy Boys mystery. Eventually I spotted the bales on the ground.

I learned then that I had a unique ability to find things. It's more than that. If you show me something on the ground, I'll find it from the air, and if I see it from the air, I'll find it on the ground. Later, when I scouted airfields in jungles all over Colombia, that ability came in handy.

We sold the marijuana bales for $25,000. Back then $12,000 was a year's income to me. From then on, when it came to smuggling, you could count me in. I learned to fly, but I never got a license. I worked as a kicker, as a mechanic, as a navigator.

Even though I didn't smoke marijuana, I saw no reason why the government should tell people what to do with their lives. To me, it was a waste of everyone's time and money to have the government out there chasing people like me. My word for all the agencies that were hunting us—police, DEA, Customs Service, Coast Guard—was the "Competition." I dedicated myself to being better than the Competition.

I learned that success starts with logistics. Most smugglers didn't have backup plans. I wouldn't pick one place to land our plane. I'd pick three or four so we'd have alternates. I'd give radios to my crew so they could all communicate. If I needed one radio, I brought three in case the first two had heart attacks. If all the radios died, the people on my ground crew had flashlights and knew basic Morse Code so they could still communicate.

I picked my crew from friends who worked at repair garages and tire shops and from the black motorcycle club. They were all solid individuals. One of my biker friends liked to fish. I put my prime landing fields by canals. I'd send him out on a bass boat with a pole and a cooler of beer, plus a radio and binoculars so he could watch the access roads and keep an eye on the Competition.

I'd do everything possible with my planes to increase their capacity for distance, speed, and payload. I'd crank up the horsepower.

When you do that, your propellers will cavitate—which is like a car spinning its wheels. You mitigate against cavitation with a longer propeller, but if we put big propellers on little planes, it might make the Competition suspicious. To make the propellers look smaller, I installed tri-blades made for turboprops. You couldn't tell they were turboprops, and they made my planes appear to have the right proportions.

To increase my range, I found a company that made rubber fuel tanks for racing cars. They were like water beds. You could fold them up, put them inside the plane, and fill them when you needed to. Fuel is key. You run out of gas in the sky, you can't put down your kickstand and park on a cloud.

Putting the extra weight in my planes made them sit wallered down. I put in nitrogen shocks so even fully loaded, my plane would sit high and proud, the way a plane should look.

Deception was critical. I did everything I could so my planes, my boats, my cars all looked average. Every time I painted a car, I'd tell my painter, "I want you to paint it well, but I want it to look like it's two, three years old."

I also believed in speed on the ground. When my planes landed in the fields we used around Florida, my crew could refuel them in under three minutes. The trunks I built in my cars could hold six 15-gallon jerry cans. I'd carry 180 gallons in two cars. I put four fuel fillers on my planes. When we met the plane, I'd have four people gassing it up simultaneously. It takes forty-three seconds to empty a jerry can. Sometimes we'd fill a plane in just over two minutes. That's getting up there with NASCAR pit crew speeds, okay?

My crew carried toothbrushes. We'd clean every crevice inside the plane after we took the cargo out. We carried extra seats to the landing fields and installed them in the cargo area after we emptied the plane. That way, when the plane returned to the airport, it would look like it couldn't possibly have been flying anything but tourists on a fishing trip.

The Competition did very little to stop us in 1978. But by 1980, when Dad and I started doing some flights for Max, they were getting better—studying airports, aircraft, pilots, docks. Smugglers had it easy for years, and when the Competition stepped up their game, those guys went down fast. We had to step up our game.

Max was intelligent, but he didn't have the patience for new ideas. He didn't want to spend money. When I met Jon, he got involved. He wasn't afraid to try new ideas. He understood we had to continually improve.

J.R.: Mickey did amazing things. He ran tourist flights from Miami to the Bahamas. He'd pay women to go on chartered tours. He and his pilot would dress up in uniforms and fly them to a luxury hotel. When the girls checked in, Mickey and the pilot would fly out and smuggle drugs for four days. Then they'd clean the plane, put on their uniforms, pick up the girls, and fly them back to Miami. Mickey called the girls he used the "cover girls."* Eventually he shut down the Bahama route because they started searching every plane. But Mickey made fools of all the big-shot government lawmen for years. What an evil mind Mickey had, despite his talking like the all-American kid.

He was always coming up with new ways to trick people. When cops in Dade County got aggressive about stopping cars and searching trunks, Mickey came up with the idea of buying a tow truck company. When we moved cars around the county with drugs in the trunks, we put the cars on flatbed tow trucks. The drivers had work orders. It never occurred to the cops to stop a tow truck and search the car it was towing.

---

* The federal indictment of Jon and Mickey offers this version of the "cover girl" scheme: "The Munday Organization utilized as one of its transportation methods a Piper Navajo aircraft, N9096Y (hereinafter 'Navajo'), which was flown by its pilots from the United States to the Bahamas carrying various female passengers known as 'cover girls,' who were paid to travel to facilitate entry of the Navajo through Bahamian and United States Customs. The pilots frequently wore uniforms to create the appearance that each flight was a legitimate charter flight. The cover girls would remain in the Bahamas while the Navajo was flown to Colombia to pick up drugs."

One of the greatest things Mickey did was situate secret landing fields in the last place anybody expected them—on government property. Mickey brought in most of our coke at old U.S. military bases. What a twisted guy. Don't be fooled by Mickey's little happy smile.

MICKEY: The government locations I found were abandoned Nike missile sites.* These were built with a high standard of quality, from the missile silos to the access roads. They made terrific landing fields.

When I started exploring the Nike sites, I'd go out with a fishing pole and a small cutting torch in a knapsack. These sites went on for miles, and they had fences everywhere. I rode on a Honda 70 minibike light enough to toss over the fences. That way I could climb over the fences and keep riding.

The grass was maintained beautifully at these sites. They were empty, but the lawns were still cut regularly. In case of nuclear attack, no one could have complained that the lawns weren't well kept. Everything was gated and locked.

The military used a padlock that looked like a number five Master Lock, but the key had a groove on the side. I had a friend who supplied me with identical locks. When I found an area I wanted to come back to, I'd cut off the government lock with my torch and replace it with one of mine. Now I could come and go as I pleased.

When I replaced a government lock with one of my own, I made sure that there was a secondary way in. That way when caretakers came to the site, and their key didn't work in one lock, they could enter through another gate. They might file a report about

---

* Nike missiles were nuclear-tipped tactical weapons designed to detonate atomic bombs off of America's coastline in the event of a Soviet attack. They would theoretically destroy incoming missiles or planes. The system was dismantled in the late 1960s when officials realized that detonating hundreds of small nuclear bombs over America's coastline might be as bad as or worse than the Soviet attack they were designed to thwart.

a "malfunctioning lock," but being the government, it would be months or years before anyone would look into the matter.

The other sites I found to land planes on were federal lands along the Aerojet canal. In the 1960s when they started the moon rocket program at Cape Canaveral, they dug a canal through the Everglades to move rocket motors up there made by Aerojet.* They shut down the program and closed the Aerojet facilities along the canal. When they dig a canal in Florida, they always make a "spoils bank" alongside it—a pile of excavations that is graded flat and turned into a road. The Aerojet facilities had miles of spoils-bank roads that made excellent landing strips. These were fenced off like the Nike sites, so I just put in more of my own locks so I could come back and visit whenever I needed to.

The Nike and Aerojet sites gave me numerous 12,000-foot-long runways. That length was my holy grail, because you needed only 6,000 feet to land or take off. When my plane landed, my crew met it in the middle of the 12,000-foot runway. When my pilot took off again, he didn't need to turn his plane. That saved time. We could land the plane, unload it, fuel it, clean it out, refit it, and get it in the air in under six minutes.

There were workers who came onto the government sites we used, but they worked government hours—nine to five, at best, and all the holidays off. The rest of the time these sites belonged to me.

J.R.: After we landed drug planes on the government property, we still had to fly them to airports and service them. Mickey got the idea to make his own service hangar. We bought a 280-acre farm in Lakeland about two hundred miles north of Delray in the middle of nowhere, with barns Mickey converted into secret hangars. We started a fake crop-dusting company and kept the planes there. Sometimes Mickey's pilot did crop dusting for farmers, so no one could say it wasn't a real business.

---

* Aerojet, now a division of Rancho Cordova, California–based Gencorp, remains the nation's leading builder of civilian and military rocket motors.

At times, the Colombians would put thousands of kilos of coke on a fishing trawler and send the vessel into the Gulf of Mexico. Then we'd send speedboats out to unload it.

Ultimate Boats was the boat shop Mickey started to make smuggling boats.* His boats were the opposite of Don Aronow's. Instead of being made for getting laid, they looked like garbage. Mickey built boats that, I guarantee you, no girl would get on, with or without Quaaludes. But he put huge engines in them and secret cargo holds. Mickey was so sure of his boats that one time, when he was driving in a load of coke and saw a Coast Guard boat that was having engine trouble, he threw the Coast Guard a line and towed them in. This, with a half-ton of cocaine in his boat. Of course, Mickey was friends with half the Coast Guard because he went for all the voluntary boat inspections and took special classes they gave in boat safety.

Mickey put spotters everywhere. He had people watching Homestead Air Base, where the Customs Service flew its jets, to tell us how many were in the sky. He had people watching their docks. We rented an apartment overlooking Haulover Cut in Biscayne Bay and put a girl there to watch and tell us when the government boats were coming in. When we had a drug plane returning from Colombia, Mickey sent up spotter planes to look for government jets.

What put us over the top was Mickey's listening in on government radios. Mickey tuned in to them and recorded them twenty-four hours a day. We knew when they were sending patrols and where. If they were going south, we went north. If one day they were looking for a red smuggling plane, we made sure to fly only green planes.

We had a radio room at Ultimate Boats. For entertainment I'd go there and listen to the idiots in the Customs Service talk about what they were doing that day to stop us.

---

* Ultimate Boats was located in an industrial area of Miami at 3254 N.W. 38th Street.

MICKEY: I didn't know about radios when I started in the smuggling business. One of the best schools I found was the local RadioShack store. My education began when I bought a police scanner, and the people who worked there explained how you could tune it in to the Coast Guard. The key was finding what frequency their radios were on. It turned out, RadioShack sold a book for five dollars that listed frequencies used by most government agencies.

The FAA gave public tours of its main air traffic control center in Miami. They'd show you their radars and maps and radios. You could ask questions, and I'd ask about their radios. That was very helpful.

All the agencies kept some channels they used a secret. But I took public tours of Coast Guard facilities and boats, and I noticed that Coast Guard radio operators wrote down the frequencies they used to talk to the Customs Service on pieces of tape that they stuck to their gear. One time I brought a lady I knew who was an accountant and had almost a photographic memory for numbers. She was also a very chesty young lady, and while the sailors were ogling her assets, she was ogling their frequency numbers and memorizing them.

Something basic to radios is that the frequency you communicate on determines the length of your antenna. I started driving around to different Coast Guard and Customs Service facilities around Florida and visually measured their antennas. I couldn't get the exact lengths, but I got close enough to know what range of frequencies I should be tuning in to.

Then I found a device called a frequency scanner. If you get a line of sight to an antenna and aim it, this scanner will tell you the exact frequency of whatever radio is hooked up to it. Lo and behold, the Customs Service had one of its main antenna farms near the old Dupont Plaza Hotel.* I could rent a suite in the Dupont Plaza that gave me line of sight to the Customs Service antenna farm. I'd check

---

* The Dupont Plaza Hotel was a landmark property at 300 Biscayne Boulevard Way that closed its doors in 2004.

in there every few weeks with my frequency scanner and pick off the latest frequencies they were using.

As I collected more radio frequencies, I built radios that I connected to voice-activated recorders. Any one channel might only have people talking on it for a few minutes in a twenty-four-hour period. When I had a lot of chatter on one tape, I learned to fast-forward but still pick up key words.

The Customs Service and Coast Guard would talk to each other and to local police. They talked openly about operations they were running against us. They'd gripe about things that the DEA and FBI were telling them to do. They had no idea anybody was listening. They didn't even encrypt their channels.

Sometimes I'd miss what they were doing even while listening to the radios. But I also watched the local news stations, and they'd show a press conference where some bigwig in the government would announce, "This weekend we're launching operation Orange Thunder"—they always picked corny names—"to stop drug smugglers along the coast." They wouldn't say where they were going to be operating, but since the idiots gave out their code name for the operation, I'd go back through my tapes and listen for "Orange Thunder" to get the details of where they were setting their traps for us.

I liked it when the Competition mounted really big operations. We'd just stand down for the week or ten days they ran it and let them catch the other smugglers. When it was over, I knew everything would be wide open, because they'd have to bring in their boats and planes for maintenance. Their personnel would have burned up their overtime. The agencies would have used up their budgets for extra fuel. They'd drop to skeleton operations for the next month.

All the agencies were jealous of each other. Customs would bicker with the Coast Guard. And they'd both trash-talk the DEA or the FBI or the local police. The Customs Service was really out for glory. They hated the other agencies because they'd spend weeks tracking a smuggling ring, and at the last minute the FBI or DEA would swoop in, make the arrests, and steal the credit. Everyone would fight over who was going to get to be on camera in the press conference.

As much as Jon and I argued at times, we didn't have those problems. We weren't as infantile. To be clear, I don't want to bad-mouth the Coast Guard here. They were always more focused on the safety of boaters and on disaster response than on arresting smugglers. Every person in the Coast Guard is a hero every day of the week, as far I'm concerned.

I could make fun of the Competition because we beat them time and time again. But when we beat them, they went home at night. If they beat us once, we were finished. I lost sleep over that. I focused all my waking hours on the Competition.

J.R.: One thing Mickey could not do was speak Spanish. It used to irritate me. I believed he purposefully didn't learn it so that he would have an excuse to not deal with the Colombians. That fell to me.

MICKEY: Rafa was one crazy little son of a gun. Everybody was scared to death of Rafa. Max was terrified of him, and Rafa was in charge of Max. What Rafa said was the equivalent of Pablo Escobar's word.

Rafa barely spoke English, and he had his bodyguard, Flaco, who spoke none. One of the worst times I ever had was going to Max's house and having to tell Rafa there was a problem with a plane of mine being delayed. When I came in, the Colombians in the house were really nervous. Max was out, and Rafa was in the dining room at a long table with Flaco. It was filled with smoke because they were smoking cocaine, and they were wound up.

I started to tell Rafa I had a little problem with a plane—a *problemo*. Rafa began shouting in broken English to me and in Spanish to Flaco. Flaco started shouting back. It became increasingly ter-rifying because the more Rafa shouted, the less I could understand what he was saying. It wasn't the kind of situation I ever wanted to be in again.

J.R.: Mickey came to me and said, "The less I deal with Colombians, the better."

I could handle Rafa. I could handle Max. All Max wanted was to sit on his fat ass, and a couple times a week I'd bring him shoeboxes of money. The key was to always defer to him as the great king, *El Jefe*. The key to Rafa was to smoke coke with him and never show him weakness.

The more Mickey and I worked together, the less we told Max. We didn't tell him where our farm was or where I put the stash houses. Nothing. Mickey and I just made everything work. Mickey's job was technical things. I was the people person.

MICKEY: Jon was a tough guy. He had gone through a lot of craziness in Vietnam, and it showed. Jon had some anger. People feared him. I'm nonviolent. I didn't allow my pilots to carry guns on the planes. I saw guns as having the potential to make most situations worse. Jon could handle difficult situations. My job is to get the packages from point A to point B. One reason we worked well together is, Jon was really good at what he did and I was really good at what I did.

Let me get something clear. I never did it for the money. Little green pieces of paper mean nothing to me. I did it because I got to play with awesome toys, and it was one heck of an adventure.

J.R.: That's one difference between Mickey and me. I'm a criminal and I know it. Mickey, he believed he was a pirate. He was kind of like a child. We succeeded because it was like combining someone who lived by my father's philosophy with a Boy Scout. We were almost unbeatable together.

MICKEY: If you added up all the money I spent on radios, boats, cars, and aircraft, it probably didn't exceed $5 million a year. Jon and I had no more than forty people helping us. By contrast, the Competition had thousands of people. When they declared the "War on Drugs," they committed hundreds of millions of dollars a year to stopping us. I hate to sound arrogant, but they were seldom a worthy opponent.*

J.R.: The joke of it was, the harder the government tried to stop smugglers, the better it was for us. When they arrested smugglers, they eliminated our competitors. When Mickey and I started together in 1981, there were a lot of other smugglers. By 1985 we were it. The "War on Drugs" helped make the Cartel into a true monopoly.† Thank you, government.

---

* In contrast to Mickey's contemptuous assessment of government efforts to interdict his smuggling flights, the American government's appraisal of his efforts, as laid out in its indictment of him and Jon, has an almost breathless quality: "The Munday Organization provided spot or cover planes to conduct countersurveillance activities. The Organization used sophisticated electronic equipment to monitor law enforcement radio communications, communicate with its aircraft and boats, and locate the shipment of drugs. The Organization also sought the design, development, manufacture, and testing of a remote-controlled electronic beacon device to be placed with hidden loads of drugs to facilitate the pickup of the drugs by boats. The Organization also acquired, possessed, and used other electronic devices, including night-vision goggles, radar detectors, forward-looking infrared devices and radios which scrambled communications in order to avoid detection by law enforcement agencies in the United States."

† From the early to mid-1980s—the period when Jon and Mickey and Max came together to run the Cartel's transportation efforts, it rose to control an estimated 80 percent of the U.S. cocaine market.

57

J.R.: When the Colombians saw me working with Max, Fabito stepped back. I dealt more with Rafa. But I still ran planes with Barry Seal and worked with my pilot, Roger. I helped Mickey with radios. I moved the coke on the ground and ran the stash houses. I was going in eight different directions at once.

The most annoying part of my job was dealing with Max. If I could have overthrown Max, I would have pushed a bullet into his fat head with my bare fingers, but because of his marriage that was impossible. Even though we were taking on more of the work, Max would sometimes have to throw his weight around as *El Jefe*.

He did this by calling meetings with me at strange times. These were ridiculous because we kept Max in the dark about what we were doing. What could he possibly tell me in a meeting? But to humor him, I'd always say, "Sure, Max. Let's talk."

One time Max called me in the middle of the night to insist we meet as soon as possible.

"Okay, Max. Come up to my house in the morning. I'll make breakfast."

The next day he shows up late in the afternoon. Max arrives in the backseat of his Mercedes station wagon, with Rafa beside him. Rafa's guy, Flaco, is at the wheel. Flaco gets out of the car laughing. Flaco had a reputation as a real bad guy. When he had to kill somebody, they said he liked to put his knife in the person's face and cut a smile into it. That was his joke. Flaco himself wasn't a smiley kind of guy. But on this day he's laughing. He whispers to me, "Max and Rafa got surgery this morning."

"What happened? Did they get shot?"

"No, they paid a doctor to vacuum the fat out of them."

"Get out of here."

Flaco explained he took them to a doctor, and he stuck tubes in them and sucked out their fat. This was before I'd ever heard of liposuction.

"They had a doctor suck fat out of them with a hose?"

Flaco opens the back door, and Max and Rafa can hardly get up. He has to pull them out. They're both howling in pain. Rafa points to his stomach and says, "The doctor did *bliff bliff bliff*," which I guess was the sound the liposuction made.

"But Rafa, you're skinny."

Max explains that when Rafa heard Max was going to get surgery, he decided to get it done for "fun."

When we get in the house, Rafa lifts up his shirt. He rips off a bandage and shows me these disgusting holes in his stomach. That's where the doctor stuck the suction hoses in. Rafa starts yelling, "That fucking doctor. I'm gonna kill him!"

I get them lying on the floor with pillows. I sit down and say, "Okay, Max. What did you want to talk about?"

"Jon, I can't talk at a time like this. It hurts too much."

That was it. He never told me what the meeting was about. There was truly no need for Max to have any kind of meeting, but by calling one, it made him feel important.

After they left, Rafa checked into a hospital. His surgery got infected, and it nearly killed him. He was Pablo Escobar's man in Miami, and Max nearly killed him with unnecessary surgery.

ANYTHING MAX tried to do on his own ended in disaster. One time Max met a guy who told him if he came to Mexico, he could set him up with guys who could smuggle coke into Texas. Max went to Mexico and brought his wife. As soon as they checked in to their hotel, the *federales* busted into his room and demanded a ransom. The whole thing was a setup. It took Max two days to raise the money. The whole time the *federales* had him in the hotel, they were having a party—ordering liquor, whores, you name it—putting it all on Max's tab. After Max paid the ransom to the *federales,* the hotel held him until he raised a second round of money to pay the bill.

Obviously, Max never found a way to smuggle through Mexico.

PART OF what Max did to remind everybody he was married into the Cartel was to have all these illegal Colombian kids stay at his house. He claimed that everyone in the house was somehow related to Pablo Escobar or Don Ochoa. In reality, most were just peasants from the mountains. They would mow his grass, wash his cars. Some would move on to become bodyguards for the Colombian distributors in Miami or other cities.

One time Max told me I needed to give his "nephew" a job. This kid was different from the peasants who stayed at Max's. He was soft. He looked like a rich kid. None of the Colombians wanted him. Max told me I needed to train him as a driver.

I went in the room where the kid was staying. He was twenty years old, watching *Sesame Street* on TV, laughing at the big bird. I shut the TV off and told him to meet me the next day in blue jeans, a work shirt, and a baseball cap. I explained that I'd pick him up, drive him to a car. He was to drive that car to a Burger King and leave the keys in the bathroom.

"Oh yeah, man. That's real easy. No problem," he said.

The next day I pick up Max's asshole nephew in my Buick

Riviera that I used for work. He's got the cap on, the jeans, the work shirt. Very good. I drive him to the car he's going to take to Burger King. It is one of Mickey's special cars with half a ton of cocaine in the trunk. I handed this turd the key and told him, "Okay. Drive it to Burger King."

The kid freezes. He won't even close his hand over the key.

I say, "Good-bye!"

I reach over to push the kid out, and he starts slapping me like a girl.

The Buick Riviera has a wide center console and a fat gearshift. I take the kid by the hair and I smash his face into the center console. I bounce his head a couple times and knock him out. I drive down a side street and push him out. If you won't work, you're fired.

I ended up running the car to Burger King myself. I didn't like it, but I had no choice. When I finished, I called Max and I said, "I'm going to tell you something. You're a fat fuck. Your nephew's a piece of shit. You're all assholes. Have a nice day."

The next day Rafa has me meet him at a dive bar on the Miami River, where a lot of the Colombian smugglers used to hang out. He says, "Come on, let's go get laid. Let's go get high."

We go inside the place in the middle of the day. We do a few lines, send the whores away. I ask him what's going on.

Rafa says, "The Jewball is very upset."

Rafa had started learning English, and his new nickname for Max was "the Jewball."

"What's wrong with Max?"

"The Jewball's crying that you beat up his nephew."

I explain to Rafa what happened. Instead of cooling him down, now he wants to kill Max's nephew. "That kid is a piece of shit. He's a nobody. I'm gonna take care of him. Fuck the Jewball."

"Rafa, forget about that kid. He got a beating. It's over."

But there was no reaching Rafa. I never saw that kid again. In the end Max couldn't complain because, as much as he tried to throw his weight around, everybody knew he was nothing on the inside.

• • •

THE WORST part of working with Max was his parties. Sometimes he'd have them at his farm in Davie. The centerpiece of a Max party was when he would put on a Spanish *caballero* outfit and hoist his big ass onto a Paso Fino and greet everybody like a cowboy clown. Max had a picture of Don Ochoa on a horse like this, and in his mind he was trying to show everyone he was the same kind of guy.

Part of the reason I didn't like going to Max's parties was that many of the people who attended were the Colombian distributors I delivered coke to. Everything was set up—using different cars, having the drivers drop the keys at restaurants—so I'd never have to see them. The distributors were the ones going wild in the streets. They all had heat on them. I didn't want them to know my face.

But I went to the parties to keep Max happy. One time I was in his house, and I saw Rafa talking to an older lady, maybe thirty-five. She reminded me of a Colombian version of Phyllis, but this lady wore gaudy clothes. One thing about her intrigued me. Normally, when Rafa talked to a woman, he was either flirting with her or bossing her around. With this woman, he was subdued.

I went up to Rafa and said, "What's her story?"

He said, "Forget about her. That's Griselda."

Griselda Blanco ran a gang that was moving hundreds of kilos a month. It was coke that I delivered to her guys, but I'd never met her. I later found out that she knew Rafa from back in the slums in Colombia. She supposedly committed her first murder when she was eleven. In the early 1970s she came to New York and worked as a whore. When Rafa showed up in Queens in 1976, she became one of his first big distributors. Rafa and Griselda were very loyal to each other. Rafa treated every woman I saw him with like garbage, but Griselda was his princess. She could do no wrong. I did not know when I met her that she was already wanted for the Dadeland

Massacre or that she was well on her way to supposedly murdering two hundred people.* Had I known this, I would have been furious that Max had her at a party because a woman that scandalous would have a lot of heat on her.†

But when I asked Rafa about her, all he said was "That bitch is a little bit crazy."

I couldn't keep my eyes off of her, which made no sense. Griselda was already going fat. In a couple of years she'd lose all her looks and turn into a real beast. Despite her not being the most attractive woman at the party, she turned me on. I couldn't put my finger on it. There's something about a woman in her killing prime.

I told Rafa I was going to pick her up.

He said, "Jon, they call her the Black Widow because after she uses a man, she kills him."‡

"Come on. I'm not going to let her kill me." I'm thinking, *A bitch that mad might give the best fuck in the world.* I went over to Griselda and started talking. She said, "I've never talked to a gringo who speaks Spanish so natural. You must be a funny gringo."

It was a stupid joke, but I laughed along with her because I was going out of my mind for this broad. My balls were aching for her. I guess I'm just weak for evil women. Rafa came back over and pulled me away. He said, "Jon, forget her. If you fuck her, it is bad for our business."

Can you believe it? Rafa was the voice of sanity.

---

* In 1979 Griselda Blanco and her crew are believed to have ambushed Cubans from a rival coke gang at the Dadeland Mall, raking several shops and a nearby parking lot with gunfire from automatic weapons. The brazen daylight shoot-out, which resulted in three deaths, was dubbed the "Dadeland Massacre." Authorities believe that Blanco and her crew killed as many as two hundred people. Her top enforcer admitted that when murdering a rival, they'd often seek out his wife and children and kill them, too.

† Contrary to Jon's worries, police had no idea who Griselda was until years after her Miami murder spree ended, when she was arrested for another crime. Only then did one of her accomplices fill in police on the full extent of the gang's activities.

‡ Griselda is reputed to have murdered three of her husbands.

· · ·

My last social event involving Max was his Christmas party. Max wanted me to bring Toni Moon with me. What a farce. I wasn't going to bring her to a gathering of Colombian psychopaths. Max liked to think of himself as a Jewish version of Joe Kennedy. I didn't even know who Joe Kennedy was until Max told me he was the father who founded the family's fortune by smuggling liquor and using the money to make his son the president. Max always talked about Joe Kennedy. I don't think he planned to make his stepkids president, but in his mind Kennedy was his hero because he proved that being a smuggler was respectable.

I didn't care if what I did was respected by society or not. My idea of a party was a bunch of Playboy Bunnies on Quaaludes in the back room of the Forge. But Max had a different idea. For his Christmas party he'd decked out his house with lights. There was Christmas music. There was mistletoe. Max wore a Santa Claus hat to entertain the little kids crawling around the carpets, who belonged to the Colombians. When I arrived at his house and saw Max in his Santa hat, I thought, *This is going to be a terrible party.*

The food was good. Colombians don't have turkey on Christmas, or a normal ham you slice up. They served *arepas,* beans, rice, long sandwiches with cheese and olives on them. They laid the food out in a buffet, and that part was good.

Everybody started drinking, getting high. I ate some food, had a few laughs, and told Max, "Okay. I need to go."

"Come on, Jon. Stay."

"All right, Max. Half an hour more."

Twenty minutes later I heard *bang bang.* Normally, if somebody shoots a gun in a crowded room, women will scream. But everybody goes silent. I see at one side of the room, one of Max's party guests is on a table with his face blown off. Rafa is standing a few feet away with a gun, talking to himself and laughing. He's out of his mind, smoking bazookas. Nobody says anything because they know Rafa. Nobody wants to make a noise and be the next person he shoots.

Rafa lowers his gun and says, "It's okay. Don't worry."

Some people try to go back to acting normal, talking and laughing, like *Hey, what a fun Christmas party this is.*

I see Rafa talk to Max, then Max comes over to me, smoking his cigarette like mad, and says, "Jon, he wants me to help move the body out. You've got to help me."

"Fuck you, Max. I wanted to leave half an hour ago."

I go over to Rafa and said, "Is it okay if I leave?"

Rafa says, "Hey, man. Thanks for coming."

As I walk outside, Max and Flaco are dragging out the body of the guy Rafa shot. Max is whimpering like a little puppy because he's so fucking terrified.* I say, "Enjoy your Christmas, buddy."

Two days later I see Max at his farm. He's got five cigarettes going at one time. He tells me Rafa and Flaco drove him around all night long in a van with the dead Colombian. Every time they found a good place to dump the body, they would stop, get the corpse halfway out, and Rafa would change his mind. Rafa would give Flaco orders to drive to a different spot. At dawn Max said they finally drove back to his house to chop the body up in the garage. Rafa and Flaco then fed it to a swamp somewhere. Max told me the guy Rafa shot was married to a woman Rafa knew. He'd offended Rafa by disrespecting his wife. Honor is important to Colombians like anybody else.

In the end, the shooting benefited me. I always had it to hold over Max. Now, whenever he asked me to do something idiotic, I'd say, "Is this gonna be like your Christmas party, Max?"

The other good part was I had an excuse to never go to another party at Max's.

---

* In the previously cited book *The Man Who Made It Snow*, Max places this Christmas shooting in 1978 and cites it as a turning point in his becoming Rafa's virtual kidnapping victim—a sort of Patty Hearst—forced to run Cartel operations in the United States. Jon places the shooting in 1981. He says that Max moved up the date so he could better make the "ridiculous claim" in his book that he was kidnapped into cocaine smuggling.

58

J.R.: Obviously, when you're in an illegal business, you need to assert your dominance with enough force that nobody will fuck with you. The Colombians took this idea too far.

One time Rafa asked me to help collect from a Colombian who owed him money. We were out driving around one night, and Rafa found out that the guy was in a bar. "Go in the bar, Jon. Make friends. Tell him you have good coke. He'll trust you because you're a gringo. When he comes out the door, Flaco and I will grab him and get our money."

"Okay, Rafa. We'll see what happens."

I spent one hour with the guy in the bar, and in that time Rafa changed his mind. I walked out the door with him, and two Indian fuckers—the peasants with flat faces who Rafa used to do his dirty work—hopped off of a motorbike. They walked up with MAC-10s and shot the guy five feet behind me.* Rafa's thought process was, he'd rather kill a guy than get the money the guy owed him.

You can imagine how angry I was. I could have been shot. When I found Rafa the next morning, I said, "You crazy fucker. Where would you be if you got me killed?"

"Jon, I got carried away."

That's how they were. The Colombians were aggressive. One time Griselda sent her guys to blow up the car of someone she had a feud with. They put so much dynamite in the car, it blew up the house it was parked in front of. That was the Colombian way.

People in Miami got very uptight about all the bodies piling up. The Colombians got a reputation for being crazy. At the street level Colombians fought among themselves. Higher up, there were guys like Rafa who smoked a little too much cocaine and went crazy sometimes. Despite their balls, the Colombians could not dominate the streets in Miami. They were outnumbered by the Cubans twenty to one. In the long run the Cubans would always kick their asses.

From the start, smart Colombians like the Ochoas understood they could not work alone. They were happy to sell to Cubans, Italians—anybody with money. They weren't completely irrational people.

In my view, the Colombians weren't more murderous than other people. They just were more open about it. They'd shoot people and leave them on the streets. They didn't pick up after themselves.

I WAS in no position to look down my nose at the Colombians for being violent. Look how we took care of Richard Schwartz at his hamburger shop. People could say we did that killing for Gary Teriaca's honor, to avenge his little brother's murder. But we were no better than the Cubans or the Colombians.

In the early 1980s, Bobby Erra got involved in the jukebox and

---

* The MAC-10 was a small, wildly inaccurate machine gun that was popular among Miami's killers in the 1980s because of its compact size and its ability to take a long silencer tube, making it not much louder than a whisper.

pinball machine industry. When some pizza shops wouldn't pay him what he wanted for his coin machines, Bobby hired Albert to blow up all their pizza shops.* All this over coin machines. The money was nothing to Bobby. He just wanted to impress people by showing he could blow up their businesses.

Gary Teriaca found out about a guy in Miami's diamond district who was importing cocaine with some Colombians we'd never heard of. Gary didn't like this diamond guy because he was trying to sell coke to the same people in Miami that Gary sold to. Gary wanted to rob him.

Gary was really out of his mind by this time. He was the first "cocaine junkie" I'd ever seen. He had been such a good-looking athletic kid. Now he was pale and skinny, his nose would start bleeding, and there was no way to stop it. He'd plug his nose with tissues, and the blood would bubble out of his mouth. He was a mess. I told him many times he should start smoking bazookas like Rafa. That way, at least, his nose would get a rest.

But Gary was right about the diamond guy. He was getting hundreds of kilos of coke. And he was bringing it in in a very smart way. He found a factory that made plastic shoe hangers—bags you hang in your closet for holding shoes. He got the factory to make special shoe hangers with seams in the back that they could put a kilo of coke in. They'd flatten the kilo so you wouldn't even feel it in the plastic. They'd send these shoe hangers to Colombia empty, and the Colombians would ship them back loaded.

The diamond guy was a competitor, so it made sense to rob him. You always want to fuck up your competition. I wasn't at a point in life where I wanted to be ripping off people in Miami, but I had an idea.

My ex-brother-in-law, Henry Borelli, was always begging to do business with me. We'd left on good terms after the incident at the

---

* In the "Pizza Wars," from 1980 to 1983, ten bombs were detonated at Pizza Shops in and around Miami. Erra's and San Pedro's roles in the bombings emerged in the 1986 cocaine-trafficking case against San Pedro.

International Inn where I had to kneecap his guy, and I was happy to do Henry a solid. I invited him to come down and rob this diamond guy for us. He'd make out and nobody would connect the robbery to us.

Henry came down with a couple of his guys. *Boom. Boom.* They ripped off the guys working for the diamond guy. A man of his word, Henry gave a cut to Gary and me. End of story.

The weak link in this was Gary Teriaca. He ended up bragging about his New York heavies he called in to do the rip-off, and this got back to the diamond guy, who had his own heavies. A couple weeks later Gary was walking down 79th Street in broad daylight, and somebody opened up on him. Gary was hit three times. He was fortunate that though they shot him in the chest, they missed his heart.

Unfortunately, Gary never really recovered mentally. He'd never been the same since his little brother got shot at the Forge. Being shot on the street weakened him more. When guys get weak, people inevitably start to turn on them.

ALBERT SAN PEDRO feared weak people. Gary had become very important to Albert. Gary was buying hundreds of kilos a month from him to ship out to Colorado. Some went to his friend Steven Grabow. A lot went on to Joey Ippolito or other guys in California. There were some months people in California took a thousand kilos. That meant a great deal to Albert. When he saw Gary, his main partner in this, with his nosebleeds, getting shot up on the street, it made him uptight.

Albert got so uptight, he called me over to meet him one day and asked me if I'd have a problem if he got rid of Gary and Bobby. He reasoned that since Bobby and Gary were old friends and had become strong partners in the Colorado cocaine scheme, Bobby wouldn't let it stand if Albert killed Gary.

"Would you take my side in this, Jon?"

I didn't think he was wise to go after Bobby. He was part of the Mafia, and his father had been very strong. But Albert was stubborn, and he felt strong enough to take out Bobby. Albert's idea was that with Gary and Bobby gone he'd take over the route to Colorado.

Albert's plan put me in an awkward spot. I was loyal to Bobby and Gary. We'd had good times together. But the fact was, Albert was the guy buying coke from the Cartel, and I was with the Cartel. Albert was my customer—not Bobby and Gary—and the customer is always right. On top of this, Albert had more force on the street than Bobby.

I told Albert, "If you want to get rid of Gary and Bobby, bring in an outsider."

Albert had liked Joe Da Costa, my dog guy, ever since he'd sold Albert his dog, Sarge. Joe was also a shooter. I went to New Jersey to meet with Joe to see about his killing Bobby and Gary. Joe wanted to hit them in New York.

A couple times a year Bobby and Gary went up to New York to visit family. They liked to stay at the UN Plaza Hotel.* When they made their next trip, Joe went looking for them.

The problem with hit men is, it's not like the movies. They don't just pull out their sniper rifles and wack the guy from a rooftop. Professional shooters, even a nasty fucker like Joe Da Costa, could be very finicky. Everything had to be just right.

Joe Da Costa spent three days watching Gary and Bobby at the UN Plaza Hotel. Finally he called me and said, "Man, it's going to be a bloody mess. They hardly come out of their room. There's girls going in and out. I don't want to kill like five, six people just to get those two."

I went to Albert and told him killing Bobby and Gary was not going well. Albert was so nuts, he said, "Good. I don't want to kill Bobby. I changed my mind."

I was relieved. Can you imagine what it's like being friends with two guys and having to hang out with them all the time so you can figure out how to get a hit man the chance to kill them? It's not easy, bro.

---

* Still located at One United Nations Plaza on 44th Street.

Gary and Bobby were my best friends in Miami. The last good time the three of us had together was the second Duran-Leonard fight.* We watched on the big-screen TV at the Cricket Club, and when Duran quit the fight, Bobby threw a bottle of Cutty Sark at the screen and caused a mini-riot. We laughed our asses off. It was just a good time.

UNFORTUNATELY FOR Gary, Albert cut a deal with Bobby to take over the route to Colorado. They started squeezing him out. By then Gary had moved out of his house with Carol Belcher and was living at a condo in Bay Harbor. Gary had gotten so paranoid, he removed the normal front door of his condo and installed a steel door like something you'd see on a bank vault. He'd lock himself in that condo for days at a time.

Late in 1981 there was a night he tried calling me a bunch of times, and after that no one ever heard from him again. Albert and Bobby told me he'd stolen $800,000 from them because he was mad that they were taking over his Colorado coke business. Then my lawyer Danny Mones told me that if anyone ever asked, I should tell them, "Gary had run off to Europe." I knew that was bullshit.

I believe Albert and his guys killed Gary. But no one ever found a body. Later the cops tried to make a case that Albert and his guys went into Gary's apartment and beat him to death.† I found out that

---

* The fight took place on November 25, 1980.

† Gary Teriaca is believed to have been murdered in early October 1981. His disappearance was ruled a homicide during the 1991 racketeering investigation of Albert San Pedro. Federal investigators involved in the case discovered that shortly after the disappearance of Gary Teriaca, Albert San Pedro had hired an off-duty Hialeah police crime-scene investigation unit to scrub the apartment clean, then had it repainted. In 1991 FBI forensics examiners stripped the newer layers of paint from Teriaca's former apartment and found blood that possibly matched his in spray patterns on the bedroom walls and ceiling. Witnesses identified San Pedro as having led a group of men who, around the time of Teriaca's disappearance, broke down the front door of his apartment with a pry bar, after which loud screams were heard coming from within. Among the group of men who came to Teriaca's apartment at the time of the murder, witnesses identified San Pedro's enforcer Ricky Prado. Other witnesses identified Prado as the driver of San Pedro's car on visits he made to the apartment

I was the last person Gary ever called, and it made me feel bad, that I never picked up the phone.*

After he died, it broke me up inside a little bit. I had no heart for Gary, but I don't like picturing him being so alone. When they were coming to get him, I was the only person he could think of to reach out to, and a year earlier when Albert asked for my help I'd been just another guy ready to kill him.

I get tired of hearing about how the Colombians were such animals in the 1980s. We were all animals. Everybody was making corpses. I'd risen above the streets and become more like a businessman. I was the upper management of the Cartel. But I was in a business where if the Cartel were a Fortune 500 company, and you looked in the boardroom, you'd see that the CEO and all the presidents were carrying guns or bats. One minute they'd be discussing a merger, and the next they might be knocking somebody's brains in. That's the kind of businessman I was.

---

in the days after the murder. Prado moved from Miami and entered the CIA approximately four weeks after the murder of Gary Teriaca. Investigators leading the racketeering investigation of San Pedro planned to include the murder of Gary Teriaca as a predicate act—an earlier offense that can be used to enhance a sentence levied for a later conviction—in their case, and to include Ricky Prado in the indictment, but were prevented from doing so by the prior immunity agreement San Pedro had negotiated with U.S. Attorney Dexter Lehtinen. The state of Florida—not bound by San Pedro's immunity deal—considered filing separate murder charges against San Pedro and Prado, but San Pedro's attorney Fred Schwartz filed suit alleging misconduct among Miami-Dade police serving on the federal task force that investigated San Pedro. Schwartz's suit was thrown out, and he was disbarred for misconduct in another case, but the state declined to pursue the matter any further. In 2010 I interviewed San Pedro's ex-wives—Lourdes San Pedro and Jenny Cartaya—who presented new evidence that they believe further implicates San Pedro and Prado in the murder of Gary Teriaca. Police involved in the investigation of Teriaca's murder remain optimistic that charges will be filed against San Pedro and Prado. Bobby Erra was never implicated in the murder of Gary Teriaca, but in 1990 he pleaded guilty to racketeering charges based in part on the cocaine trafficking business he and Albert took over from Teriaca in 1981. Erra served nearly a decade in prison and today has an interest in Mezzaluna, a chain of high-end Italian restaurants in South Florida.

* Police reports from the investigation of the Gary Teriaca murder indicate that Jon's number was the last he dialed before his death.

59

We started arresting low-level Colombian dopers who
would tell us about a bearded gringo. They'd say the
"bearded gringo" was there when they landed the plane.
The "bearded gringo" was in the room with the money.
The "bearded gringo" was everywhere.

"Does he have a name?" we'd ask.

"John."

For years, we were looking for "John, the bearded
gringo."

I never thought he might spell his name without an "h."

We'd get little pieces of information. He was a
psycho Vietnam vet. He was extremely violent. He
traveled with a giant.

"A giant? Are you kidding me?"

They'd insist, "The gringo works with a giant by
his side."

That's what we went on for years: John. Gringo with
a beard. Travels with giant.

—Mike Fisten, a former lead investigator for the Miami-
Dade Police Department–FBI organized
crime task force, 1986 to 1995

J.R.: I grew out a beard in the 1980s because many mornings I didn't have time to shave. I had to focus on the job. Rafa was always telling me we needed to get more coke. I had to deal with Toni and our life in Delray. I had Mickey. He was a genius, but he would never move more than four hundred kilos of coke at a time, and he only moved it when everything was right. He didn't have to deal with the Colombians always telling him we needed more. I still had my pilots, Barry Seal and Roger, who I was managing. I had the drivers to run and the stash houses. Everything involved different people.

My sister used to complain how hard she worked managing personnel in the corporate world, and I'd laugh at her. Now I was starting to understand what she meant. A lot of my job was managing people. When something went wrong with a person—this guy doesn't show up, this kid tries to rip us off—it fell on me.

I was on the phone constantly. If I was discussing specific details of a work project, I'd use pay phones. For general calls, Max and I had radio phones put in our cars. Later we got the early Motorola cell phones. Driving back and forth between Delray and Miami, I lived in my car.

As convenient as you'd think it would be owning a helicopter and having a pilot, it was hard to find places to land in Miami outside of the Palm Bay Club, where they had a landing pad. The helicopter was great for flying around in the country and going to farms to look at racehorses. It was a great pussy wagon. You offer a girl a ride in a helicopter, she'll put out. There's something about heights that makes women excited. But mostly for my work I was driving everywhere.

I needed a driver. Danny Mones used to tell me that I needed a bodyguard, if only to keep me out of fights. I needed a guy who was reliable, someone I could trust enough to know my business. I needed a guy who could be as feared as I was. What I really needed was an executive assistant who fit in my business world.

I found all of this in Bryan Carrera. Bryan was a knockabout Italian kid raised in Florida. I met him through Bobby Erra, who'd give him odd jobs collecting debts. Bryan was a couple years younger than I was. He was large. He was six foot six and weighed about 300 pounds. He was a freak of nature. He could squat 600 pounds. Bryan was crazy about steroids. His legs looked like something from an elephant.

When Bryan and I first met, we mostly worked out at the gym together. Sometimes I'd give him little jobs. He was the guy who went to the International Inn and helped me deal with Henry Borelli when I had to shoot out his guy's knees. We slowly built trust between us, and by the early 1980s he became my full-time driver. Bryan had a heart as big as his monster body. He was the most loyal guy I'd ever had with me.

God Almighty, was he big. Bryan was once seated behind me in my car while I drove. There was an accident ahead of us, and when I slammed on the brakes, Bryan broke the seat behind me and nearly crushed me to death.

MICKEY MUNDAY: You remember Luca Brasi, the goon in *The Godfather*? Bryan was Jon's Luca Brasi. Bryan would shadow Jon. It was like he and Jon communicated telepathically. If you were with Jon someplace, he would stand up to leave, and Bryan would appear outside with the car. No words would have passed between them. It was unreal.

Did Jon tell you what Bryan's day job was? He was a pro wrestler. He dressed up in a costume, went to arenas, and wrestled as a character named The Thing.

J.R.: Kids loved Bryan. He'd work for me during the week, then Saturday nights he'd go to an arena or gym somewhere and put on his show. He wore his costume. He had a following. He'd give out autographed pictures. He was nuts in the ring. Bryan would put razor blades in his gloves and cut his own face, so he'd bleed and make the fight look better.

Bryan was truly insane. He got addicted to horse steroids. I blame myself for this. I had my racehorse business that I started in order to launder money, and Bryan spent time in the stables with me. Back then they had a drug called Equipoise that you'd give to your horse to make him stronger. Equipoise was not just a steroid, it had horse testosterone in it. You would give it to a gelding—a horse with his nuts cut off—and it would give him back his male hormones. It was a heavy, oily juice that came in IV bags. You'd hang it by the horse and drip it into his veins. I came in the barn one day, and Bryan had a bag of Equipoise hooked into his arm with the needle.* He juiced himself with horse testosterone and steroids every couple of weeks. You can imagine where the guy's mind was at, to get the idea to do this. After years of shooting up that shit, he had very little mind left.

I'm not judging Bryan, but if I unleashed him on somebody, he would go nuts. I only used Bryan if I absolutely needed him. By the 1980s I went out of my way to avoid trouble. If a guy accidentally bumped my car on the street, I wasn't going to jump out and kick his ass. Even if the accident was his fault, I'd buy the guy a new car so later on if he ever found out I did illegal things, he'd think, *Wow. This guy bought me a new car. I saw him do something illegal yesterday, but I'm not going to tell on him, because he took care of me.*

That was my theory. Treat people good. I didn't bully people unless they really decided to fuck with me. If you want to fuck with me, I will make sure that is the sorriest day of your fucking life.

IT WAS always these pissant, nothing guys who'd end up giving me the biggest problems where I'd need Bryan's help. One time it was a couple kids I hired to drive a boat. The Colombians had a commercial fishing trawler in the gulf with several thousand pounds of cocaine. Mickey was tied up with a smuggling job, so instead of using

---

* Equipoise, an anabolic steroid that mimics the effect of equine testosterone, is sold in Canada with the warning "For horses only. This drug is not to be administered to horses that are to be slaughtered for use in food."

his boats, I found freelancers with their own boats. Most people who worked for me had fear—either because of my personality or because they knew I was involved with insane Colombians.

Somehow I'd failed to instill sufficient fear in these two kids I hired. They went out to the fishing boat, picked up their load, put it in a car, and left it where they were supposed to. They picked up another car with their fee. The problem was, these kids got wise. Instead of leaving the 400 kilos in the trunk of the first car they'd picked up, they left only 310.

We didn't count the pieces until after these clowns had already been paid. They claimed that 310 kilos was all they got off the boat, then they went into hiding. They reasoned that I couldn't call up the fishing boat and ask what had really happened, so that made them feel protected. They could hide out a few weeks, and I'd forget about them. Wrong.

The Ochoas ran a tight system. If I ever had a serious problem, I could call Fabito or his brother Jorge in Colombia. I could talk directly to Rafa, but I didn't always trust him to handle bad news.

The way I reached the Ochoas in Colombia was funny. Their family had a restaurant called Las Margaritas. The main one was in Bogotá, and the Ochoas had a phone there that was for my calls. When I rang it, I'd get a guy who worked for Fabito and Jorge.

So after I got shortchanged on the kilos, I called the Ochoas' guy at the restaurant and told him about the problem. The next week I got Fabito on the phone. Fabito used to call me *cabron,* which means "friend." He said, "*Cabron.* We checked with everybody, and they gave four hundred kilos. You know I wouldn't lie to you. The problem is with your guys."

It fell on me to make up those ninety kilos that those kids stole. By this time in my life, the $5 million—or whatever it was that I was out—wasn't a big deal. It was the principle of the matter. Two punks believed they could rob me. I sent Bryan all over Miami looking for them. But it was like they'd never lived on the planet.

Months and months passed, and one day Bryan and I are driving out on the turnpike in a new AMG I'd just picked up. Even though I called Bryan my driver, he usually sat beside me. He was my extra set of eyes. Out of nowhere Bryan says, "Jon, it's those kids."

They zoom up in a little piece-of-shit Japanese car to our right. They see Bryan's fat head in the seat next to me and try flooring their car. I let them pull ahead. I'm in an AMG. No way will they lose me. I say, "Bryan, roll your window down and duck, so I can shoot them."

This was the first time I'd ever tried to shoot somebody from my car with Bryan next to me. Guns were not Bryan's forte. His strength was in his hands.* He could pick somebody up with one hand and choke him.

I get up beside the kids' car, and Bryan tries to bend down, but he's such a big lug, he goes down like two inches. I fire one round, but it makes me uneasy, with Bryan filling up the window.

"I'll get in the backseat, Jon." He tries climbing over the back, but he's got no flexibility.

"Fuck it, Bryan. I'm going to cut these motherfucking kids off and crash them."

We're going eighty, ninety miles an hour. Not a cop in sight, thank God. The kids try running their car onto I-95. I cut over to tap their car from the side. If you lightly tap the rear tire of another car with your bumper, you can spin it out of control. As I'm getting closer, *boom!* The kids fire a shotgun.

It misses us, but it makes me so mad, I slam into their bumper. The AMG is so much heavier than their car, they fly off sideways. They spin a half-mile down the road, bouncing off the guardrails.

When we stop behind their car, it's wrecked, and I can't see through the broken windows to tell if the kids are alive or dead. They still have a shotgun.

Bryan jumps out.

I say, *"Think,* Bryan. They got a shotgun."

---

* Bryan Carrera was arrested numerous times for assault and was convicted the first time in 1978. None of his arrests included use of firearms.

He don't care. He reaches in the driver's side and pulls one kid out by the neck. I go carefully to the other side of the car with my gun.

But the kid in the passenger seat is knocked out. I open the door, grab the shotgun at his feet, and pull him out. I drop him to the ground and smash his face with his shotgun. I beat him and beat him. I don't check his pulse when I'm done, but I believe he isn't going to wake up and steal anybody's coke again. I look across at the kid Bryan's been strangling, and he's gone from red to blue to white. Bryan drops him. He says, "I want to strangle your guy."

"You don't have to, Bryan. He's not moving."

"I want to strangle him anyway. I want to see the difference in how their necks feel."

To Bryan, strangling was like a science experiment. That was his mentality.*

BRYAN WAS extreme. One time Bryan made a guy eat his gun. I'd never seen anything like this. It happened with a Cuban who thought he was an actual wiseguy, but was really just another punk. Somehow Rafa got hooked up with this Cuban and wanted me to sell him some coke. By the 1980s Cubans had moved onto 79th Street and were taking over the old Italian clubs. This guy wanted to meet me in an old Italian place now run by greaseball Cubans. When I sat down, this clown started arguing with me about the price, trying to beat down what he'd already negotiated with Rafa. I told him, "If you don't like it, nobody's forcing you to buy from us. Good-bye. Nice knowing you."

As I walk off, this punk said, "If you don't sell to me, I'm gonna fix your ass."

I say something back to this greaseball turd, and he follows me

---

* A former Florida law-enforcement official who reviewed this passage stated that records indicate an incident like this did take place in the early 1980s. He noted that there was a report from a witness who described seeing two men, one of whom was "extremely large," assaulting one or more motorists at the scene of an accident by the freeway. Police who responded found a wrecked car and evidence of a struggle, but no bodies.

outside to shoot his mouth off. Bryan, who is waiting for me outside, sees this guy reach for something. Bryan comes up beside the guy and wraps his hand around his hand. Bryan's hand is so big, the other guy's hand looks like it belongs to a tiny baby, but inside that little hand is a little .38 snub-nosed revolver.

Bryan squeezes the Cuban's hand harder and says, "What do you got there?"

"Nothing, man."

"It feels like a gun."

Bryan uses his other hand to lift the guy by his throat and jam him against the side of the building. He pulls the gun from the guy's hand—which I'm sure was already broken—and holds up the gun. Bryan says, "I'm not real sure how to use a gun. Is this what you do with it?"

Bryan pushes the barrel into the guy's mouth. I've seen that before, but then Bryan does something new. He pushes the pistol all the way in the guy's mouth. It don't go all the way in until Bryan pounds it with the flat of his hand. That gun disappears down the guy's throat. His jaw must have been broken. He's got blood pouring out of his mouth. He's trying to kick Bryan and fight him off, but with a gun jammed in his throat, he's already going weak.

I say, "Bryan, don't do that. Just pull the trigger."

"Jon, I don't like guns, man."

What Bryan used to love was to pick people up and throw them on the pavement. He liked to see if he could bounce them. So now he lifts the guy over his head and starts bouncing him.

I say, "Bryan, careful that gun don't go off in his throat and shoot one of us."

Bryan throws the guy and looks at me, laughing. *Ha ha ha!* He picks him up and bounces him again. Bryan is like a big dog with a toy he doesn't want to let go of.

Don't get the wrong idea about Bryan. He did more than just mangle people. He had a brain. He was no Mickey Munday, but he could count numbers. He could remember things I told him. When

I had orders for my drivers, he was the guy who gave them. He became my face.

Bryan was not a person you looked at and thought, *There must be some kind of nice part to him.* The older he got, the steroids and horse testosterone and the cutting of his face with razors made Bryan an increasingly scary-looking guy. Most people who saw him could perceive it was best to stay the fuck out of his way, and if they set him off, whatever was going to happen with him was going to happen.

But because Bryan could count very well, and he had a good memory, he helped me count the kilos at the stash houses. I kept three or four going at all times.

All my stash houses were owned by people who had regular jobs. The houses didn't look like drug houses on the outside. I'd come by during the day when the owners were at work. I'd have my own remote control for the garage. We'd park my car and go in.

I kept the stashes in secret closets that were about half the size of a bedroom. We kept them locked to protect the house owner from temptation. His mind wouldn't have to bother with how much coke or cash was stored there.

I'd go from house to house every week to divide up loads for the different distributors I was moving the coke to. When we were taking loads out of the house, I'd have Bryan bring the empty car to the garage, and we'd fill the trunk.

Only one time did I have a problem. Bryan and I were carrying kilos to load a car in the garage, and Bryan said, "These pieces feel funny, Jon. They're light."

Back then we didn't have these magical little electronic scales you could carry in your pocket. In every stash house I kept a triple-beam scale like you'd find in a high school chemistry lab. I got out the scale and started weighing the kilos and found every one was five to ten grams light. Bryan had been exactly correct.

His ability to feel the kilos and notice they were a few grams off shows that, despite looking like a monster, he was on the ball.

I sometimes wondered if taking horse hormones gave him sharper senses, like those of an animal.

When the Ochoas sent a kilo, it was always exactly one thousand grams. I knew I had a rat in that house. The kid who owned the house was a smart guy. He ran a successful sign-painting business in South Beach, and he got paid $10,000 a month by me to rent his closet. But something made him go stupid. He'd figured out a way to break into the closet we'd made, and he'd poked a straw into each kilo. He'd cut into each package along a seam and put a piece of tape on the fold, so it was difficult to see what he'd done. If he did it to a thousand kilos, that was five or ten thousand grams he'd stolen—five or ten keys.

Bryan and I drove right to his place of business. It was lunchtime when we walked in. "What do you want?" he asks.

"Relax," I tell him. "I'm taking you to the Forge."

We drive him to the restaurant. We make small talk. I'm looking at this kid, trying to see in his eyes how scared he is, but he's not showing anything. We go into a private dining room. We order our food. Bryan, because he's had all that horse testosterone pumping in him, eats like a horse. You'd order a meal and start eating like a civilized person, and Bryan would shout to the waiter, "Hey, bring me my third lunch."

Bryan's shoveling food in his face, but in the atmosphere of the fine dining room the kid relaxes.

That's when I say, "I've noticed you're breaking into my closet, stealing my coke."

"I'm not doing anything like that," he says. "It's got to be your drivers."

I've already thought of that. But my drivers, even if they wanted to steal, didn't have the time to carefully poke a tiny hole in each bag and reseal it. It has to be this kid is the rat. I say, "I pay you good money, and now you lie to me?"

I don't say nothing else. Bryan grabs the kid by the neck with his left hand and, while squeezing him, keeps eating.

This kid is in his twenties. He works out. He's 190 pounds. But he can't budge Bryan's hand. He's swatting at him, kicking. His eyes are bugging out.

I look at the kid and say, "Before he fucking kills you, admit what you did."

Bryan relaxes his grip, and the kid nods.

"Thank you very much," I say.

The kid starts to speak, and Bryan decides to give him one last squeeze. Just a flick of his fat fingers, and I hear a sound like when you tear apart a raw chicken. It's the gristle in the kid's neck tearing.

I tell Bryan, "Stop! Not in the restaurant."

When he lets go, the kid drops into his plate. Bryan grabs him by the hair and slaps his face. He's lifeless. I run to the front desk and tell the maître d', "Call 911! My friend's choking on his food!"

By the time the ambulance gets there, the kid's breathing. But he's out of it. The medics start giving him oxygen, and they see the horrible marks on his neck.

"What happened here?" The medics look at me and Bryan like they're ready to call the cops. The kid points to Bryan and gasps, "He's my friend. He showed me a wrestling maneuver before lunch, and I moved wrong, so I got hurt."

The medics don't believe our story. Then one of them looks at Bryan and says, "Are you The Thing?"

"Yeah," Bryan says. He puts his hands up and makes his Thing face that's popular with his fans.

"My son loves you," the medic says.

Now the medics are all joking and laughing with us. Bryan always carries pictures of himself dressed up in his Thing costume in case he runs into fans. He goes out to my car and gets them, and by the time he comes back and signs them, the medics are having the time of their lives. The medics still have to take the guy Bryan choked to the hospital, but there's no longer any question of their calling the cops.

Lucky for me, kids loved Bryan.

60

J.R.: The Ochoas were so smart. Their cartel did something I would never have thought of in a million years. If I had a business, and I had a competitor, I'd get rid of him by getting rid of him. But the Ochoas handled it differently: they sold cocaine cheaper than anybody else. Instead of killing off people one at a time, they undercut everybody's price.

I saw this when I brought them Albert as a customer. Fabito told me they'd sell him kilos at any price to win him over. At times I saw them sell coke for $3,500 a kilo—less than what they paid me to transport it. Once they had a customer locked in, they could start raising the prices. They destroyed more people by cutting their prices than with guns. They had a reputation for violence. But it was price that made them so dominant.

My father's belief that evil is stronger than good worked on the streets. But the idea of killing my competitors by offering the lowest price? My father would never have thought of that in a million years. The Medellín Cartel was beyond evil. They were like Walmart.

Transportation was the key to their dominance. They needed volume to keep their competitors down. Rafa was always coming to me and saying, "You've got to move more, more, more."

Early on Rafa told me his boss, Pablo Escobar, wanted to meet me to discuss how to increase our volume. Mickey had already met Pablo, and he believed such business meetings were a waste of his time.

MICKEY: I had better things to do. If you traveled with Max and Rafa, they'd get two feet out of town and immediately call 1-800-GET-A-WHORE. That was their mentality. "We're away from our wives, let's have a party."

J.R.: I believed Mickey's contempt for the Colombians was partly an act. The less he got along with them, the more I had to deal with them. Mickey was no dummy. And trust me, he was not a complete Boy Scout. If a rat crossed the street and showed him its pussy, Mickey would chase after it, just like any other normal guy.

So not only did I have to deal with Rafa in Miami, I had to take time to go see Pablo for meetings. The first one I had was in Panama. Pablo felt safe there because he was friends with General Noriega, who was rising up as the dictator of Panama then.*

Because Max insisted on coming, and since Max—the *El Jefe* of smuggling—was afraid of flying in small planes, we had to fly

---

* Colonel Manuel Noriega seized control in Panama in 1981 after his boss, Omar Torrijos, the Maximum Leader of the Panamanian Revolution, aka the dictator of Panama, died in a plane crash—one that Noriega's lieutenants claimed was caused by a bomb he placed on the aircraft. Noriega cemented his grip on power in 1983 when he stole a national election, promoted himself to general, and became the new dictator of Panama.

commercial. I had a fake passport. I flew under the name "John Epstein" and ate kosher with Max.

Max liked the Holiday Inn in Panama because the rooms had little strips of paper on the toilets that said "sanitized for your protection," and he thought this meant the whores in that neighborhood were cleaner, too. Mickey was right about one thing. You always had to add extra travel days with Max so he could get in his whore time before going back to his wife.

We met Pablo at an American coffee shop near the hotel. He had a couple guys with him who sat at tables nearby, but he was lowkey. He felt safe in Panama because of his friendship with General Noriega.

Even though Pablo Escobar was from the street, he was a goodlooking guy—a little on the heavy side—and he was more polished than I expected. He asked me a few personal questions. Was I married? Did I like soccer? He asked how Mickey was doing. Pablo and the Colombians I met had a high opinion of Mickey. To them, he was like a German scientist who built their moon rockets. It's too bad Mickey looked down on them. If he'd asked, they would have given him his own island to control like a mad-scientist bad guy in a James Bond movie.

Pablo was very confident, very focused. He reminded me of Albert, but not as psycho. In that first meeting he brought up what I'd learn was his favorite theme. He wanted us to move more coke. He was making more and more in his factories.

Then he hits me with his big idea. Pablo says, "What about using dolls? Put cocaine in dolls and ship them."

"That's a great idea," Max says. If Pablo had told him to get on the floor and lick his asshole, Max would have been on all fours with his tongue out.

"Dolls?" I say. "I've seen plastic shoe hangers used for smuggling."

"No, I was thinking dolls. Mickey could do it."

"Mickey should focus on planes. If you have a guy who wants to work with dolls, I'll talk to him. Let's not distract Mickey. We don't want him playing with dolls."

"Okay," Pablo says. "Maybe I got a guy you can talk to about dolls."

That was my first meeting with Pablo Escobar. We talked about dolls. I never ended up talking to his guy who knew how to make them, and he never brought them up again. That's how upper management is in a big organization. Everybody's got to jump when they come up with a bright idea, no matter how dumb it is.

THE PROBLEM Mickey had, and the problem my pilot Roger had when I sent him to Colombia, was obtaining fuel to fly back into the United States. Roger wanted to do more flights. I sent him there for another try after Yeehaw Junction, but when he landed in Colombia, they kept him on the ground for a day waiting for fuel. Barry Seal was the only pilot I worked with who didn't need fuel when he landed in Colombia. That's because he had deals at other airports in Central America where he'd stop along the way to top off his tanks.*

What made the fuel problem worse was that many times pilots couldn't find landing strips in the middle of the jungle. They'd fly around burning gas while looking for the place they were supposed to land. Mickey finally went down there and mapped out the whole country to make it easier for our pilots.

MICKEY: Many landing strips were in triple-canopy jungle. There were no GPSs then. The Colombians would mark the fields with cars pointing like arrows, or they'd light flares. But pilots couldn't see through the coverage. We had planes come back empty because the pilot couldn't find the field.

Eventually I flew down to Colombia with Dad, my pilot, on a commercial flight. We carried fishing gear and rented a plane, as if

---

* Barry Seal was familiar with Central American airports from his days flying arms for the CIA in the 1960s and early 1970s.

for a fishing trip. We flew around the general areas where the Colombians put landing strips. I brought standard navigational charts and marked them with supplemental terrain features that could assist pilots looking for a particular spot.

Back then planes used radio compasses as navigational aids. There were stations around the world that broadcast navigational signals. A radio compass tunes in to those stations and tells you where you are relative to the signal strength. In Colombia there were places where these signals were weak. So I also looked for normal, commercial AM radio stations in Colombia that put out strong signals. If you charted the exact position of the AM radio station, you could use its signal as a navigational aid.

Dad and I spent a week flying around Colombia, adding to the charts every supplementary navigational aid I could find. Once I'd marked the charts, I pinned them to the wall in my hotel and photographed them. Then I burned the charts and flew back with the film in my camera. I didn't develop the film until I was home in the USA.

With the charts I'd made, pilots I sent to Colombia could locate landing strips anywhere in the jungle. But fuel remained a problem. It had been this way since before I worked with Max.

The first time I flew on a smuggling mission to Colombia, my pilot and I came in low and found a landing strip that looked like a junkyard. There were crashed planes strewn on either side of it—piloted, probably, by Colombians flying drunk or high. They had a sloppy attitude through and through.

When you landed, the Colombians would ride out in old farm trucks. We'd want to load the plane, and they'd want to have a party. They'd offer us drinks, girls. I'd say, "Gas. Petrol. Fuel."

That first time, the Colombians pointed down a trail in the jungle. There was an old tractor pulling a trailer tank for pesticides that they'd loaded with avgas. It was moving so slowly, there was a guy walking next to it, and he had to stop now and then so the tractor could catch up.

When the tractor pulled the fuel tank alongside our plane, another guy ran up with a portable pump—basically a fire hose on a water pump powered by an old lawn mower engine. It had no muffler and was throwing sparks everywhere. But why worry about sparks? The fuel guys were all smoking cigarettes anyway. After they started the piece-of-poop pump, they let go of the hose, which started dancing around like an anaconda snake, spraying fuel everywhere. They covered the entire side of our plane with avgas.

When we took off, I crouched behind my pilot with two fire extinguishers—one aimed at him, the other aimed at me. If I saw one spark, I was going to set them off, so we'd at least get a half second to outrun the fireball that would have erupted around our plane.

Those Colombians could screw up a wet dream. From then on I built out the fuel tanks in my planes so in a pinch they could make the round-trip without gassing up. I gave my pilots handheld pumps. I put a kit in every plane with tools and spare parts.

Jon has a high opinion of the Colombians. I have a low one.

J.R.: Mickey always complained about the Colombians. Great as Mickey was, his planes never carried more than four hundred kilos. I had pilots like Roger and Barry who were carrying two-thousand-kilo loads by 1982. Mickey's planes carried so much gas and extra engine parts, he barely had room for cocaine. It was an advantage that Mickey's planes would always get through while my other pilots had to wait for weeks sometimes to get in, but I got sick of Mickey's looking down on the Colombians.

The coke factories Pablo ran were unbelievable. The first one they ever took me to was in the middle of the jungle. It was bigger than Don Aronow's boat factory. They had vats for fermenting the leaves that were as big as swimming pools. They had one room containing hundreds of microwave ovens that they used to bake the coke. There were power generators, guys walking around in masks and chemical hazard suits, dormitories for workers. One factory could make something like a thousand kilos a day.

The chemicals from the factory were so strong, you could smell them from high up in an airplane. They'd run a factory for a week, then shut it down and switch to another. They could take the factories apart and move them in trucks to a new location. The Colombians weren't idiots. They didn't do things like Americans. They weren't in air-conditioned offices, with their tools all lined up on workbenches, as Mickey would have them. But when they decided to do something, nobody could stop them.

I STARTED traveling to Colombia every few months. Rafa owned a car dealership in Medellín. The showroom had like one 1980 Cadillac, one 1979 Corvette, one Audi with no VIN numbers on it. They all leaked. A couple times a day, kids who worked there would push the oil around with a mop.

Rafa had an office upstairs. There was a kitchen next to the office with a long table, and that's where I had my next few meetings with Pablo Escobar. The question was always the same: "Can you move more coke?"

On a couple of visits Pablo had me stay an extra day so one of his guys could show me around Medellín. Medellín was like a frontier town compared to Barranquilla or Bogotá. But Pablo was very proud of the soccer fields that he'd paid for in the slums. Pablo was vain about his charitable work. He'd run for congress in Colombia and won.* He was a politician in addition to being a criminal, no different than an American judge or congressman.

At night Rafa always wanted to go out to a disco where they played terrible, terrible Spanish rock. Even in the early 1980s before it got really bad, there was a lot of violence in Medellín. Inside the discos we'd have so many bodyguards, it was never relaxing.

One night we were driving to the disco when we pulled up to a light and I saw kids on the street run up to the car. They reached in the window and grabbed the driver's arm to steal his watch. When he put up a fight, one of the kids chopped off his hand with a machete. That's how they stole a watch in Medellín.

---

* In 1982 Escobar was elected as a representative in Colombia's national congress.

• • •

My third or fourth meeting with Pablo, he said, "Can you get me chemicals—acetone or ether?"

Those chemicals were used to make cocaine. Pablo explained that the U.S. government had restricted selling them in Colombia. I was thinking, *What do I know about getting industrial chemicals?* Colombians had an inflated view of Americans—it was as if we had magical powers.

"If you help me with this, you'll be my friend for life."

Obviously he was a treacherous motherfucker, and I didn't believe a word he said, but I told him I'd do my best for him.

When I got back to Miami, I asked everybody about these chemicals. I asked doctors who bought coke from me. I asked pilots. Weeks later I was visiting my friend Bernie Levine in San Francisco, and I asked him about getting chemicals. He said, "I got a cousin in Germany who trades all kinds of shit for factories."

It turned out Bernie's cousin knew a guy who could buy thousands of gallons of this shit and send it on a boat from Germany to Colombia.

Danny Mones set up a dummy firm to place the orders and get them through the port at Colombia. For about six months we did a huge business. We got Pablo so much acetone, he finally said, "Stop. I've got enough for fifty years now."

Getting Pablo his chemicals brought me respect in the Cartel.

Fabito started inviting me down to Colombia for more social visits. I'd visit him in Bogotá, where the Ochoas had one of their family restaurants—the one I used to call to reach Fabito or his brother, Las Margaritas. They served incredible steaks. Fabito's father, Don Ochoa, started as a rancher, and they served his cows.

What made Las Margaritas unique was that it had a ring inside where they'd bring out a live bull and kill him while the customers were eating their steak. To the Colombians this was elegant dining.

Myself, I don't want to see a bullfight when I'm eating. I like fishing, but you won't see me gutting a fish at the dinner table.

Fabito took me up to his family's *finca*—or ranch—to meet his father, Don Ochoa. The *finca* was on thousands of acres. To me, it was like driving into a real-life Ponderosa. If there ever was a true-life Cartwright family, the Ochoas were it. They had the ranch, the father, and the loyal sons all running the family business.

Their *finca* was like its own town. The family had so much money flowing in that the sons were building their own mansions across the land. There were bulldozers and cranes everywhere. Fabito's brother Jorge was building a garage that could hold his collection of two hundred cars and motorcycles. It was ridiculous, the money this family was making.

The place where Don Ochoa lived was just a big country place that looked almost like a fancy barn. When we went there, Fabito said, "We can't do any shit in front of my father."

In front of his dad, he was like a little kid on his best behavior. We had a couple of sit-down dinners there. Nobody mentioned cocaine. There were no orgies or whores running around like at a Miami party. Men dressed like gentleman cowboys. Women wore conservative dresses, or fancy riding clothes.

The big entertainment in the house was watching Don Ochoa ride his Paso Finos. He got fatter as the Cartel grew and must have weighed more than four hundred pounds when I last saw him. Everybody would stand outside at sunset and watch the big man climb on his horse. Then he'd canter past, and everybody would applaud and talk about how good his form was, insisting that he was a true *caballero*. They should have been clapping for that poor horse that had to carry his fat ass.

Whenever I went there, Don Ochoa would make a point to come over to me and ask about racehorses. Fabito had told him I owned some racehorses. We'd talk a little bit about the kind of horses I liked, and Don Ochoa would laugh. Colombia didn't have horse-racing tracks like we have in America. Every time we spoke about American racehorses, he'd say, "Why do the horses always run around in a circle?"

He'd wave his finger in a circle and laugh. I'm not saying he was an imbecile, but I never had an intelligent conversation with him about anything. A few times he said, "I know you do a good job." But that was it.

The guy sat on top of the most successful criminal organization there was. He had people like Escobar, his sons, Rafa, Griselda Blanco, Mickey Munday, and me doing all the dirty work, and the money just flowed. Don Ochoa was one of the happiest people I've ever seen. Everything was a joke to this man. They say crime doesn't pay. What a farce.

61

J.R.: In some ways Mickey had it easy. His job was clear-cut. Either the plane had enough gas or it didn't. Most of what I did was manage relationships. Everybody had to be massaged. If situations weren't handled properly, things could blow up.

After Gary Teriaca got killed, Bobby Erra and Albert took over distributing coke to Steven Grabow in Aspen, Colorado. Joey Ippolito came to me. He didn't want to buy the coke he was selling in L.A. through Bobby Erra. He didn't want to pick it up anymore. Gary Teriaca had been his friend, and now that he was gone, he wanted to get it direct from the Cartel.

But I wanted him to buy from Bobby and Albert and keep running it through Colorado because this kept those guys happy, and I wanted to keep them happy because I had to share Miami with them.

Joey argued that Steven Grabow in Aspen was no good now that his friend Gary was gone. To keep Joey happy, I promised to go out to Aspen and check up on Grabow. I had to do this to show Joey respect.

It turned out that my dog Brady, whom I'd had all these years, got cancer of the jaw. My vet in Miami sent me to the Angell Clinic in Boston to treat Brady.* But when I flew him there, they said the best clinic for him was at Colorado University. So I took Brady out there on a chartered jet and arranged for Grabow to pick me up in Denver.

After we took Brady to the clinic, I went with Steven to Aspen. He didn't know for sure that his friend Gary Teriaca was dead. I didn't know exactly what had happened to him either, but I knew the story we were telling people—that he was traveling in Europe—was bullshit.

When I looked in Steven's eyes, I could see him growing a little nervous when I brought up Gary, but other than that he seemed fine. He was a blowhead like Gary, but he wasn't strung out. He had a good life in Aspen with his lovely wife, Linda. We went out a few nights and had some meals. Grabow sold the coke Bobby and Albert shipped to him to the beautiful people in Aspen. But mostly his job was holding the coke that had been sent up in cars from Miami so guys from California could pick it up and take it to L.A. for Joey Ippolito and other distributors. The guys from California brought money to Steven that he put in the cars returning to Florida. He did a good job. He used garages at a few different condos to hold the cars and make the transfers. He was moving a good amount by then—two or three hundred kilos a month. That was half a billion dollars a year in coke passing through his hands, and nobody ever had a problem.

Even after he lost his friend Gary, I could see he was still steady.

I went back to Joey Ippolito and said, "Don't rock the boat. You got a good thing going in Aspen."

---

* The Angell Animal Medical Center in Boston is one of the foremost veterinary hospitals in the world.

Unfortunately, I learned on that trip that Brady couldn't be treated for his cancer, and I had to fly him back and put him down.

JOEY IPPOLITO couldn't complain how I handled him. But he never gave up trying to worm out of me a direct connection to the Cartel. He used to come to Miami all the time and work on me. Joey was a good friend of Donny Soffer's, who built the Turnberry Towers* and most of Aventura. In the past Danny Mones and I had put money into Soffer's business when he had trouble getting normal financing. Joey Ippolito had done the same.† In the early 1980s, when Soffer reached out for more financing to expand his Turnberry properties, Joey talked me into going in with him on condos in one of the towers. When the building was finished, we got our money back plus four corner units in a tower. My thought was to flip the condos.

But Joey had another thought: "How about we fix them up nice and rent them to celebrities I know from L.A., so they got a nice place to stay when they visit Miami?"

Joey introduced me to a broad who claimed she was an expert decorator. She met me at one of the condos we were going to fix up. It was brand-new, but the lady decorator wanted to put in a sunken

---

* The Turnberry Towers form the heart of a luxury residential resort built by Soffer in Aventura in the 1970s and 1980s. In 2007 Soffer built a similar tower complex, also named the Turnberry, in Las Vegas.
† While Jon has not provided proof of his or of Joey Ippolito's alleged financial dealings with Soffer, Ippolito is reported to have lived in one of the Turnberry Towers and to have had a relationship with Soffer, who was no stranger to controversy. A close friend of boatbuilder Don Aronow, Soffer, like Aronow, was alleged to employ high-end party girls to entertain prospective customers, investors, and other friends. In 1987 leading presidential hopeful Gary Hart, a married man, saw his campaign implode when photographs were published of him on a yacht cavorting with party girl Donna Rice (now a prominent antipornography crusader). At the time of the scandal, Rice was reportedly a part-time employee of Soffer's whom Hart had met at a party at the Turnberry. *Monkey Business*, the yacht on which the scandal took place, was owned by Soffer. Soffer was the subject of a fascinating profile written by Mark Muro for the *Boston Globe*, "Turnberry Isle: Where Stars Play and Also Fall," May 31, 1987.

floor and bigger windows and buy furniture suitable for movie stars. She said, "I can do it for a hundred thousand dollars."

I said, "Lady, that's more than the condo cost."

"You'll make up for it when you charge more for the rental."

I said, "Okay. But I got one condition."

"What's that?"

"You're a very attractive decorator. I'll hire you. You can decorate your brains out. When you're done, you're going to take me here, and I'm going to fuck the shit out of you."

"Deal."

This broad really hustled me. By the time she was done, I paid way more than her quote. Before I could see the place and make her fulfill her end, I got called out of town on business. When I got back, Joey said, "Good news. I rented our place to my friend Jimmy."

I don't know who Jimmy is, but great, if he signed a two-hundred-year lease, maybe I'll make up what that lady decorator cost me. A month later Joey calls me, "Can you bring your boat down to Turnberry Isles Marina and pick up me and Jimmy, our tenant? I want to take him out and show him a good time."

"Okay, Joey. You're my friend. I'll be there."

Coming into Miami and getting my boat out from my marina was a hassle, but Joey Ippolito isn't just a friend, he's business. When I dock at the Turnberry, Joey walks down with Jimmy, our tenant. The guy is halfway familiar, but I can't place him.

Jimmy shakes my hand and says, "Hiya, Jon," like we're old friends.

I figure it out. "Jimmy" is James Caan, the actor. That's why Joey was hot to have me come down. He wanted to show off getting James Caan as our tenant.

Soon as we get out on the water, Joey asks if I brought some coke. I always have something on my boat for recreation. Joey has brought some girls. Everybody does some lines. We're all laughing. The vial I'd brought my coke in is sitting on a mirror tray where everybody has just done their lines. Out of the corner of my eye, I see

Caan put a straw up his nose and stick it in the vial. The movie star is sitting there like a slob snorting up all my party-blow.

Joey sees me looking at Caan and says, "I'm sorry, Jon. The guy's a Hoover. I can't believe he don't got holes in his nose."

Soon as he finishes my blow, Caan starts to jones. "You got any more?"

"That's all I had, bro."

"Take me over to the Palm Bay Club. I can get some. People give it to me because of who I am."

"Okay, chief."

I drive the boat over to the Palm Bay, and as we dock, Caan says, "You're a great guy. Gimme your number for when I come back. I want to be able to call you when I'm in Miami."

"I ain't giving you my number."

"Why wouldn't you give me your number?"

"Because I want you to leave me the fuck alone."

Caan's in a bathing suit and flip-flops, but he steps up to me like he means something. "You've got a piece-of-shit attitude."

"I remember you in *The Godfather*," I say, "and I remember you beat up some guy with the garbage cans or whatever the story was, but you're not a tough guy. You may think you're a tough guy because you're wacked out of your mind on coke, but you're just an asshole in flip-flops."

Caan says nothing, just turns and steps off the boat. Joey says, "Jon, you really blew it. Jimmy don't like you now."

"Joey, that guy's beneath you."

Jimmy remained a tenant the next couple of years. After he went back to L.A. that first time I met him, I called up that lady decorator and reminded her she still owed me her end of our deal. "But the place is rented," she said.

"The tenant's out of town, and I got the master key."

"Okay."

When we meet at the apartment, she says, "I hope you don't think anything of me, but sometimes to loosen up I like to take a Quaalude. I brought some."

"How about I mix them up in some drinks?"

"That would be delightful."

I throw a bunch of Quaaludes in the blender. We toast her beautiful decorating job, and half an hour later she turns into a total freak. She's touching herself. She's begging me to eat her pussy. She's incredible. We fuck for hours like we're in a porno movie. At four in the morning I need to get home to Toni in Delray, so I carry this broad down to my car and drive her to her place.

The next day she calls. "Jon, I don't remember a thing about last night. I know we must have had fun. I'm sore all over. I hope I did nothing too unladylike."

"Not a bit. All we did was I fucked you in your ass for about seven hours in James Caan's bed."

"Goodness," she says.

That was her word, "goodness." It made me laugh.

Much as I liked spending time with Joey and having our little adventures together, he was work because he bought ridiculous amounts of coke from Bobby and Albert. I had a dozen other relationships like this that I constantly had to manage.

IN 1983 Steven Grabow got arrested on a cocaine charge in Aspen.* He didn't give up Albert or Bobby or Joey or me, but nobody was taking any chances. He got blown up outside his gym. They put a

---

* Grabow was charged with trafficking seven hundred kilos of cocaine during a three-month period. He admitted to police that the source of his cocaine was in Miami, but he didn't name his source. He was released on bond, pending trial.

† Grabow was blown up on December 8, 1985, by a powerful bomb placed in his car outside the Aspen Club, whose motto is "health, fitness, and pampering." It was the first fatal car bombing in the history of Colorado. Reporting in the December 17, 1985, *Lewiston Journal,* Don Knox and Chance Conner quoted Grabow as having once said, "I'd rather be broke and washing dishes in Aspen, than be the king of France," though their article noted that "Grabow had a penchant for fast sports cars, fancy suits, and good food. He drank from Waterford crystal glasses." His murder was never officially solved, but when Miami investigators working on the 1991 racketeering case into Albert San Pedro discovered that he and Bobby Erra had been supplying Grabow with cocaine, they came to Aspen. They discovered, among other facts, that the bomb used to kill Grabow was similar to the type used in the attempted murder of Forge restaurant owner Al Malnik when his Rolls-Royce

bomb in his car, and that was it.[†] The police found a pile of shit in his car, and his body in the bushes.[‡]

His arrest was a close call for all of us. I was sure he would have talked, had he lived, because he was facing a lot of prison time. Getting rid of him was the right thing to do. But I felt bad for the kid.

The one guy it worked out for was James Caan. Joey Ippolito and I had introduced him to Steven Grabow and his wife, Linda, when they were visiting Miami. Caan had liked Linda from the moment he met her. After Steven got blown up, Caan gave her a shoulder to cry on, and they eventually married.[*] Good for him.

By the early 1980s, my work life was so hectic, I needed something to take my mind away from it all. I found that escape in racehorses. This was a passion I shared with Toni in the life we built together. No matter how crazy my work got, I made time for our horses.

was blown up in 1982. Investigators planned to include Grabow's murder as an additional predicate act in their racketeering case against San Pedro, but this avenue was closed to them following the discovery of his immunity deal.

[‡] According to police reports I examined, Grabow was seated over the bomb when it detonated. His intestines were blown from his body. Nevertheless, he managed to run seventy-five feet while screaming for help before dying.

[*] Caan married Grabow's widow, Linda Stokes, in 1996. They have two children.

62

When Jon Roberts looks at horses he might buy, the ears have it.

"I love horses with big ears," Roberts says. "The first time I laid eyes on Best Game, she was a yearling, standing in a field. She was a big, good-looking filly, very rough. She took off like a lightning bolt. I had to have her."

In a little less than six weeks Best Game won a division of the Poinsettia. Best Game is the only filly in the world to have won two Hibiscus Stakes in 1983.

Roberts says, "If she runs good in New York there's a $100,000 grass stake in California."

Another claim Roberts made four years ago was equally fortuitous. He took Noholme's Star for $30,000. The gelding has gone on to become a stakes winner with lifetime earnings of $170,369, winning 18 races.

"When he won the Florida Turf Cup, it was the biggest thrill I've had," Roberts says. "He bowed in both legs and came back to run his heart out for me."

Roberts was born in the Bronx 34 years ago and grew up in lower Manhattan. He moved to Miami in 1973 and sold cars. "I owned several car lots," he says. "I met Danny Mones, who became my lawyer and my business partner. We bought a run-down building, very cheap, fixed it up and sold it. We made a real score and went on from there. We've done real well in real estate ever since.

"I've never married. I don't have any children. The horses become like children to me. I love going to Ocala and buying horses. It's one of the prettiest spots in Florida, and some day I'm going to have a farm up there. My girl, Toni Moon, loves horses as much as I do."

Miss Moon, a very attractive lady, is a model and actress and appears in television commercials.

"I've been offered half a million for Best Game but I don't want to sell. Think what her babies will be worth. Breeding is what I'm most interested in now. I'm going to start building up a broodmare band and go from there."

Roberts's first experience in breeding horses was sending his mare Winning Fate to Cerf Volant. "The foal came out with very crooked legs but I wouldn't let them put her down. We raised her and I gave her to Toni for a riding horse."

—Art Grace, "The Best Game in Town," a profile of Jon Roberts published in *Florida Horse,* June 1983

APRIL 2009—AVENTURA AND BAY POINT ESTATES

E.W.: The extent of Jon's involvement in horse racing didn't hit home for me until one night at Padrones, an upscale Cuban restaurant in Aventura. We were walking out with takeout food when a deep voice boomed, "Papa! Papa!"

The owner of the voice—a small, dapper man—came up the sidewalk with his arms open. Jon said, "That's Angel Cordero. The little son of a bitch calls me Papa."

Cordero, regarded as one of the greatest jockeys who ever lived, threw his arms around Jon. The two spent half an hour trading stories. When Jon owned Mephisto Stables, Cordero was one of his top jockeys. When they met again that evening in 2009, Cordero burst into tears while discussing the death of his wife, and Jon patted his shoulders to comfort him. As we left, Angel said to me, "Papa was one of the good guys."

It was a surprise to witness Jon outside the context of his life of crime and see him regarded as a beloved figure. Up until that point in interviewing Jon, I'd assumed racehorses were mostly about laundering drug money.

After meeting Cordero, Jon arranged for me to meet Seymour "Sy" Cohen, who helped run Mephisto Stables. At the time he worked for Jon, Cohen was a columnist for the now-defunct *Miami News* who specialized in handicapping races. Cohen was also a fixture on the Miami social circuit. At Palm Bay Club, he was known as a fierce competitor on the tennis courts and played frequently with Oleg Cassini and Robert Duvall. Cohen helped advise the renowned painter and racehorse enthusiast Frank Stella in his purchases. As we drove to Cohen's house, Jon explained, "The genius of Sy wasn't just in looking at a horse. He knew where to run them so they'd win."

Cohen lives in Bay Point Estates, the same gated community where Gary Teriaca once stored cocaine in his home. After Jon and I are cleared for entry at the security gate, we drive past expansive homes set back from the road. Lawns are tended by small armies of gardeners whose gas-powered machines fill the air with buzzing. Cohen's house has a brightly painted iron lawn jockey in front. When we enter, the housekeeper escorts us down a hallway where the paneled walls are covered by framed photographs of horses. Jon points to a picture of his younger self standing by a horse with Sy, a tall man with a confident grin. "That's Sy," Jon says. "See what a good-looking guy he was?"

"I still am, you motherfucker," booms Sy's voice from a room nearby.

We enter the back bedroom. Sy, seventy-six, lies propped up on pillows on his bed. Wires and tubes dangle from nearby medical machines. He's recently undergone surgery. Though his face is ashen, he pushes himself up and greets Jon, "What's happening, baby?"

Jon slips into banter with him that sounds like dialogue from a movie set in an old Miami Beach nightclub. It's pure Rat Pack.

"God Almighty, you look good, kid," Jon says.

"Sure, babe. I still have a cocktail in the evening."

"Just one? Don't lie to me, you cocksucker."

They bring up good times at the old Palm Bay Club, which in the 1990s was converted into a residential community. Sy turns to me and says, "Kid, you should have been there. The Palm Bay was a real live joint."

Jon sits by the bed and takes Sy's arm. I notice several Frank Stella paintings—hanging off-kilter and covered in dust—on the walls. I ask, "Are these real?"

"Of course they're real, kid. I help Frank buy his racehorses."

"Jesus, I studied him in college."

"College," Jon says, amused and disdainful. He rolls his eyes to Sy, then turns back to me. "Frank was a madman. Frank liked to party. He gave me a bunch of those pictures he used to make, where he'd take squares and other shit and put all the shit together. Of all the famous people I ever was friendly with, Frank Stella was the only person who ever gave me anything. He was a good guy."*

"I hope you still got those paintings, Jon," Sy says.

Jon shrugs. "Those went away when I lost everything."

I ask Sy what Jon was like when he met him.

Sy reflects a moment, then says, "When Jon asked me to help him with Mephisto Stables, he was serious. Jon wanted to learn. He made an intense effort. He listened explicitly and almost never second-guessed me. Later on, of course, he started to get his own opinions."

"Fuck you," Jon says, laughing.

---

* Intrigued by Jon's Frank Stella connection, in the summer of 2010 I phoned the artist at his studio to ask about his relationship with Jon. Stella recalled knowing Jon, but phoned me back a day later in a highly agitated state to say, "Please, don't ever ask me about Jon Roberts again. He's a very, very dangerous man. My wife is terrified that we are even speaking about him."

"You want the truth, don't you?"

"You're right, Sy. I got my own opinions, and I should've stayed with you."

Sy explains to me. "Jon got involved with that girl, Toni Moon. Jon thought she knew something about horses. It started to happen that I'd find a horse for Jon, and this girl would tell me that she didn't like it. I wasn't ready for that."

"I was an idiot, Sy. I should never have let a girl get between us."

"We ran some good races, kid. People still talk about Mephisto Stables in Ocala."

"They really do, Sy?"

"I wouldn't lie to you, babe."

As we get in the car to leave, Jon says, "I love that man to death because he gave me the most pleasure I had in my life through the horses."

Jon drives past the Bay Point security gate, lost in thought. He says, "How can I explain a horse to you? Honestly, if you compare racing a horse to fucking the most beautiful woman, it might only last a few minutes with the woman. Even if you screw that beautiful woman for hours, and your horse wins a two-minute race, you'll still have better memories from the horse. There's nothing stronger than a winning horse."

J.R.: Horses were the one good thing my father turned me on to. He loved the races. After I made my first big score selling coke to Bernie Levine in California, Danny Mones told me racehorses were a good way to launder money. Many horse sellers would take partial payment in cash. I'd claim the horse for a fake price that was low, and write a check for that amount. Then I'd give the owner cash to make up the difference. When I sold the horse later on, I'd sell it at its real price and pay taxes on the profit. Now my money was clean and legal.

Danny Mones and I started Mephisto Stables in 1977. Buying

horses was different from buying condos. I liked to look at horses. I liked to watch them run. I liked to talk to the people in the stables. I liked to think about them.

Gary Teriaca introduced me to Sy Cohen at the Palm Bay Club. Sy gave such good advice about horses, I made him the president of my stables. He started taking me to Kentucky, Louisiana, California, and New York to buy horses. It got to where I was flying horses all over the country to run them in races. Obviously I met a lot of good pilots this way who I also got to help with my coke business.

Dealing cocaine had promoted me into high society. Owning racehorses took me into the stratosphere. The first time Sy took me to Lexington, we were picked up at the airport by his friend Judge Joe Johnson,* who hosted horse auctions. Judge Johnson drove us himself in a stretch Mercedes limousine. This judge was drunk off his ass. We blew through red lights and stop signs. Nobody stopped him. He owned the cops. It was nuts. I was in a limo with a shoebox of coke money being driven by a drunk judge.

We stayed at Judge Johnson's house. He hosted buyers from all over the world. He had Japanese coming in, Arabs. We'd go to claiming races, which was where you'd bid on the horses. Judge Johnson took me under his wing and explained to me how to work cash payments in Kentucky. The judge didn't know what I did for a living. He helped all his friends out this way. Even normal rich people need to launder cash now and then.

Judge Johnson was the good kind of judge. He was what was called a "Kentucky hard boot." He spoke his mind. He was drunk when he went to bed at night. He was drunk at the breakfast table, and he was a hell of a guy. I stayed with him for years. It was through

---

* A Fayette County judge from 1968 to 1992, Joe Johnson was descended from local coal barons, and was known for eccentric statements he made from the bench, such as urging local police to shoot robbers on sight and threatening to arrest reporters he didn't like. "He had this cowboy image, but he was a thoroughly honorable, forthright, trustworthy man," a Lexington bloodstock consultant and longtime friend was quoted as saying in his obituary published April 3, 2008, by the *Lexington Herald-Leader*.

him that I got friendly with Cliff Perlman, who owned Caesar's Palace. When I'd go to Caesar's and get comped, everybody assumed it was because of my Mafia connections. No, I was connected to Caesar's Palace by a Kentucky judge.

Horse-racing people were very genial. They made the rich doctors I used to do coke with look like garbage. No matter how high I rose in Miami, I was always "the coke guy." In the horse world, I was just a man with a lot of money. One thing I truly learned about America is that once you have enough money to get in with the top, richest people, nobody asks where it came from. That's one rule rich people live by as a courtesy to other rich people. Don't ask, don't tell.

IT TURNED out that Toni fit right in with these people. We ended up becoming friends with Al Tanenbaum and his girlfriend, Gloria. Al was a guy who'd made it big in stereos.* He and Gloria were an older couple we met at an auction in Ocala. Al and I were strangers standing next to each other at an auction, and out of the blue he asked if I wanted to go in on a horse with him. I said yes and bid on the horse. I ended up fronting Al $40,000 because he couldn't write a check that high that day.

"Gentlemen's agreement," he said. "I'll send you the check when I get back to New York."

"No problem," I said. Maybe he was a con artist, but I was curious to find out.

A few days later the check came in the mail. After that we all became great friends. Al and Gloria lived in a suite at the Regency Hotel in New York.† Toni and I started going up there, and Al would send his driver to pick us up. All of us would go to Toni's favorite

---

* As noted in his *New York Times* obituary published June 26, 1991, Alvin "Al" Tanenbaum was an industrialist who founded Yorx Electronics. "An innovator in the electronics business, Mr. Tanenbaum introduced the Space Saver, a compact stereo system, and other audio concepts." The obituary makes no reference to his girlfriend, Gloria.

† Now the Loew's Regency at 540 Park Avenue.

‡ The Russian Tea Room and Elaine's epitomized New York sophistication and glamour in the 1980s.

places—the Russian Tea Room and Elaine's.‡ One night after Al had a few drinks, he said, "Jon, men should never ask this, but I feel I know you. What's your game?"

It was very classy, the way he asked me. So I said, "All I'm going to tell you is this. I do real estate. I have my stables. But sometimes I also work in the importation business."

Al laughed. "Bolivian marching powder?" Funny guy. That was the phrase he used.

"I guess you could say so."

"Money is money, Jon. Once you have it, what does it matter?" He pointed to his girlfriend, Gloria, and said, "Did you know that she's divorced from a man who has more money than you and I combined? She's so wealthy that she has a car and chauffeur just to take her little fucking dog on a drive around the park so he can look at the trees out the window. All the starving people in the world, and that's what she does with her money. Who are we to judge her?"

These people didn't give a fuck about anything. They didn't judge me. They didn't want anything from me. They just wanted to have a good time.

We bought several horses together and started running them in Saratoga Springs in upstate New York.* We'd stay at Al's house up there, and he and Gloria would come down to Delray and stay with us. It was the best social relationship I'd had with anybody, and it lasted for years.

IT WAS through Al that I became friendly with another very interesting man, Judge Tom Rosenberg, who was a top guy in Cook County.† Judge Rosenberg was a houseguest at Al's place in Saratoga Springs when we met him. He ended up coming down to

---

* Saratoga Springs is home to one of the oldest racetracks in the country.
† Judge Thomas Rosenberg served twelve years on the circuit court in Cook County, retiring in 1981. Before that he'd been an alderman for the 44th Ward, closely allied with Mayor Richard Daley.

Florida, and we went in on some horses together. He was a real gambler,* and I turned him on to Bobby Erra, who would take bets on anything. At the end of Judge Rosenberg's first visit to Miami, I took the judge to Joe's Stone Crab for dinner, and he said, "I insist you visit me in Chicago. Come to Sportsman's Park.† There's a race called the Color Me Blue that you're going to love. Bring one of your horses."

A few weeks later I had my stables send my horse Best Game up to Chicago. The afternooon Toni and I fly in, Judge Rosenberg has us picked up at the airport by a security detail of cops. They take us to a hotel by the Water Tower.‡ After we rest, the cops escort us to a restaurant. Inside, it is like the Roaring Twenties. Everybody is dressed to the nines. Judge Rosenberg is sitting like a prince at a table surrounded by ass-kissers and beautiful women. When he stands up to greet us, it is like the parting of the seas. Everybody in the room steps back and stares at him, then at me and Toni. Mostly at Toni, because she was always at her finest surrounded by money. After dinner the judge says, "I'm going to take you to a place I know you'll like."

The cops chauffeur us across town to a cabaret theater. One of the goons at the door says, "Good evening, Judge. Would you like your table by the bar, or are you going upstairs?"

"We'll be going upstairs," he says.

We went upstairs to big double doors. The bouncer standing there says, "How are you tonight, Your Honor?"

The bouncer opens the doors, and inside there are green tables with every game you'd see in Las Vegas, except this place is classier. There are guys in tuxedos, women in jewels. Everybody comes up to say, "Hi, Your Honor."

---

* In his obituary published on August 21, 1999, in the *Chicago Sun-Times*, his son Tom says of his father, "He was a wild man. There was no minute that wasn't filled with entertaining, politics or gambling." Tom Rosenberg is the Oscar-winning producer of *Million Dollar Baby*, who was also named as an extortion victim in the 2008 trial of crooked Chicago financier Tony Rezko.

† The racetrack outside of Chicago was demolished in 2003.

‡ An actual water tower near Miracle Mile that has become a landmark.

Judge Rosenberg turns to me and says, "I'm going to get you some chips. The way it works is, nobody walks out of here with money. If you win, I'll have somebody bring your cash tomorrow."

I shot craps for hours. That's my favorite game, but doing it with Toni and Judge Rosenberg and all these people who looked like they were in the movies—it was a trip and a half. At the end of the night, I was up $50,000. Next day, good to his word, Judge Rosenberg had one of his cops bring me my winnings.

A day later we went to Sportsman's Park to run my horse Best Game. When the race started, he didn't break right. My heart went to my stomach. Judge Rosenberg must have noticed the look on my face, and he leaned over and said, "Don't worry about it, Jon. It's just a horse race."

Judge Rosenberg wasn't just classy, he was a gracious man. I knew he'd bet on my horse, but he was trying to put me at ease. All my worrying was for nothing. Best Game pulled ahead and won.

We all had a terrific time in Chicago. At the time the judge was hosting me, my partner Ron Tobachnik and I were moving a couple hundred kilos every month in the city. Not that I'd ever mention this to the judge. I'd been some kind of gangster my whole life, but the first time I ever lived like one—like the way I pictured Al Capone living in his heyday—was during those nights in Chicago when Judge Rosenberg took me around town.

WHEN I first started buying horses, they were like pieces of meat to me. Whether they won or lost, I made money—because I was using them for laundering. But early on I became interested in winning. I had horses gushing cash. I bought a horse called Noholme's Star for $30,000, and he earned $850,000 for me.

Sy taught me how to train horses so they'd run their hearts out. But I also learned how to fix races. There were many tricks. I hired what they called witch doctors—crooked vets—who could take a nothing horse and give him hops so he'd run his brains out. In the early days, *hops* meant heroin. They'd give it to injured horses so they'd run hard on injured legs. Of course, once a horse runs a race or two on hops, there's no more horse left. By the late 1970s witch doctors were coming up with all sorts of exotic dope. There was the testosterone that Bryan used to shoot up. There was a drug called Sublimaze* that made horses fly like Superman. When they banned it in the United States, I found a guy in Colombia who could get it for me, and I'd fly it up with coke shipments.

The tracks got wise to doping, and they made a rule that winning horses had to get tested in a "spit barn," where officials would test their piss. The guys overseeing the spit barns at Florida tracks were state employees. I could usually find one I could bribe into switching the piss cups. That way I could win with a doped horse, no problem.

If there was no way to pay off the guys at the spit barn, I found a mad-scientist doctor who, the morning before the race, would remove all the horse's blood and replace it with oxygenated blood. I had another guy who employed a very simple trick. Before the race, he'd blow pure oxygen into the horse's ass. The oxygen feeds all the veins up there, and the horse will run like a motherfucker, but he won't test dirty.

There was always the old-fashioned way to fix a race: pay off the jockey. Some jockeys would sneak charging sticks up their sleeve. A charging stick is like a stun gun. When the horse gets shocked, he runs faster.

A really good jockey can hold a horse when he's running him. He'll whip him like crazy with his crop, but secretly he's holding back the horse. If you do this with the same horse several races in a row, everybody thinks he's a nothing horse. The odds go long, then you run him to win.

Albert San Pedro was into racehorses, and so was Bobby Erra. One time we put our heads together and decided, "Let's fix a race at Calder by buying off every jockey."†

---

* Sublimaze is a narcotic painkiller that when blended with amphetamines and illegally injected into racehorses came to be known as "rocket fuel."
† Calder Race Course—which now is also home to a casino—is in Miami Gardens.

We paid off every jockey and picked the trifecta.

It went perfect, at first. Everybody hit their marks. Bobby and Albert and I were all slapping hands. It's one of the few times I ever saw Albert smile. Then, in the final stretch, *bam,* the lead horse steps in a tiny hole and breaks his leg. He goes down, and the whole pack crashes into him. Horses are falling everywhere, jockeys flying in the air. Disaster. You plan and you plan, and at the last minute your horse slips his foot in a little hole.

IN MY early days, I ran my horses like I ran my life. If there was an evil way, I'd find it. I got my rewards, and the good people got punished. At Calder I had a jockey named Nick Navarro who worked for me. He was one of the good guys. He wouldn't hold horses or charge them or run them on dope. He was very skilled, and when I ran my horses clean, I used Nick.

One day in 1977 he ran a race for me at Calder. I walked up to him after he finished. He put his hand up to wave, and there was a powerful explosion. A bolt of lightning came out of the sky and hit him. It blew him to pieces. It split his helmet in half, threw him out of his boots.* He was one of the best guys. He had a wife, a couple of kids. And there's me a few feet away. God sends a lightning bolt down. Instead of hitting me, He hits the good guy. Please. Don't tell me the wicked are punished.

In the early days there were many things I did that I'm not proud of. Sometimes you'd dope a horse, and then when you used him up, you'd kill him for the insurance. There was a guy who was a hit man for horses. He'd come to your barn and give your horse lethal drugs that couldn't be traced. It would look like the horse had a seizure. The last time I did this, I put the injection in the horse myself. I went out to eat, came back, and saw the horse legs up in the stall. This dead horse had a terrible look on his face. Even though he was dead, he was looking up at me. I could see in

---

* The incident made the national wires that day, December 28, 1977, in a UPI story, "Jockey Killed by Lightning."

his eyes that in his last minute on earth, I gave him agony, and all he'd ever given me was pleasure.

I never killed a horse after that. Part of what changed my attitude about horses was Toni Moon. She loved horses. She liked riding them, and she had an eye for racehorses. When she came along, she and Sy got into a pissing match over how to run my stables, and she won. He still bad-mouths the horses she picked, but that's sour grapes. Toni had good instincts, and she really cared for the animals.

When you care for your animals they can break your heart. This happened to me with a horse named Desperado. Toni and I found him in Kentucky. We were out at a farm early in the morning. The sun was barely up. There was a heavy mist. Out of it a horse came running. Desperado. He was gray with black dimples.

Toni and I looked at each other. We knew this was the horse. I'd always had the fantasy of winning the Kentucky Derby. I could dominate many tracks, but winning against all those blue-blood assholes at the Kentucky Derby? There'd be nothing greater. I felt Desperado was my winner.

He was still a baby when I got him. He hadn't been trained how to run, but he could already fly on the grass, and he had good instincts. He didn't like other horses. You don't want a sociable horse. They stay in the pack. You want a horse who likes to run in front of all the other horses. Desperado was a killer.

I named him Desperado because I saw myself in his eyes. We took him down to Ocala, because Ocala is the best place in the world to raise baby horses. There's no snow on the ground to slip and hurt themselves. Ocala's built on limestone that leaches minerals into the water, and when the baby horses drink, it makes them strong.

The legs on a baby horse are tender. If you give the horse his head too soon and start running him early, he can buck his shins and injure himself. We found a trainer who was patient, Juan Sanchez. Juan had worked for Horatio Luro when he trained Northern

Dancer, which many people believe was the best racehorse that ever lived.*

I raised Desperado the opposite of how my father raised me. That horse was my son, and I gave him the best. There were carrot farms near my house in Delray. You could pay farmers to walk on their land and pull carrots from the ground. I used to get up early and pull bunches of carrots and fly up to Ocala in my helicopter to feed Desperado.

After months and months Juan and I put a boy on Desperado and ran him. We had the boy hold him back, but Desperado moved like lightning. Juan turned to me and said, "He's really full of himself. He knows how good he is."

We decided to breeze him—give him an easy, full run—the next morning. Desperado decided to show off. He took all his head and ran full out. He broke the track record in the morning. We ran him again, and he broke the track record for the afternoon.

I looked at Toni and said, "We're going to the Kentucky Derby."

A few weeks later we were breezing Desperado out for his first race, and I guess he got cocky. He broke from the gate and twisted his leg. He went down. I ran to him. He tried again and again to get up, but his leg couldn't hold him. He didn't understand. I had to hold his head to stop him from fighting to get up. When I looked him in the eyes, that poor horse could see in my face it was over for him. To see this horse go from proud to broken, it's the worst thing I've ever seen.

That horse killed me inside. But I was never mad at him. I tried to let him know he hadn't disappointed me. I paid for an operation to try to remove a bone chip from his knee. I sent him to a rehabilitation farm where they swam him in tanks. But he was never the same. In the end I gave him to someone who let him live on a farm outside Ocala. I still brought him carrots.

---

* Horatio Luro is regarded as one of the best trainers, in part because Northern Dancer, the horse he trained with Juan Sanchez, is one of the winningest horses in history.

Toni gave me the idea that I should retire from my business in Miami. She wanted to buy a farm up north. I'd become certified as a horse trainer. We had a vision of living up there and breeding horses.

I was thirty-four or thirty-five years old then. I had millions and millions of dollars. Since I'd come to Miami less than a decade before, I'd become, along with Max Mermelstein, one of the top two Americans in the Medellín Cartel. I'd helped them build their empire. I'd survived while a lot of people around me ended up in the dirt. A smart man might have walked away, but that wasn't me. I believed I could have both worlds—my business life with the Colombians and my life with Toni—and this life would never stop.

But it don't work that way, bro.

63

When Jon moved into the neighborhood, people talked
about him because he was a New York boy. I'd always
see him talking at pay phones along the main road.
I wondered about that, but I believe what makes this
country great is people are free. Soon enough, we
became good neighbors.

—Earl, Jon's redneck neighbor from Delray*

J.R.: When I moved to Delray, I never imagined how
well I'd get along with rednecks. I still had my New
York prejudice. I believed that most rednecks had an attitude, that they were out there shooting black people
and were closed-minded. It took time to know them, but
I found out that my redneck neighbors were very open.

---

* Jon's former neighbor, whom I interviewed in 2010 outside the
Hole in the Wall feed store, still lives in Delray. He asked that he be
identified simply as "Earl" or as Jon's "redneck neighbor."

When they realized I was in the drug business, it wasn't the end of the world. Several of them got involved.

Our first few months in Delray, nobody talked to us. Then one day a big man in overalls came to our door and introduced himself as Earl. If you could imagine a Hells Angel in overalls with a hick accent, that was Earl. He was a pig farmer.

Earl came over to discuss "the gator problem." Alligators were overrunning a canal that went from his property to mine. Earl wanted to know if I minded him killing gators at night.

"No problem, man. Kill away."

"Good. Come with me Tuesday night, and we'll kill the gators together."

This could be a kick, I thought. I show up at Earl's house Tuesday night. We drag a canoe and a case of beer into the water and get in. Earl hands me a thirty-aught-six rifle, with a flashlight wired to it. Earl says, "When you see the gator, shine the light in his eyes and blow him away. Hit him in the eye, because if you hit him anywhere else, you're not going to kill him. The skin on a gator is like metal."

Earl passes me a beer and starts canoeing. "One more thing. Gators got red eyes. When you point the light at him, his eyes are going to be bright red."

Sure as shit, within about five minutes, I see these fucking red eyes. I aim my rifle, pull the trigger, and *boom,* I'm pretty sure I hit the motherfucker in the eye. To be safe, I fire another shot. Earl tells me, "Don't waste bullets. He's hit."

Earl jumps into the water. I hear splashing. I can't see nothing because my flashlight is attached to the rifle and I don't want to point it at Earl and accidentally shoot him. The last thing I want is to be alone in a canoe surrounded by angry alligators. I hear *bang,* and the canoe starts tipping side to side. Earl has thrown the gator in the canoe. Its tail is kicking at my feet.

"Get it the fuck out of here, man!"

Earl is standing in the water next to the canoe, clamping the gator's mouth shut with his arms. Earl is very calm. He says, "Jon, behind the beer cooler, I got my machete. Take my machete and chop him behind the neck where his nerve is."

I look at the tail thrashing in the canoe and think, *Fuck it*. I point my rifle barrel at the gator's head.

"If you're going to shoot him, don't shoot into the canoe. You'll sink it," Earl says. He calmly pulls the gator's head over the water. I press my gun down into its angry red eye and pull the trigger. One good blast directly in the eye stops him.

Earl whoops, "Yeehaw!" Then he says, "Let's get some more. Use only one bullet next time, not three. You got that, boy?"

Rednecks are cheap.

Hours later we go back to Earl's house and carry three dead gators into his shed. Earl starts chain-sawing the heads off. "Okay, neighbor, next comes the fun part. I'm gonna skin the tails, filet the meat, marinate it, and have you over for dinner."

A week later Toni and I went over for a cookout. Earl had soaked the meat in brine for days, then smoked it. I thought it would taste like garbage, but it was delicious. Then Earl did something I'll never forget. He'd mounted the gator's jawbone with its teeth showing, and he handed it to me and said, "This is my friendship gift to you." Later he took me to a guy living in a trailer who turned the skin from the tail into very fine boots.

After we bonded over killing gators, Earl introduced me to another side of Delray.

He came by my house one night and said, "Let's go."

"Get the fuck out of my life, bro. I ain't going gator hunting tonight."

"No, neighbor. Tonight is party night."

We took his truck up to the shithole diner by the feed shop. I knew the diner because it had pay phones in front that I used to call Max and Rafa from. What I didn't know was that after closing, the two sisters who ran the diner put on a party. They'd cook up fried chicken and serve beer and untaxed liquor. They brought in girls who did lingerie shows. The main event was a poker game that went all night. The diner owners did this a couple times a month. Earl, two of his brothers, a deputy sheriff, and other farmers all came. A couple of these guys were Baptists. To them this was sin city. By my standards, the stakes were nothing. But this was the local redneck power structure, and I'd been allowed in.

I found out that one of my gambling neighbors was an old-time marijuana smuggler who'd fallen on hard times because of oversupply in the weed market. I hired the weed smuggler and Earl and his brothers to help me out with cocaine. They found abandoned sheds out in the middle of nowhere that I could use as stash houses. I started flowing kilos of coke to one of these guys that he moved in places like Georgia and Alabama. I eventually had these guys moving hundreds of keys a month in the Deep South.

AT ONE POINT I got frustrated with Mickey for moving coke too slowly. There was a two-month period where he shut down shipments to rebuild his planes. My pilot Roger believed he'd learned to beat the Customs Service air patrols as effectively as Mickey, and to prove it he offered to pick up eight hundred kilos in his King Air. The twist was, I had him drop it a couple miles from my backyard in Delray.

My redneck neighbors ran the operation. One of the farmers hired a low-flying crop duster plane the morning of the airdrop to mask the sounds of Roger's King Air coming in. Roger was going to drop the eight hundred kilos in the Everglades. Earl and his brothers organized canoes and ATVs to pick up the load and bring it to a stash house.

The morning of the drop, I watched Roger's plane come in as I cooled off in my pool. I swam laps while my army of rednecks picked up all the coke.

I had a level of trust with these hicks, and not just because they'd done a little pot smuggling in the past. The fact is, they all hated the government. They believed it was almost their patriotic duty to show they couldn't be pushed around. Even the one sheriff's deputy who played cards with us felt the same way. We didn't involve him in our smuggling, but all these hillbillies got off on beating the government just as much as I did.

I only did two coke drops in my neighborhood. I didn't want to push my luck. What mattered was, I had good neighbors. I controlled the rednecks.

IT WAS so safe up in Delray, I used it as a hideout for Griselda Blanco, who by 1983 had murdered so many people that she had to run from Miami. She was one of the Cartel's oldest and biggest distributors, but she burned up her luck. Rafa, though, was loyal to this beast of a woman to the end. When everybody wanted her dead, he came to me and asked if I could help her hide.

I found a house down the road whose owner took $250,000 in cash and let me have it. Earl had some guys put up a fence and brought in Rottweilers to run in the yard. When Griselda came up to the house, she looked like a pig. She'd packed on forty pounds of ugly. She was shacked up with an Argentinean guy who claimed to be a doctor and shot her up with tranquilizers twenty-four hours a day. He probably kept her medicated hoping she wouldn't kill him like she usually did with her men.

Griselda and her boyfriend wouldn't leave the house. I had Bryan bring them groceries. Griselda, the feared killer, lived in terror. She nailed boards over the windows and hid in the dark. I went there once with Bryan. The house smelled worse than a truck-stop toilet. Once inside, I gagged. Griselda flicked on a nightlight. I saw her in the corner, this fat, stinking bitch with red eyes.

My impulse was to shoot her in the eye like a gator. I should have. When she went into hiding in Delray, Rafa cut her off from distributing. Griselda lashed out. She ended up stealing 150 kilos from one of Fabito Ochoa's cousins and killing her. That finished Griselda. You can't kill an Ochoa.

Rafa could no longer protect her. Even then he let her flee. Crazed as he was, Rafa had a heart for her. Griselda ran to California and continued her thieving and murdering until they caught her.*

I was just glad the rotten bitch was gone. She was a blight on the neighborhood.

TONI AND I built up our house year by year. We had her little brother, Lee, living with us. Toni's mom moved in. She brought her stepdaughter, Amber. Amber was the daughter of an ex-boyfriend of Toni's mom. Amber was fourteen. She was just a sweet schoolgirl who ran around with the kids in the neighborhood. I made sure that Bryan or Lee got her to school every day, and that she didn't miss her homework.

Bryan loved Delray. Even though he was Italian, he'd grown up in Florida, and the redneck way of life had soaked into him. He and Earl became the best of friends. They hunted gators together all the time. Bryan liked to try to beat them to death with his bare hands.

We added on to the barn to make room for more horses I was buying. I kept my main barn for Mephisto Stables at a racetrack. But I moved my most prized horses to Delray. I had a staff come in every morning to work for me.

LISA "BITSY" BENSON: Just about my whole family worked for Jon and Toni. My father was a trainer for Jon.† My cousin Chris, who was fifteen, rode for Jon. My boyfriend was his blacksmith. I had a company that did cold-laser therapy for his horses.

---

* Griselda Blanco was arrested in California in 1985. Though authorities suspected Griselda and her crew of having been involved in dozens, or hundreds, of murders, and one of her top enforcers testified against her, legal technicalities prevented them from pursuing murder charges. She was convicted on federal drug-trafficking charges, imprisoned until 2004, and deported to Colombia. Recently, photographs purporting to show Griselda alive and well in Colombia have surfaced. Some feature a woman in her late sixties who bears a resemblance to her. Jon believes such look-alikes may be relatives of Griselda but could not be her. As he put it, "Trust me, that bitch was so despised, she was killed the second she stepped off the plane in Colombia."

† Harry Benson remains an active trainer and breeder in Florida.

Jon and Toni were an awesome couple. Toni was so fucking hot, it wasn't even funny, and Jon was straight with everyone who worked for him. He loved the horses, and he treated us well because we took care of them.

Jon said he was in real estate, but we knew. One time workers were digging by the barn, and they found a bag with $300,000 in it. When Jon came out, he acted like it was no big deal. People said he was involved with drugrunning. But those were the days of *Miami Vice*. It seemed glamorous to me.

Jon and Toni were glamorous. They had everything, and they seemed so much in love, even when things got stormy. And they would. They definitely had their fights.

J.R.: I'd slam a door. Toni would kick it down. One time she tried to run me over. I'd pulled up in the driveway, and I saw Toni's black Mercedes racing toward me. She crashed into my car, and I chased her around the property until our cars couldn't drive. We destroyed everything in our path. That was a spat for us.

It's how we communicated. We'd laugh about it afterward. We did all kinds of crazy things in the house. I used to put on a helmet when I watched the football games on my big-screen TV. If my team was losing, I'd destroy the TV by running into it. I had a carpenter who lived behind the barn. He'd just follow Toni and me around, rebuilding things behind us.

Our house was *Wild Kingdom* inside. When you have a couple of dogs and a 150-pound cat like Cucha, things will get broken. Cucha was good with people. You could have little kids or babies in the house, and she was fine. The one thing that freaked her out was jockeys. I guess in her cat mind she could understand the concept of a child or a grown-up, but jockeys—five-foot-tall grown-ups—made her crazy. Jockeys were like catnip to her. Whenever you had a jockey in our house, she'd start creeping around, wiggling her tail, getting ready to pounce.

Angel Cordero used to come by to give Toni riding lessons. It's no secret Angel liked to smoke out. He's in our house one day after a lesson, smoking a fat one, when he stands up to get something to eat. I thought Cucha was out in the pen. But *boom*, the floor shook from the force of that cat's hind legs jumping up. I see Cucha flying in the air. Angel thought he was going to grab a munchie. Cucha decided he was the munchie. With all the bad things I'd done, I wasn't going to go down as the guy whose cat ate one of the greatest jockeys who'd ever lived. Luckily, I had a new Doberman, Apollo, who was protective of Angel. He jumped up and blocked Angel. You had 100 pounds of dog hitting 150 pounds of cat. They broke a wall when they collided.

Angel just stood there, still holding his blunt. "Wow" was what he said.

MICKEY MUNDAY: I don't understand how they kept all those animals. It wasn't just the cats, the dogs, and the birds. Toni would rescue critters from the side of the road.

Toni was a special person. With her looks she could have been stuck-up, but she was friendly to everybody. She was a tomboy at heart. She was like a frontier gal. She could ride, shoot, cuss. In that house, she was the alpha animal. That's why those animals didn't slaughter each other like they should have by the rules of nature. Toni bossed them around. She'd give a look, and that cat would slink off.

They had one hallway in the house that must have been a hundred feet long. Jon and I were standing there one day talking, and over his shoulder I see his favorite bird walking down the hall. Jon was very fond of this bird. It was a green parrot with clipped wings that made it walk like a penguin. Then I saw Cucha, down low behind the bird, stalking it. I said, "Jon—"

"Don't worry, Mickey."

How could Jon be so calm? I watched as that cat leaped. There was 150 pounds of death in the air. Then I heard Toni shout,

"Cucha!" The cat fell to the floor, turned, and skulked off. The bird kept walking. It had no idea how narrowly it had escaped being eaten.

Toni ruled that house. It was clear. She was a force of nature.

J.R.: At her best, Toni could handle anything. When she went riding in the morning, she'd carry a hunting rifle or one of our AK-47s to deal with gators. My new dog, Apollo, loved riding with her. He was the trailblazer. He'd run ahead to show the horse the way.

One morning Apollo ran into a gator. He'd been trained by Joe Da Costa to believe he was invincible. However big a dog's heart is, a dog-on-alligator contest isn't going to end well for the dog. A dog can't even bite a gator because of its skin being like metal.

Apollo did his best. That gator sliced his stomach open with a hole so big, his intestines fell out. This mighty dog did not give up. He bit with all his strength and locked his fangs in the gator's back. The gator shook him off and broke Apollo's fangs. They were stuck in his skin.

That gator didn't count on Toni. She charged at him with her AK and emptied the whole banana clip into him. Toni put thirty rounds into that gator. He was done.

After the attack Toni came off the trail with the horse behind her. She was carrying Apollo in her arms, holding his intestines in with her hands. That was Toni at her best. In the animal kingdom, she was fierce.

We got a vet to come out immediately. Apollo got stitched together, and he healed fine within two months. Unfortunately, he had no fangs.

I knew a cokehead dentist who I thought could help. He was a human dentist, but I persuaded him to take Apollo as his patient. We brought him in on Sundays so his normal patients wouldn't freak out at seeing a dog in the dentist's chair. It took a few weekends, but we got beautiful gold implants made where Apollo's fangs had been.

Apollo completely recovered and the rest of his life was happy with his gold teeth.

WHEN I first moved to Delray, my aim was to keep our home insulated from my work life. But then I got the neighbors involved, and I had Toni's brother, Lee, working as a driver for my transport cars. Lee ended up working very closely with Rafa's enforcer, Flaco. You never would have predicted it, but Lee and Flaco became the best of friends, even though neither spoke a word of the other's language. Flaco was a psychotic killer from the jungle. Lee was a big, all-American *Dukes of Hazzard* kid. But they were thick as thieves. It worked out good for me. I didn't have to deal directly with Rafa as much. Flaco would give Rafa's directions to Lee about who was getting what from which stash house, and everything got taken care of. It was crazy watching Flaco and Lee work things out. They communicated in a mangled language that wasn't English or Spanish. It was a mutant way of talking, but they understood each other perfectly. I came to understand that the soldiers Rafa brought from the hills were just Colombian rednecks. Despite all the differences between Lee and Flaco, they could talk to each other redneck to redneck.

There was only one time that mixing my home life with my work ever caused a problem. I'd let Toni's jerk-off English pilot friend Shelton Archer talk me into flying loads for me. Shelton had started working with another piece-of-shit Englishman who was his kicker and organizer. He was like a poor man's Mickey Munday. I got them flying loads from Louisiana out to Bernie Levine in San Francisco. Big mistake.

Even though Bernie was one of my oldest friends, he was an untrustworthy guy. Put him with a dirty Englishman like Shelton, and bad things were bound to happen. My mistake was giving Shelton responsibility for bringing back the money from California that Bernie owed the Cartel.

One thing I did not do was count money. Rafa had guys to count it. Even Mickey counted money sometimes. I don't want to see counting machines. I don't want to touch the money. I walked into rooms filled to the ceiling with cash ten times a week. That much cash stinks. It has BO from all the humans that have been touching it and perspiring on it. There are germs on it. People roll up bills and stick them in their noses to snort coke. Who knows what other disgusting things they've done with our drug money?

When distributors such as Bernie got coke from me, the price was set by the Cartel, and it was up to them to put the right amount of money in the bags they sent back. I told them to bundle the money in $100,000 packs, sometimes even in $1 million bricks. I'd count out my share of the bundles and pass the rest on to Rafa for the Cartel.

I knew Rafa took his bundles apart and counted each bill. I didn't bother with mine. I knew if there was a problem, Rafa would catch it on his end. I never had a problem with my distributors shorting the cash they owed—until Shelton met Barry.

I didn't catch the problem directly. It was Rafa who did. In a safe house, he piled up $10 million or $15 million that had come from Barry and counted it one weekend. He found that each bundle was short a couple grand. It added up to a few hundred thousand dollars, stolen.

Instead of telling me what the problem was, Rafa went crazy. He put together a Colombian death squad and sent them to my house in Delray.

What saved me was the close friendship between Lee and Flaco. One morning they were out picking up a car, and Flaco told Lee that Rafa believed I'd ripped him off. According to Flaco, Rafa was sending a "death squad" to my house. Lee called me right away and said, "Jon, Rafa has an *escuadrón de la muerte* on his way to the house."

Escuadrón de la muerte—death squad—was the term Griselda

used to use when she'd get a bunch of her guys together to kill someone. Somehow Lee'd picked up the term from Flaco. They'd kill everyone in the house—children, dogs. If there were fish in a fish tank, they'd pour bleach in the water. Apparently Rafa had the same thing in mind for me. He used to come up with ideas like this when he smoked too many bazookas.

Soon as I hung up with Lee, I tried to call Max. As I'm dialing, I see Rafa coming up my driveway with three cars following his. He gets out with a bunch of armed Colombians from the hills.

By this time, I had so many people working on the property that the gate was never closed. If I fired the tear gas, these Colombians would all start shooting. I had to deal with the situation. I had Toni in the house. I had Bryan in the kitchen eating. There were a couple guys in the barns, and a Cuban maid who worked for us in the laundry room. That was my army. If there was going to be a shoot-out, we were done. Toni saw the cars from the window. I told her to get her guns out, and I went downstairs.

I got Bryan and walked out to meet Rafa. He walked up to me with his guys fanning out behind him. "Jon, you know why I'm here."

I actually didn't know at that time what he was specifically accusing me of stealing. Lee had been unable to figure out from Flaco exactly what it was I was supposed to have done. But if you showed weakness to a Colombian, that was it. They'd run you into the ground. You could not back up an inch. I said to Rafa, "You better think before you make the mistake of your life."

"I'm not here to talk about my mistake, Jon."

As I'm thinking of what to say next, I look over Rafa's shoulders and see pickup trucks, ATVs, horses coming up behind him. Toni has called Earl, and he's organized every redneck in the neighborhood. They've formed a cavalry. Earl's brothers are on horseback with hunting rifles. There are two pickups with all their inbred nephews riding on the cabs and pointing shotguns. Rafa's soldiers see them coming and make a hissing sound with their teeth, nudging each other. Then I see the window open in our bedroom, and

Toni leans out with an AK. This is like a scene right out of *Bonanza*, where the Indians come to do a massacre but the settlers turn the tables and surround them.

Toni shouts from the window, "You motherfuckers. Get the fuck off my land."

Rafa looks from Toni to the armed hillbillies coming up behind him and gets a funny look. As insane as he is, he's worried. He's stirred up an angry mob of white people.

"Rafa," I say. "Please. It's not relaxed here. Let's talk about this at Max's."

"Okay, Jon."

"Thanks, Rafa. You're a good friend."

They all get in their cars and drive off.

I met Rafa the next day at Max's, and it was like nothing had happened between us. He told me about the accounting error. I told him I'd correct it.

I knew Shelton was responsible. For six years Bernie had never shorted us a dollar. Shelton started flying his loads, and suddenly they were a few dollars light. I suspected Bernie was also involved because it seemed to me the money had to have been pulled out of the bundles before they were wrapped and put on the plane.

I knew if I confronted Shelton, he'd lie his English ass off. Bernie would act offended, and the matter would remain an unsolved mystery. When you think a person has wronged you, but you can't prove it, sometimes the best thing is to make your point a different way.

I had Bryan pick up Shelton's running mate, the guy who worked as his kicker. Bryan tied him up with electrical cord and put him in the trunk of his car. There was a canal in the wilds of Delray where we kept a rowboat. What Bryan did to scare people who caused me aggravation was to drag them behind the rowboat. He called it "gator-dragging." He'd row a guy past the mud islands where the gators hung out. If I wasn't too mad at the guy, Bryan would row him back without letting the alligators catch him. We'd pull him out, and the guy would have an adventure story for his grandkids.

With Shelton's guy, we just wanted to scare him. I wanted him to go back to Shelton and relate his experience as a warning. If Shelton had done something wrong, it would make him think twice. Even if by some chance Shelton was innocent, the dragging would still make the point that I was unpredictable, and that he should always be careful of me.

I came out to meet Bryan the day he was going to gator-drag Shelton's guy. When I got there, I saw Bryan rowing his ass off. He was rowing so fast, the nose of the little dinghy was pointed up like a speedboat. Every five or six rows, Bryan turned around and beat his paddle on Shelton's guy. It looked like Bryan was beating the poor asshole to death for fun.

Then, as the boat got closer, I saw it was being chased by an alligator who was biting the guy's feet. Bryan was trying to fight it off. He ran that boat up to the edge of the canal and dragged the guy from the water. Shelton's asshole buddy was screaming, "My toes, my toes!"

Bryan holds him up with one hand like a fish. His one foot is chewed to pieces.

"Bro, forget your toes. You don't got no foot."

I laughed my ass off. This man set a good example for Shelton. After the guy got out of the hospital, Shelton paid me back. He never admitted to stealing. He said he'd "misplaced" the money. I never had a problem with him or with Bernie Levine again.

That was the beauty of Delray. I had my life with Toni. I had the rednecks. I even had the alligators helping me. I was untouchable up there.

64

J.R.: In my smuggling operations I did every job at
least once. I flew as a kicker and pushed the loads
out of the plane. I drove coke cars and money cars. I
flew with Roger and Barry Seal, and I took the controls
of their planes when we were flying easy, straight lines.
But it was unwise to get too involved. After I saw what
a job was like, I'd stay in the background as much as
I could.

One job I couldn't stay away from was working the
radios. I truly loved Mickey's radio rooms. You could
follow the whole smuggling mission. At Ultimate Boats,
Mickey's shop in Miami, the radio room was upstairs in
a little garret. There was a narrow staircase to get to it,
and a catwalk. Inside there was a table with the radios
and tape recorders, and a bed in the corner. I sometimes
spent twenty hours in there, following the progress of a
load coming in. Every time one of our loads got past all

the government assholes in their boats and planes and hit American soil, I got off so hard I could feel it in my balls.

That's why I couldn't stop smuggling. I had to keep getting off.

THE COLOMBIANS also couldn't stop. Their addiction wasn't psychological. It was economic. The more successful we were in smuggling, the less money they made per kilo. That was the twist of it. We flooded the market with so much cocaine that by 1983 the wholesale price of a kilo kept dropping. It had gone from $50,000 in the late 1970s to as low as $6,000 a kilo at one point. That meant that to make the same amount of money in 1983 as they did in 1978, the Colombians had to move almost ten times as much coke.

By combining the efforts of Mickey, Barry Seal, Roger, and the occasional guys I had running coke in boats that came in off the Cartel's fishing trawlers, I had months where I moved ten thousand kilos. Some months it went down to a trickle, but we always got something through.

The Cartel made life more difficult for itself in some ways by their freewheeling way of distributing coke. They'd sell to anybody. They had their own distributors around the country, and they'd take on anybody else. My distributors—Bernie in San Francisco, Ron Tobachnik in Chicago, my rednecks in Delray, my uncle Jerry Chilli on Miami Beach, Albert and Bobby Erra in Miami as well as people in L.A.—were all together moving a thousand kilos a month just for me. I'd also cut one-off deals where a guy I knew would take five hundred or a thousand kilos in one bump. Now and then, I used to do this with John Gotti in New York and other wiseguys.

But of course the Cartel had many more distributors than me. Most of the coke I imported was for their guys, not mine. They didn't care if they sold to ten guys in the same city. Their philosophy was that by selling to everyone, they owned the market. What ended up happening, though, was that all their distributors in a given city competed against each other. In Miami this caused wars in the streets. In other cities it just made the prices drop.

From where the Cartel sat, their business would have almost

been better if the government had been able to shut down our smuggling for a few months. That way the prices would have gone back up.

But the government couldn't stop us.

MOSTLY, IT couldn't stop Mickey Munday. By 1983 the DEA and Customs Service had banded together with the air force to use their radars and spy planes. They tried to build an invisible wall around the coast of Florida.

Pilots I had flying into Florida like Roger and a couple guys he worked with would shut down for weeks at a time. They wouldn't fly. When they did make a run, they used Super King Air planes that could carry two thousand kilos. Rafa and I would stock up. We filled our stash houses with enough extra coke to keep everyone supplied for months.

Mickey's philosophy was different. He'd do his four-hundred-kilo loads every week or two. Sometimes he slowed down, but he never stopped. He liked the challenge. If someone had told him he could only smuggle one kilo in a plane, he would have done it, just to do it. In this way, Mickey was the same as me. He smuggled to get off.

When the government tried to wall off Florida with radar and spy planes, Mickey found a hole in their plan. The government had decided to track planes coming into Florida from Colombia. Law enforcement would even track seaplanes if they landed on the water off the coast and tried to hand their coke off to a boat. I knew that because a few times we used seaplanes and had problems with them being chased.

But Mickey came up with an idea. He decided to have his planes air-drop bags of coke into the water. People had done this with weed near the coast. But Mickey's idea was to do it twenty or thirty miles out to sea. The plane would drop the coke and fly back to Colombia, or land in Florida at an airport as if it were returning from a tourist trip.

When the coke was on the water, Mickey's idea was to send out a fishing boat to pick it up. If a boat went twenty or thirty miles out on the water, fished for a day, and came back, it didn't look suspicious to the government because the boat hadn't stopped at an island or met a seaplane on the water like it would have done if it were picking up coke.

Nobody imagined we could drop coke thirty miles out on the ocean and find it a day later. It was impossible to do that—for anyone but Mickey.

MICKEY: The easy part was dropping the cocaine in the water. As long as it's in waterproof wrapping, cocaine will float. The hard part is finding it. Even if your pilot and kicker knew the exact coordinates where they dropped the coke bales, the bales would drift several miles in a few hours.

So I built radio beacons in buoys that we could track from the radios in our boats. At that time I'd also started working with military night-vision goggles. These weren't easy to get, but I obtained a few sets to help find our way to airstrips when we were moving at night. The other nice feature of night-vision goggles is that they pick up infrared light that's invisible to the naked eye. When I built my beacons, I attached an infrared strobe light to each one. When you put on the night-vision goggles, you could see the infrared strobe lights flashing from nearly a quarter-mile away on the water.

After I built my beacons, the ocean drops were simple. We bundled the coke into 50-kilo bales, tethered them together, and attached the beacons that we could track no matter how far they drifted on the water. It was basic American ingenuity at work.

J.R.: The one problem we had was that the coke packages the Colombians wrapped for us leaked in the ocean. Mickey tested all kinds of ways to wrap the product. He came up with the exact type of plastic to use, how to fold it and seal it, but he couldn't get the Colombians to follow his directions.

MICKEY: I made a comic book showing every step needed to seal the packages. I found a Colombian girl with a very sultry voice. She was so sexy, when you rang her up and she said hello, your ear would just melt. I had this gal narrate into a tape recorder the directions that I'd laid out in the comic book. I had her talk like wrapping coke was an erotic experience: "Slide your finger under the flaps. It's tight, isn't it?" I sent my books and the tapes of this girl narrating them to Colombia, but the guys who did the wrapping still didn't get it right.

J.R.: That's because they were too busy jerking off to those stupid tapes Mickey made. Because Mickey didn't speak Spanish, he didn't get the girl to explain properly in Spanish. The tapes were gibberish. I flew to Colombia and went to Pablo's guys in a coke factory and showed them in person how to wrap the coke. Once I did that, we had no more problems.

MICKEY: Then I decided to take it to the next level. The Competition began conducting random stops of boats as they were coming into the harbors. So I built a stealth boat that I could sneak in at night. I saw an article in an aviation magazine about a new kind of airplane the military was building, the stealth plane. It had a low profile and asymmetrical carbon fiber surfaces that reduced its radar signature.

I decided to build a boat that followed the same principles. It was probably the neatest toy I ever made. My boat was twenty feet long and eighteen inches high. She was like a pancake. I rigged her with a racing car seat that had me lying back, like I was on a luge. I hung a pair of 300-horsepower engines off the back with twin-reverse screws, and I built asymmetrical carbon fiber cowlings to go over them. I put in reversible bilges so if I was spotted, I could flood my boat and sink her in under five minutes. When I ran her, I wore a wet suit and had a scuba tank. If I had to scuttle her, I could swim away.

She could hold 400 kilos of cocaine and do 80 miles an hour, and I'd wired her with a state-of-the-art stereo, integrated with my radios, so I could listen to tunes through my headphones while monitoring my communications. For my first run, I made a ninety-minute extended mix tape of my favorite Phil Collins song, "In the Air Tonight," and took off. That boat was a rocket. When you're eighteen inches on the water doing 80 miles an hour, you can see your speed in the waves whipping past your eyes. It's like Scotty* jamming the *Enterprise* into warp speed on *Star Trek*. Everything melts.

We ran water-drop missions for an intense three-month period when the Competition had deployed all their resources to seal off the coast. After they caught a bunch of other smugglers and held some press conferences, they declared victory. They stood down their effort to block off the coast, and we went back to landing our planes at the Nike sites.

J.R.: Great as Mickey was when it came to basic things, he was very obstinate. One time I needed to fly a bunch of coke from Florida to Los Angeles. It was a simple domestic flight. I asked Mickey if his pilot could do it. He said, "No. That's impossible right now."

It was easy for Mickey to say no because he was insulated from the Colombians. For me, it wasn't so easy. I'd already promised Fabito I'd get the coke moved. Luckily, I had a brainstorm: air ambulances. I saw them at airports all the time when I flew on horse-buying trips. An air ambulance resembled a regular plane, but it was outfitted with a stretcher. All you needed to make it legit was a nurse, a sick person, and a note from a doctor saying the medical team had to get to a hospital in the city they were landing in.

---

* Chief Engineer Montgomery "Scotty" Scott, played by James Doohan in the original *Star Trek* series.

I got a crooked doctor friend in Miami to fill out all the papers. He gave me his nurse. We dressed one of my drivers in bandages, and we put the coke in medical trunks that we drove out to the airport in an ambulance. The pilot of the plane we hired didn't even know he was flying coke for us. It worked out so good, I must have done it eight or ten times. We flew out of the Fort Lauderdale–Hollywood airport. One time we even dressed up Bryan in the bandages, but he was so big, they had a hard time rolling him on the stretcher. Mostly I was just happy to prove to Mickey that the thing he said was impossible could be done.

Every time the thought came to me that I should quit smuggling, a new challenge came along. With Mickey and me combining our ideas, there was very little anyone could do to stop us. And we couldn't stop ourselves because we were having so much fun.

65

J.R.: When I visited Don Ochoa at his ranch in late 1982, he told me he was having a terrible problem with Communists. They were coming down from the hills and stealing his cows and trying to stir up the people against him. They even kidnapped one of his daughters. This made the Cartel stronger because the families in it banded together to fight the Communists.* To do this, they needed guns. They also needed guns to protect coke factories and fight little wars in the streets. The Colombians couldn't get enough guns. They wanted guns from America because here they're easier to get than in Colombia. Plus, many gun dealers in Florida took cash.

* In 1981 Don Ochoa's daughter, Martha Nieves, was kidnapped by M-19, a left-wing revolutionary group. In response to the kidnapping, the Ochoas joined with other Cartel leaders and wealthy landowners to create a paramilitary force called *Muertas a Sequestradores*—Death to Kidnappers. The rise of this and other private armies helped destabilize Colombia for the next two decades.

The Colombians could launder money with guns the same way I did with racehorses.

Mickey would not fly guns. It went against his philosophy of nonviolence. So I got into this business with Max. The one thing Max proved good at was buying guns. He obtained caseloads of AR-15s and other excellent weapons.* Max had an in with a dirty cop on the Miami Police Department bomb squad. When the cops impounded exotic weapons such as plastic explosive or machine guns, they sold them to Max out the back door of the station.

Once a month I'd have Roger come down with his King Air and fly guns to Colombia. The flights were easy. The heat was looking for drugs coming in, but nobody cared about guns going out.

WHEN I earned more trust with the Cartel by shipping the guns, they asked me to help fly their money out of Florida. Up until about 1982 the Colombians had crooked banks in Miami that they could walk into with trash bags full of cash and make deposits. Everybody did this. In the late 1970s my friend Bebe Rebozo had a bank where he let me deposit shoeboxes of cash, no questions asked.† By the early 1980s the heat was starting to watch Florida banks because of all the cash coming in.‡ There were many months when I brought Rafa a half ton of cash—hundreds of millions of dollars—as payment from the distributors. Stash houses were overflowing.

Finally, General Noriega, who was friends with Pablo Escobar, said the Cartel could use his banks in Panama to hold their dollars. Laundering money was his specialty.§

---

* The AR-15 is the civilian version of the U.S. military's M-16 infantry rifle.

† The banker and close confidant of former President Nixon whom Jon spoke about in chapter 37.

‡ In 1982 the Federal Reserve Bank reported that Miami banks had taken in more than $2 billion of cash that couldn't be accounted for by lawful economic activity.

§ The CIA used banks in Panama to launder money and secretly finance its activities throughout Central America in the 1980s. Noriega, who emerged as one of the Agency's top money-laundering facilitators in Panama, offered similar services to drug smugglers, as outlined in Larry Collins's July, 23 1991, *New York Times* story "Banker of Choice to the Company."

Rafa asked me to run cash flights to Panama. He promised it would be easy to land there. Noriega would give our planes military protection at the airport.

I used Roger on the first run. We took a few boxes with $50 million as a test load. As soon as we landed, army trucks surrounded our plane. Soldiers got out showing guns. A big guy with acne grooves in his face came forward. Then a nasty little woman in a military uniform walked in front of him. This did not look promising. But the woman said, "We will take you to the bank."

The soldiers unloaded the plane, and we drove to the bank in a motorcade with sirens blaring. Then the guy with grooves on his face drove Roger and me across town to a big house. He walked us into an office to meet General Noriega. Like our escort, Noriega had holes in his face from bad skin, and I wondered if the two men were related. But Noriega was short. He was a troll. He wanted me in his office to witness his signing off on the bank deposit, so I could tell the Colombians how serious he took his job as a banker.

On my next trip Noriega warmed up to me. He invited me to his house. He wanted to show me a room where he kept some of his favorite mementos. He had shelves of pictures showing him in military school in America* and a couple of paintings that looked expensive. I told the general how nice his paintings were and asked where he got them.

He made a funny smile and said, "I stole them."

His most prized possessions were photographs of him with Vice President Bush.† Noriega's favorite one was really strange. It showed

---

* As a young Panamanian military officer in the 1960s, Noriega received U.S. military training at bases in Panama and in the United States at Fort Bragg.

† Bush the elder met frequently with Noriega beginning in the mid-1970s, when he was the director of the CIA. As reported in the May 16, 1991, *Chicago Tribune* article "Files Detail Noriega CIA Connection," prior to Noriega's 1992 trial for racketeering, trafficking, and money laundering, his defense claimed he had been paid more than $10 million by the CIA. During the trial, the U.S. government's lead prosecutor, U.S. Attorney Dexter Lehtinen, disputed that figure, arguing that Noriega had been paid only about $300,000 in the form of monthly paychecks that he received from approximately 1971 to 1986—meaning it cost about $1,500 a month to bribe the dictator of a third world country in that era.

him sitting in Bush's lap.* He'd point to the picture and laugh. "See? I am America's best friend. Bush is my boss."

I didn't care who his friends were, Noriega was a disgusting person. On one trip to Panama, I went to a party at a government mansion. It started off normal—everybody was doing lines, beautiful Latin women everywhere. I walked into a corner, and there was Noriega on a couch with a couple of little girls, maybe nine years old, on either side of him, and he was petting them. He had a funny smile on his face like when he showed me his stolen art.

But whatever his faults, the U.S. government believed he was dependable. He was Bush's friend, and at his parties, when he wasn't putting the moves on nine-year-old children, you'd see him talking to clean-cut Americans from the embassy.

When Noriega told me I could open my own accounts at his banks and that he'd personally take care of me, I saw it as an opportunity. Over the next two to three years, I gave him $150 million of my own money—cash that I dug up from hiding spots around Delray. I had the trusted dictator of an important country working as my personal banker. The only thing crazier would be if the U.S. government hired me to be a smuggler.

But that would be impossible, wouldn't it?

---

* Jon is likely referring to a photo of Bush and Noriega taken in the 1970s. In the photo, Bush and Noriega are seated extremely close together on a couch, and perhaps through an accident of perspective Noriega appears to be sitting in Bush's lap.

66

Dear Mr. Roberts: I am delighted to inform you that at the last membership meeting of the National Republican Reelection League, your name was placed in nomination by Representative Ted Jones, and you were accepted for membership.

—letter from the National Republican Reelection League* to Jon, 1984

J.R.: I've never met a politician who didn't put his hand out when I met him. One night in 1983, after I started running the Cartel's money flights, I took Toni out to Joe's Stone Crab. I'm sitting there with Toni and Bryan when the maître d' brings over a bottle of wine. I

---

* The National Republican Reelection League is a pseudonym for a real Republican fund-raising organization to which Jon was a contributor. Evidence of Jon's participation in the organization appears to be authentic, but due to the prominence of its members, the name has been changed here.

ask who sent it, and he points to an older man at a corner table surrounded by guys in suits. "Representative Ted Jones."*

I said, "What's the congressman drinking?"

The maître d' named a shit wine, and I told him to send the congressman two bottles.

Then a man in a suit came over from the congressman's table.
He told me the congressman would like to meet me.

I'd lived by Senator Smathers on Indian Creek, and he'd never
caused any trouble, but he was retired. This congressman was still
on the job, which meant he had power to do bad things. Sending his
goon over to get me made me uptight.

I went to his table. Congressman Jones stood. He was not a big
guy, but he stuck his hand out with confidence. When I told him my
name, he said, "I know all about you."

That made me sweat a little. Then he laughed and said it was a
pleasure meeting me, but he couldn't accept my "generous gift"—
of the shit wine I'd sent to his table. He could give me a gift, but I
couldn't give him one. That was the rule. He handed me his card
and said to call him anytime.

"Okay. Nice meeting you," I said.

I got back to my table as fast as I could. I didn't like a congressman saying he knew about me. I couldn't enjoy the rest of my crabs.
I noticed when the congressman left that his goons were carrying
the unopened bottles of wine I'd sent. Somebody could accept gifts.

I STARTED getting letters asking me to donate money to Congressman Jones and the National Republican Reelection League. They
were form letters, but they made me uptight. I never gave out my
address. I wasn't registered to vote.

I went to my lawyer, Danny Mones, and showed him the letters.
He told me to relax. The congressman probably got intrigued when

---

* Representative Ted Jones is a pseudonym for a congressional leader who was
one of the most powerful figures in Washington in the 1980s. There is evidence
Jon had contact with him, but the allegations of wrongdoing that Jon makes
against him cannot be proved.

he saw me with Bryan and Toni and asked the waiters about me. Getting my address would have been easy.

"So what do I do with these goddamn letters?"

"Send these cocksuckers their money," Danny said, laughing. "This congressman's extorting you. Now that he knows who you are, you can't tell him no. He's got a good racket."

I had Danny send a check in my name for $5,000—the maximum amount allowed. Danny said, "Now you got to call him. Tell him you're happy to help him out."

I called the number on the congressman's card and got a flunky. I told him I'd made a contribution. A couple days later the congressman calls me and thanks me. Next, he asks if I like fishing. Before I know it, I've agreed to meet the congressman and some of his friends for a fishing trip on Hilton Head Island in South Carolina.

When I told Danny Mones, he got very excited. "This is good. You should bring some cash money."

"How much?"

"Fifty thousand dollars is good for a U.S. congressman. It's not a fortune, but it shows you're sincere."

I flew to Hilton Head with Bryan and a tackle box with $50,000 in it. When I went to the marina, one of the congressman's flunkies was waiting in the restaurant. He told me the congressman had had some business come up. I put the tackle box on the table and said, "Too bad. I brought something for him."

"I'll make sure he gets it."

The congressman called me a few days later and apologized for not making the fishing trip. The flunkies in his office set up several more trips. He never showed. I always brought tackle boxes of money. On my third or fourth trip, the congressman's flunky took my tackle box and said, "It's better from now on if you don't have contact with us."

That was fine with me. These shakedowns were an aggravation.

BUT THE Republican bigwigs I'd sent my check to weren't done with me. They said that I was now a member of the Reelection League.

They invited me to a luncheon in Washington for all the people like me who they were squeezing so we could shake hands with Vice President Bush. It almost made sense that I should meet Bush. We had people in common. Don Aronow and General Noriega were both friends of his. Why not me?

I flew up with Bryan. The lunch was being held at a Marriott banquet room. Inside, a couple hundred stooges milled around in suits with name tags, waiting to get their handshake with the vice president. Bryan just wanted food. As we were walking into the main room, three guys came up to me. They looked like FBI agents. The hair stood up on my neck. I'm thinking, *This whole thing has been a scam to entrap me,* but the main FBI-looking asshole smiles and says, "Jon? You've got a lot of friends. They told us about you."

His asshole buddies all smile like he cracked a joke. He says, "Do you mind if we talk?"

I leave Bryan in the banquet room. We walk out in the hall. One of his guys mentions my friendship with Representative Ted Jones, and they all smile again. These are the happiest government assholes I've ever seen.

"I barely know the guy," I say.

"What do you think about the war in Nicaragua?"

"I don't follow the news."

One of the government assholes says, "Well, Jon. There are problems in Nicaragua. Some real bad guys have taken over. Other people want to fight them—'freedom fighters'—and they need our help. But Congress passed a law that says nobody can help them.* We don't think that's right."

"That's very interesting. But what's this got to do with me?"

"We want you to help."

"You want me to help freedom fighters?" I'd never heard a more insane idea.

"Would you be willing to meet some friends of ours in Miami?"

---

* Between 1982 and 1984 Congress passed a series of laws known as the Boland Amendments forbidding the U.S. government to provide weapons to the Contras, who were then fighting the Sandinista government in Nicaragua.

What could I say?

Bryan was in a bad mood when I got back to the banquet room. The food they served to League members wasn't up to his standards. We flew back to Miami that afternoon to get a decent meal.

I never did get to shake the vice president's hand.

A WEEK later I met two new guys at the Fontainebleau Hotel to talk about helping the freedom fighters in Nicaragua. We met in the lobby. One of the guys looked like Steve McQueen. The other one was older. I told the older guy to get away from me. I'd only talk to one of them.

My uncle Joe used to tell me that when you meet people connected to the government, you should only talk to one guy. Two guys from the government can make up lies against you and claim you said things that you didn't. If you go to court, they'll back each other up. Even if they record you on a wire, if it's only one guy you talked to, you can claim that there's things you said that the wire didn't pick up, which make you look less guilty. Government assholes usually come to you in pairs. If you can separate them, not only does it give you more protection, but it also makes the guy who gets left out feel like a jerk. The more you can make people from the government envy and mistrust one another, the better.

I walk outside with the guy who looked like Steve McQueen, and he says, "You have friends in high places."

"All that's got me so far is shakedowns and shitty banquet food. What do you want?"

"I work for an agency that thinks you can help us."

"With the freedom fighters?"

"We need someone who can help with airplanes."

"Bro, I'm not a pilot."

"We want you to work with Barry Seal."

His naming a smuggling pilot I worked with makes me uptight.

"Relax," he says. "We don't care about your business. Here's my question: Are you a true American and a good American?"

I say, "Stop with the American shit. Just talk frank and tell me what the fuck is going on here."

He says, "We're going to give you a great deal on planes. We have some C-123s.* You can put twenty thousand pounds of anything you want in them."

"What do you want me to carry in them?"

"Guns to help the freedom fighters in Nicaragua."

"Why me?"

"You're a smuggler."

It made sense. If you're a good guy who works for the government, and you need to break the law, you need to hire somebody like me who does illegal things. It was logical, but I wanted to know who had told these assholes I was a smuggler. When I asked him, he gave me an answer.

"Ricky."

"Ricky?"

"Ricky. He says you might remember him as 'Albert's guy.'"

Albert San Pedro's "guy" was Ricky Prado, who'd helped kill Richard Schwartz. This about knocked me over. I knew Ricky had left Miami. What could he have to do with these assholes? Was he an informant?

The Steve McQueen look-alike said, "Ricky and I work together helping the freedom fighters in Nicaragua. We get them guns.† Ricky says you're reliable. He thinks you could be a good asset."

This was a lot of information to take in. Ricky used to move

---

* The Fairchild C-123 was a military cargo plane, smaller than the C-130s and C-17s used today by the military, but still large enough to drive a small armored vehicle into or to carry seventy armed troops.

† Prado's initial assignment in the CIA, after being hired in 1981, was to help train and equip the Contras. Recently, Prado has publicly stated that he was the "first CIA officer living in anti-Sandinista Contra camps." In his capacity as a CIA employee living abroad, he appears to have maintained ties with members of the Miami underworld and to have attempted to leverage these contacts for his CIA mission. In the 1991 racketeering investigation of San Pedro, investigators interviewed a Miami gun dealer with a criminal history who informed them that he had met with Prado in Central America and that Prado had asked for his help in acquiring weapons in Miami and shipping them to Central America—presumably as part of his CIA job.

coke and cash for Albert and me, but I'd never talked to him about smuggling. Albert knew what I did, and he and Ricky were still very close.* You never imagine that a guy you've worked with on the street will end up in the government. It's dirty. Ricky could tell anybody in the government anything he knew about me from the street. Maybe he'd obtained immunity for things he did with me in the past because he worked for these guys, but I didn't have that.

First these rats shake me down for contributions to the Republican fund. Next they want me running guns. This was worse than dealing with my uncle Joe in the Mafia.

THE NEXT time I met the Steve McQueen look-alike, I picked the coffee shop at the Best Western Thunderbird Hotel as the location. It was my uncle Jerry Chilli's domain. He had a crew of old, bent-nose wiseguys who'd sit in the coffee shop playing gin all day long. I felt secure there.

The government guy explained that they wanted me to set up a company that could get the C-123 planes to Barry Seal. The government had weapons in Texas that I had to deliver to Seal so he could fly them to a landing strip in Nicaragua. They'd give us radio codes for the planes so we could fly back into the United States with no problem. I'd get $100,000 for every load we delivered, to cover costs, including what I paid Barry.

I still had one question. "Why did they send a congressman after me in the restaurant?"

"Jon, we don't send congressmen out to recruit guys. That was a coincidence. We were going to talk to you before you met him. It doesn't hurt that he thinks you're a good American."

"Do I get any protection here because of my helping you?"

"Now, we all know you're a good American. I think that's a lot."

---

* During the 1991 racketeering investigation of Albert San Pedro, investigators learned that San Pedro placed calls to foreign embassies where Prado was stationed as a CIA officer through the 1980s and early 1990s. In a 1991 interview with federal investigators at CIA headquarters, Prado admitted he visited with San Pedro in Miami even after San Pedro had been convicted of cocaine trafficking and bribery of a public official.

Tackle boxes of cash to the congressman and several checks to the Republican League, and that's what it bought me. I'm a good American.

I WENT to see Barry Seal in Louisiana and laid it out. "Barry, there's government guys who want to give me some C-123 military cargo planes so we can fly guns on them to some freedom guys in Nicaragua."

Barry said, "Get the fuck away from me, Jon. There's something very wrong here. Forget about this."

Barry usually liked a big challenge. It appealed to his blowhard personality. I was taken aback. I explained to him that I didn't think I had any choice in the matter. I had a U.S. congressman extorting money from me. I had other guys twisting my arm, calling me a good American.

Barry laughed. He said, "Okay, Jon. I'm no stranger to this kind of work.* Let's get the C-123s up here. But I have one condition."

"What is it?"

"If I fly guns, I'm not moving coke with you."

I thought his condition was weird at the time, but I let it pass.

DANNY MONES helped set up a dummy company to take the C-123s from the government and get them to Barry in Baton Rouge. I got the codes for the radios from a guy I met at a gas station outside Homestead Air Force Base.† The codes changed every week, so every time Barry flew to Nicaragua and back, I had to drive to Homestead and get new ones.

The guns would come from a National Guard armory in Corpus Christi, Texas.‡ They were going to be in two rental trucks parked

---

* Barry Seal's history as a CIA-connected weapons smuggler is noted in chapter 47.
† According to a former CIA official I interviewed, Homestead is home to one of the CIA's oldest domestic stations. It was opened in South Florida in the late 1950s to oversee preparations for the Bay of Pigs invasion.
‡ According to an FBI report I viewed, as early as 1959, the CIA directed operatives to steal weapons from domestic military bases in order to supply its various anti-Castro activities.

outside a shopping center near the armory. The trucks were from a company called ATI.

Before our first run, the Steve McQueen–looking asshole said, "You need to bring drivers who aren't going to be drunk or fucked up."

I was a little offended. My drivers had moved thousands of kilos of coke all across the country for years, and I'd never had a problem. I didn't like being treated like a stooge.

I mapped out the route with a TripTik road map from the Automobile Club of America and flew with Bryan to Baton Rouge. We met our drivers there and drove two rental cars to Corpus Christi. When we arrived that afternoon, the ATI trucks were in their spot by the market. There was a government guy in a car parked nearby who gave me the keys. He said, "You need to get started now."

I said, "My guys got to eat first."

"Those trucks can't sit there."

"How about you shove these keys up your ass and drive the trucks yourself."

I didn't like getting attitude from this jerk. The more I thought about it, I was doing the government a favor. Not the other way around.

I fed Bryan and my drivers, and we got going after dark. Bryan and I followed the trucks in the rental cars. We got back to Barry Seal's hangar early the next morning and unloaded the trucks. The weapons we were giving to the freedom fighters in Nicaragua weren't the kind you could buy in Miami. There were M-60 machine guns, M-79 grenade guns, LAWs rockets,* and ten thousand pounds of ammo.

We split the weapons between the two C-123s. Each plane was

---

* The M-60 is a belt-fed machine gun used by infantry or mounted on helicoptors that was widely used by the U.S. military in Vietnam; the M-79 is a single-shot grenade launcher also used in Vietnam; the LAW rocket was also used in Vietnam. The LAWs provided to the Contras had a design flaw that caused them to occasionally blow up when launched, which was detrimental to the person launching it.

a little over half full, but they carried big bladders of extra fuel. Barry and his guys did one run successfully.

The next run I flew with Barry to see Nicaragua for myself. We landed on a farm. The freedom fighters we met were dressed in rags. They were peasants, none over five feet tall. They had women with them, tough little broads with guns. They helped unload the planes. One of the men told me the women fought by their side, even though some had babies with them. In Vietnam a girl in a village might have had a gun, but these freedom fighter broads were out living in the mud. They had heart. We stayed an extra couple hours just to see the broads test-fire an M-60. They were sensational.

After that trip I distanced myself from the operation as much as I could. Barry moved the C-123s to a new airport he had in Arkansas. Bryan took over getting the guns from different National Guard armories. The one thing I had to do was get the radio codes from Homestead. The government guys wouldn't give them to anyone else.

I didn't like smuggling guns for the government. I didn't get any kick from it. It was the opposite of a kick. The government made everything difficult. They initially promised to pay me in a convenient bank in Panama. But they changed their minds. They paid in cash—bulky small bills. It's probably just a coincidence, but the amount they paid me to smuggle was about equal to what I'd paid the congressman. It was as if I'd paid for them to hire me and Barry.

I never flew cocaine for the Cartel on the government planes. The radio codes we got meant we could fly back into the United States with impunity. But I never trusted the government not to trick us. I just stuck to flying their illegal guns.*

---

* Jon first told his story of helping the CIA arm the Contras to an attorney in 1986—more than a decade before Prado was outed as a CIA officer. Law enforcement officials involved in the racketeering investigation of San Pedro believed Jon's statements regarding Prado's alleged role in the murder of Richard Schwartz were credible. His statements regarding his alleged involvement with Prado in the arming of Contras were not examined as part of that investigation. But three Miami-Dade detectives I interviewed who served on the task force that led the investigation of Prado told me that the U.S. Attorney's office in Miami was pressured

After a half-dozen runs, they told me we should leave the planes in Honduras. They were changing their smuggling operations, and they didn't need me no more.

I did my part for the country. I wrote checks to the Republican League. I gave cash to the congressman. I smuggled guns. Nobody could say I wasn't a good American. I'm still waiting for my hand-shake from Vice President Bush.

---

by the CIA to stop looking into Prado on the grounds that their case threatened to "reopen the Contra scandal." One assistant U.S. Attorney I interviewed who dealt with the matter recalled that he had meetings with CIA associate counsel E. Page Moffett regarding Prado. But this Assistant U.S. Attorney could not remember what he discussed with Moffett, or why a subpoena his office had served Prado to compel him to testify was quashed. When I asked Dexter Lehtinen—the U.S. Attorney at the time of the investigation—about the matter, he vigorously rejected the notion that his office would ever bow to pressure from the CIA. Jon's assertions about helping to arm the Contras are plausible because of his previous relationship with Prado, but he has provided no additional supporting evidence. I have attempted to ask Prado about this, but he has not responded to my inquiries.

67

J.R.: There were many strains on my relationship with Toni. One of the biggest was her dream to be a movie star. When we met, she'd got a small part in a film with Ryan O'Neal called *So Fine*. It was a stupid movie about a guy who invents jeans with plastic windows in the back to show off people's asses. Toni had maybe one line in the whole movie. But because she was so beautiful—and because her ass was so good—when *So Fine* came out in 1981, they put Toni in the movie poster with Ryan O'Neal. That little success played with her mind, and Toni kept nursing her Hollywood dream.

We were both busy in Delray—with my business and our work with horses—but with that Hollywood dream still burning bright, Toni still did her modeling in New York, and after *So Fine* she traveled to Los Angeles for auditions. When I went with her, we'd stay at the Beverly Hills Hotel.* They had bungalows where we could bring

* Still located at 9641 Sunset Boulevard in Beverly Hills.

dogs. Toni and I would hit our favorite spots—Mr. Chow's and Spago*—and we'd work. She had auditions, and I had my business. I'd usually take Bryan with us, and we'd make sure everything was running smooth with the planes I was landing at Van Nuys airport. Sometimes I'd hold my coke in suitcases in the Beverly Hills Hotel luggage room and do transfers around town. I used Nate 'n Al's† deli in Beverly Hills because I liked the food, and there was a city lot nearby where my coke cars could be safe. Nobody stole cars in Beverly Hills.

Toni auditioned for *Red Sonja,* a movie where they wanted a big blonde to run through the jungle in a cape. Toni was perfect for the part, but they gave it to Sylvester Stallone's girlfriend, Brigitte Nielsen.

It was the same outcome with *Clan of the Cave Bear*—a film where they wanted a big blonde to run around with wild animals. Toni did a few readings, but it went to another giant blonde, Daryl Hannah.

My friend Joey Ippolito had connections at a company called TriStar Pictures through his coke business. He introduced me to some executives there. I told them, "Let me buy a fucking movie for my girl so she can star in it."

They agreed to help. What was even better was, these guys liked cash. I gave them a couple million dollars in shoeboxes. I even unloaded a box of small bills on them that I got from the government for flying the guns. These guys didn't care. Throw in a couple extra bricks of coke to keep them happy, and we were in the movie business. They got a writer to make up a script. Ryan O'Neal agreed to play a role in the movie. But in the end it never got shot.‡ I believed those guys fleeced me, but Joey Ippolito said, "Jon, who the fuck

---

* Both establishments were celebrity hotspots in the L.A. of the 1980s.

† Officially called Nate 'n Al of Beverly Hills Delicatessen, it remains a popular spot on 414 North Beverly Drive.

‡ Jon Roberts's untitled film project of the early 1980s involved a successful producer-screenwriter still active today, and according to other sources I interviewed, Jon sank two to three million dollars into it.

knows? It's Hollywood. It's not like the coke business where a kilo's a kilo."

I worked every angle for Toni. When they started filming *Miami Vice* in our hometown, I had a friend introduce me to Don Johnson. We met at a club in Coconut Grove called Mutiny on the Bay. The whole club was glass inside so people could snort coke on any surface. It was blowhead heaven, and I'm in there with people who got to be stars playing cops and smugglers on TV. My friend walks me over to Don Johnson and the black guy who played Tubbs* and says, "Jon, meet the guys who pretend to be hunting you every week on TV."

Nose powder makes us all instant friends, and the next night we're at a fish restaurant in South Beach. The black guy tells me, "Don and I are so famous, I can do anything. I can get any part I want. I'm bigger than the Beatles."†

As I remember, the black guy wasn't doing coke like the rest of us, but he sure was high on himself. Fame can delude people as bad as drugs. I say, "Are you a fucking wacko? You're the fucking black-guy sidekick on the TV show. Fuck you."

Don Johnson says, "I'm sorry about my friend, man. Is there anything I can do to make you forget the dumb shit he's saying?"

"Can you get my girl a part on TV?"

To his credit, Don Johnson tried, but all Toni got were background parts. Once I hung out with the director and watched him film a show. He gave me a spiel about how he brought realism to TV. "Don't you think so?"

"You're filming a drug dealer opening the trunk of a car with coke in it in the middle of the street. That's amateur shit."

This jackass director says, "No, they do it this way. I have an expert who advises me."

"Okay. You're the Hollywood guy. What do I know?"

I told Toni she was better off not making it in the movies if it

---

* Philip Michael Thomas.
† Thomas released two albums in the 1980s, neither of which did quite as well as efforts by the Beatles.

meant dealing with these full-of-shit morons. But she went to auditions until her dream crushed her. The last time in L.A., I left her alone at our hotel for a week while I went to Mexico on business. When I got back, she was a mess. She'd taken a suitcase from storage with some kilos in it. She got a straw and poked through the kilo packs. They looked like Swiss cheese. I said, "Did you have a good time?"

She was high. She said, "Yeah! I've had months of great fun out here."*

I said, "Come home to Florida. Your actressing career is finished."

Someone had to tell her the truth. *Smokey and the Bandit III*—that was the only movie she got after *So Fine*. Nobody was giving her an Oscar for being Background Girl Number Two in a *Smokey and the Bandit* sequel.

OUR LIFE in Delray was becoming tense. Toni couldn't get out of bed sometimes. When my sister visited, the aggravation was endless. Those two didn't get along.

JUDY: I first met Toni when she and Jon came to New York. She had a group of men who fawned over her—the writer Noel Behn and Bob Fosse†—and I remember seeing Jon with them at the Russian Tea Room, thinking she'd really spun his head around. With her looks and figure, she was quite the package. But I wasn't impressed. She was friends with literary people, but I didn't think she was very well read or educated.

And forgive me for saying this, Toni was a lousy housekeeper.

Everything my brother did was to make that woman happy. Jon

---

* Toni remembers these incidents differently and disputes the veracity of Jon's account.

† Behn was a playwright and novelist best known for *The Kremlin Letter* and for his work at the Cherry Lane Theater in the 1950s and 1960s. Fosse was the choreographer and Academy Award–winning director of *Cabaret* and *All That Jazz*.

is insecure about himself. Don't let his macho side fool you. Inside, he is a little boy who doesn't think he has enough to offer people. This is why money was always so important to him. He believed it could make up for the things he thought he lacked. Toni was a woman who knew how to press all his buttons.

On one of my visits they had a terrible fight. The next morning I went to Toni and said, "If you kept the house a little better, my brother would be happier, and you wouldn't argue as much."

That woman threw me out of the house. Jon did nothing to stop her. I was very hurt. I still am.

J.R.: My sister didn't help things in our house. Toni's mind started to get unstrung. She was prone to rages of jealousy. At first it was over imaginary women, even when I wasn't cheating. She'd get paranoid that I was hiding girls in the closet. She'd come in the bedroom when I was sleeping and shout, "Where are they?"

One time Bryan was in the driveway, and she ran out and made him open his trunk at gunpoint because she thought he was smuggling girls in there. Another time she set off the tear-gas cannons by the front gate to chase imaginary girls from the bushes. She got extreme.

Toni decided to put me in my place by having an affair with one of the grooms in my barn. When I found out, that sorry asshole ran off and disappeared off the planet. On principle I would have to give him a beating, but I didn't take it personally. I was more mad that I'd lost a good groom.

I saw more and more cocaine inside our house going into people's noses.

LISA "BITSY" BENSON: When I first started working for Jon, I didn't know he and Toni did coke. Then my dad started dating a girl who was closer to Toni's age, and they became friends. They'd invite me into the house, and those ladies really racked up the rails. Toni wore a chain on her neck with a gold pickax for breaking up the coke. The more she chopped with the gold pickax, the wilder it got. Toni would get paranoid and break out guns, and we'd have to march around the yard searching for intruders. She called it "rat patrol."*

J.R.: Toni and her family were excessive people. Liquor ran freely through that family. Anybody that tells you that alcoholism doesn't run in the genes is full of shit.

Toni's mother got completely wacked out on booze. I sent her to doctors. I sent her to AA classes. Finally I told Toni's mom, "If you can stay without a drink of alcohol for a month, I'm going to buy you a brand-new Mercedes."

That woman put all of her will into it. She struggled. She was shaking for days. But she finally got the poisons out. At the end of that month, I'd never seen her look so good. I had a guy send up a new Mercedes. She cried when she saw it.

I said, "You deserve it. You stayed clean. God bless you."

She said, "I'm going to show all my friends the car."

She drove off, and the next morning I got a call from a cop in Delray. He said, "We found your mother-in-law pulled over by the road. She told us that spiders had filled her car and made so many webs that she couldn't see."

The poor woman had gotten drunk, and with her body clean as it was, it made her flip. They had to give her special injections at the hospital to bring her mind back.

To GET away from the madness in Delray, I started an affair with a girl from Fort Lauderdale named Karen. She was a little stripper, with dark hair and a sweet heart. When Toni would go nuts and chase me around the house kicking down doors, I'd escape in my helicopter. I'd pick up Karen. We'd fly to a place by Cape Canaveral

---

* Toni remembers these incidents differently and disputes the veracity of Bitsy's account.

where you could skim over the water to watch the porpoises. That was my out.

But it never lasted. I was in the barn one day and found burned Coca-Cola cans that someone had poked holes in. I asked one of the kids who worked in the barn what they were for. "They're home-made pipes for smoking crack."

I'd never heard of crack. He explained it was cocaine made into special rocks so you could smoke it easily. That was a new one on me.

It turned out that Toni's brother, Lee, was smoking it in the barn with some other guys who worked for me. At first I didn't think nothing of guys blowing off steam, smoking a little crack.

Then my stepdaughter, Amber, whom I'd helped raise, told me someone had stolen the ATVs that I'd bought for her and her friends to play with. I went into the barn to ask the guys in there if they knew about the missing ATVs. At ten in the morning, they were smoking crack. I knocked them around and said, "Where are my ATVs?"

They told me Lee had sold them to some guys in town to buy crack cocaine. This was a shocker. Lee was moving hundreds—sometimes thousands—of kilos for me a month. He was one of my most trusted drivers. I also had an airport security guy I'd bribed at Fort Lauderdale airport to let Lee pass through the screenings without a hassle. A couple times a month I sent Lee to Chicago with forty keys in his luggage.

I put it together that Lee was a smart enough kid that he wouldn't steal from my business. But he was such an addict that he was steal-ing shit from around the house to sell to dealers. I started to worry that he'd given crack to Amber. All I needed was the whole family on drugs. I wanted to make an example of Lee. I'd blow his brains out and show them that's what happened when you got hooked on drugs. I went a little nuts.

FATHER BRADLEY PIERCE: I'd received the strangest call from Jon. I'd barely heard from him since I'd entered the seminary.

Jon was in torment. He said he had a family member involved in drugs. He wanted to lash out at them for stealing from him and bringing drugs into his house. I'll never forget what Jon said, "Help me. Save me from killing this person."

We talked for a few minutes. He thanked me and abruptly hung up.

J.R.: I didn't kill Lee. I went in the barn and beat the shit out of his friend. I made him tell me where the crack dealer was who had my ATVs.

I drove to the guy's house with Bryan. We went inside, and it was the worst thing I'd ever seen. There were people wacked out everywhere. There was trash. There were bottles filled with urine because these guys were too high to get up and piss in a toilet. Bryan and I knocked them around and found my ATVs in the garage. Some crackhead had taken them halfway apart, like he thought he was going to strip them for parts. He was such a moron. You could sell a stolen ATV as is and get more money for it. These guys had no brains left.

After we got the ATVs in my truck, I lit the garage on fire. We drove off with crackheads running out of the burning house.

That was my part for community improvement.

I was trapped by Toni. I never talked to her about my business, but she knew enough that, if I left her, she could make real problems for me. The only proper way to break up with her would be to put her in the ground along with her whole family. I didn't have the stomach for that. So I lived like a hostage in my own house.

68

J.R.: My business functioned almost mechanically. The planes and boats made it in. The coke got pushed out. The money got flown to Panama. Sometimes I'd have to beat on somebody.

I started making little dumb mistakes. One time I was in San Francisco with Bernie Levine. He mentioned some asshole in Marin County who'd ripped him off. The guy had been a partner in Bernie's recording studio, and when they closed it down, this jerk stole a gold record from the wall.

Bernie thought it would be funny if he brought me to the guy's house for a drug deal, and I pretended to rob them in order to take back his gold record.

I hadn't done a rip-off in years. Why not, for old times' sake?

We drove up to the guy's house in Bernie's Volvo. He'd introduce me as a new supplier, and I'd do my thing. Then I'd "steal" Bernie's car, and he'd meet me later.

The victim had a beautiful hillside house. Big sliding-glass doors with a wooden deck hanging over a canyon. The gold record was in a frame in the living room. We sit down, exchange some chitchat, and I reach into a briefcase for my gun, and *bang*—as I'm pulling it out, I hit the trigger and shoot out a window. The guy jumps up and runs right through a glass sliding door. He smashes the glass out and runs off the deck. I go out and see him rolling down a cliff into a culvert. He was a real Houdini.

I go back inside, and Bernie is panicking. "Oh my God! Let's go."

I smash the frame to grab the record, but Bernie screams, "Leave it!"

"Leave the gold?"

"It's not made out of actual gold, Jon."

We tore out of the neighborhood with Bernie worrying the whole time. "How could you try to shoot him?"

"How could you not tell me the gold record wasn't actual gold?"

"I live here, and you tried to kill him?"

"What's the worst these pussies do in San Francisco? Not invite you to a wine tasting?"

Bernie never forgave me. He was a criminal but not violent. Years later, after Bernie quit the drug business, he committed crime by scamming rich ladies. He was fifty years old, but he'd date seventy-five-year-olds. He took ballroom dancing lessons so that he could make these old biddies happy and take their money. Bernie had the same criminal mind as me, only he used dancing shoes where I used a gun.

The one thing I never admitted to Bernie was that I'd shot the gun by accident. I'd embarrassed myself. My reflexes were dull.

MY JUDGMENT was slipping, too. Mickey and his friend Delmer—"Dad"—kept hiring a kicker who'd freeze up when the time came to push the loads out of our plane. Two times we almost had to ditch our loads. Mickey and Delmer tried to cover it up, but I knew about it from listening on the radios.

If we'd lost those loads, it would have been up to me to explain the loss to the Colombians, not them. I didn't pay this half-wit to fly around in the sky and enjoy the view. I found out that Mickey and Delmer kept hiring the guy because he was some kind of cousin of Delmer's.

I decided to fire him. I go down to Ultimate Boats on a day when I know the guy is working on boats with Delmer. I walk up to this half-wit cousin—a stringy kid in a Lynyrd Skynyrd T-shirt— and say, "You're a piece of shit, and if it was up to me, I'd beat the piss out of you. Unfortunately, your cousin is Mickey's partner. But you'll never go in a plane again."

This kid is so stupid that he pulls a knife on me, but instead of stabbing me, he runs to the stairs to the radio room. He gets about five feet up the stairs and I yank him down by his foot. He flips backward onto the floor. I say, "Whoops. I was wrong. It looks like you did fly again."

I kick the half-wit in the face, and then I lose my head. A kicker needs good hands to throw the loads out. I wanted to make sure this kid never got put on a plane again, so I stomped his hand bones. I broke both his hands to pieces.

It was the right thing to do, because this kid put my ass on the line with the Colombians. If he screwed up bad enough, they'd break more than my hands.

But it was the wrong thing to do because he was Delmer's cousin. That poisoned things for me. Delmer never talked to me the same again. It was bad judgment to strain my business like that, and it did cause problems for me down the road.

I should have beaten Delmer's relative in private.

I GOT lackadaisical because it didn't feel like I could get caught. I saw this in Bryan, too. One day we worked out together at the gym. I walked out past his car, and there was a terrible smell coming from it.

At the time Bryan drove the smallest car he could fit in, a Nissan

Z car, with the hatchback. I got twenty feet from his car and smelled a terrible stink. I said, "Bryan, did you leave some workout clothes or shoes in there?"

We walked up to the hatch on the back. I saw some towels in the window. I opened up the hatch, lifted the towels, and there's a corpse stuffed in the back. There's matted hair, dried blood—the whole thing was bloated and congealing.

"Jesus Christ, Bryan."

"Jon, I forgot. I'll take care of it."

That's how casual we were getting. Bryan killed a guy and decided it was more important to work out at the gym than dump the body.

THE LAST gun battle I ever had was at a disco at the Coconut Grove. It was started over the honor of a TV star a friend of mine was dating. It was one of the stupidest things I ever did.

One of my running mates was a kid named Eddie Trotta. Eddie was a wiseguy, but mostly he was into the Florida life of women, boats, and fun.* When I needed to get away from Toni, I'd run with Eddie. He loved strippers like I did. Unfortunately, he got hooked up with a girl who got famous for being on a TV show where she'd spin around in a tight dress.† This idiot TV star was very hot and she tamed Eddie down for a while. When we'd go out, I'd bring my stripper girl, Karen, and we'd make it a foursome.

We're in the Coconut Grove disco one night when some jerk comes over to Eddie's girl and says, "I'd like to spin you like you spin on TV."

Eddie and I don't want to have a fight with this nothing guy. We

---

* Eddie Trotta now owns Thunder Cycle Design, a premier custom motorcycle shop in Fort Lauderdale. Trotta is a two-time winner of the Discovery Channel's Biker Build-off. He described his winning design philosophy this way: "I always design my bikes like women, with a waistline. And then the fat tire in the back becomes the big butt."

† The identity of this 1980s TV icon has been omitted at the request of Eddie Trotta.

let him walk off. But his celebrity girlfriend starts digging into this. "What did he mean, 'spin' me?"

Eddie says, "Maybe he meant to spin you like on a merry-go-round."

She's not buying it. "Eddie, should I be offended?"

Eddie can't take it. "Are you offended that guy said he wanted to fuck you?"

"Is that what he meant by 'spinning' me?"

"Yes. He wants to spin you around his dick. Everybody does who sees you. That's why you're on TV," Eddie said.

Eddie's girl runs over to the table where the guy is and starts giving him a piece of her mind. She doesn't have much, but it's enough that she gets the guy who wanted to spin her and a bunch of his friends to chase her back to our table. Eddie and me should have left the club then. I had my business to think of, and he had his own legal issues.*

Instead of leaving, we get into a sloppy fight. The next thing you know, one of these jerks has a gun, and I take out mine and shoot one of his friends in the stomach. Another guy gets shot in the shoulder, either by Eddie or someone else.† Who knows? It was madness in the disco.

I was lucky that Karen got rid of my gun when she fled with Eddie's girl. There were no witnesses to my shooting anybody. Even the guys who got shot were no use because they'd been drunk out of their heads. So ended the Battle of the Idiot TV Star in Coconut Grove.

But I was the one who got arrested.

I didn't own the cops in Coconut Grove. I couldn't reach a lawyer for hours. But what saved me was my almost nonexistent

---

* At the time, Trotta had recently been arrested for his role in smuggling four tons of marijuana in Long Island. He would later do several years in federal prison for tax evasion.
† Trotta denies shooting anyone in a club in Coconut Grove but allows, "Maybe I was shot at outside a club."

criminal record. I'd lived a decade in Miami, but all I had were speeding tickets. To the cops, I didn't look like a bad guy. I told them I didn't know what happened at the disco. They believed me.

It was 1984. I was a top American in the most wanted drug cartel in the world, and they let me walk out of the station after I shot a guy in the stomach.

Dumb luck.

69

.R.: By 1984 the senior partners of the Cartel were having problems. They were starting to fight an open war with the Colombian government.* Pablo Escobar and Jorge Ochoa were on the run. The U.S. government was also going after them with indictments in the hope of putting them on trial in American courts.

I wasn't worried, though. I grew up looking at my uncles and Gambino. They proved that when you got big enough, you could live with an indictment on your head. As long as nobody inside your circle ratted, you could beat almost anything.

You could go crazy worrying about the government getting you, or guys on your own side. I've never had

* In April 1984 the justice minister of Colombia—equivalent to the U.S. Attorney General—was gunned down by assassins controlled by Escobar and his associates. An estimated thirty thousand police and military were soon engaged in hunting Cartel labs and fighting their private armies.

a paranoid mentality. My heroes were Al Capone, dying with a fishing pole in his hands, and Meyer Lansky, walking the beach to his last days. I couldn't see myself living in the stinking darkness like Griselda. My attitude was, you do your best and when you've done everything to protect yourself, don't run around like a scared chicken.

Mickey was the same as me. He was cautious, but he always focused on moving forward.

Max was the opposite. He got more scared every day. He began constantly calling on his car phone to say he was being followed.

"Max, if you're truly being followed, thank you for calling me and alerting the people following you, you moron."

As long as nobody in the top of the Cartel ratted, we'd be fine forever.

WE ALL knew we'd have to stop smuggling through Florida eventually. At some point the heat would be too ridiculous even for Mickey to handle.

Mexico was the obvious place to go. The Ochoas had a guy named Gacha who smuggled through Mexico.* The Mexicans had always been good at weed smuggling. They missed out on cocaine only because they couldn't grow the leaves or process it there.

In 1982 my pilot Roger introduced me to a friend of his who'd flown planes for Rafael Quintero, a top Mexican weed smuggler. I'd met Quintero in the early 1970s on my vacation in Mexico with my French girlfriend. Roger's friend reintroduced me to Quintero in early 1983. He was very eager to help the Colombians with coke. There was no competition between the Mexicans and the Colombians because they needed each other. The Colombians had coke, and the Mexicans had good ways to smuggle.

---

* José Gonzalo Rodríguez Gacha, a Medellín Cartel member, was listed by *Forbes* magazine as the eighth-richest man in the world in 1987, right below Pablo Escobar. Gacha was attacked in his fortified compound by more than one thousand Colombian soldiers and gunned down in 1989.

Mexico was wide open. The whole Mexican air force had like two planes. The beauty of Mexico wasn't just that everybody was corrupt. The fact was, the higher-up guys in the police departments resented America on principle. When I started working with Quintero, we'd go drinking with *federales* he owned, and they'd complain about how American officials, like from the DEA, looked down their noses at them. The Mexican cops loved making the stupid gringos look like fools by helping out smugglers.

When Quintero started helping me, he'd get part of my transport fee, or I'd have the Cartel give him X number of kilos per load that his guys could sell on their own. Quintero helped set up airstrips in Mexico that Roger could fly to from Colombia. Once there he'd refuel and fly over the Pacific into California. Southern California was out because they were watching it. But in a Super King Air, Roger could carry almost 2,000 kilos to northern California. We did a few runs like this, but they had such a big marijuana-growing industry in northern California that the cops were always looking for cars moving any kind of cargo. It made me uneasy.

In 1984 Quintero told me he had a better way to move coke. He'd built a tunnel for weed smuggling that went from Mexico into Laredo, Texas. I don't mean a little rathole like the gooks built in Vietnam. This tunnel had lights, paved floors, and elevators at both ends. It was all made by Mexican peons. They'd dig it, and when they were done, Quintero would just shoot the motherfuckers and shove them in a hole in the desert, so only a few guys would know where the tunnels were located. That was the Mexican way of doing a nondisclosure agreement in business. Shoot the poor assholes.

Now that we had access to a tunnel, we'd fly the coke into Mexico and drive it to an old metal barn by the border with Texas. Inside the barn there was an elevator. We'd use it to haul the coke underground, and then, using the tunnel, we'd push $20 million of coke over the border in a handcart. It came out in an auto paint shop on the Texas side. It worked beautifully.

Unfortunately, Rafa bragged about my tunnel to Max. I liked to keep Max in the dark about how I was earning his shoeboxes of money for him, but he insisted on seeing the tunnel. We were still making fun of Max for having gotten kidnapped in Mexico, and it probably made him jealous that I'd found a tunnel and he hadn't. Max had to see it.

Max decided to go on a beefalo hunting trip in Texas, then drive into Mexico when he was done. I met him in a bakery with some of Quintero's guys. I was always embarrassed to introduce Max as my "partner," especially that day. Max walked into the bakery in a corduroy safari suit wearing some kind of Sherlock Holmes hat. I guess that's how gentlemen hunters dressed in Texas. It only got worse when he started explaining to the Mexicans the concept of hunting beefalo penned up on farms. They couldn't believe this guy.

I told the Mexicans we'd play a joke on Max. I had them take him into the tunnel and tell him there were no lights. I wanted Max to go through in the dark so I could surprise him from the Texas side of the tunnel and say, "Hey, Max. Welcome to Texas."

I drove over to Texas and got in the tunnel first. I waited in the dark until I heard Max and the Mexicans. I could see a little ember glowing as Max puffed on his cigarettes. Then I heard Max's scared voice saying, "*¿Donde le luces?*"—Where are the lights?

When he got a few feet from me, I jumped up and said, "Max—"

Max screamed like a girl. One of the Mexicans flipped on the lights. When Max saw me, instead of calming down, he started running back to Mexico. I had to chase him down and grab him. Max was shaking. He was soaking wet. I don't know if it was sweat or he'd pissed himself. He had a look in his eyes like I'd only seen in Toni's mom when she thought spiders were chasing her. He was gone.

The great thing about Mexicans is they love to fuck with people. A couple of them came up to us, and one of them said, "Hey, man. Is that how you hunt a beefalo? You run fast?"

They laughed their asses off. My partner was now the laughing-stock of Mexico. It was embarrassing.

But I missed the point. Why was Max so afraid? He was beyond reasonable. Having a partner crack up simply from fear of the dark should have been a warning that something was wrong with him, but I totally missed it.

70

J.R.: In late 1984 Max experienced a crisis that was even worse than nearly having a heart attack in our Mexican drug tunnel. Rafa came to us and told us we had to kill Barry Seal.

What I'm going to tell you will blow your mind. In the summer of 1984 Barry Seal flew one of my C-123s, loaded with cocaine, into Homestead Air Force Base. He was also carrying pictures of Pablo Escobar personally loading cocaine into the plane at an airfield in Nicaragua, with guys from the Sandinista government helping him. Barry set up Pablo and the whole government of Nicaragua. It turns out that Barry had been working as a DEA snitch since the middle of 1983.

What happened is, in April 1983 the DEA busted Barry at Fort Lauderdale airport when he tried to

* Following his 1983 arrest, Seal's name was published in local Florida papers, but they printed his legal name, "Adler Berriman

fly in a load of counterfeit Quaaludes.* They hadn't even targeted Barry. They'd been going after a big Quaalude smuggler, and Barry had taken a job flying his plane for fun. Barry loved to fly.

Once they got Barry on the Quaalude charge, they forced him to set up Pablo Escobar. We learned all this late in the summer of 1984, when there were a bunch of news stories about it.* Max was beside himself over this. He had seldom worked directly with Barry Seal, but the story put Pablo Escobar more in the news.

You might think I'd be freaked out that Barry turned snitch. Looking back, it's clear that I'd started working with Barry to smuggle guns to Nicaragua a few months after he'd become a DEA snitch. I'd worked with him running guns until about four months before he used a C-123 to set up Pablo.

But I wasn't worried. Barry had told me at our first meeting about the C-123s that he didn't want to smuggle coke with me. Now I understood why. Barry didn't want to snitch on me. There are two types of snitches: the kind with rat blood who'll sell out anybody at any time and the kind who's got his balls in a vise with the government and has been told the only way out is to snitch out specific guys. Barry set up Pablo because that's what they told him

---

Seal," which neither Jon nor his Colombian cohorts recognized at the time, since they knew him as "Barry," or by another alias, "Mackenzie." Criminal aliases used to confuse police may also confuse criminals. Had the Cartel known Seal was arrested in 1983, they would have killed him then.

* As Jon said on the previous page, in 1984 Barry Seal flew a C-123 to Nicaragua. Instead of delivering guns to the Contras as he had been doing, he landed at a government airfield. The CIA, working with the DEA, had equipped Seal's plane with concealed cameras. As the cameras snapped photos, Pablo Escobar and members of the Nicaraguan government loaded the plane with cocaine. Seal had set them up on behalf of the U.S. government. He delivered the plane and the photos to Homestead Air Force Base. Two stories were published about Seal's CIA-backed sting operation of July 1984, in *The Wall Street Journal* and in *The Washington Times*. It was picked up on television news outlets, and on March 16, 1986, President Reagan displayed the photographs taken by the C-123 cameras during an Oval Office speech in which he exposed the Nicaraguan government's role in cocaine smuggling.

to do, probably to work off his charge for the Quaaludes. If Barry had wanted to snitch me out, he would have said, "Let's smuggle a bunch of coke this month." But he said the opposite of that.

I wasn't worried about having worked with Barry to fly guns to Nicaragua, either. The one time I flew with him to Nicaragua, I had told him I was uptight. Barry had laughed and said, "Don't worry, Jon. We're working for Vice President Bush."

I didn't literally believe what Barry said about working for Bush.* But I understood that someone in the government had hired criminals like Barry and me to fly their guns to Nicaragua because they didn't want the government to get caught doing what was against their own law. The last thing in the world they wanted was for us to get into trouble over flying their guns to the freedom fighters. They wanted to keep that shit out of the news.

The government people had twisted my arm by saying that Ricky Prado had recommended me for the job. They probably had twisted Barry's arm with that Quaalude bust hanging over his head. Maybe Barry thought he could score brownie points with the government by flying the guns and get out of his trouble with the Quaalude bust.

I was glad when they told me they didn't need me anymore. Obviously, they did not let go of Barry Seal. They used him to set up the Cartel. It made no sense to me that Barry was able to fly one of our C-123s to Nicaragua and load it with cocaine, with Pablo Escobar personally helping him. Even today, it makes no sense. I never heard of flying cocaine out of Nicaragua. I never heard of Pablo personally loading one of our planes. But it's a fact Barry got him to do this and took pictures of it.

---

* Perhaps Jon should have taken him literally. Richard Ben-Veniste, esteemed Washington attorney who was President Clinton's chief counsel during the Senate Whitewater hearings and later served on the 9/11 Commission, also represented Barry Seal after his 1983 Quaalude bust. Ben-Veniste claims he introduced Seal to Vice President Bush after Seal's 1983 Quaalude arrest, believing the smuggler could be a useful asset. Speaking of Seal in a 2004 interview with *The Wall Street Journal*, Ben-Veniste said, "I did my part by launching him into the arms of Vice President Bush, who embraced him as an undercover operative."

I couldn't care less that Barry Seal was still flying around in a C-123 after we'd ended our arms-smuggling partnership. Barry could do anything he wanted with those planes except set up Pablo Escobar.* For that, Barry would have to be killed.

MAX WAS beside himself when the Barry Seal situation came up because it made it more difficult to be around Rafa. He was very angry about Barry Seal setting up Pablo. He took it personally because Pablo was his boss. Plus, Rafa, like other Colombians, had an inflated view of Americans. Rafa never imagined that a trusted gringo would be a rat. What Barry did had lowered Rafa's opinion of all gringos.

Rafa did more and more things to fuck with Max. I went to Max's house in Sunny Isles, and Rafa had set up an ice chest in the garage that he filled with wet phone books. He used these to catch bullets he was test-firing from MAC-10s. The whole house was filled with smoke. We're on a suburban street, and Rafa's in the garage shooting machine guns. Even with silencers, they make an awful racket. I go in, and Rafa's smoking a bazooka and lecturing Max while ripping rounds from the guns. "It's your job, Max"—*brrrp!* "You're the boss"—*brrrp!* "You got to take care of the traitor"—*brrrp!*

---

* There is no dispute that Barry Seal set up Pablo Escobar, and that he did so in a sting operation probably run jointly by the CIA and DEA. The sting not only satisfied the U.S. government's objective of discrediting Nicaragua's Sandinista government, it also nailed Escobar, a top enemy in the nation's "War on Drugs." As a clandestine operation, it was a stunning success. Jon's assertion that Seal also flew weapons for the CIA Contra program has been widely speculated about since the 1980s. Adding fuel to this speculation is the fact that on October 5, 1986, a C-123, like that flown by Seal to set up Escobar—possibly the same plane—was shot down while delivering arms to the Contras. That Seal seems to have played a critical role in several major U.S. intelligence operations being run at the same time is astounding. But the most baffling part of Seal's story is simply that after serving as an instrument of American clandestine policies, the case against him for Quaalude smuggling pressed ahead, with the result that Seal was ordered to live in a Baton Rouge halfway house for drug addicts, with scant police or federal protection. As Seal put it, he felt the government had made him a "clay pigeon"— a marked target.

Max ran to me with a shoebox filled with $250,000 and asked me to hire a hit man. Of course, it's never that easy.

By late 1984 Barry Seal was like a celebrity. He was facing trial in Baton Rouge for his Quaalude bust, but he was testifying to Congress about the Cartel and on the news every night. Professional hitters didn't want to kill a guy testifying to Congress. The truth is, most professionals like to go after low-hanging fruit, like some bookie or accountant no one's ever heard of.

I sent a couple different shooters to Baton Rouge to look for Seal. He was out on bond, but they claimed they couldn't find him. Max kept crying to me that we had to find him. I said, "I'll go to Baton Rouge myself and find out where he is."

"I'm coming with you," Max said.

"What are you going to do, stand over my shoulder and tell me to adjust my aim because the breeze is blowing five degrees to the west?"

"You're not going to shoot him, are you?"

"Of course not, you fat piece of shit. I'm not taking no gun."

"Then I'm coming."

I HATED traveling with Max. Soon as we hit the Holiday Inn in Baton Rouge, he wanted to get a whore.

"Baton Rouge hookers, Max? I'll take you to the dog pound. Anything you fuck there will be better than the escort they'll send from the Baton Rouge Yellow Pages, trust me."

I made Max drive around with me for two days, so he could do some work for once. I didn't know where Barry was staying, if he had U.S. marshals with him, or what. I went to restaurants he and I had been to, gas stations, a propeller shop. Not a hair of the man did we see. All I got was the smoke of 20 million cigarettes smoked by Max in our rental car.

Every time we crossed the town, I'd swing past the Airport Road Waffle House. Barry loved that greasy southern fast food. On the third day I see him walk out of the Waffle House and get into his

Eldorado. The only secretive thing about him is that he'd replaced his convertible with a coupe. I jam the gas and drive after him. I don't see any protection on him. I get excited. "Boy, I wish we had a gun."

"Are you crazy?" Max says.

"Just think of him as a beefalo."

I let Barry drive way ahead. I don't have a Ricky Prado disguise kit on me, and I don't want him to see me. Barry had good eyes. I knew that from flying with him.

He makes a quick turn on a side street. I speed up to catch him.

"What are you doing?"

"Maybe we can do something here, Max."

"But he's under federal protection."

"So was Kennedy, you asshole."

I'm not the greatest follower, but we pick up Barry's car again. We're on a street of metal shops where they sell parts for planes. Barry is slowing down. He's a block ahead. There's no moving traffic, just workers' cars parked by the little factories. I floor it.

Max starts to whimper.

I've decided to run into Barry. I'm thinking: *We'll smash his car. I'll jump out and kill him with my hands, and then we get away before an ambulance comes.*

"What are we doing?"

"Shut up. We're running him over."

Max screams "No!" like he's being thrown off a cliff.

He locks his hand on my wheel. I punch him in the face. He can't fight, but Max is a fat pig, and he has all 280 of his pounds hanging on the wheel, and he isn't letting go.

Max won. I slowed down, and Barry turned into the shop. We drove past and that was that. Barry got to live another day.

71

J.R.: You know the comic book with the four superheroes? The chick who could make herself invisible, the guy who could skate on ice across the sky, the old guy whose arms could reach to the moon, and the kid who could burn shit with his eyes? Max was like the opposite of all them combined. His superhero power was to sit at home on his fat ass, stick his face into boxes of money, and fuck everything up.

One day in 1985 Max called me from his Jaguar. He always thought he was being followed, but this day he sounded more scared than usual. "Jon, there's a car coming after me. There's a roadblock. They're getting me."*

That's how I heard they arrested Max. The moron called me on my phone to tell me. The phone was not in

---

* Max was arrested on August 27, 1985, while in his Jaguar, speaking on the phone with Jon.

my name, but please—don't give the cops more little clues to help them investigate me.

Why did they arrest Max? It wasn't because they caught a single plane, boat, or car that Mickey or I had moved. It wasn't because any of the hundred guys who worked for Mickey or me had been caught doing something. Nobody found a stash house with $100 million in it or a money plane flying to Panama. It was nothing we did. Mickey and I had a perfect record. So did Roger.

Not even Barry Seal, testifying to Congress, ratted Max or me out.

Max got arrested because he was an idiot, and that is a statement of fact.

WHEN I first met Max in the happy times when he was sending me swing sets and beefalo meat, he came to me once and asked if I wanted to get into the exotic-car business. I'd just sold off a car lot I ran with Ron Tobachnik, but Max told me he had a line on a new kind of car. They were going to call them DeLoreans.*

Max wanted to go into business selling DeLoreans. When he asked me, I said, "That car's a piece of shit. It's got a slow engine. Who needs it?"

I never thought of DeLorean cars again until after Max's arrest in 1985. That was when I found out DeLorean was the reason Max got arrested.

John DeLorean was the businessman who got caught in 1982 trying to move coke to raise money for his car factory.† It turned out that the guy who sold DeLorean his coke had bought it from Max. Every time Max went out on his own to do a business deal, it always blew up in his face. The DeLorean deal was no different. After DeLorean got arrested, Max's guy ratted on him.

---

* The cars best known from the *Back to the Future* films.
† John DeLorean was a former GM executive who founded DeLorean Motors. He was arrested in 1982 in a sting in which he was videotaped doing a coke deal to raise cash for his car company after Wall Street financing had dried up. DeLorean was charged with narcotics trafficking but was found not guilty after his defense argued he'd been entrapped by the FBI.

They indicted Max in 1981. It was a sealed indictment. That's an indictment that they keep secret until right before they arrest you.* But there's no way Max couldn't have known something might be up. The DeLorean case was all over the news.† Max must have known his guy had been arrested.

All of this explained why Max was so terrified all the time—beyond just being a normal pussy. That mystery was solved.

Every person in an illegal business encounters problems. I was wrong to say my cocaine-trafficking record was completely perfect. One time Toni's brother, Lee, got arrested outside the airport in Chicago with forty kilos he was moving for me. But I took care of it. I called my friend in Chicago, Judge Rosenberg, and found out which lawyer to hire. I found out who to pay off. I made the charges go away. Lee never went back to Chicago. We never shipped cocaine there the same way again. That's how you deal with problems.

When you're a professional criminal, being indicted for one thing or another is not the end of the world. Look at Meyer Lansky. The guy had federal indictments on him for decades. He fought the government in the courts. He was very careful how he did his business, and he died a free man, running his empire to his last breath.

What Max did, though, made no sense. After DeLorean got in the news, Max never hired a lawyer. He never put out feelers to the prosecutors or to his partners who were on trial. He did nothing.

---

* Max was charged with cocaine trafficking in a sealed indictment in 1981 in California, with three men who were involved with supplying cocaine to DeLorean. It is unclear from the record whether Max supplied the cocaine involved in the DeLorean matter, or whether his co-defendants later cooperated in the sting operation aimed at DeLorean. Either way, Max was unaware of the indictment, and the federal law-enforcement agencies who brought the indictment failed to prosecute or investigate Max for nearly five years.

† DeLorean was spoofed on *Saturday Night Live* regularly after his arrest in 1982. He then became a featured character in Garry Trudeau's *Doonesbury* comic. In 1983 *Hustler* magazine publisher Larry Flynt leaked FBI tapes to the media of DeLorean's arrest, resulting in Flynt's trial for theft regarding the government's DeLorean tapes, which became its own media event when Flynt showed up in court dressed only in a diaper made of the American flag.

He rode around in his cowboy suit on his farm in Davie and played make-believe *El Jefe*.

But that's why if you tapped him on his shoulder, he'd nearly shit his pants every time. He feared he was a marked man.

WHEN THEY arrested Max, they didn't know who he was. They arrested him on a four-and-a-half-year-old indictment from the De-Lorean case. When they went to Max's house, they were fishing. Unfortunately, Max gave them something. They found a bag with $250,000 in unlaundered drug cash in his bedroom. A bag of unreported cash, even if the cops have nothing else on you, is almost an automatic money-laundering charge.

FORMER MIAMI-DADE POLICE DETECTIVE MIKE FISTEN: That arrest was almost a fluke. The 1982 indictment of Max Mermelstein in the DeLorean case sat in a filing cabinet for years in a federal office in California. I served on a federal task force in Miami, and we asked the DEA every month to send us relevant information about traffickers in our area. The DeLorean arrest was a major trafficking case, but nobody sent us the Mermelstein indictment from that case until approximately five months before it expired. The squad that arrested Mermelstein had to act with haste. They didn't have the time to properly develop an investigation. He probably would have walked except for the bag of cash they found in his house.

J.R.: My lawyers believed the original indictment against Max was going to be tossed, even after they found the money in his house. A year before they arrested Max, a judge threw out the case against DeLorean. That case was old news.

What we thought was, Max might get two years on a money-laundering charge from the cash they found in his house. Just as likely, if he kept his mouth shut, he could bond out and fight the laundering charges for years. That's how any normal criminal deals with a nothing arrest. They had DeLorean on tape buying kilos of cocaine, and he walked. That's how it's done.

Everybody had confidence in Max. As much as I say he's a moron, he was a smart guy. He'd survived in that psycho Colombian family for years. He of all people would know that if he crossed the Cartel, they'd slaughter him. Being related to Pablo by marriage wouldn't save him. It would make them despise him more for his personal betrayal.

Mickey and I were confident of another thing. Max didn't know the details of the smuggling we did. He didn't know where the farm was where we kept the planes. He didn't know the guys driving my cars, or where the stash houses were. We made it easy for him to be ignorant if he was ever questioned by a cop.

To be safe, Mickey and I shut down everything after Max's arrest. We turned the lights off and went dark. Neither of us was worried.

Max couldn't be so stupid as to talk.

72

J.R.: After Max's arrest I had unfinished business with Barry Seal. Fabito slipped into Miami to emphasize how important it was to kill him. Whatever damage Barry had done to the Cartel was done. He'd spoken. At this point, getting rid of him was symbolic. Any successful group of criminals has to kill guys like Seal on principle—just to show what happens to a rat.

The Cartel wasn't the only group that wanted Barry Seal dead. The U.S. government gave him a death sentence, too. Look how they treated this guy. They bust him for flying in some Quaaludes, and so he can work off his charges, they get him and me flying guns to freedom fighters. Then they send him to Nicaragua in a plane with hidden cameras to take pictures of Pablo Escobar loading cocaine. Pablo's supposed to be the most dangerous man in the world, and they parade Barry Seal on the news as the guy who ratted him out? A normal guy who sets up a top criminal gets witness protection.

What do they give Barry? A federal judge in his Quaalude case orders Barry to move into a Salvation Army halfway house a couple miles from the airport where he used to meet the guys who are now coming to kill him. The government did everything but put a bull's-eye on Barry's back.

Barry was a freewheeling guy. He didn't worry about personal protection. But even with a guy who doesn't want security, if he's an important witness, the government will order him into protective custody. Not Barry. The government practically put the gun in our hands.

I knew why we wanted him dead. I don't know why they wanted him dead. Was it for smuggling guns to Nicaragua? They never came after me for that. I don't know what Barry did to piss them off, but it probably had something to do with the fact that he went on TV and talked about flying our C-123s for the CIA.*

When Rafa brought hit men from Colombia to kill him, I told him they could find Barry driving his Eldorado on Airport Road between the Waffle House and the Salvation Army. They were nearly across the street from each other. I had Rafa draw them a map.

MICKEY: I met the Colombians whom Rafa had brought to kill Barry Seal. They were about as bright as Huey, Dewey, and Louie or the Three Stooges. They weren't hit men. They were gofers with guns.

J.R.: Rafa gave these wild Indians a pair of MAC-10s that he'd test-fired in Max's garage,† and they flew commercial to Baton

---

* In 1985 Peabody-award-winning journalist John Camp filmed Seal in an interview he gave aboard a C-123. Seal disclosed details of his role in the CIA sting against the government of Nicaragua, and the interview aired on WBRZ in Baton Rouge in 1985.

† Ballistic tests matched the guns used to kill Seal with shell fragments found in Mermelstein's garage.

Rouge. They checked the guns through. They took the map we gave them and followed Barry from the Waffle House to the Salvation Army. They shot him in his Eldorado.* The Colombians were arrested within hours. They all got convicted for life. They never talked. They were good Colombian rednecks.

People say that a search of the briefcase Barry Seal was holding turned up a piece of paper with Vice President Bush's direct phone number written on it.† A lot of good that did Barry.

---

* Seal was shot to death on February 19, 1986.
† The story of Bush's phone number being on Seal when he died was widely reported but has never been verified.

73

J.R.: Everything quieted down after Barry Seal was killed, and eventually Mickey and I both got restless. We wanted to get back into smuggling. I flew down to Colombia and met with a new group of Colombians. Despite the war on the Cartel, they still had their factories going. These other guys were helping the Cartel move its coke.* So I got into business with them.

MICKEY: I never thought about quitting. I still wanted to run the ideal mission. I wanted to use some small islands that are in Biscayne Bay, so close to Miami that nobody believed anyone could smuggle on them. My

---

* By this time, Jorge Ochoa had been arrested in Spain. He was extradited to Colombia, where the government subsequently released him. But the Medellín Cartel was in disarray. Jorge would be rearrested in 1991 and would serve just five years in prison. Pablo Escobar was gunned down in a joint Colombian-U.S. military raid on his hideout in 1993.

fantasy was to drop coke in the water behind the islands and race out from the beach in my stealth boat to get it. I wanted to say I did it. But I never got the chance.

J.R.: We did a dozen smuggling flights after Max got arrested. One night in 1986 I was working in the radio room at Ultimate Boats when Delmer came in and offered to take over. Mickey was at the farm that night, where we had a pilot bringing in a load from Colombia. The plane wasn't due for another few hours, so I left.

But I didn't feel like going home to Toni in Delray. I decided to go back to the radio room. I wanted be there when the plane came in and we stuck our thumbs in the government's eye one more time.

At four A.M. I started to get excited. The plane was coming. Then there was an explosion. The building shook. A bunch of cops in their stupid Darth Vader suits drove an armored truck through the doors of our shop. They charged up the staircase with their guns out.

You should take it calmly when they come for you. I saw my dad do that when the government men came to our house and deported him out of our living room.

They handcuffed me on the ground. All these cops had radios on their belts. I could hear other cops talking on the radios about raids they were doing all over.* I heard them say they were moving on our farm. I'm wondering how they'd found our farm.

Then, over their radios, I hear all hell break loose. Cops are screaming about a helicopter crashing, fires, a shoot-out. The cops arresting us look a little freaked out. They pick up their radios and ask cops on the other end what's going on.

---

* More than 250 local and federal law-enforcement personnel were involved in coordinated raids on facilities used by Jon and Mickey. They hit a total of 17 locations and seized 12 airplanes, 21 cars and trucks, and 28 boats used in their smuggling operations.

We hear cops yelling, "He's getting away. He's escaped. We lost him."

I don't know what the hell is going on. But I realize they are talking about Mickey. He got away.

I'm sitting there chained on the floor, and that makes me laugh my ass off.*

---

* Jon was arrested on September 21, 1986, in the radio room of Ultimate Boats. Keeping with his habit of not identifying himself by name when he was working, other men arrested in the boat shop claimed not to know who he was. Jon initially refused to provide his name to arresting officers. In initial reports he was simply identified as "an individual with a beard and pelicans on his T-shirt."

74

E.W.: A warm, blue-sky day. Jon pulls into a line of mostly Range Rovers jamming a narrow road outside an exclusive private school in Miami. The parents create a minor traffic jam every afternoon as they arrive to pick up their children. Jon drives Noemi's Cadillac SUV because it has enough space for Julian's hockey gear. The boy has practice every afternoon. Sometimes Jon drives other boys on the team. "I'm a hockey dad," Jon says.

"Julian can't stay late. He has extra math homework," Noemi says from the passenger seat.

Jon curses the Range Rover ahead. "Wait all day, you stupid moron."

"Take a breath, Jon."

Noemi tries to calm Jon with tips learned in a parenting class they recently took. Jon prevailed against a suit his previous wife had filed to alter their custody arrangement with Julian, but he, Noemi, and his previous wife were ordered to attend parenting classes. Since finishing the class, Jon has complained that one of the evaluators described him as "domineering and aggressive." Or as Jon puts it, "Can you believe I had to pay that cocksucker to tell me I'm a bully?"

"Jon, you are a bully sometimes," Noemi says.

"I am?" Jon seems surprised. Then, without warning, he jabs the accelerator, turns sharply, and speeds past the line of cars, driving on the grass to grab a parking spot that has opened up. Jon says, "You said Julian's got extra math homework. We can't wait in the line all day with those jerks."

As Jon and Noemi get out, I'm curious to see how they will blend in with the other parents. Jon has recently been hanging out with his friend Akon and the rapper Lil Wayne, and he wears baggy shorts, a cap, and gold chains that show the hip-hop influence. Noemi recently shaved her head into a Mohawk and is wearing a plunging tank top with tiny red shorts that seem painted on.

I notice that many—perhaps a majority—of the other mothers flash tattoos and cleavage that would be the envy of the waitstaff at Hooters. The prep-school moms seem proof that the shimmering, excessive Miami of Jon's Playboy Bunny–infused past has not so much vanished, but become the new normal.

One feature of the parents waiting outside the school is very 1950s. There are almost no men among them. Jon is the only father standing on the curb.

When Julian sees his dad, he runs into Jon's arms. Jon kisses the top of his head. Noemi throws her arms around him, and they walk to the car playfully, jostling each other with each step. The other children walk beside their parents, some holding their hands, most not.

In the car, Julian plays with his Nintendo. It *bleeps,* and Jon says, "Julian, put that away."

Jon says to me, "I don't want him to turn out like me. I want him to learn in school." Then to Julian, he says, "How was your spelling test today?"

"I missed one word."

"What word?"

"*Emptying.*"

"How did you spell it?"

"E-M-P-T-Y-"

"Julian, it's *empting.*" Jon pronounces it with a New York accent that elides the *y*. He spells it for him: "Julian, it's E-M-P-T-I-N-G."

"Dad, I think there's a *y* in there."

"Julian, don't be wise with me. You need to learn. I love you, okay?"

Jon says to me, "That's the one thing I learned in prison. I never loved someone. That's what I missed in life. It took getting arrested to figure that out."

75

J.R.: Months before I was arrested, I knew Max was cooperating. You couldn't miss that. They made his entire family disappear. The feds put Max into a "submarine"—that's what they call a place where nobody can touch a witness. It could be a Days Inn in Topeka, but they call it a submarine. For Max, it was a very crowded submarine. He went into it with his wife and fifteen of his Colombian in-laws. Max lived in a submarine for the rest of his life.*

Everybody said Max cooperated because he was a coward and couldn't face two years in prison. But I had my own theory. By the time Max was arrested, nobody treated him like *El Jefe*. We all talked to him like he was a moron. But the cops would have treated him differently. They would have made him feel powerful, told

* When Max died in 2008 of cancer, he had lived his last twenty-three years in witness protection, with much of that time spent in Tennessee.

him he was so smart. They'd have to say that, because he was the main part of their case. Once Max got in the submarine with the cops, they probably treated him like the mastermind of the Cartel.

Mickey and I knew Max could give them a lot of stories about the Colombians, but what he had to say about us would be garbage. We hadn't told Max where the farm was, about the radio rooms, the Nike sites, what planes we used, the radio beacons. Nothing. I showed him a tunnel once in Mexico, but that was shut down and buried the day Max got arrested. Obviously Mickey and I were overconfident about Max's ignorance. We should have stopped working. I guess we just loved our work too much.

It took them a year to find out where the farm was. They infiltrated Mickey by having a DEA agent act like he was a mechanical gearhead the same as Mickey. This guy hung out at a machine shop Mickey hung out at, and they became friends. Mickey's weakness was, he wanted to show off the farm to the guy—and he flew him over it so he could see it. That's when they had all the pieces they wanted and did their raid.

They raided the farm with over a hundred cops. Mickey escaped when some cops flew their helicopter into a power line and crashed. The cops on the ground thought it had been hit by a missile, and they ran in all directions. Mickey shot some flares at them, and it was more confusion than the cops could handle. That's the mayhem I heard on the cop radios when I was cuffed on the floor of our radio room.

In the detention center, my criminal lawyer told me that Mickey's friend Delmer wanted to cooperate against me. That was his payback for how I'd fired his moron cousin. But everybody had to do what they had to do.

Having Mickey on the run gave me my opportunity. I made a deal with the prosecutors that if they let me bond out, I'd help them capture Mickey. That's how I walked out of jail.

I had Danny Mones sell a commercial building I owned, and we took cash from that and posted it as my bond, and I went home to Delray.

76

When I saw the mug shot of Jon, I thought, *Here's the mysterious "bearded gringo."* I put in a request to interview him. By the time it was processed, it was too late. He was gone.

—Former Miami-Dade Detective Mike Fisten

J.R.: As bad as you'd think it would be having my partner Max snitching against me, it wasn't that bad. The cops had nothing on any of my guys—Lee, Bryan, Roger, my redneck neighbors, or Albert. They'd searched the house in Delray and got nothing. Toni made sure there was no coke, no illegal guns. They couldn't touch the house. We kept our horses.

I spent weeks jerking the FBI around about Mickey. I'd drive to pay phones and pretend to call Mickey and pass codes to him. I'd tell the FBI agents, "Mickey's going to snorkel into the lake tomorrow to meet me. You better have your guys in scuba gear hiding under the water."

I led them on chases all over the state. Meanwhile I got my affairs in order. Danny Mones had $20 million in properties of mine that he controlled. I had $150 million in Noriega's banks. I had $30 million in cash buried all over the county, and a few million in bank safe-deposit boxes under fake names.

I took a couple million dollars in cash and had Roger fly me to Colombia.

NINETEEN-EIGHTY-SEVEN WAS a bad year to hide out in Colombia. Half the Ochoa family was in hiding. Pablo was trying to blow up the government. I went to go meet Rafa, and somebody shot his brains out. Compared to this, the days when they'd just chop a guy's arm off at a stoplight to steal his watch were the good old days.

I caught a plane to Mexico after a few months there. My friend Rafael Quintero had been arrested in 1985 for kidnapping and torturing to death a DEA agent.*

But Quintero had friends who helped me find a place to live by Mazatlán, which is a beautiful city. I got a little house behind a gate. My face had gone up on FBI most-wanted posters, and these circulated in Mexico. I hooked up with two nineteen-year-old whores and moved them into my hideout. I reasoned that I'd be staying indoors a lot, and that two girls would be better than one. They were best friends in the whorehouse, but when we moved in together, they started to compete and get jealous. I liked them both, but they didn't see that.

There was a show on TV that was like the Mexican version of *America's Most Wanted*. One day they put my face on this show and warned viewers I might be in Mexico. The girls saw this on a day that one of them was feeling jealous, and she called the Mexican police.

---

* Undercover DEA agent Enrique Camarena was kidnapped by Quintero, who tortured him during a three-day period during which Quintero employed a physician to prolong Camarena's life. Quintero recorded the torture sessions on audiotape and sent copies to friends and enemies alike.

I'd been on the run for almost two years and had burned through most of my cash. The Mexican police took the rest of it on my way to prison.

IN A Mexican prison, the warden is like the CEO of a business. His business is to get as much money from the inmates as he can. The good side to this was that, as a gringo, I was viewed by the warden as a good potential source of income. The prison officials didn't report me to the U.S. embassy. The bad side was that during my first week they put me in a section of the prison that was probably about as comfortable as being aboard an old African slave ship. We were chained to the floors. Everybody was covered in their own filth. At night the guards pulled me out and shocked me with wires connected to a car battery. This was how they warmed me up for the shakedown.

After a week they hosed me off and brought me in to see the warden. He put his hand out, and I told him that if he let me use the phone, I could have somebody bring money.

I had no intention of paying this crook. If I did that, he'd hold me longer to squeeze more out. I called my sister with a plan.

JUDY: Jon told me he was in a Mexican prison and he needed me to come down there dressed like a nun so I could smuggle him clothes and documents to help him escape.

I did what any sister would do. I found a priest and told him I was making a humanitarian effort that required me to impersonate a nun. He gave me papers I'd need and sent me to a costume store in Manhattan to rent a habit.

I took some vacation days from work and flew to Mexico. I entered the prison as a nun. When I saw the filthy conditions they were holding my brother in, as if he were an animal, I was outraged. I wanted to pull my brother out of there with my hands. But all I could do was pass him the clothes and fake passport I'd smuggled in under my habit.

J.R.: I had everything I needed to escape. But an inmate turned me in. They sent me to the warden. This time I noticed he had a picture of a racehorse on the wall. The warden was into racehorses. We got more friendly, and he named a price for my release: two Kentucky-born sprinters.

I got Toni to drive them to the border in a trailer. She was met by some corrupt *federales* loyal to the warden, and they brought them to his farm. The warden released me, and we went to his farm. The man cried, looking at those horses I got him. I stayed a few days at his house to teach his guys how to feed the horses and take care of them. The warden wasn't a bad guy. But that's Mexicans. Once you're a friend, they have a lot of heart.

THE WARDEN had some *federales* drive me to an illegal border crossing by San Diego. I walked into the United States with a few pesos in my pocket. It was just my luck that the year I came back President Bush invaded Panama and arrested his old friend and my banker, General Noriega. The U.S. government took over Noriega's banks. I lost $150 million.*

I avoided my criminal friends like Joey Ippolito. When you're a fugitive, you're a get-out-of-jail-free card to anybody who's got charges over his head. If they turn you in, they can get everything wiped clean.

The one guy I could trust in California was Larry Barrera. His father, Laz Barrera, had helped train some of my horses in Ocala. Laz was, of course, the greatest trainer who ever lived.† His son Larry was a great kid. I could depend on him, but he was a heroin addict.

Larry let me move in with him. He had a shack in the Hollywood Hills. Larry had an old lady who lived in a nearby house. He used to help her out—get her mail, bring her milk from the store.

---

* The 1989 U.S. invasion of Panama was undertaken chiefly to seize banks that contained billions of narco-dollars and prevent the cartels from using the country as a finance hub.
† Laz Barrera trained Affirmed, the last horse ever to win the Triple Crown, in 1978.

About a month before I showed up, the old lady had died. She was a shut-in with no visitors, so Larry left her mummifying on the couch, picked up her mail, and cashed her checks. He ran an extension cord from his shack to her place for free electricity. That's how we lived.

You won't believe this, but Larry was married to Joe DiMaggio's niece. They were separated, but Larry was still friendly with her uncle, Joe DiMaggio. When Joe was in town, we'd go to a sporting goods store, steal a box of baseballs, and then visit him. He'd sign the balls, and when there was a Dodgers game, we'd sell them in the parking lot.

I didn't call Judy or Toni when I got to California because the FBI had started watching them. I contacted my old friend Al Tanenbaum. When I asked him to loan me $20,000, he hung up on me. So much for rich assholes.

I phoned a girl who'd worked in my barn when she was seventeen. Her name was Eleanor Roosevelt, just like the president's wife. Eleanor had always liked me. Now she was twenty-five and living in her parents' house in Delaware. I asked her to send me $500.

Instead of sending it, she drove across the country and picked me up. She took me to her parents' house in the suburbs. She introduced me to her parents but used a fake name. They were very friendly. I told them I was from Chicago and had come east to find a job as a stable hand.

The next morning I woke up alone in the house. I was curious about who her parents were, so I went in their bedroom to poke around. I noticed that in the closet her dad had a thick, black belt with a holster on it. Then I saw a big Smokey-the-Bear hat, a nightstick, a gun, and a badge. Her dad was the assistant warden of the county jail.

But her dad liked me. I got a job in the stables at Delaware Park Racetrack.* I liked coming home to dinners with the Roosevelts. I'd been on the run for so long, it was enjoyable having a family.

---

* Now a track and casino called Delaware Park Racetrack and Slots on 777 Delaware Park Boulevard in Wilmington.

I looked exactly like my wanted poster, but these people didn't see me as that guy. I was almost a son-in-law. Eleanor's parents helped us get an apartment. Her father picked me up one day and drove me to the county jail. He wanted me to consider getting a job there. I told him I'd think about it.

I lived with Eleanor until March 1992, when I got recognized by a kid at the racetrack. He'd lived in Florida and was with that little group of kids who were smoking crack with Toni's brother in my barn. He had a grudge because I'd fired all his friends. I got turned in by an angry crackhead.

A small army of FBI agents, backed by a local SWAT team, took me from the apartment I had with Eleanor.

I'd lasted five years as a fugitive. That's not bad. Mickey beat me. Before his house arrest, he spent nearly seven years in Norfolk, Virginia. He opened a motorcycle-repair shop, moved in with a single mother, and helped raise her kid.

77

J.R.: I was facing nearly three hundred years in prison, based on my indictment. They put me in the Tampa County Jail while the feds tried to figure out what to do with me. The Tampa County Jail was so disorganized that there weren't even race gangs like a normal prison. It was a free-for-all. My first month there I got into a scuffle with three black inmates, and they threw me off a second-story tier.

I spent a few weeks in the infirmary. Every week they gave sick inmates an ice cream. They took away our ice cream sticks when we were done eating, but you could buy them back from a crooked guard. I bought three sticks. When I got well enough to stand, I sharpened them by holding them against the wall when they let us walk in a circle around the roof pen every day.

There's only one place to hide sharpened ice cream sticks when you leave the infirmary. It's not a comfortable place, bro. But when I reentered the general population, I had my sticks ready. A few nights after I got back, I attacked the three guys who threw me off the tier. I got them in their sleeping racks. One guy, I scratched his head. One guy, I jammed a stick into his ear and nose before it broke. And the third guy, I got the stick into his eye and blinded him. I lucked out with him because the moron leaped toward me and ran into my ice cream stick.

They wanted to charge me with aggravated assault, but there was a jurisdictional fight because I was in the county jail on federal charges. They put me in the hole, then moved me to Dade County Metro Jail.

THE FEDERAL indictment charged Max and me with being "the American representatives" of the Medellín Cartel. They said that working with Mickey and Delmer, we'd smuggled $2.3 billion worth of coke.* If you're ever indicted, don't get worked up over things they write in the indictment, or the numbers they throw out. A three-hundred-year sentence? Please. Nobody wanted me to do three hundred years. Nobody wanted a trial. What everybody wanted was a negotiation.

In a situation like this, they want you to give them things. You got things you can't give them, but some things you can. They want things from you that are so good, they'll feel good knocking down your time. And when they feel good doing that, you feel good, because you're out sooner.

The best way to start is to feel them out, let them come to you with all the things they want, then figure out the things you can't give them. For me that was easy. The Ochoas. Albert San Pedro.

---

* The $2.3 billion figure was one estimate used by federal officials based on evidence provided by Max about smuggling flights he supervised—both before and after he began working with Jon and Mickey—that led to the importation of fifty-six tons of cocaine. There were many other flights Jon and Mickey supervised independently of Max. Given that the wholesale value of cocaine fluctuated wildly, reaching an exact figure is next to impossible. The $2.3 billion figure is at the low end. Other estimates from government officials placed the value of cocaine imported by Max, Jon, and Mickey at $15 billion. By any measure, they supervised the bulk of the cocaine smuggled into the United States by the Medellín Cartel during its peak in the first half of the 1980s.

They were out. They were still strong. Other things I could help them with. General Noriega—that was easy. He was a pedophile who'd lost $150 million of my money. Plus, he didn't even have a country. He wasn't coming after nobody. Anything they wanted on him was okay.

They wanted Ricky Prado on the Schwartz murder. I had no problem giving him up. He was a rat who went to work for the government. They gave me immunity on the Schwartz murder for my proffer statement saying how he shotgunned Schwartz.

For my cooperation, they knocked 297 years off my sentence. I never testified against Noriega because they realized I contradicted another witness. A few months after I cut the deal on Prado, they dropped the case against him. I got 297 years off for next to nothing. As a bonus, they let my state assault charges for the ice-cream-stick incident disappear.

I did three years in prison. I'm not going to lie to you and say that was a tough time. After all the things I've done to people, that amount of time is a joke. But one thing did happen that stuck with me. I was lying in my cell one night thinking about how other guys in prison had mothers or sons or somebody they thought about. I had people who would do things for me. My sister visited me. But lying in that cell, there was nobody I'd think about. Because there was nobody I ever thought about, I was completely alone. I don't mean lonely, or by myself in a prison. Rather, I realized I was alone on this earth.

78

J.R.: When I got out of prison, I had no plans. I worked at the old Beachcomber Hotel* on Miami Beach. Having the job was a necessary condition of my parole.

The money I thought I had in Miami was gone. People had spent ten years in Delray with shovels and backhoes treasure-hunting cash I'd buried in plastic buckets. Neighbors, people from the barn, guys who'd driven for me—anybody who knew that I buried money was up there digging away. When I went back to Delray, the places where I thought I'd put buckets in the dirt were looted or had washed away. I know of one neighbor who found $400,000 in the rafters of an old barn I used as a stash house. He moved away.

While I was on the run and then in prison, my lawyer Danny Mones had transferred or sold the property I had owned. Just as I was confronting him, he died almost

---

* The Beachcomber is a two-star dive at 1340 Collins Avenue.

overnight of cancer. I saw him one time. He promised to straighten everything out, and he was dead a week later. If you knew Mones, the guy was such a thieving piece of shit that he probably was happier dying of cancer than giving back something he'd stolen.

I went to a bank where I'd left a million dollars in a safe-deposit box under a false name. It took me a year to remember the name I'd used and to get a fake ID made to match it. When I got to the bank, the building was gone. I went to the main branch, presented my fake ID, and they said they'd saved my box from the building they'd torn down. When I opened it, there was a letter from the IRS—addressed to the fake name I'd used—saying I owed a quarter-million dollars in back taxes. Who knew that when they tear down a bank, the IRS opens unclaimed safe-deposit boxes and taxes the contents?

There were some kids I knew—sons of wiseguys I used to run with—who asked me to help them smuggle weed. I had a friend fly us to Mexico, and I introduced them to people, and when we got the weed into California through a tunnel, I showed them how to put it in five-gallon paint cans and get UPS to ship it anywhere it needed to go. Smuggling's just as easy today as it was then. There's just as much cocaine. It's the same price or cheaper. Nobody won any war on drugs. Drug traffic keeps people employed on the streets and in cop cars. That's all.

I retired from the industry.

When I found my old bodyguard Bryan in 1997, he could only move with a walker, and he barely knew who I was. He died at the age of forty-two. They said it was cancer, but it was probably the horse hormones.

In 1999 I hooked up with a dancer from Venezuela, and she got pregnant. She had my son, Julian. When he was born, I was proud I'd made a baby, but I had no what you call "human empathy" for him.

I never cared about my father, and I don't believe he cared about me. I had no expectation that I'd care about my son. Julian's mother ended up leaving the country for a while. At that point I was in the apartment alone with this little baby. I was feeding him and changing his diapers.

I had nobody else to take care of him. I couldn't leave him. I couldn't be flying to Mexico carrying him with me through the tunnel with the dope trolley. I needed a job where I could stay nearby and work flexible hours.

I knew a guy in New York who ran an escort service in Miami. He was a fat piece of shit who reminded me of Max, only he didn't smoke. He hired me to straighten out his business.

The way an escort service works, whether it advertises itself in the phone book or in newspaper ads or on the Internet, it's all the same. They book the girls from the main office. The customer calls and orders a girl for *x* number of hours. They have a driver take the girl to the job. He's there to protect the girl, and to watch her.

The guy who hired me had a problem. His girls were ripping him off. Some of these girls were great fucks. They'd fuck the guy's brains out, and he'd ask for a second hour or a third hour. The girl was supposed to report that to the company, so they'd get their end of the extra hours. The drivers were supposed to be watching the girls to make sure they didn't cheat. But the girls were paying off the drivers. So the owner, whose fat ass was sitting up in New York, was being robbed blind.

He hired me to watch his drivers. What I did was follow these guys around, and when I caught them cheating the owner, I'd beat the piss out of them. You put the fear of God into a couple of these guys, and nobody rips off the escort agency owner no more. Now, my job was, I'd just ride around and watch everybody, help the whores out if they got into a jam. I'd start at eight o'clock and be done at four in the morning.

It worked out perfectly because I put a baby seat in my car. It was nice and quiet in there. Julian could sleep. I could feed him, change him. Most of the time I was just sitting outside a hotel somewhere. All the whores fell in love with Julian. One whore had a baby his age. We'd go in together on shit, like buying a thousand diapers from Costco and splitting them. So Julian was raised in my car with whores.

I did this for maybe eighteen months. I was with Julian every hour. His mom came back, and I dumped him onto her. I figured, now I can have some fun. I was done trying to be the perfect dad.

A week went by, and I felt sick. Something was wrong with me. I went to visit Julian at his mom's house. I went in the door. Julian was way across the room. That little fucker could hardly walk. His face lit up. You should have seen those legs spinning and kicking when he ran to me. I grabbed him and looked in his eyes. I realized I was all he had, and he was all I had. I'd never felt that way about a person before. I went from having nobody to having somebody. I was no longer alone on this earth.

But I'm not saying I'm a good person now. Please. I still believe if I need power in a situation, I'll choose the evil over the good. The only thing different today is that sometimes I look in Julian's eyes and I know he'll lose me someday. That's nature. But I fear how much it could hurt him not to have a father. I don't want him to ever feel that. That's the worst pain I can imagine. I'd rather suffer torture than have my son feel that pain, or any pain. For a lifelong bad guy like me, these feelings I have for my family are not usual. They are probably what normal people call love. It's not an easy thing to feel. Evil is much simpler.

Acknowledgments

I WOULD not be here today if it were not for my wife, Noemi. She is young in years but old in wisdom. She helped me have a better relationship with my son when there were some very hard times between us. She made me understand things and see things about people that I never would have realized before or ever known. She tried to make my relationship with my sister better, which is a very hard task. Noemi gave me a heart with which to feel. She made me think positively and showed me that whatever time I have left in life I should relax, enjoy, and try to be at peace with myself. This all sounds great, but with a person like me, it is more or less a miracle that Noemi could change me, even a little bit. I owe Noemi everything. I am sure when I leave this earth to see the Devil, who I'm sure will be my partner in Eternity, that any good I've found in myself now will disappear forever. But I'm glad that in this small, last part of my life I've been able to follow and listen to Noemi's wisdom, for this brought me closer to my son, Julian. He is my soul, and Noemi is my light for seeing him. That I get to enjoy their love now is probably unfair to all the people I abused, but that's life. It's not fair, and maybe if my son reads this when he's old enough, he won't make the decisions I did.

— JON ROBERTS

Evan Wright wishes to express his gratitude to Alfred Spellman and Billy Corben, authentic Cocaine Cowboys, whose insane vision got the ball rolling. He wishes to acknowledge Mike Fisten, Steve "Hollywood's Hollywood" Saito and Joanne Chu for their unstinting support in preparing the manuscript. Thanks to Richard Abate, Rick Horgan, Nathan Roberson, and Melissa Kahn, who actually made the book happen; and to Alex "The Bow Slayer" Kohner, who makes everything else happen. And to Los Bulls a message from El Borrego: you will never win, but *muchas gracias* for preordering the book. Finally, to Zari, thanks for the gangsta memories. We will always have Lord Barrington.

— Evan Wright

Index